Study Guide

to accompany

Java Concepts
for AP* Computer Science

BICENTENNIAL
1807
WILEY
2007
BICENTENNIAL

THE WILEY BICENTENNIAL—KNOWLEDGE FOR GENERATIONS

*E*ach generation has its unique needs and aspirations. When Charles Wiley first opened his small printing shop in lower Manhattan in 1807, it was a generation of boundless potential searching for an identity. And we were there, helping to define a new American literary tradition. Over half a century later, in the midst of the Second Industrial Revolution, it was a generation focused on building the future. Once again, we were there, supplying the critical scientific, technical, and engineering knowledge that helped frame the world. Throughout the 20th Century, and into the new millennium, nations began to reach out beyond their own borders and a new international community was born. Wiley was there, expanding its operations around the world to enable a global exchange of ideas, opinions, and know-how.

For 200 years, Wiley has been an integral part of each generation's journey, enabling the flow of information and understanding necessary to meet their needs and fulfill their aspirations. Today, bold new technologies are changing the way we live and learn. Wiley will be there, providing you the must-have knowledge you need to imagine new worlds, new possibilities, and new opportunities.

Generations come and go, but you can always count on Wiley to provide you the knowledge you need, when and where you need it!

WILLIAM J. PESCE
PRESIDENT AND CHIEF EXECUTIVE OFFICER

PETER BOOTH WILEY
CHAIRMAN OF THE BOARD

Study Guide

to accompany

Java Concepts
for AP* Computer Science

5th Edition

FRANCES P. TREES
Drew University

JOHN WILEY & SONS, INC

* *AP is a registered trademark of the College Board, which was not involved
in the production of, and does not endorse this product.*

EXECUTIVE PUBLISHER	Don Fowley
ASSOCIATE PUBLISHER	Dan Sayre
EXECUTIVE MARKETING MANAGER	Christopher Ruel
PROJECT MANAGER	Cindy Johnson
COVER DESIGNER	Howard Grossman
COVER ILLUSTRATOR	Susan Cyr
ANNIVERSARY LOGO DESIGN	Richard J. Pacifico

* AP is a registered trademark of the College Board, which was not involved in the production of, and does not endorse this product.

To order books or for customer service, please call 1–800–CALL–WILEY (225–5945).

ISBN 978-0-470-18161-4

10 9 8 7 6 5 4 3

PREFACE

This Study Guide is designed to assist high school students preparing for the AP Computer Science Examination. It is organized and designed to accompany *Java Concepts for AP Computer Science, 5th ed.,* by Cay Horstmann and published by John Wiley & Sons, Inc. The Guide may also be used with *Big Java, 3rd ed.,* also by Cay Horstmann.

To the Student

Advanced Placement Computer Science is a college level course. As a student in an AP course, you are expected to understand college level material and to read a college level textbook. Because versions of this text may be used in multiple college courses, they contain material that is not tested on the AP Computer Science (CS) Examinations. This guide identifies and stresses the content that is tested on the AP CS Exams. This does not imply that you should skip the additional material in the text. Your teacher may include the additional material in your course and hold you responsible for that material. Some of the material that is not tested on the exam is extremely useful and may be included in your course. By following this guide, you will be able to focus on the topics included in the AP CS 2007-2008 Topic Outline and the elements of the AP Java subset that will be tested on the exam. You should visit the College Board Web site in the beginning of the school year to see if there are any updates or changes to the Topic Outline or AP Java Subset. Because the guide is designed for students taking either the A or the AB Computer Science exam, topics covered on the AB Exam are marked "AB only." If you are participating in an AP CS A course, this should not discourage you from reading these sections; it merely indicates that those topics will be tested on the AB Exam and not the A Exam.

Features of the Study Guide

This guide is organized to help students recognize and master those topics that will be tested on both the A and AB examinations. Where applicable, each chapter includes:

Topic Summary
This section parallels the material in the textbook, adding additional examples and explanation of topics presented in the text. Students will find special emphasis here on topics likely to be tested.

Expanded Coverage of Material That Is Not Found in the Text
Any topics in the AP CS Topic Outline or the AP Java subsets that are not covered in the text are presented in this section.

Topics That Are Useful But Not Tested
This section alerts students to sections of the textbook that present useful features of the Java language. Although these sections are not required for the AP Exam, they address features of Java programs that students are likely to encounter, or that they will need to progress in their programming ability. Although the student is encouraged to stay within the AP Java subset when

writing solutions to free-response questions, a correct solution that implements Java features not in the subset will not be penalized.

Things to Remember When Taking the Exam
Each chapter restates important concepts and provides suggestions for avoiding common errors.

Key Words
Vocabulary used in the chapter is listed alphabetically for student review and reference. Each key word is accompanied by the page number(s) where it is defined and/or discussed in the text.

Connecting the Detailed Topic Outline to the Text
This listing links the topics presented in the guide to the pages in the text where the same topics are covered.

Practice Questions (Multiple Choice and Free Response)
A large number of practice questions, modeled after those on the AP exam, are included in each chapter. The questions use the multiple-choice and free-response formats that students will encounter on the exam. In addition to the practice questions, there are cumulative reviews included after Chapters 7, 13, and 17. Answers to all practice questions are in Appendix A.

AB Examination Topics
Any sections (and practice questions) that cover topics that will not be tested on the Computer Science A Exam are clearly marked "AB only." Students who are preparing for the AB exam should be sure to complete these sections.

Web Resources
The reference materials that students may use during the AP Exam are available from the College Board's Web site at http://www.collegeboard.com/student/testing/ap/compsci_a/exam.html?compscia (AP CS A) and http://www.collegeboard.com/student/testing/ap/compsci_ab/exam.html?comsciab (AP CS AB). These reference materials contain a listing of the classes, interfaces, and methods contained in the Java subset covered by the AP Exam and references and source code for the case study tested on the exam.

The AP Computer Science Topic Outline is available at:

http://www.collegeboard.com/student/testing/ap/compsci_ab/topic.html?comsciab.

This Topic Outline and the AP Java subsets may be revised from time to time, so you are encouraged to check for the most current version of these documents in the AP Computer Science Course Description on the College Board site:

http://www.collegeboard.com/prod_downloads/ap/students/compsci/52435%20APCompSci-Locked.pdf.

Web sites associated with this guide and with *Java Concepts for AP Computer Science, 5th ed.,* and *Big Java, 3rd ed.,* are another important resource for users of this guide. Cay Horstmann's site, http://horstmann.com/bigjava.html, includes a section, *Compiler Help*, that provides installation tips and getting started instructions for the most commonly used Java compilers and environments. You will also find source code for programs in the text(s), solutions to selected exercises in the text(s), frequently asked questions, a programming style guide, and more.

Many of these same items are also available from the Wiley Web site for the text at http://www.wiley.com/college/horstmann. Also available at the Wiley Web site are instructor resources not available to students.

Acknowledgments

It has been a sincere pleasure and honor working with Cay Horstmann's material in developing this guide. Dr. Horstmann is truly a master computer scientist and teacher.

Many thanks to Cindy Johnson and her staff at Publishing Services for their hard work, support, and patience throughout. I am extremely grateful to Greg Volger and Joe Kmoch, whose reviews offered many valuable comments and suggestions.

My energy and enthusiasm for teaching computer science are constantly renewed by the many AP CS teachers that I work during AP CS workshops and summer institutes.

Finally, thanks to Eli for his patience, encouragement and support.

CONTENTS IN BRIEF

*Numbers in parentheses indicate the corresponding chapters in *Java Concepts for AP Computer Science, 5th ed.*

CONTENTS

CHAPTER **1**

Introduction

■ Topic Summary

1.1   What is Advanced Placement?

The Advanced Placement (AP) Program is a joint educational undertaking of the College Board, secondary schools, and colleges. This program provides a means by which secondary schools and colleges collaborate to develop college-level course descriptions and exams which are accessible to high school students. By participating in an AP course and taking the AP Exam, you have an opportunity to earn college credit, placement in higher-level courses, or both. You will gain confidence and develop skills that will be indispensable in college.

The AP Program currently offers 37 courses.
- *Art History*
- *Biology*
- *Calculus AB* and *Calculus BC*
- *Chemistry*
- *Chinese Language and Culture*

1

- *Computer Science A* and *Computer Science AB*
- *Economics: Macro* and *Economics: Micro*
- *English Language & Composition* and *English Literature & Composition*
- *Environmental Science*
- *European History*
- *French Language* and *French Literature*
- *German Language*
- *Government & Politics: Comparative* and *Government & Politics: US*
- *Human Geography*
- *Italian Language and Culture*
- *Japanese Language and Culture*
- *Latin Literature* and *Latin Vergil*
- *Music Theory*
- *Physics B, Physics C: Electricity* and *Magnetism,* and *Physics C: Mechanics*
- *Psychology*
- *Russian Language and Culture (under development in 2007)*
- *Spanish Language* and *Spanish Literature*
- *Statistics*
- *Studio Art: Drawing, Studio Art: 2D Design,* and *Studio Art: 3D Design*
- *US History*
- *World History*

Each offering is the responsibility of a development committee appointed by the College Board. The committee members include both high school AP teachers and college professors from the respective academic discipline. Committee members represent a variety of types of secondary schools and colleges and a diversity of knowledge and points of view in their fields. This committee, as a group, plays a critical role in making subject-matter decisions in the course description and the exam development.

1.1.1   Computer Science as an AP Subject

Although AP Exams were first offered in the early 1950s, the first Advanced Placement Computer Science (AP CS) Exam was not administered until 1984. The early 1980s were a time of significant change in the computer industry, with many companies manufacturing personal computers (PCs). PCs became more accessible and affordable; computer science departments flourished in universities; the number of college students interested in computer science increased rapidly. In response to this, the College Board added computer science to its list of Advanced Placement offerings. In 1984, a total of 4,263 students took the first AP CS Exam. In 2002, the number of AP CS Exams administered was close to 23,500, and in 2006, 19,602 AP CS Exams were taken.

Since 1984, Advanced Placement Computer Science has undergone many changes. These changes parallel the changes that have taken place in the computer science curriculum in colleges and universities. The most recent is the change in the implementation language from C++ to Java. The first AP CS Exam using Java as the delivery language was administered in May 2004.

1.2   Who Takes AP Courses?

In 2003, more than 1,700,000 AP Exams were taken in more than 80 different countries. In 2005, 2.1 million AP Exams were taken at more than 15,000 schools in 100 countries and in 2006 more than 2.3 million AP Exams were taken. A variety of initiatives have been undertaken to make the AP Program accessible to all. The federal AP Incentive Program provides monies in the form of grants to encourage low-income students to participate in AP. Some states use their own resources to provide support by encouraging or requiring AP courses in high schools and assisting with students' AP examination fees.

There is no risk in taking an AP Exam and there are numerous benefits. In addition to experiencing the academic demands of a college-level course, students who succeed on multiple AP Exams could earn enough credits to enter college with sophomore standing. Any credits earned can free valuable course time so more electives can be taken or a dual major pursued. It is up to the specific college to grant placement or credit.

1.2.1   Who Takes AP Computer Science?

The intent of AP CS is to parallel the goals of the introductory sequence of courses for computer science majors in colleges. It is not expected that all students taking the AP CS Exam will major in computer science. In fact, AP CS can benefit students majoring in just about any area that involves problem solving and analysis.

Although AP CS is intended to be an introductory course, some secondary schools offer pre-AP courses that serve as prerequisites for AP CS. Students enrolling in AP CS should have skills in problem solving, writing, and algebra. The suggested prerequisite courses are usually designed to sharpen these skills and are taught in a variety of implementation languages.

1.3   What is the Difference Between AP Computer Science A and AB?

Advanced Placement Computer Science is intended to be an introductory course in computer science. The content of AP Computer Science A parallels that of most first-semester college courses. The content of the AB course more closely corresponds to the first two semesters of college computer science. Additional topics covered in AP CS AB include formal analysis of algorithms, advanced data structures and algorithms, and a more detailed design of classes and their relationships and responsibilities.

AP CS A covers less material but should not be considered an easier exam. Offering two separate AP CS Exams allows secondary schools to choose the appropriate course offering based on the school's environment and resources. Many schools do not have the time, resources, and/or enrollment to offer both AP CS A and AP CS AB. Others have an extended computer science curriculum offering multiple computer courses including both AP CS courses.

1.3.1   AP CS Course Organization

There are two essential parts to any computer science course: lecture and lab. In the lecture portion, the course material is presented. In the lab portion of the course, you apply what you have learned to solving problems on the computer. Lab time is handled by different schools in different ways. Time on the computer does not have to be part of class time but is an essential element of successful completion of the course. You should spend as much time as possible working on AP CS lab assignments. The more experience you have, the more knowledge you will absorb.

1.4   Which Elements of Computer Science Are on the AP Exam?

The elements of computer science that will be tested on the AP CS Exams include basic programming concepts (branches and loops, method calls), object-oriented programming (classes, interfaces, inheritance), data structures, and algorithms. The focus of the exams is not the Java programming language. Java is a very large language and cannot be mastered in the AP course. The exams cover the elements of computer science. Object-oriented design is a major focus in the AP CS curriculum.

The tested materials are well defined in College Board documents. These resources are: the AP CS Topic Outline, the AP CS Java Subsets, the Quick References for the Java AP subset of classes, and the current case study documents. Before taking the exam, you should be familiar with the material contained in these documents.

1.4.1   Format of the AP CS Exam

The AP CS Exam is divided into two parts. Part 1 contains 40 multiple-choice questions which must be answered in 1 hour and 15 minutes. Part 2 contains 4 free-response questions with a time limit of 1 hour and 45 minutes. The two parts of the exam are weighted equally when determining the final AP score. The following documents are provided for use during both sections of the exam:

- Quick Reference for A Exam *or* Quick Reference for AB Exam
  - A list of methods from the Java library that may be included on the AP Exam
- Case Study Materials
  - Class Summary
  - Testable API
  - Source Code for the Testable Classes

1.5   Strategies for Taking the AP CS Exam

You first should decide which AP CS Exam you are prepared to take, A or AB. If you are enrolled in an AP CS A course and you are following that curriculum then there really is no decision and you should sign up for the A exam. However, if you are enrolled in AP CS AB, or if you are enrolled in AP CS A and doing additional work on the AB topics, you need to make a decision. The A exam is not necessarily easier then the AB exam but it does cover significantly less material. In order to feel comfortable with the AB exam, you need to be very, very comfortable with designing classes, and understand and be able to apply advanced data structures and algorithms.

You will be given supplemental materials that you may use during both parts of the exam. These materials are available to you throughout the entire year. Do not wait until the exam to become familiar with them. On exam day, briefly scan over these documents so that you are familiar with the official resources that you will be able to reference.

1.5.1   Strategies for Part 1

The first part of the exam contains 40 multiple-choice questions. Usually the questions are in a somewhat increasing order of difficulty but sometimes questions that are not difficult for one person may be difficult for another.

- Read each question carefully. If you do not know the answer, circle the question, skip it for the moment and go on. Come back to that question later if you have time.
- Do not haphazardly guess on the multiple-choice questions. There is a deduction of one-quarter of a point for each wrong answer. Omitted questions do not add or subtract points from the total. If you can eliminate two of the possible choices, then your odds of choosing the correct answer are better.
- Review all possible answers before choosing one.
- If there is code in the question, read the entire question before reading the code.
- There may be several questions dealing with one code segment or problem specification. If you do not know the answer to the first question in a series, do not assume the following questions in the series are more difficult. Read them all.
- Remember, you have 1 hour and 15 minutes to answer 40 questions. That averages to less than two minutes per question. Watch your time.

1.5.2   Strategies for Part 2

The second part of the exam contains four free-response questions. Each of these four questions is weighted equally. Usually the questions are in a somewhat increasing order of difficulty but, as with the multiple-choice questions, what is difficult for one person may not be difficult for another. If the first question seems difficult, go on to another.

- Don't panic if the question seems extremely long. Read the question introduction and the comments in the code. Many times the comments outline an algorithm that solves the problem.
- Read the question carefully before you begin to write your answer. Read the question again after you answer the question to make sure that you satisfied the problem specifications.
- Most of the free-response questions have more than one part. If you do not know how to answer the first part, do not give up on the entire problem. Read all parts of the problem. Sometimes the last part of the problem is the easiest part to answer. In most problems, each part is graded independently from other parts even if they seem to depend on each other to work.
- In a multiple-part free-response question, part (b) or part (c) may indicate that you may use a call to a method you wrote in part (a): "Assume that this method works as intended regardless of what you wrote for part (a)." This is usually a hint that the call to the method from part (a) will be useful. You may be able to answer this part of the question even if you skipped the previous parts.
    - Do not write code that you are told exists and works as intended. If your solution reimplements the functionality provided by methods given in the problem definition, or by methods written in previous parts of the problem, you will not receive full credit for your work. Rather than reimplementing these methods, you should appropriately invoke them.
- Do not worry about the efficiency of your algorithm unless explicitly told to do so.
- Do not include "extra" code in a solution.
    - Do not add `System.out.println` statements unless required by the problem. This is considered to be a side-effect and will probably be penalized.
    - Do not write code to check preconditions. Assume preconditions are satisfied.
- Though not an absolute rule, stay within the AP Java subsets when writing code.
- If you are told to justify your answer, you need to provide an explanation. The explanation need not be lengthy. Points will be deducted if you do not include a justification.

- Strive for clarity in your code.
  - Indent properly.
  - Use meaningful variables names that are distinguishable from class names by more than case differences. (Do not name a `String` variable `string` or a `Person` variable `person`.)
- Don't try to write overly clever code!
- Use braces where needed and for clarity. Comment only when absolutely necessary.
- The first solution on your paper is the solution that will be graded. If you rewrite a solution to a problem, be sure to cross out the unwanted solution. Do not waste time erasing.
- If you are running out of time, write as much code as you have time to write. Do not write comments on how you would solve the problem if you had time. No credit is given for comments!
- The exam answer booklet provides plenty of blank space for all of your answers. You should not run out of room. But, if you do, continue your work on a blank page in the back of the booklet. Clearly label the page with the problem number and indicate in the original space provided where the exam reader can find your answer. If there are no blank pages and you use additional paper, your paper has to be appropriately labeled. Your exam proctor should provide you with information on how to do this. Do not just include an unlabeled piece of paper in your answer booklet.
- Remember, you have 1 hour and 45 minutes to answer 4 questions. That averages to about 26 minutes per question. Watch your time.
- Be neat! Real people have to read your answers!

1.5.3 *Materials You Should Bring to the Exam*
- Several #2 pencils.
- Erasers: Bring erasers that erase! Incorrect multiple choice answers need to be completely erased.
- A watch: If the start time and end time are not clearly stated on the board, take note of these on your exam booklet. Look at your watch frequently.
- Your social security number for identification purposes.
- A photo I.D. if you are taking the exam at a school other than your high school.

1.5.4 *Last Minute Reminders*
- Get a good night's sleep.
- Eat a good meal before your exam.
- Don't rush! If you are prepared, you should have sufficient time to answer all questions.
- Try to relax! Enjoy the exam. You worked very hard all year to prepare for this day!

1.6   How Are the Exams Graded?

The score on the multiple-choice part is equal to the number of questions answered correctly minus one-quarter of the number of incorrect answers. This part of the exam is graded by computer.

The free-response questions are graded by a group of experienced AP computer science teachers and university computer science professors. Each of the four questions is scored on a 9-point scale. A grading rubric is developed at the reading and used to insure that the student solutions are graded in a consistent manner.

The multiple-choice section and the free-response section are weighted equally when determining the composite score. A corresponding AP Grade (1–5) is then assigned.

Meaning of AP Grades

AP Grade	Possible Interpretation
5	Extremely Well Qualified
4	Well Qualified
3	Qualified
2	Possibly Qualified
1	No Recommendation

1.6.1   Special Recognition for Doing Well

The College Board recognizes excellent student performance on AP Exams through the AP Scholar Awards. In 2006, over 247,000 students were designated AP Scholars. This distinction is based on the student's average AP Exam grades (from that year and previous years) and the AP grade requirement for the specific award. There are 8 different AP Scholar distinctions including Scholar, Scholar with Honors, State Scholar, and International Scholar. You may cite the AP Scholar Awards among your achievements on college applications.

The Siemens Foundation recognizes America's most promising science and mathematics students by awarding monetary scholarships to 24 students, two females and two males in each of the six College Board regions. These awards are presented to the students who have earned the greatest number of scores of 5 on AP exams taken in grades 9, 10, and 11 on the following AP Exams: *Biology, Calculus BC, Chemistry, Computer Science, Environmental Science, Physics C (Physics C: Mechanics* and *Physics C: Electricity and Magnetism* each count as half), and *Statistics*.

1.6.2   College Credit or Placement

The College Board AP Program offers high school students the opportunity to take college level courses while still in high school. More than 90% of colleges and universities have an AP policy regarding credit and/or placement for students receiving acceptable scores on AP Examinations. These policies differ among different universities. AP credit and placement policy information for many colleges and universities is provided through the College Board Web site, http://www.collegeboard.com/ap/creditpolicy.

1.7   How Should This Guide Be Used to Prepare for the AP CS Exam?

This study guide is intended to be used in conjunction with *Java Concepts for AP Computer Science,* 5th ed. (written by Cay Horstmann and published by John Wiley & Sons, Inc.). Because this text is identical in content to the first sixteen chapters of *Big Java,* 3rd ed. (a college-level text), it includes material that is not tested on the AP CS Exam.

This study guide will lead you through the chapters of the text, focusing on the topics that will be tested on the AP CS Exams. The elements of each chapter are:
- Topic summary
- Expanded coverage of material that is not found in the text
- Topics that are useful but not tested (if applicable)
- Things to remember when taking the AP Exam (if applicable)

- Key words (with references to the text)
- Connecting the topic outline to the text
- Practice questions

1.8 Where Can I Get More Information?

You can access general information about the Advanced Placement Program at:
http://www.collegeboard.com/ap/students/index.html

Information about the AP Scholar Awards can be found at:
http://www.collegeboard.com/student/testing/ap/scholarawards.html

Siemens Foundation Award information can be found at:
http://www.siemens-foundation.org/awards/

Specific information about AP Computer Science can be found at:
http://www.collegeboard.com/student/testing/ap/subjects.html

Information on university credit and placement policies can be found at:
http://apps.collegeboard.com/apcreditpolicy/index.jsp

1.8.1 Where Can I Get the Text Ancillaries?
The student companion site for *Java Concepts for AP Computer Science,* 5th ed., or *Big Java,* 3rd ed., can be found by clicking on the appropriate link at:
http://www.wiley.com/college/horstmann

Cay Horstmann's site for *Big Java,* 3rd ed., and *Java Concepts*, 5th ed., is:
http://www.horstmann.com/bigjava.html

1.9 Are There Other Suggestions for Success in AP CS?

- The AP Computer Science Examinations will include questions based on the current AP CS case study. Chapter 18 of this guide describes why and how the case study is used in AP CS courses and on the AP CS Exam. Begin reading the case study documents early in the year so that the materials will be familiar to you *before* the day of the exam.
- Keep good notes of your teacher's lectures.
- Practice *writing* code. Actually writing code on paper is different than typing code into the computer!
- Keep your graded programming assignments and review your teacher's comments on the assignments. Don't just look at the grade on the paper and throw it away!
- Do not be afraid to ask for help on your assignments or to seek alternate solutions to problems.
- Volunteer to help your classmates debug their programs. Looking at someone else's code is not as easy as looking at your own code and may help you when exam time comes around.

CHAPTER

(Covers Java Concepts for AP Computer Science Chapter 1)

Introduction to Hardware and Software

■ Topic Summary

For the AP CS Exam, you are expected to have a working knowledge of major hardware components, system software, and responsible uses of computers. This chapter will review some commonly used vocabulary that may be included in multiple-choice questions.

2.1   What Is Programming?

Many people use computers for specific everyday tasks such as sending and receiving e-mail, conducting online banking activities, online shopping, playing games, and many other interesting and not-so-interesting activities. In order to attend to our every need, computers must be programmed. A computer program is a sequence of instructions that tells the computer how to complete a task. To use a program, you do not need to know how to design and develop the program. To develop a computer program, you need to attain a set of skills for which this course will provide a foundation.

2.2   The Anatomy of a Computer

The basic hardware components of a computer include
- the Central Processing Unit (CPU)
- primary memory (or storage)
- secondary memory (or storage)
- peripheral devices

The Central Processing Unit (CPU) is the "brain" of the computer. The CPU processes individual commands or statements of a program. The CPU consists of a chip or a small number of chips. Each chip contains transistors that send and receive electrical signals that control program execution, data transfer, and arithmetic operations. Processors execute machine instructions and processors from different companies (e.g., Intel Pentium, Sun SPARC, Motorola PowerPC G5) have different sets of machine instructions.

Primary, or main, memory stores software and data while it is being used. Primary storage, or Random Access Memory (RAM), loses its data when the power is turned off.

Secondary memory stores data in a permanent way. It is much cheaper and slower than primary memory. Some secondary storage devices popular today are the hard disk, the compact disc (CD), the digital video disc or digital versatile disc (DVD), the floppy disk (diskette), and the USB keychain memory device.

Input/Output (I/O) devices, or peripheral devices, enable us to communicate with the computer. Input devices such as the keyboard or the mouse are used to input data and programs. Monitors and printers are used to display information. Other computer peripherals include speakers, digital cameras, scanners, light pens, and barcode readers.

Many of us own single-user systems. A single-user system is a self-contained unit. Many computer labs are permanently connected to a local network. These computers are connected together so that information can be shared among them. The Internet is a world-wide network.

2.3   Translating Human-Readable Programs to Machine Code

A compiler translates a program written in a high-level language into machine code. An interpreter is similar to a compiler but translates and executes a small segment of code (perhaps one statement) at a time. Usually, a Java program is entered into the computer through an editor. It is then submitted to the compiler. The editor and compiler may be part of an integrated development environment (IDE). The compiler checks the program and reports any syntax or grammar errors such as missing semicolons. If the program is free of compilation errors, the compiler translates the Java program code into Java bytecode. The bytecode is written for the Java Virtual Machine (JVM). A JVM has been written for every major operating system. The JVM is like a simulated CPU that runs inside a particular operating system. The JVM is the reason that the same Java program will run on different operating systems such as Windows XP, UNIX, Linux, or Mac OS X. The JVM reads the bytecode and executes the program.

The operating system manages the computer resources. The operating system is software that automatically starts when the computer is turned on. Typical services provided by an operating system include deciding the priority in which programs are to run, loading the programs into memory, managing files, and printing. It is the operating system that makes the computer user-friendly (easy to use). *Random Fact 9.1* on page 406 of your text discusses operating system tasks in detail.

2.4 The Java Programming Language

Java was designed so that a developer could create either stand-alone applications or programs that can be executed through the Internet using a browser. The programs that are executed using a browser are called applets. Java has many security features, including some that ensure that running an applet will not harm your computer. Because of Java's portability, the same program will run on various operating systems.

2.5 Becoming Familiar with Your Computer

You should be familiar with your computer and its operations before you proceed. Section 1.5 of your text discusses the basic logistics involved with organizing your files and folders on the computer. If your AP class works in a computer lab, your teacher will explain what you should do to organize and save your work. In this course, you will be writing programs using the Java language. These program files will have a .java extension and will be stored in a folder (or directory) on your computer. Maintaining an organized file and folder system on your computer is important. Be sure to understand where your programs for this course will reside.

2.6 Compiling a Simple Program

Section 1.6 of your text introduces the traditional "Hello World!" program and explains the basic syntax of a trivial Java program. The program prints a string to the screen using the System.out.println method. You should enter and compile this simple program using the guidelines in Sections 1.6 and 1.8 in your text. By doing so, you will become familiar with the environment in which you will be programming. Example 2.1 below illustrates another simple Java program.

Example 2.1

```
public class TrivialProgram
{
   public static void main(String[] args)
   {
      System.out.print("This prints a line.");
      System.out.println(" This stays on the same line.");
      System.out.println("Now we are on the next line.");
   }
}
```

will print

This prints a line. This stays on the same line.
Now we are on the next line.

2.6.1 Java Comments

The types of comments that you may see on the AP CS Exam are the single line comment:

```
// This is a comment
```

the multi-line comment:

```
/*
   This is a comment
   This is another comment
*/
```

and the javadoc comment:

```
/**
   This is a javadoc comment used to give
   the purpose of a class or method.
*/
```

These comments are discussed in your text in *Advanced Topic 1.1*, page 22, and in Appendix A.

2.7   Errors

Our first attempt in writing, compiling, and executing a program is not always perfect. Many of our errors can be classified as syntax errors. A *syntax error* is a violation of the rules of the programming language. The compiler will detect syntax errors. Missing semicolons and missing or unmatched braces and parentheses are examples of syntax errors. We may also have an error that causes a result other than the result that we originally intended. This is called a run-time or logic error. A *logic error* causes a program to take an action that the programmer did not intend. The program doesn't do what it is designed to do. The compiler does not detect run-time errors or logic errors. It is up to you, the programmer, to test your programs for logic errors.

2.8   The Compilation Process

If you have typed a program into the computer, you may have experienced compile-time errors. After you correct all of your errors, the compiler is able to translate your Java program, your source code, into *class files*. The class file contains a translation of the instructions that you wrote and is stored in a .class file. The Java Virtual Machine loads the instructions for the program that you wrote, starts the program, and loads any other necessary library files. The Java Virtual Machine is the reason that you can execute a compiled Java program on machines with different operating systems. Figure 13 on page 26 of your text illustrates this process.

■ Expanded Coverage of Material That Is Not Found in the Text

- Included in the AP CS Topic Outline is "Responsible Use of Computer Systems." This topic is one that you deal with every time you access information on your computer. Responsible use of the computer and ethics dealing with computers and computer work apply to everyone, including students and teachers. Some materials available to you on this topic are listed below.

- The Association for Computing Machinery (ACM) has a Code of Ethics and Professional Conduct that every member of the ACM is expected to uphold. This Code of Ethics is accessible online at http://www.acm.org/constitution/code.html and best summarizes the issues related to this topic in the AP CS curriculum. Also included in this online document are Professional Imperatives and Leadership Imperatives. The General Moral Imperatives expected to be upheld include:
  - Contribute to society and human well-being.
  - Avoid harm to others.
  - Be honest and trustworthy.
  - Be fair and take action not to discriminate.
  - Honor property rights including copyrights and patents.
  - Give proper credit for intellectual property.
  - Respect the privacy of others.
  - Honor confidentiality.
- The Computer Ethics Institute has written "The Ten Commandments of Computer Ethics" which can be accessed at http://www.brookings.edu/its/cei/cei_hp.htm.
- The Computer Professionals for Social Responsibility is a public-interest group of computer scientists and others concerned about the impact of technology on society. General information about papers and projects can be accessed at http://www.cpsr.org/cpsr/about-cpsr.html.

- Documents and materials addressing privacy issues, legal issues, and intellectual property include:
  - The Fourth Amendment of the U.S. Constitution: "The right of the people to be secure in their persons, houses, papers, and effects, against unreasonable searches and seizures, shall not be violated, and no Warrants shall issue, but upon probable cause, supported by Oath or affirmation, and particularly describing the place to be searched, and the persons or things to be seized."
  - The Privacy Act of 1974 is designed to be a "code of fair information practices" that attempts to regulate the collection, maintenance, use, and sharing of personal information by the federal government. More information is available at http://www.usdoj.gov/oip/privstat.htm.
  - The Computer Matching and Privacy Protection Act of 1988 amended the Privacy Act to include requirements for government agencies to follow when conducting computer-matching activities. More information is available at http://www.usdoj.gov/oip/1974compmatch.htm.
  - Copyright Law of the United States: The Congress shall have Power to promote the progress of science and useful arts, by securing for limited times to authors and inventors the exclusive right to their respective writings and discoveries. More information can be found at http://www.copyright.gov/title17/. Information about United States Copyright Law Limitations on exclusive rights regarding computer programs can be found at http://www.copyright.gov/title17/92chap1.html#117.

■ Topics That Are Useful But Not Tested

- Becoming familiar with your computer system and the Java compiler is the first important step toward a successful programming experience. Sections 1.5, 1.6, and 1.8 of your text guide you through writing, compiling, and executing your first Java program.

- *Productivity Hint 1.2* on page 16 of your text discusses how to develop a strategy for keeping backup copies of your work before disaster strikes. (The key word is *before*.)

■ Things to Remember When Taking the AP Exam

- Although points are not deducted for missing semicolons on the free-response part of the AP CS Exam, try to remember to write clear, correct code in answering all questions.
- Time is limited during the AP CS Exam. Do not spend time writing comments in your free-response answers unless your solution needs to be explained or you are specifically instructed to include comments.

■ Key Words

You should understand the terms below. The AP CS Exam questions may include references to these terms. The citation in parentheses next to each term identifies the page number where it is defined and/or discussed in *Java Concepts for AP Computer Science*, 5th ed.

backup (15)
case sensitivity (17)
chip (4)
class (18)
comments (20)
compiler (9)
computer program (3)
Central Processing Unit (CPU) (4)
editor (25)
file (14)
integrated circuit (4)

Integrated Development Environment (IDE) (13)
Input/Output (I/O) devices (6)
Java Virtual Machine (JVM) (8)
library packages (11)
logic error (23)
main (19)
method (19)
network (4)
peripheral (6)

primary storage (4)
Random Access Memory (RAM) (4)
removable storage device (5)
run-time error (23)
secondary storage (4)
statement (20)
string (21)
syntax error (23)
transistors (4)
variable (9)

■ Connecting the Detailed Topic Outline to the Text

The citations in parentheses identify the pages where information in the outline can be located in *Java Concepts for AP Computer Science*, 5th ed.

- What Is Programming? (2–3)
- The Anatomy of a Computer (3–8)
- Translating Human-Readable Programs to Machine Code (8–10)
- The Java Programming Language (10–12)
- Becoming Familiar with Your Computer (12–16)
- Compiling a Simple Program (17–22)
  - Java Comments (20, 22–23)
- Errors (23–24)
- The Compilation Process (25–27)

■ Practice Questions

Multiple Choice

1. Every Java application contains a class with

   a. a `main` method
   b. a `System.out.println` statement
   c. a compiler
   d. a string
   e. comments

2. A syntax error is a violation of programming language rules. Syntax errors are detected by

   a. the operating system
   b. the compiler
   c. the Java Virtual Machine
   d. antivirus software
   e. the CPU

3. Which of the following is **not** a fundamental task carried out by the Central Processing Unit (CPU)?

   a. locating and executing the program instructions
   b. carrying out arithmetic operations such as addition, subtraction, multiplication, and division
   c. fetching data from storage and input/output devices
   d. sending data back to storage and input/output devices
   e. translating high-level programs to machine code

4. All of the following are examples of peripherals except

   a. mouse
   b. microprocessor
   c. keyboard
   d. printer
   e. monitor

5. A _____ translates programs written in a high-level language to machine code.

   a. CPU
   b. microprocessor
   c. compiler
   d. Java Virtual Machine
   e. storage device

6. What is printed as a result of executing the following Java program?

   ```
   public class Tester
   {
       public static void main(String[] args)
       {
           /*
               System.out.println("This is a test.");
   ```

```
            This is another test;
    */
  }
}
```

a. *This is a test.*
b. *This is a test.*
   This is another test.
c. *This is another test.*
d. Nothing is printed. The compiler reports an error.
e. There is no error reported but nothing is printed.

7. The hardware of a computer consists of all of the following except

   a. processor
   b. memory
   c. input and output devices
   d. storage
   e. operating system

8. "Intellectual property rights" refers to rights relating to which of the following?

   I.   literary, artistic, and scientific works
   II. scientific discoveries
   III. computer software

   a. I only
   b. II only
   c. III only
   d. I and II only
   e. I, II, and III

9. Refer to the Java statement:

   ```
   System.out.println("Hello");
   ```

   Which of the following statements is **not** true about the code printed above?

   a. `System` is the Java class that contains the `out` object.
   b. `out` is an object that represents the console window.
   c. `"Hello"` is a parameter to the `println` method.
   d. `System` is a string object.
   e. `println` is a method applied to the `System.out` object.

10. Which is the U.S. Government directive that requires government agencies to comply with legal norms for the collection, maintenance, and distribution of information in databases?

    a. The First Amendment
    b. The Fourth Amendment
    c. Copyright Law of the United States
    d. The Privacy Act of 1974
    e. Computer Matching and Privacy Protection Act of 1988

    (Note: It is not likely that the AP CS Exam will include questions referring to content of specific legal documents.)

CHAPTER

(Covers *Java Concepts for AP Computer Science* Chapter 2)

Using Objects

■ Topic Summary

3.1 Types and Variables

In the last chapter we introduced a simple Java program whose task was to print a string to the console window. Consider the Java statement below.

```
System.out.println("Hello");
```

"Hello" has the type String and System.out has the type PrintStream.

A variable is a storage location that has a type, a name, and contents.

```
String myFishy = "Nemo";
int testGrade = 92;
double hourlyPay = 15.25;
```

myFishy is the name of a variable of type String that refers to the string "Nemo". testGrade is a variable that holds the integer value 92 and hourlyPay is a variable that holds the floating-point number 15.25. Each of these three statements declares a variable and assigns a value to the variable when it is declared. After these declarations are made, the variables can be used anywhere they can be legally accessed in the program to refer to the assigned values. A variable can also be declared without explicitly giving it a value.

```
int quizGrade;
```

Before using the variable `quizGrade`, a value must be assigned to it. The combination of the previous statement and the statement

```
quizGrade = 92;
```

would declare and initialize `quizGrade` for use in the program.

The compiler checks type mismatches and will report an error for the declaration

```
int number = "one";
```

You cannot assign a `String` value to the `int` variable `number`.

There are rules and conventions used in naming variables. These rules and conventions are described in Section 2.1 of your text.

3.2   The Assignment Operator

Values of existing variables can be modified by using the assignment operator.

```
int testGrade = 92;    // testGrade has the value 92
testGrade = 94;    // testGrade now has the value 94
```

The compiler checks type mismatches and will report an error for the assignment

```
testGrade = "one";
```

3.3   Objects, Classes, and Methods

Object-orientation is an important approach in software development and design that supports the development of programs that are easy to understand, can be adapted to different situations, and can be reused in multiple contexts. *Objects* and *classes* are the central concepts of object-oriented programming and are a primary focus of the AP Computer Science courses.

You can think of a *class* as a factory for objects or a blueprint from which an object is created. Many objects can be created using the same blueprint. An *object* is an instance of a class that you can manipulate in your program. Each object has *behavior* and *state*. In Java, every object belongs to a class. The class defines the behavior and state of objects of that class. You access the behavior of an object by calling methods. Some methods may result in changes to the object's state. The statement

```
System.out.print("This prints a line.");
```

in Example 2.1 of this guide illustrates the `System.out` object being manipulated by its `println` method.

3.4   Method Parameters and Return Values

`String` objects can also be manipulated by methods.

Example 3.1

```
1     int numCharacters;
2     String myFishy = "Nemo";
3     System.out.println(myFishy);
4     numCharacters = myFishy.length():
5     System.out.println(numCharacters);
```

Line 1 declares the variable `numCharacters` that can hold an integer value.

Line 2 declares and initializes a `String` variable named `myFishy` whose value refers to the `String` "Nemo".

Line 3 invokes the `println` method on the `System.out` object. The object `System.out` has the type `PrintStream`. The `println` method has one explicit parameter, `myFishy`, which is of type `String`. The implicit parameter of the method call is `System.out`. Line 3 results in *Nemo* being printed to the console window.

Line 4 calls (or invokes) the `length` method defined in the `String` class on the `String` object `myFishy`. The `length` method returns an integer value that represents the number of characters in this `String` object. Since "Nemo" has 4 characters, the integer *4* is the return value of this method call. This integer value is assigned to the `int` variable `numCharacters`. The `length` method has no explicit parameters. The implicit parameter of the method call is `myFishy`.

Line 5 invokes the `println` method on the `System.out` object. The `println` method has one explicit parameter, `numCharacters`. The `println` method does not return a value. Line 5 results in the number *4* being printed to the console window.

In the example above, the `println` method is called twice, once with a `String` parameter and once with an `int` parameter. When a class defines two methods with the same name and different explicit parameter types, we say the method is *overloaded*.

Lines 4 and 5 in Example 3.1 could be simplified to

```
System.out.println(myFishy.length());   // 4 is printed
```

Some methods, such as the `length` method for a `String` object, *return* values. `myFishy.length()` returns the value *4* because the string "Nemo" has length 4. A method does not always return a value. The `println` method does not return a value. We will see later that a method that does not return a value has the return type declared with the reserved word `void`.

3.5   Number Types

Most Java programs require us to work with expressions and to define variables. Each expression and each variable has a type. These types can be primitive data types or class types. The primitive number data types that you are responsible for are `int` and `double`. Primitive types are not classes. Numbers are not objects. Numbers have no methods.

The objects that are tested on the AP CS Exam are strings, arrays (which are covered in Chapter 7 of your text and Chapter 8 of this guide) and objects instantiated from existing classes (which are introduced in Chapter 3 of your text and Chapter 4 of this guide).

3.6   Constructing Objects

Up to now, we have only used the `System.out` object (of the `PrintStream` class) and the `String` class in our programs. Your text introduces the `Rectangle` class from the Java class library. Although the AP Exam will not ask you questions about this particular class, we will use it to discuss a few general ideas about objects and classes.

An object of type `Rectangle` describes a rectangular shape. The `Rectangle` object is not the rectangle itself. The state of the `Rectangle` object is defined by the *x*- and *y*- coordinates of its top-left corner, its width, and its height.

In order to manipulate an object, the object needs to be created by using the `new` operator. A *constructor* is called to create, or construct, a new `Rectangle` object.

```
new Rectangle(5, 10, 20, 30);
```

The top-left corner has coordinates 5 and 10; the width of the rectangle is 20 and the height is 30. Remember, these values are stored, not the rectangular shape itself. The four values (5, 10, 20, 30) are called *construction parameters*. The call

```
new Rectangle();
```

also constructs a `Rectangle` object. This constructor creates a new `Rectangle` object whose top-left corner has coordinates (0, 0), width 0, and height 0.

Because the `new` expression is not a complete statement, we usually construct an object and assign its value to a variable.

```
Rectangle box = new Rectangle(5, 10, 20, 30);
Rectangle anotherBox = new Rectangle();
```

Because we can construct a `Rectangle` object by invoking either of these two constructors, we say the `Rectangle` constructor is *overloaded*. One constructor has no parameters and the other constructor has four integer parameters.

3.7   Accessor and Mutator Methods

A class defines the behavior of its objects by supplying methods. A method either changes the state of the object or it does not. Methods that change the state of an object are called *mutator methods,* or modifiers, and usually have a `void` return type. An example of a modifier is the `Rectangle` method `translate`.

```
box.translate(15, 25);
```

The `translate` method moves the `Rectangle` object `box` a distance of 15 in the *x*-direction and a distance of 25 in the *y*-direction. This will result in changing the coordinates of the top-left corner.

The method `getWidth` returns the width of a `Rectangle` object without changing the state of the object.

```
box.getwidth();
```

returns the value 20. A method that accesses an object and returns some information about the object but does not change the state of the object is called an *accessor method*.

3.8   Implementing a Test Program

In order to test the behavior of an object, you can use an interactive development environment such as BlueJ or you can write a simple test program. Testing some objects requires us to import Java classes from packages. A package is a group of Java classes that are usually related in some way. The `Rectangle` class is contained in the `java.awt` package. In order to include a `Rectangle` object in our program, we need to import the `java.awt.Rectangle` class.

```
import java.awt.Rectangle;
```

This tells the Java compiler that the `Rectangle` class belongs to the `java.awt` package in the Java library. Without the `import`, we would have to use the fully qualified name for `Rectangle` by specifying the Java library package `java.awt` each and every time we refer to the `Rectangle` class.

```
java.awt.Rectangle box = new java.awt.Rectangle();
```

The steps you follow to write your test program, and the procedure used to import packages, are explained in Section 2.8 of your text.

3.9   The API Documentation

The API is the "Application Programming Interface." The API documentation documents all of the classes in the Java library and is available at http://java.sun.com/javase/6/docs/api/index.html. The AP CS course includes a very small percentage of the material included in the Java API. Although the API itself is not tested, understanding how to read and write comments found in the API (documentation comments) are included in the AP subset. This type of comment is discussed in Section 3.3 of your text. Being able to navigate the Java API is a valuable skill in programming.

3.10   Object References

In order to do anything with the object that we created, we must store a reference to the object in an object variable.

```
Rectangle box = new Rectangle(5, 10, 20, 30);
```
or
```
Rectangle anotherBox = new Rectangle();
```

The object variables `box` and `anotherBox` store references to `Rectangle` objects. There can be many instances of a class. Each object (or instance) has its own memory that contains specific information about it. An object variable stores the object's location. Every variable has a type that identifies the kind of information it can contain. `box` contains a reference to a `Rectangle` object; once declared as a reference to a `Rectangle` object, it cannot reference a `double`, a `String` object, or any other type of object.

```
String student = "Anne";                  // This is OK
Rectangle cerealBox = new Rectangle();    // This is OK

Rectangle crate = "Davis";                // WRONG!
String csStudent = 4.35;                  // WRONG!
double num = new Rectangle();             // WRONG!
```

You can choose any appropriate variable names for object variables. Rules for naming variables are discussed in Section 2.1 of your text. Object variables must be initialized before you access them. In the declaration,

```
Rectangle box;
```

box is not initialized. The new operator creates a new object and returns its location.

```
Rectangle box;
box = new Rectangle(5, 10, 20, 30);   // Now initialized
```

You can have multiple references to the same object.

```
Rectangle anotherBox = box;
```

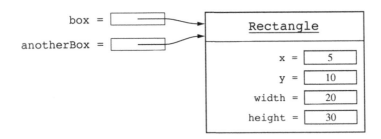

Because box and anotherBox reference the same Rectangle object, after the statement

```
box.translate(15, 25);
```

is executed, both variables, box and anotherBox, refer to the same object that has been moved.

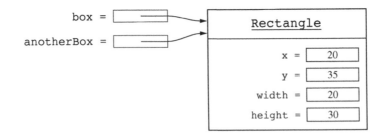

A variable that is a primitive type, like a number, stores the value, not a reference. This is illustrated in Section 2.10 of your text. You should understand that numbers are different from objects. Number variables are *not* created with new.

■ Topics That Are Useful But Not Tested

- The String methods toUpperCase and replace may be useful if your program deals with String objects. These methods are explained in Sections 2.3 and 2.4 of your text.
- The classes and methods of the Java library are listed in the API documentation. Although you are not explicitly tested on the Java API, you should be familiar with it. Navigating through the API documentation is explained in Section 2.9 of your text.
- Section 2.11 of your text introduces you to graphical applications using Java libraries. Although the AP Exam doesn't include material on graphics, working with simple graphical

elements can be fun. Page through the material in Sections 2.11–2.13 to see some very simple graphics applications.

■ Things to Remember When Taking the AP Exam

- Initialize all objects and variables before you access them.
- When deciding on a variable name, choose a name that describes the purpose of the variable.
- Do not name the variable with the same word as the class name.

```
Rectangle rectangle = new Rectangle(5, 10, 20, 30);   // BAD
```

Although this would compile, it is very confusing to those grading your exam!

- Follow the Java conventions when naming variables, classes, and methods.
- Do not try to reset an object by calling a constructor. You cannot invoke a constructor on an existing object.

```
Rectangle box = new Rectangle(5, 10, 20, 30);
box(10, 5, 30, 20);   // WRONG
box = new Rectangle(10, 5, 30, 20);   // OK
```

This is explained in *Common Error 2.1* on page 46 of your text.

- When calling methods from a test class (client program), include the implicit parameter (object reference) in the call.

```
box.getWidth();   // This is OK
getWidth();   // WRONG! You need to supply an object reference
```

- Do not use a class name when an object name should be used.

```
Rectangle box = new Rectangle(5, 10, 20, 30);
System.out.println(Rectangle.getWidth());   // WRONG
System.out.println(box.getWidth());   // This is OK
```

■ Key Words

You should understand the terms below. The AP CS Exam questions may include references to these terms. The citation in parentheses next to each term identifies the page number where it is defined and/or discussed in *Java Concepts for AP Computer Science*, 5th ed.

accessor (46)	import (49)	package (49)
assignment operator (36)	integer (43)	parameter (40)
class (38)	method (37)	primitive type (43)
constructor (46)	mutator (46)	private implementation (39)
double (43)	new (45)	public interface (39)
explicit parameter (40)	object (37)	return value (40)
floating-point number (43)	object reference (53)	type (34)
identifier (35)	overloading (42)	variable (34)
implicit parameter (40)		

■ Connecting the Detailed Topic Outline to the Text

The citations in parentheses identify where information in the outline can be located in *Java Concepts for AP Computer Science*, 5th ed.

- Types and Variables (34–36)
- The Assignment Operator (36–37)
- Objects, Classes, and Methods (37–39)
- Method Parameters and Return Values (40–43)
- Number Types (43–44)
- Constructing Objects (44–46)
- Accessor and Mutator Methods (46–47)
- Implementing a Test Program (47–50)
- The API Documentation (50–53)
- Object References (53–56)

■ Practice Questions

Multiple Choice

1. Which of the following statements about *classes* is true?

   a. Classes are examples of objects.
   b. Classes are factories or blueprints for objects.
   c. Every class belongs to an object.
   d. The public interface of a class is hidden from the user.
   e. The new operator is used to construct a new class.

2. Constructors are always invoked using

   a. a println statement
   b. a return statement
   c. the new operator
   d. an = sign
   e. overloading

3. An object location is stored in

   a. an object variable
   b. a class
   c. a parameter
   d. a String
   e. another object

4. If two methods have the same name and different explicit parameters, the method name is

   a. overloaded
   b. encapsulated
   c. implemented
   d. an implicit reference
   e. illegal

5. Which of the following statements about objects and classes is **not** true?

    a. Object locations are stored in object variables.
    b. All object variables must be initialized before you use them.
    c. An object reference describes the location of an object.
    d. Multiple object variables can contain references to the same object.
    e. Every class has a particular type that identifies what kind of information it can hold.

6. The implicit parameter to a method call is

    a. the object on which the method is invoked.
    b. the object returned as the result of the method being executed.
    c. the public interface of the method.
    d. the class in which the method is defined.
    e. the constructor of the method.

7. The `PrintStream` class defines the `println` method as

    ```
    public void println(String output)
    ```

    Which of the following statements about this definition is **true**?

    a. The return type of the `println` method is `String`.
    b. The implicit parameter of the `println` method is `void`.
    c. There is no value returned by the `println` method.
    d. `output` is the name of the object on which the `println` method is invoked.
    e. The return value of the `println` method is of type `String`.

8. Which of the following results in the integer variable n having the value 54?

    I. ```
        n = new int(54);
        ```

    II. ```
        int n;
        n = 54;
        ```

    III. ```
        int n = 54;
        ```

    a.  I only
    b.  II only
    c.  III only
    d.  II and III only
    e.  I, II, and III
        ```

9. Consider the following methods of the `Rectangle` class.

    I. ```
       public void translate(int x, int y)
       // Translates this Rectangle the indicated distance,
       // to the right along the x-coordinate axis,
       // and downward along the y-coordinate axis.
       ```

    II. ```
        public void setRect(double x, double y, double width,
                double height)
        // Sets the bounds of this Rectangle to the specified
        // x, y, width, and height.
        ```

    III. ```
         public void grow(int h, int v)
         // Resizes the Rectangle so that it is h units larger on both the
         // left and right sides, and v units larger at both the top and
         // bottom.
         ```

    Which of these methods are modifiers (mutators)?

    a. I only
    b. II only
    c. III only
    d. I and III only
    e. I, II, and III

10. Consider the following methods of the `Rectangle` class.

    I. ```
       public void setSize(int width, int height)
       // Sets the size of this Rectangle to the specified
       // width and height.
       ```

    II. ```
        public double getY()
        // Returns the y-coordinate of the top-left corner
        // of the Rectangle.
        ```

    III. ```
         public double getHeight()
         // Returns the height of the Rectangle as a double.
         ```

    Which of these methods are accessors?

    a. I only
    b. II only
    c. III only
    d. II and III only
    e. I, II, and III

CHAPTER

(Covers Java Concepts for AP Computer Science Chapter 3)

Implementing Classes

■ Topic Summary

4.1 Levels of Abstraction

4.1.1 Black Boxes

Section 3.1.1 of your text describes the difference between *using* a device and actually building (or fixing) the internal workings of that device. The term *black box* refers to inner workings. The black box hides these internal workings from those using the device. The process of hiding the implementation details is called *encapsulation*. Encapsulation is very important to us in real life situations. We do not have to know how to build or fix internal circuitry in order to use an electronic device such as a radio. In fact, many electronic devices warn against opening the box that contains this circuitry with a statement such as "This device should be serviced only by a certified professional. If you open this panel, you will void your warranty." A radio is designed in a way that it is easy for you to use. Someone, other than yourself, came up with the right black box so that your radio is easy to use. You see the radio controls. You do not see the inner workings. The *right concept* for a device is discovered through abstraction. Abstraction is taking away inessential features, until only the essence of the concept remains. For example, "radio" is an abstraction. "Car" is an abstraction. We are not looking at or thinking about the details of this device. Abstraction permits us to focus on the essential functionality of a class without being distracted by complex implementation details.

4.1.2 Object-Oriented Design

The focus of the AP CS curriculum is an object-oriented approach to programming. At this time, the most common approach to structuring programming is an object-oriented approach. The black boxes from which we manufacture programs are called objects. Sometimes you will use objects that others have designed and sometimes you will design objects that others will use. The AP Exam will test on both of these aspects.

4.1.3 Crawl, Walk, Run

In Chapter 2 of your text and Chapter 3 of this guide, you learned to use objects such as String objects and the object System.out. Although we will continue to *use* objects, we will also design and implement our own classes to allow our objects to carry out behaviors we define. Think of your design process as creating a black box where the operations are visible (the radio controls) and the data and implementation are hidden (the inner circuitry).

4.2   Specifying the Public Interface of a Class

Section 3.2 of your text describes the design of a BankAccount class. The three behaviors defined for a BankAccount object allow users to deposit money, withdraw money, and get the current balance of the account. Behaviors defined for a bank account define the methods for the BankAccount class. A BankAccount object has a state (a current balance). The state of a BankAccount object can be changed by a deposit or a withdrawal. Therefore, the methods deposit and withdraw are mutator methods (or modifiers). These methods do not return a value so they have a void return type. The getBalance method does not change the state of our BankAccount object and is therefore an accessor method. The method getBalance will return the current balance of the BankAccount object so it will have a double return type (because we usually use floating-point numbers to represent money). The return statement is a special statement that instructs the method to terminate and return a value to the statement that called the method. Example 4.1 below is an overview of the BankAccount class.

Example 4.1

```
// Class definition
public class BankAccount
{
   // Constructor
   public BankAccount()
   {
      // Code here
   }

   // Constructor
   public BankAccount(double initialBalance)
   {
      // Code here
   }

   // Accessor
   public double getBalance()
   {
      // Code here
   }
```

```
// Modifier
public void deposit(double amount)
{
    // Code here
}

// Modifier
public void withdraw(double amount)
{
    // Code here
}

    // Private instance fields here
}
```

The `BankAccount` class definition above has the following format.

```
accessSpecifier class ClassName
public class BankAccount
{
    Constructors: There are two constructors in our BankAccount class
    Methods: There are three methods in our BankAccount class
    Instance fields: The private data (instance) fields will be discussed later
}
```

The public constructors and methods of a class form the *public interface* of the class. The access specifier `public` indicates that the users of our `BankAccount` class can create and manipulate `BankAccount` objects through the public constructors and the public `deposit`, `withdraw`, and `getBalance` methods. Example 4.2 below demonstrates this manipulation.

Example 4.2

```
BankAccount momsChecking = new BankAccount(10);
momsChecking.deposit(510);
System.out.println(momsChecking.getBalance());
momsChecking.withdraw(100);
System.out.println(momsChecking.getBalance());
```

A `BankAccount` object is created with an initial balance of $10. A deposit of $510 is made. The current balance (520) is printed. $100.00 is withdrawn and the new balance (420) is printed.

4.3   Commenting the Public Interface

When you define classes, you should include documentation of your methods and constructors. Section 3.3 and Productivity Hint 3.1 of your text explain how to use the `javadoc` utility and implement documentation comments. In the examples presented in this guide, we use `javadoc` (documentation) comments. The AP CS Java subset includes `/* */`, `//`, and `javadoc` comments. Only the use of `@param`, `@return`, and `@throws` in `javadoc` comments is included in the subset. `@param` and `@return` are demonstrated in Section 3.3 of your text. Examples of `@throws` are in Section 12.2 of this guide.

4.4　Instance Fields

An object of a class has its own set of instance fields (instance variables or attributes) that define its state (data). These instance fields are usually hidden from the programmer who uses the class (the client program). As mentioned in Section 3.1 of your text, the process of hiding details (the private information or data) and providing ways to access the information (public methods) is called *encapsulation*. We will be designing a black box where the operations are visible and the data and implementation are hidden. *Information hiding* refers to the idea that the client, or user, of a class does not need to know about the inner workings of the class in order to use it. To remain true to the meaning of object-oriented programming, our data (or instance fields) should be declared `private`. Access to this data should be allowed only through the methods defined in the class. Declaring instance fields as `private` does not permit access from methods outside the class. In the AP Java subset, all instance fields are declared as `private`. Example 4.2 accesses the balance of the `BankAccount` object `momsChecking` through the public method `getBalance`.

```
System.out.println(momsChecking.getBalance());
```

The implicit parameter of a method is the object on which the method is invoked. The implicit parameter in the call to `getBalance` in the above statement is the `BankAccount` object `momsChecking`. The private instance field is defined in the `BankAccount` class and each object of a class has its own set of instance fields. An object stores its data in these instance fields. A field refers to a storage location inside a block of memory. An instance of a class is an object of the class. There may be many instances of a class (e.g., many `BankAccount` objects). Thus, an instance field is a storage location that is present in each object of the class. Figure 5 in Chapter 3 of your text shows two `BankAccount` objects, each with its own instance field, `balance`.

Example 4.3 below shows an incomplete definition of a `Student` class. The attributes (data) are declared as `private`. The `public` method `getId` returns the value of the private instance variable `id`.

Example 4.3

```
public class Student
{
    // More code here

    public String getId()
    {
        return id;
    }

    // More code here

    private String firstName;
    private String lastName;
    private String id;
    // More code here
}
```

A client program (or test class) containing the statements

```
Student artStudent = new Student("John", "Smith", "111111");
Student mathStudent = new Student("Ann", "Dunn", "222222");
```

creates (or constructs) the two student objects below.

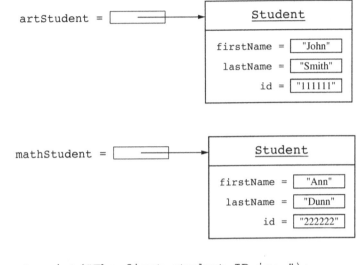

```
System.out.print("The first student ID is: ");
System.out.println(artStudent.getId());
System.out.print("The next student ID is: ");
System.out.println(mathStudent.getId());
```

would print

The first student ID is: 111111
The next student ID is: 222222

The expression `artStudent.getId()` calls the `getId` method of the `artStudent` object. The id of `artStudent` is returned to the client program or calling method. The expression `mathStudent.getId()` calls the `getId` method of the `mathStudent` object. The id of `mathStudent` is returned to the calling method.

4.5   Implementing Constructors and Methods

Example 4.4 contains the complete implementation (code) of our `Student` class.

Example 4.4

```
/**
    A Student has a first name, a last name, and an ID number.
    When a student grade is entered, it is added to sumOfGrades and
    the numberOfGrades is incremented by 1.
*/
public class Student
{
```

```
/**
    Constructs a Student with the given information.
    @param first the student's first name
    @param last the student's last name
    @param idNumber the student's identification number
*/
public Student(String first, String last, String idNumber)
{
    firstName = first;
    lastName = last;
    id = idNumber;
    sumOfGrades = 0.0;
    numberOfGrades = 0;
}

/**
    Constructs a Student with default values.
*/
public Student()
{
    firstName = "";
    lastName = "";
    id = "";
    sumOfGrades = 0.0;
    numberOfGrades = 0;
}

/**
    Gets the first name of the Student.
    @return the first name of the Student
*/
public String getFirstName()
{
    return firstName;
}

/**
    Gets the last name of the Student.
    @return the last name of the Student
*/
public String getLastName()
{
    return lastName;
}

/**
    Gets the ID number of the Student.
    @return the ID number of the Student
*/
public String getId()
{
    return id;
}
```

```
/**
   Modifies sumOfGrades and numberOfGrades
   to include new grade.
   @param grade new grade to add to student record
*/
public void addGrade(double grade)
{
   sumOfGrades = sumOfGrades + grade;
   numberOfGrades = numberOfGrades + 1;
}

/**
   Gets the grade average of the Student.
   Assumes that the number of grades is greater than 0.
   @return the average grade of the Student
*/
public double getGradeAverage()
{
   return sumOfGrades / numberOfGrades;
}

private String firstName;
private String lastName;
private String id;
private double sumOfGrades;
private int numberOfGrades;
}
```

The Student class in Example 4.4 contains five private instance variables. When implementing the Student class, we need to think about what attributes a student has. To begin, a student has a first and last name, and an ID number. We include methods that will retrieve this information for the client program (test class). The methods that return the first name, last name, and ID number have String return types because these instance variables are of type String. The student also accumulates test grades throughout the term. We include a method addGrade that allows the user to add a grade for a student. This method increments numberOfGrades and adds the grade to the sumOfGrades. The method addGrade has a void return type because no value will be returned. We then have a method getGradeAverage that returns the average of the student grades (an easy calculation—if we assume that each grade has equal weight!).

4.5.1 *Implementing Constructors*

We include two constructors in the Student class. Constructors contain instructions to initialize the instance fields of objects. Our Student object has five private instance fields that will be assigned values in the Student constructor. A constructor has the same name as the class and does not have a return type. The syntax for a constructor is:

accessSpecifier ClassName (parameterType parameterName, ...)
{
    constructor implementation
}

The *accessSpecifier* of the constructor is public. In Example 4.4, the first Student constructor has three String parameters. The values of these parameters are used to initialize the appropriate private instance fields firstName, lastName, and id. The instance fields `sumOfGrades` and `numberOfGrades` will change in the lifetime of the object and are not part of the information passed to the constructor. We initialize them to 0. We will see how these values change a little later.

The second constructor has no parameters. A constructor with no parameters is called a default constructor.

```
emptyStudent = new Student();
```

This type of constructor initializes the private instance fields with default values where `""` denotes an empty string, as shown below.

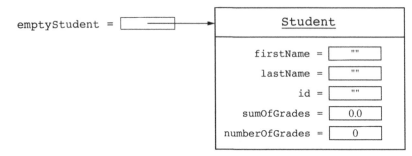

When the same name is used for more than one method or constructor, we say the name is *overloaded*. Constructors are commonly overloaded. Methods can also be overloaded provided that their signatures are different. The *signature* of a method is determined from the number, types, and order of its parameters. The return type of the method does not matter and is not included when referring to the method signature.

4.5.2 Implementing Methods

The methods `getFirstName`, `getLastName`, and `getId` are accessor methods. They require no parameters to do their tasks. Each of these accessor methods has a `String` return type because the information returned to the calling method is a `String`. The `getGradeAverage` method has a `double` return type. The method `getGradeAverage` calculates and returns the average of the student's grades. The `addGrade` method changes the value of the private instance fields, `sumOfGrades` and `numberOfGrades`, of a `Student` object. This method is a modifier (or mutator).

```
public void addGrade(double grade)
{
    sumOfGrades = sumOfGrades + grade;    // Adds grade to
                                          // sumOfGrades
    numberOfGrades = numberOfGrades + 1;  // Increments
                                          // numberOfGrades by 1
}
```

Consider the following sequence of statements and resulting student diagrams.

Example 4.5

```
Student goodStudent = new Student("Jamie", "Brown", "222333");
```

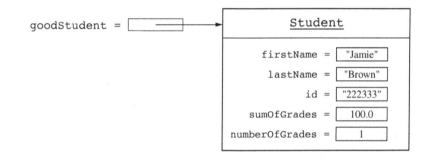

The constructor initializes the private instance fields.

```
goodStudent.addGrade(100);
```

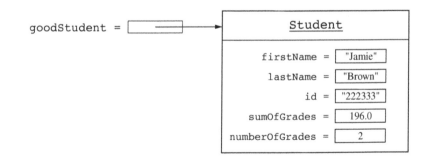

A grade of 100 is added to sumOfGrades. numberOfGrades is incremented from 0 to 1.

```
goodStudent.addGrade(96);
```

A grade of 96 is added to sumOfGrades. numberOfGrades is incremented from 1 to 2.

```
System.out.println(goodStudent.getGradeAverage());
```

The method getGradeAverage returns 98.0 (196.0 / 2) to the println method of the System.out object. *98.0* is printed to the screen.

4.5.3 Designing and Implementing a Class

Steps in designing and implementing a class are highlighted in *How To 3.1* on page 99 of your text. You should read this section carefully. The AP CS A and AB Exams may ask you to design and implement a class given a certain problem description. You should follow the steps below.

- Decide what you are asked to do with an object of that class.
- Write the public interface for the class.
  - Decide on methods, return types, and parameters.
  - Decide on what information you need to construct an object and if it is appropriate to have more than one constructor.
- Document the public interface.
- Decide on the private instance fields.
- Implement the constructors and methods.
- Test your class.

Due to the time restriction, the AP Exam usually will not require that you document your classes. However, you should always document your classes when not in an exam situation.

4.6 Unit Testing

In order to test your class, you can use an interactive development environment such as BlueJ or you can write a simple test class. This is discussed in Section 3.6 of your text. If you choose to write a test class, a good organizational technique is to name the test class with the name of the class you are testing followed by the word "Test" or "Tester". For example, a test class for the `Rectangle` class will have the name `RectangleTest`. A test class for the `Student` class will have the name `StudentTester`. The `StudentTester` class will be in a separate file named `StudentTester.java`. Example 4.6 might be a test class for our `Student` class.

Example 4.6

```java
public class StudentTester
{
    public static void main(String[] args)
    {
        Student goodStudent = new Student("Jamie", "Brown",
                "222333");
        goodStudent.addGrade(100);
        goodStudent.addGrade(96);
        System.out.println(goodStudent.getGradeAverage());
        System.out.println("Expected Value 98.0");
    }
}
```

4.7 Categories of Variables

The `Student` class demonstrates the use of two types of variables: instance fields (`firstName`, `lastName`, `id`, `sumOfGrades`, `numberOfGrades`) and parameter variables (`grade`). The implementation of the `BankAccount` class in Section 3.5 of your text is another example of a simple class. The `BankAccount` class demonstrates the use of three types of variables: instance fields (`balance`), local variables (`newBalance`), and parameter variables (`initialBalance` and `amount`). Instance fields and parameter and local variables have two major differences:

- Life span: Instance fields belong to an object and live as long as some client method refers to the object. Parameter variables and local variables belong to a method. They die (go out of scope) when the method is over.
- Initialization: You must initialize all local variables. If you do not initialize local variables, the compiler will generate an error. Parameter variables are initialized with the values that are supplied in the method call. All instance fields should be initialized but if they are not, those instance fields that are numbers are initialized to 0 and those instance fields that are object references are initialized to a special `null` value. The AP subsets do not include the rules for the default initialization of numbers to 0, references to `null`, and `boolean` variables to `false`. We will discuss `boolean` variables in Chapter 6 of this guide.

4.8   Implicit and Explicit Method Parameters

In Example 4.4, the `addGrade` method changes the value of the private instance fields, `sumOfGrades` and `numberOfGrades`, of a `Student` object. Each `Student` object has its own instance fields. If, for example, `artStudent` and `csStudent` are references to two `Student` objects, calls to `addGrade` could be

```
artStudent.addGrade(90);
artStudent.addGrade(96);
```
or
```
csStudent.addGrade(85.5);
```

The object whose `sumOfGrades` and `numberOfGrades` will be set is determined by the method call. The statement

```
sumOfGrades = sumOfGrades + grade;
```

will add `grade` to the current object's `sumOfGrades`. The *implicit parameter* of a method is the object on which the method is invoked. The `this` reference denotes this implicit parameter.

```
sumOfGrades = sumOfGrades + grade;
```

is equivalent to

```
this.sumOfGrades = this.sumOfGrades + grade;
```

When an instance field is used in the implementation of a method, the compiler automatically applies the `this` parameter. Every object method has one implicit parameter. The parameter `grade` in `addGrade` is an *explicit parameter*, because it is explicitly named in the method definition.

■ Topics That Are Useful But Not Tested

- The `javadoc` utility produces HTML files from the documentation in your code. Most of the comments included in your text use `javadoc` comments. This utility is explained in *Productivity Hint 3.1* on page 93 of your text. Your IDE may provide a tool that will produce the HTML files from your `javadoc` comments. Although the AP CS subset includes `javadoc` comments, how to produce the resulting HTML files is not part of the subset.

- If you are not using an integrated development environment, you can invoke the editor, the compiler, the linker, and the program to test manually by using command line editing. This is explained in *Productivity Hint 3.2* on page 104 of your text.
- You can call one constructor from another constructor of the same class using a short-hand notation. This is explained in *Advanced Topic 3.1* on page 110 of your text.
- Section 3.9 of your text explains how to build complex graphical objects using an object-oriented approach. Although not tested on the AP CS Exam, building such graphical objects is another example of designing and implementing classes.

■ Things to Remember When Taking the AP Exam

- Initialize all objects before you access them.
- Instance fields are initialized with default values if you do not initialize them but it is a good habit to explicitly initialize all instance fields within the constructor. The AP Exam will not test default initialization rules.
- The `return` statement in a method returns the specified value and exits the method immediately. The type of the value you are returning must match the return type of the method.
- When calling an object method from a test class (client program), you must supply an object reference on which to invoke the method.

```
artStudent.getId();   // This is OK.
getId();   // WRONG! You need to supply an object reference.
```

- Do not name parameter variables of methods with the same variable name as your instance fields. A parameter variable with the same name as an instance variable leads to complications when referencing the instance variable in the method.
- Remember to include a `return` statement if your method is to return a value.
- Do not attempt to access `private` data or methods from outside the class. If you need to use the value of an instance field, look for an accessor method that returns the value of the instance field. If there isn't one, then there probably is no need for you to access that private value outside the class.

■ Key Words

You should understand the terms below. The AP CS Exam questions may include references to these terms. The citation in parentheses next to each term identifies the page number where it is defined and/or discussed in *Java Concepts for AP Computer Science*, 5th ed.

abstraction (83)	initialization (106)	`private` (86)
access specifier (86)	instance fields (93)	`public` (86)
black box (82)	`javadoc` comments (90)	public interface (88)
constructor (87)	local variables (104)	`return` (97)
encapsulation (83)	method body (86)	return type (86)
explicit parameter (107)	object-oriented (83)	`this` (108)
implement (85)	parameter variables (104)	type (86)
implicit parameter (108)		

■ Connecting the Detailed Topic Outline to the Text

The citations in parentheses identify where information in the outline can be located in *Java Concepts for AP Computer Science*, 5th ed.

- Levels of Abstraction (82–85)
    - Black Boxes (82–83)
    - Object-Oriented Design (83–84)
    - Crawl, Walk, Run (85)
- Specifying the Public Interface of a Class (85–90)
- Commenting the Public Interface (90–93)
- Instance Fields (93–95)
- Implementing Constructors and Methods (95–101)
    - Implementing Constructors (95–96)
    - Implementing Methods (96–98)
    - Designing and Implementing a Class (99–101)
- Unit Testing (102–104)
- Categories of Variables (104–107)
- Implicit and Explicit Method Parameters (107–109)

■ Practice Questions

Multiple Choice

1. Which of the following statements about the public interface of a class is **true**?

    a. The public interface of a class includes the implementation for the constructors but not for the methods.

    b. The public interface of a class includes the implementation for the constructors and the public methods.

    c. The public interface of a class includes a set of methods, with specific types for the parameters and specification for the constructors.

    d. The public interface of a class includes a set of methods, with specific types for the parameters, specification for the constructors, and declarations of the instance fields.

    e. Writing the public interface should be the last step in program design.

2. Suppose the Car class has the following instance field declarations.

    ```
    private double mileage;    // Mileage on odometer
    private double mpg;        // Miles per gallon
    private double tankSize;   // Size of gas tank in gallons
    ```

    What is true about the initialization of the instance fields? **(not tested on the AP Exam)**

    a. The instance fields must be initialized in the constructor. If they are not, there will be a compile-time error.

    b. The instance fields must be initialized in the constructor. If they are not, the program will compile but there will be a run-time error when the Car object constructor is called.

    c. The instance fields should be initialized in the constructor. If they are not, they will automatically be initialized to null.

    d.   The instance fields should be initialized in the constructor. If they are not, they will automatically be initialized to 0.

    e.   The instance fields should be initialized to `null` by passing values to the constructor as parameters.

3.   The implicit parameter of a method in a class is denoted by

    a.   a `double`

    b.   a `String`

    c.   `null`

    d.   `this`

    e.   the empty string

4.   Consider the following three method headers.

```
I.   double findAnswer(String a, int b)
II.  int findAnswer(String a, int b)
III. double findAnswer(int b, String a)
```

Which of the following statements is **true** about their method signatures?

    a.   I and II have the same method signature and this signature is different from the method signature of III.

    b.   II and III have the same method signature and this signature is different from the method signature of I.

    c.   I and III have the same method signature and this signature is different from the method signature of II.

    d.   I, II, and III all have the same method signature.

    e.   I, II, and III all have different method signatures.

Questions 5 and 6 refer to the `BankAccount` class whose incomplete definition is shown below.

```
/**
    A bank account has a balance that can be changed by
    deposits and withdrawals.
*/
public class BankAccount
{
    /**
        Constructs a bank account with a given balance.
        @param initialBalance the initial balance
    */
    public BankAccount(double initialBalance)
    {
        balance = initialBalance;
    }

    /**
        Deposits money into the bank account.
        @param amount the amount to deposit
    */
    public void deposit(double amount)
    {
        double newBalance = balance + amount;
        balance = newBalance;
    }
```

```
/**
   Gets the current balance of the bank account.
   @return the current balance
*/
public double getBalance()
{
   return balance;
}

private double balance;
}
```

5. Suppose the following statements were executed.

    ```
    BankAccount b1 = new BankAccount(500);
    BankAccount b2 = new BankAccount(500);

    b1.deposit(b2.getBalance());
    b2.deposit(b1.getBalance());
    ```

    What are the balances of b1 and b2 after the code is executed?

    a.   b1 has balance = 500, b2 has balance = 500.
    b.   b1 has balance = 1000, b2 has balance = 500.
    c.   b1 has balance = 500, b2 has balance = 1000.
    d.   b1 has balance = 1000, b2 has balance = 1000.
    e.   b1 has balance = 1000, b2 has balance = 1500.

6. Suppose the following statements were executed.

    ```
    BankAccount b1 = new BankAccount(500);
    BankAccount b2 = b1;

    b1.deposit(b2.getBalance());
    b2.deposit(b1.getBalance());
    ```

    What are the balances of b1 and b2 after the code is executed?

    a.   b1 has balance = 500, b2 has balance = 500.
    b.   b1 has balance = 1000, b2 has balance = 500.
    c.   b1 has balance = 500, b2 has balance = 1000.
    d.   b1 has balance = 1000, b2 has balance = 2000.
    e.   b1 has balance = 2000, b2 has balance = 2000.

7. Which of the following statements about categories of variables is **true**?

    I.   Local variables are initialized within a method body.
    II. Instance variables are initialized in the constructor of the class.
    III. Parameter variables are initialized with the values that are supplied in the method call.

    a.   II only
    b.   I and II only
    c.   I and III only
    d.   II and III only
    e.   I, II, and III

8. Which of the following statements about categories of variables is **true**?

    I.   Local variables belong to the method and are in existence for the lifetime of the object to which the method belongs.
    II. Instance variables belong to the object and are in existence as long as there is some reference to the object.
    III. Parameter variables are in existence for the lifetime of the method to which they belong.

    a. II only
    b. I and II only
    c. I and III only
    d. II and III only
    e. I, II, and III

Questions 9 and 10 refer to the `Student` class whose incomplete definition is below.

```
/**
    A Student has a first name, a last name, and an ID number.
    When a student grade is entered, it is added to sumOfGrades
    and the numberOfGrades is incremented by 1.
*/
public class Student
{
    /**
        Constructs a Student.
        @param first the first name
        @param last the last name
        @param idNumber the Student id number
    */
    public Student(String first, String last, String idNumber)
    {
        firstName = first;
        lastName = last;
        id = idNumber;
        sumOfGrades = 0.0;
        numberOfGrades = 0;
    }

    /**
        Constructs a Student with default values.
    */
    public Student()
    {
        firstName = "";
        lastName = "";
        id = "";
        sumOfGrades = 0.0;
        numberOfGrades = 0;
    }

    /**
        Returns student's first name.
        @return the first name
    */
    public String getFirstName() { }
```

```java
/**
    Returns student's last name.
    @return the last name
*/
public String getLastName()  { }

/**
    Returns student's id.
    @return the student id
*/
public String getId() { }

/**
    Modifies sumOfGrades and numberOfGrades to include
    new grade.
    @param grade the grade to be added
*/
public void addGrade(double grade)
{
    sumOfGrades = sumOfGrades + grade;
    numberOfGrades = numberOfGrades + 1;
}

/**
    Returns student's average grade.
    Assumes the number of grades is greater than 0.
    @return the average grade
*/
public double getGradeAverage()
{
    return sumOfGrades / numberOfGrades;
}

    private String firstName;
    private String lastName;
    private String id;
    private double sumOfGrades;
    private int numberOfGrades;
}
```

Suppose the following statements were executed.

```java
Student one = new Student("Jamie", "Morris", "111");
Student two = new Student("Jan", "Smith", "222");

one.addGrade(56);
one.addGrade(34);
two.addGrade(one.getGradeAverage());
two.addGrade(99);
one.addGrade(two.getGradeAverage());
System.out.println(one.getGradeAverage());
System.out.println(two.getGradeAverage());
```

9. What is the value of the instance fields `numberOfGrades` and `sumOfGrades` for the `Student` object one after the code is executed?

   a. numberOfGrades = 3, sumOfGrades = 162.0
   b. numberOfGrades = 3, sumOfGrades = 189.0
   c. numberOfGrades = 5, sumOfGrades = 279.0
   d. numberOfGrades = 5, sumOfGrades = 189.0
   e. numberOfGrades = 3, sumOfGrades = 279.0

10. What is printed to the screen when this code is executed?

   a. *81.0*
      72.0
   b. *54.0*
      72.0
   c. *81.0*
      94.5
   d. *93.0*
      94.5
   e. *54.0*
      94.5

Free Response Questions

1. An `Employee` object has a first name (a `String`), a last name (a `String`), and a salary (a `double`). An incomplete class definition is given below.

```java
public class Employee
{
   /**
      Constructs default Employee.
   */
   public Employee()
   {
      myFirstName = "";
      myLastName = "";
      mySalary = 45000;
   }

   // Other constructor(s) here

   /**
      Returns employee's salary.
      @return employee's salary
   */
   public double getSalary()
   {
      return mySalary;
   }
}
```

```
/**
    Employee salary increased by byPercent percent.
*/
public void raiseSalary(double byPercent)
{
    // Code goes here
}

private String myFirstName;
private String myLastName;
private double mySalary;
}
```

a. Write a constructor for the `Employee` class that has three parameters: `firstName` (a `String`), `lastName` (a `String`), and `moneyEarned` (a `double`). The private instance variables should be initialized to the values of the parameters.

b. Write a method `raiseSalary` for the `Employee` class. The method `raiseSalary` will raise the employee's salary by a given percentage passed as a parameter to the method. For example:

```
Employee worker1 = new Employee("John", "Smith", 50000);
    // John Smith has salary = $50,000.

worker1.raiseSalary(20);
    // John Smith now has salary = $60,000.
```

Use the method header below to write `raiseSalary`.

```
public void raiseSalary(double byPercent)
```

c. Write a method `calculateBonusAmount` for the `Employee` class. The method `calculateBonusAmount` will calculate and return the amount of money to be given to an employee as a holiday bonus. This amount is based on the salary of the employee and the given percent passed as a parameter to the method. For example:

```
Employee worker1 = new Employee("John", "Smith", 50000);
    // John Smith has salary = $50,000.

System.out.println(worker1.calculateBonusAmount(3));
    // 1500.0 will be printed
```

Use the method header below to write `calculateBonusAmount`.

```
public double calculateBonusAmount(double byPercent)
```

2. A `Book` class is to be implemented with the following properties. A `Book` object has a title (a `String`), an author (a `String`), and a price (a `double`). An incomplete definition for the `Book` class is shown below.

```
public class Book
{
```

```
// Constructor goes here

/**
   Returns price of book.
   @return price of book
*/
public double getPrice()
{
    return price;
}

/**
   Decreases book price.
   @param byPercent the percent the price is decreased
*/
public void giveDiscount(double byPercent)
{
    // Code goes here
}

private String title;
private String author;
private double price;
}
```

a. Write a constructor for the Book class that has three parameters: a title (a String), an author (a String), and a price (a double).

b. Write the method giveDiscount that modifies the price of the book by decreasing the price of the book by a given percentage. For example:

```
Book myFavoriteBook = new Book("The Cat in the Hat Comes Back",
        "Dr. Seuss", 10.00);
myFavoriteBook.giveDiscount(15);     // price = 8.5
System.out.println("The new price of the book is "
        + myFavoriteBook.getPrice());
        // Output would be The new price of the book is 8.5
```

Use the method header below to write giveDiscount.

```
public void giveDiscount(double byPercent)
```

CHAPTER 5

(Covers *Java Concepts for AP Computer Science* Chapter 4)

Fundamental Data Types

■ Topic Summary

5.1   Number Types

In Java, every value is either a primitive or a reference to an object. We have used the primitive types `double` and `int` in the programs we have written so far. Both `double` and `int` are somewhat restrictive in that they cannot represent very large integer or floating-point numbers. Table 1 in Section 4.1 of your text gives details on the exact ranges of these types. You do not need to memorize the exact upper and lower limits for `int` and `double` numbers but you do need to know that there are restrictions. The `double` type also has a precision problem. Rounding errors occur when an exact conversion between numbers is not possible. Computers represent numbers in the binary number system. Because, in a computer, there is no exact representation of a fraction such as 1/10, roundoff errors may occur when we least expect them. Although you will probably not have to worry about this in writing answers to the free-response questions on the AP Exam, you do need to understand that these precision errors may exist. This is discussed in Section 4.1 and in *Advanced Topic 4.2* on page 137 of your text.

Let's look at converting one type to another. Consider another version of our `StudentTester` program from Chapter 4 of this guide.

Example 5.1

```
Student goodStudent = new Student("Jamie", "Brown", "222333");
goodStudent.addGrade(100);
goodStudent.addGrade(95);
System.out.println(goodStudent.getGradeAverage());
```

The above `println` statement would print the value 97.5. Suppose our grading system allowed for only integer-valued average grades to be given to the student. We have a few choices. The first of these choices is to ignore the fractional part of this grade average, in which case the student will receive 97 instead of the earned 97.5. You may not like this solution. However, if we look at a different problem description that involves the same situation, you may change your mind. Suppose you wanted to buy something from a vendor who refused to accept coins. If your total owed involved any cents (e.g., $4.95), and the vendor simple charged you the dollar amount ($4), would you like that? In Java, you can convert (cast) a value to a different type.

```
int newAverage = (int) goodStudent.getGradeAverage();
```

will cast our `double` value to an `int`. The variable `newAverage` will have the value of 97 in our example above. Of course, the other two solutions would be to round *up* to the next higher integer or to round to the nearest integer (closest integer value). These options will be discussed later.

5.1.1   Numbers in Other Bases

Roundoff errors occur when binary digits are lost in the internal representation of a floating-point number. Binary numbers are explained in *Advanced Topic 4.2* on page 137 of your text. You should be able to represent numbers in different bases. Three common bases are binary (base 2), octal (base 8), and hexadecimal (base 16).

Here is a method for converting the decimal number 100 to a binary number (base 2):

100/2 = 50 remainder 0
50/2 = 25 remainder 0
25/2 = 12 remainder 1
12/2 = 6 remainder 0
6/2 = 3 remainder 0
3/2 = 1 remainder 1
1/2 = 0 remainder 1

If you read the remainders from bottom to top you have the binary representation of the decimal number. 1100100 is the binary representation of the decimal number 100. Binary numbers contain only the digits 0 and 1.

To convert the fractional part of a number to binary, we multiply the fractional part by 2 until we get 0 or until the pattern repeats. Consider the decimal number 0.625.

.625 * 2 = 1.25 → integer part of product = 1
.25 * 2 = 0.5 → integer part of product = 0
.5 * 2 = 1.0 → integer part of product = 1

Read the integer parts going down. .625 is approximately equal to .101 in binary.

Consider the decimal number 0.375.

.375 * 2 = 0.75 → integer part of product = 0
.75 * 2 = 1.5 → integer part of product = 1
.5 * 2 = 1.0 → integer part of product = 1

Read the integer parts going down. .375 is approximately equal to .011 in binary. To convert 100.625 to binary, you convert the integer part and the fractional part separately. The decimal number 100.625 would convert to the binary number 1100100.101.

Advanced Topic 4.2 on page 137 of your text demonstrates converting the fractional number .35 to binary. This example shows a repeating pattern.

Similarly, to convert the decimal number 100 to an octal number (base 8):

100/8 = 12 remainder 4
12/8 = 1 remainder 4
1/8 = 0 remainder 1

If you read the remainders from bottom to top you have the octal representation of the decimal number. 144_8 is the octal representation of the decimal number 100. Octal numbers contain only the digits 0, 1, 2, 3, 4, 5, 6, and 7.

To convert the decimal number 100 to a hexadecimal number (base 16):

100/16 = 6 remainder 4
6/16 = 0 remainder 6

If you read the remainders from bottom to top you have the hexadecimal representation of the decimal number. 64_{16} is the hexadecimal representation of the decimal number 100. Hexadecimal numbers contain the digits 0–9 plus A, B, C, D, E, and F where A has the value of 10, B has the value 11, C = 12, D = 13, E = 14, and F = 15.

To convert the decimal number 27 to a hexadecimal number (base 16):

27/16 = 1 remainder 11
1/16 = 0 remainder 1

$1B_{16}$ is the hexadecimal representation of the decimal number 27.

You can reverse the algorithm to convert back to base 10. To convert the binary number 1100100 to a decimal (base 10) number, multiply each digit by the corresponding power of 2:

$$(0)(2^0) + (0)(2^1) + (1)(2^2) + (0)(2^3) + (0)(2^4) + (1)(2^5) + (1)(2^6) = 100 \text{ base 10.}$$

To convert the octal number 144_8 to a decimal, multiply by the power of 8:

$$(4)(8^0) + (4)(8^1) + (1)(8^2) = 100 \text{ base 10.}$$

To convert the hexadecimal number 64_{16} to a decimal, multiply by the power of 16:

$$(4)(16^0) + (6)(16^1) = 100 \text{ base 10.}$$

5.2   Constants

Sometimes it is convenient to use *constants* in our programs. A constant is used when the value of a variable remains the same throughout the life of the variable. Some examples might include:

```
MAXSEATS    // The maximum number of seats on an airplane
TAX_RATE   // Sales tax rate
NICKEL_VALUE   // The value of a nickel
```

In Java, we declare constants as `final` variables. Once a `final` variable has been given a value, that variable's value cannot be changed. Constants are usually given variable names that are all uppercase letters. `final` variables declared within a method can be used only within that method. Method `getTotal` below demonstrates the use of constants.

Example 5.2

```
public double getTotal()
{
    final double NICKEL_VALUE = 0.05;
    final double DIME_VALUE = 0.1;
    final double QUARTER_VALUE = 0.25;
    return nickels * NICKEL_VALUE
          + dimes * DIME_VALUE + quarters * QUARTER_VALUE;
}
```

`NICKEL_VALUE`, `DIME_VALUE`, and `QUARTER_VALUE` are only accessible from within the method `getTotal`.

It may be more useful to have these constants accessible throughout the class definition, in which case the `final` variables should be declared as `static` and either `public` or `private`. You declare a constant as `static` if you do not need a copy of the constant for each object. If your constant will be called only by methods within your class, then you should declare it as `private`. If you wish to allow client programs or other classes access to your constants, then you would declare them as `public`.

Example 5.3

```
public class PiggyBank
{
    public double getTotal()
    {
        return nickels * NICKEL_VALUE
              + dimes * DIME_VALUE + quarters * QUARTER_VALUE;
    }

    // Other methods and declarations

    private static final double NICKEL_VALUE = 0.05;
    private static final double DIME_VALUE = 0.1;
    private static final double QUARTER_VALUE = 0.25;
}
```

Section 4.2 in your text includes a more complete example of using constants in the `CashRegister` class.

5.3   Assignment, Increment, and Decrement

The assignment operator sets the variable on the left-hand side of the = operator to the value of the expression on the right-hand side of the = operator. Java also permits the combining of basic arithmetic operators with assignment by providing us with special assignment operators. For example, the arithmetic operation + can be combined with assignment to give us the += operator. The statement

```
total += count; is equivalent to total = total + count;
```

and will add the value of count to the value of total and assign this sum to total. The other combined arithmetic/assignment operators are -=, *=, /=, and %=.

In addition, Java provides an *increment* operator (++) and a *decrement* operator (--). The statement

```
count++; has the same effect as count = count + 1;
```
and

```
count--; has the same effect as count = count - 1;
```

Example 5.4

```
1    int numberOfCoins = 10;
2    int moreCoins = 12;
3    numberOfCoins = numberOfCoins + 1;    // numberOfCoins = 11
4    numberOfCoins++;    // numberOfCoins = 12
5    numberOfCoins += moreCoins;    // numberOfCoins = 24
6    numberOfCoins--;    // numberOfCoins = 23
```

Lines 1 and 2 assign integer values to int variables.
Line 3 increments the int variable numberOfCoins by 1 and assigns this new value to numberOfCoins.
Line 4 illustrates another method of incrementing numberOfCoins by 1.
Line 5 adds the value of moreCoins to the value of numberOfCoins and assigns this new value to numberOfCoins.
Line 6 decrements the value of numberOfCoins by 1.

Java is a strongly typed language. We must take care that the type of the value on the right-hand side of the = sign is compatible with the type of the variable on the left-hand side of the = sign. We cannot make the following assignment because Student and int are not compatible types.

```
Student goodStudent = new Student();
goodStudent = 10;    // WRONG
```

An int can be assigned to a double because an int can be stored in a double without loss of information.

```
int numberOfCoins = 7;
double taxRate = numberOfCoins;
System.out.println(taxRate);    // Prints 7.0
```

A double cannot be assigned to an int. There would be a loss of information. An attempt to do this type of assignment results in a compiler error.

```
double taxRate = 7;    // This is OK.
```

```
int numberOfCoins = taxRate;    // WRONG; This is a compile-time
            // error (failure to recognize the loss of precision).
```

Number variables hold values. Assigning a number variable to another number variable assigns its value.

```
int aNum = 5;
int anotherNum = aNum;
```

Object variables hold references. Assigning an object reference to another object reference creates another reference to the same object.

```
Car mySportsCar = new Car(20);    // mpg = 20 (efficiency)
                                  // initial mileage = 0
Car yourNewVehicle = mySportsCar;
```

Changing information for `mySportsCar` will be reflected in `yourNewVehicle`. Both object variables refer to the same object. Now that both object variables refer to the same object, they both get 20 miles per gallon! And when you *drive* `yourNewVehicle`, `mySportsCar`'s mileage goes up! This may not necessarily be your intended result.

5.4   Arithmetic Operations and Mathematical Functions

Most applications require us to write expressions that contain arithmetic operations. Computers will do exactly what we tell them to do, so take care in writing complicated algebraic expressions. Use parentheses just as you do in algebra. The order of operations shown in Table 5.1 lists operators with the highest priority at the top. If two operations on the same level are contained in one expression, these operations are evaluated from left to right, just as they would be in an algebraic expression. Sometimes splitting a complicated expression into smaller parts and combining these parts to obtain the final result enhances readability and decreases errors.

Table 5.1

Operator Precedence (top row has highest priority)

Operator Order of Precedence				
++ --				
* / %				
+ -				
= *= /= %= += -=				

The arithmetic operations involving two operands work as you would expect in most cases. However, if both numbers are integers, then the result of division is always an integer, with the remainder discarded. For example, the result of 7 / 3 is 2. The remainder of 1 is discarded. If you are interested in the remainder, use the modulus operator. The result of 7 % 3 is 1 because the remainder when 7 is divided by 3 is 1. You must be careful when dividing and using the modulus operator in arithmetic expressions, especially if you are combining doubles and integers.

Table 5.2

Arithmetic Expressions

Expression	Operand 1	Operand 2	Result	Result Type
4 + 5	int	int	9	int
14 / 5	int	int	2	int
4 / 5	int	int	0	int
14 / 5.0	int	double	2.8	double
14.0 / 5	double	int	2.8	double
14 % 5	int	int	4	int
4 % 5	int	int	4	int

Java provides a library of math functions that can help us with solutions to complicated applications. The AP CS subsets include only those math functions listed in Table 5.3.

Table 5.3

`class java.lang.Math`

Method	Method Summary
`static int abs(int x)`	Returns the absolute value of the integer x.
`static double abs(double x)`	Returns the absolute value of the double x.
`static double pow(double base,` `    double exponent)`	Returns the value of `base` raised to the power exponent.
`static double sqrt(double x)`	Returns the correctly rounded positive square root of a double number x.
`static double random()`	Returns a double in the range [0.0, 1.0). (Includes 0.0 but does not include 1.0.)

5.5   Calling Static Methods

The functions from `java.lang.Math` are `static` functions. You can see this by the word `static` before the return type in the method header.

```
static double sqrt(double x)
```

This indicates that the method does not operate on an object. To invoke the square root function, we write

```
Math.sqrt(x)
```

Because of the Java convention of naming variables, methods, and classes, we can tell that the call above is a static method. Math begins with a capital letter which designates this as a class and not an object. *Quality Tip 4.2* on page 145 and Sections 4.2 and 4.5 of your text discuss the convention of naming variables, classes, and methods.

5.5.1   *More on Type Conversion*

We have mentioned that Java is a strongly typed language. This means that the compiler will complain if we try to assign incompatible types.

```
int a = 4;
double b = 2.1;
int c = a + b;    // Compiler complains about loss of precision.
```

If we intentionally want to discard the fractional part of this result, we need to *cast* the result to an int before the assignment can be made.

```
int a = 4;
double b = 2.1;
int c = (int) (a + b);    // Compiler no longer complains.
```

You do need to realize that this results in a loss of precision. The behavior resulting from casting to an int is sometimes referred to as "truncation toward 0" behavior, because the rounding truncates (cuts off) the fractional part of the double number, the result being an integer that is closer to zero than the original double number.

Table 5.4

Truncation Toward 0 Behavior

Expression	Result
int num = (int) (3.4);	3
int num = (int) (3.7);	3
int num = (int) (-3.4);	-3
int num = (int) (-3.7);	-3

You can use this behavior to round floating-point numbers to integer values. The expression

```
(int) (x + 0.5)
```

rounds a positive floating-point number, x, to the nearest integer and the expression

```
(int) (x - 0.5)
```

rounds a negative floating-point number, x, to the nearest integer.

Table 5.5
Rounding Numbers

Statements	Rounding Result
`double x = 4.2` `int xRounded = (int)(x + 0.5)`	4
`double x = 4.8` `int xRounded = (int)(x + 0.5)`	5
`double x = -4.2` `int xRounded = (int)(x - 0.5)`	-4
`double x = -4.7` `int xRounded = (int)(x - 0.5)`	-5

Of course, `java.lang.Math` does provide a method `round`. The `double` parameter is rounded to an integer by adding 1/2, taking the integer that is less than or equal to this result, and casting the result to type `long`. Care has to be taken when using this `Math.round` method with negative numbers. `Math.round(-4.5)` returns -4. The `round` method is not tested on the AP Exams.

5.5.2   Random Numbers

The `java.lang.Math.random()` method can be used to generate integers and doubles in a specified range, as seen in Table 5.6 below. The general form for generating random integers is:

```
int numberOfNumbers = some positive integer representing the number of numbers
                         from which we are choosing
int smallestNumber  = the smallest number in the range of the random numbers

int rnd = (int)(Math.random() * numberOfNumbers + smallestNumber);
```

For example,

```
(int)(Math.random() * 23 + 3)
```

will generate a random integer in the range [3, 25].

Table 5.6
Random Numbers

Expression	Result
`Math.random()`	[0.0, 1.0)
`Math.random() * 100`	[0.0, 100.0)
`Math.random() * 100 + 1`	[1.0, 101.0)
`(int)(Math.random() * 100 + 1)`	[1, 100]
`(int)(Math.random() * 20 + 10)`	[10, 29]

5.6   Strings

Strings are one of the most commonly used data types. A `String` is a sequence of characters enclosed within double quotes. A `String` is an object. Strings can be concatenated (put end to end to produce a new string) by using the + operator. If one expression to the left or right of the +

is a `String`, then the other is automatically converted to a `String` and the two parts are concatenated. For example,

```
String s = "The number of ";
s += "Dalmatians is: ";   // Two strings concatenated
```

`s` is now the string: *The number of Dalmatians is:*

```
s += 101;   // 101 is automatically converted
System.out.println(s);
```

The number of Dalmatians is: 101 is printed.

Although the `String` class has many methods, you are responsible for those listed in Table 5.7.

Table 5.7

class java.lang.String implements java.lang.Comparable

Method	Method Summary
int compareTo(Object other)	Compares two strings lexicographically. Returns value < 0 if this `String` is less than `other`. Returns 0 if this `String` is equal to `other`. Returns value > 0 if this `String` is greater than `other`.
boolean equals(Object other)	Compares this `String` to specified object. The result is `true` if and only if `other` is not `null` and is a `String` object that represents the same sequence of characters as this object.
int length()	Returns the length of the `String`.
String substring(int from, int to)	Returns a new string that is a substring of this one beginning at `from` and ending at `to - 1`.
String substring(int from)	Returns a new string that is a substring of this one beginning at `from` and ending at `length - 1`.
int indexOf(String str)	If `str` occurs as a substring within this object, then the index of the first character of the first such substring is returned; if it does not occur as a substring, `-1` is returned.

Comparing strings lexicographically means that the strings are compared character by character according to the Unicode character set (*Appendix B* in your text). *Advanced Topic 4.5* on page 162 and *Random Fact 4.2* on page 163 of your text discuss the Unicode character set in detail.

Example 5.5 demonstrates these `String` methods.

Example 5.5

```
1   public class StringTester
2   {
3      public static void main(String[] args)
4      {
5         String greeting = "Hello";
6         String bookName = "Java Concepts";
7         System.out.println(greeting);
8         System.out.println(bookName);
9
```

```
10              String subBook = bookName.substring(5, 12);
11              System.out.println(subBook);
12
13              System.out.println(greeting.length());
14              System.out.println(greeting.substring(3));
15
16              int position = bookName.indexOf("Java");
17              System.out.println(position);
18
19              greeting = greeting + " there!";
20              System.out.println(greeting);
21          }
22      }
```

Lines 5 and 6 create `String` objects and assign values to these `String` objects.

Line 7 prints *Hello*

Line 8 prints *Java Concepts*

Line 10 creates a new `String` containing the characters in positions 5 to 11 inclusive. The first character in a string is in position 0.

Line 11 prints *Concept*

Line 13 prints *5*

Line 14 prints *lo* This prints the substring from position 3 to the end of the string.

Line 16 assigns to the integer variable `position` the index of the first occurrence of *Java* in the `String` *Java Concepts*

Line 17 prints *0*

Line 19 creates a new `String` with the value obtained from concatenating *Hello* with *there!* Strings are immutable objects. This means that a `String` object is never changed. A new `String` object is created when an assignment such as the one in line 19 is executed.

Line 20 prints *Hello there!*

The `String` methods `compareTo` and `equals` will be discussed in Chapter 6.

5.6.1   *Escape Sequences*

Some characters have a special meaning in Java and cannot be directly included as a character in a string. Two such characters are the backslash (\ ) and the double quotes ("). The backslash is used as an escape character and the double quotes character either begins or ends a string literal. Java provides escape sequences that enable us to include these characters as characters in a string. Another escape sequence that is often used to help in formatting output denotes a newline or linefeed character (\n).

Example 5.6

```
1    System.out.println("C:\\My Documents\\Hello.java");
2    System.out.println("He said: \"Hello!\"");
3    System.out.println("One\nTwo\nThree");
```

will print

> *C:\My Documents\Hello.java*
> *He said: "Hello!"*
> *One*
> *Two*
> *Three*

Line 1 uses \\ to indicate that a \ is a character in the output string. This occurs twice.

Line 2 uses \" to indicate that " is a character in the output string. This occurs twice.

Line 3 uses \n to indicate that a new line begins. This occurs twice. The output string for Line 3 is written to three different lines.

■ Expanded Coverage of Material That Is Not Found in the Text

- The `String` method `indexOf` is part of the AP CS language subset.

  ```
  int indexOf(String s)
  ```

  If `s` occurs as a substring within this object, then the index of the first character of the first such substring is returned; if it does not occur as a substring, `-1` is returned.

  ```
  String greeting = "Hello";
  System.out.println(greeting.indexOf("e"));    // Prints 1
  System.out.println(greeting.indexOf("x"));    // Prints -1
  ```

- The `Math.random` method is used to generate random numbers. This method is explained in Section 5.5 of this guide. Examples of its use are listed in Table 5.6 of this guide.

■ Topics That Are Useful But Not Tested

- `java.lang.Math` has many useful methods that will not be tested on the AP CS Exam. These methods are listed in Table 2 in Section 4.4 of your text.
- The `toUpperCase` and `toLowerCase` methods of the `String` class discussed in Section 2.3 of your text can be very useful.
- If a `String` contains the digits of a number, you can use the `Integer.parseInt` or `Double.parseDouble` method to obtain the number value. This is discussed in Section 4.6 of your text.
- Strings are composed of individual characters. Characters are values of the `char` type. The `char` type is discussed in *Advanced Topic 4.5* on page 162 of your text. The `charAt` method can prove to be quite useful when working with strings.
- Sometimes it is convenient to have values input by the person using the program. *Advanced Topic 4.7* on page 169 discusses reading input using the `JOptionPane.showInputDialog` method. On the AP CS Exam, if input by the user is required, you will see something similar to:

  ```
  double x = call to a method that reads a floating-point number;
  ```
  or
  ```
  double x = IO.readDouble();    // Read user input
  ```

- It is often important to output information in a specific format. You may wish to have a certain number of decimal places printed. You can achieve proper formatting with the `printf` method of the `PrintStream` class. This is explained in *Advanced Topic 4.6* of your text. Since formatting output is not tested on the AP Exam, `printf` will not be tested.

- The Scanner class enables you to read keyboard input in a console window. Although input is not tested on the AP Exam, the Scanner class is easy to use and gives us an option for reading input in our programs. The Scanner class is discussed in Section 4.7 of your text.

■ Things to Remember When Taking the AP Exam

- Remember to declare all variables before you use them.
- Initialize variables that need to be initialized.
- Do not use *magic* numbers in your code. Magic numbers are constants that appear in your code with no explanation. They are explained in *Quality Tip 4.1* on page 145 of your text.
- Use descriptive variable names. This is discussed in *Quality Tip 4.2* on page 145 of your text.
- Use parentheses as you would in algebra. If in doubt about the need for parentheses in an expression, use them.
- Remember that integer divided by integer equals integer. Sometimes casting an integer to a double is required to obtain a correct result.
- Remember that the first character of a String is in position 0.
- The indexOf method of the String class returns -1 if the string being searched for is not found.
- The last character of a String s is in position s.length() - 1.
- When you assign one object variable to another object variable, both object variables reference the same object.

■ Key Words

You should understand the terms below. The AP CS Exam questions may include references to these terms. The citation in parentheses next to each term identifies the page number where it is defined and/or discussed in *Java Concepts for AP Computer Science*, 5th ed.

assignment (146)	final (141)	modulus operator % (149)
binary numbers (137)	increment operator (146)	rounding error (135)
cast (136)	magic numbers (145)	static method (153)
concatenation (158)	Math.sqrt (149)	String (158)
constant (140)	Math.pow (149)	substring (159)
decrement operator (146)	Math.abs (150)	

■ Connecting the Detailed Topic Outline to the Text

The citations in parentheses identify where information in the outline can be located in *Java Concepts for AP Computer Science*, 5th ed.

- Number Types (134–140)
  - Numbers in Other Bases (137)
- Constants (140–145)
- Assignment, Increment, and Decrement (146–148)

- Arithmetic Operations and Mathematical Functions (148–153)
- Calling Static Methods (153–154)
- Strings (158–162)
  - Escape Sequences (161)

■ Practice Questions

Multiple Choice

1. Consider the following declarations.

   ```
   int a = some integer value
   int b = some integer value
   int c = some integer value
   ```

   Which of the following statements will correctly calculate the average of a, b, and c?

   a. `int average = (a + b + c) / 3`
   b. `double average = a + b + c / 3`
   c. `double average = (a + b + c) / 3.0`
   d. `double average = (double) ((a + b + c) / 3)`
   e. `double average = (a + b + c) / 3`

2. The expression

   ```
   5 + 6 * 3 % 2 - 1
   ```

   evaluates to

   a. 0
   b. 1
   c. 4
   d. 10
   e. 13

3. Given the following declarations:

   ```
   int m = 18;
   int n = 4;
   ```

   What is the value of the following expression?

   ```
   m / n + m % n
   ```

   a. 0
   b. 2
   c. 6
   d. 6.5
   e. 10.5

Questions 4 and 5 refer to the following segment of code.

```
String bookName = "Java Concepts for AP Computer Science";
String newWord = bookName.substring(18)
        + bookName.substring(4,18) + bookName.substring(0,4);
```

4. After the code is executed, what is the `String` that `newWord` references?

    a. `"A Concepts for Java"`
    b. `"AP Computer Science Java Concepts "`
    c. `"P Computer Sciencea Concepts for Java"`
    d. `"AP Computer Science Concepts for Java"`
    e. An error message is generated

5. The statement

```
System.out.println(bookName.indexOf("cat"));
```

    prints

    a. *−1*
    b. *0*
    c. *null*
    d. *1*
    e. An error message is generated

Questions 6–9 refer to the following incomplete definition of the `PiggyBank` class.

```
public class PiggyBank
{
    /**
        Constructor-initializes nickels, dimes, and quarters to 0.
    */
    public PiggyBank() {. . .}

    /**
        Adds nickels to the bank.
        @param count the number of nickels to add
    */
    public void addNickels(int count) {. . .}

    /**
        Adds dimes to the bank.
        @param count the number of dimes to add
    */
    public void addDimes(int count) {. . .}

    /**
        Adds quarters to the bank.
        @param count the number of quarters to add
    */
    public void addQuarters(int count) {. . .}
```

```
/**
    Returns total value of all the coins in the bank.
    @return the total amount of money in the bank
*/
public double getTotal(){. . .}

/**
    Takes count dimes from the bank.
    @param count the number of dimes to take from the bank
*/
public void subtractDimes(int count)
{
    // Code goes here
}

private static final double NICKEL_VALUE = 0.05;
private static final double DIME_VALUE = 0.1;
private static final double QUARTER_VALUE = 0.25;
private int nickels;    // Number of nickels in piggy bank
private int dimes;    // Number of dimes in piggy bank
private int quarters;    // Number of quarters in piggy bank
}
```

6. The code for method `subtractDimes` should be

   a. `dimes = dimes - DIME_VALUE * count;`

   b. `dimes = dimes - count;`

   c. `double amount = dimes - count;`
      `return amount;`

   d. `int amount = dimes - 1;`
      `return amount;`

   e. `int amount = dimes - DIME_VALUE * count;`
      `return amount;`

7. A client program is to print the total value of the coins in the `PiggyBank` object `myBank`. Which of the following code segments will complete the intended task?

   I. `double totalMoney = myBank.getTotal();`
       `System.out.println(totalMoney);`

   II. `double totalMoney = nickels * NICKEL_VALUE + dimes`
          `* DIME_VALUE + quarters * QUARTER_VALUE;`
       `System.out.println(totalMoney);`

   III. `double totalMoney = nickels * 0.05 + dimes * 0.10`
           `+ quarters  * 0.25;`
        `System.out.println(totalMoney);`

   a. I only
   b. II only
   c. III only
   d. I and III only
   e. II and III only

8. After the following code is executed, what are the values of c and d?

```
PiggyBank p = new PiggyBank();
PiggyBank q = p;
p.addNickels(5);
q.addNickels(3);
double c = p.getTotal();
double d = q.getTotal();
```

a. c = 5   d = 3
b. c = 0.25   d = 0.15
c. c = 0.25   d = 0.25
d. c = 0.15   d = 0.15
e. c = 0.4   d = 0.4

9. Consider the following code segment.

```
1     int numberOfCoins = 5;
2     double taxRate = 4;
3     double number = 3.0;
4     PiggyBank yourBank;
5     PiggyBank myMoney = new PiggyBank();
6     taxRate = numberOfCoins;
7     numberOfCoins = number;
```

Which of the following statements is **true**?

a. A compile-time error occurs in line 2 because 4 is an int and not a double.
b. A compile-time error occurs in line 4 because an object is not being created with new.
c. An error occurs in line 6 because numberOfCoins and taxRate are not compatible types.
d. An error occurs in line 7 because a double cannot be assigned to an int.
e. The program will compile without errors.

10. Which of the following statements about objects and classes is **true**?

a. A final variable in a class must be declared as private.
b. Multiple object references cannot contain references to the same object.
c. A client program can create only one object of a class.
d. A static method is a method that operates on an object that has been instantiated.
e. Every object belongs to a class.

Free Response Questions

1. Consider the `Car` class, whose incomplete definition is shown below.

```java
public class Car
{
    /**
        Constructs a car with given values.
        @param milesPerGal the number of miles per gallon
        @param miles total miles recorded on car
        @param gasTankHolds the amount of gas the tank holds
        @param gasTankHas the amount of gas in the tank
    */
    public Car(double milesPerGal, double miles,
            double gasTankHolds, double gasTankHas)
    {
        mpg = milesPerGal;   // Miles per gallon
        mileage = miles;   // Total mileage of car
        tankCapacity = gasTankHolds;   // Amount of gas tank holds
        gasInTank = gasTankHas;   // Amount of gas in the gas tank
    }

    /**
        Updates mileage and gasInTank to reflect numMiles being
        driven. Assumes there is enough gas in tank to make trip.
        @param numMiles number of miles driven
    */
    public void drive(double numMiles)
    {
        // Code goes here
    }

    /**
        Returns amount of gas consumed by car in numMiles miles.
        @param numMiles number of miles driven
        @return gas consumed
    */
    public double findGasUsed(double numMiles)
    {
        // Code goes here
    }

    /**
        Returns the total mileage on car.
        @return car mileage
    */
    public double getMileage()
    {
        return mileage;
    }

    /**
        Returns the amount of gas in tank.
        @return amount of gas in tank
    */
    public double getGasInTank()
    {
```

```
        return gasInTank;
    }

    private double mpg;
    private double mileage;
    private double tankCapacity;
    private double gasInTank;
}
```

a. Write the method `findGasUsed`. This method should calculate and return the amount of gas used in driving `numMiles` miles. Assume that you have enough gas to make the requested trip!

Call to findGasUsed	mpg	Value returned
findGasUsed(100)	20	5.0
findGasUsed(25.2)	25	1.008
findGasUsed(10)	25	0.4

Use the method header below.

```
public double findGasUsed(double numMiles)
```

b. Write the method `drive`. The method `drive` is given the number of miles the car has traveled as a parameter. Certain `private` instance variables need to be updated as a result of this action. You may include a call to `findGasUsed` from part a. Assume that this function works as specified regardless of what you wrote for part a. Use the method header below to write your method `drive`.

```
public void drive(double numMiles)
```

2. A `Purse`, whose definition is shown below, is used to keep track of a number of coins.

```
/**
    A purse computes the total value of a collection of coins.
*/
public class Purse
{
    public Purse()    // Constructor
    {
        nickels = 0;
        dimes = 0;
        quarters = 0;
    }

    /**
        Adds nickels to the purse.
        @param count is the number of nickels to add
    */
    public void addNickels(int count)
    {
        nickels += count;
    }
```

```
/**
    Adds dimes to the purse.
    @param count is the number of dimes to add
*/
public void addDimes(int count)
{
    dimes += count;
}

/**
    Adds quarters to the purse.
    @param count is the number of quarters to add
*/
public void addQuarters(int count)
{
    quarters += count;
}

/**
    Gets the total value of the coins in the purse.
    @return the sum of all coin values
*/
public double getTotal()
{
    return nickels * NICKEL_VALUE + dimes * DIME_VALUE
        + quarters * QUARTER_VALUE;
}

/**
    Returns the total value of the coins in the purse in
    pennies.
    @return the value of coins in purse in pennies
*/
public int totalInPennies()
{
    // Code goes here
}

/**
    Returns the number of whole dollars in the purse.
    @return the number of dollars in purse
*/
public int getDollars()
{
    // Code goes here
}

/**
    Returns the number of cents in the purse. If the total
    amount in the purse is $7.56, getCents will return 56.
    @return the number of cents in purse
*/
public int getCents()
{
    // Code goes here
}
```

```
        private static final double NICKEL_VALUE = 0.05;
        private static final double DIME_VALUE = 0.1;
        private static final double QUARTER_VALUE = 0.25;
        private static final int PENNIES_PER_DOLLAR = 100;

        private int nickels;    // Number of nickels in the purse
        private int dimes;    // Number of dimes in the purse
        private int quarters;    // Number of quarters in the purse
    }
```

a. Write the method `totalInPennies` that returns the total value of the coins in the purse in pennies. In writing your solution, you may not include calls to `getCents` or `getDollars`. You may include calls to other methods defined in this class.

Total value of coins in `Purse`	Value returned
2.14	214
0.30	30
2.00	200

Use the method header below.

```
    public int totalInPennies()
```

b. Write the method `getDollars` that returns the number of whole dollars in the `Purse` as an integer. In writing your solution, you may include calls to `totalInPennies` from part a. Assume `totalInPennies` works as intended. Examples of calls to `getDollars` appear below.

Total value of coins in `Purse`	Value returned
2.14	2
0.30	0
2.00	2

Use the method header below.

```
    public int getDollars()
```

c. Write the method `getCents` that returns the number of cents in the `Purse` as an integer. In writing your solution, you may include calls to other methods defined in this class. Examples of calls to `getCents` appear below.

Total value of coins in `Purse`	Value returned
2.14	14
0.30	30
2.00	0

Use the method header below.

```
    public int getCents()
```

CHAPTER 6

(Covers *Java Concepts for AP Computer Science* Chapter 5)

Decisions

TOPIC OUTLINE

■ Topic Summary

6.1   The `if` Statement

The `if` statement is used to control the flow of a program based on a condition. Examples 6.1, 6.2, and 6.3 are the general forms used most often in AP CS.

Example 6.1

```
if (condition)
    statement1;
```

If *condition* evaluates to `true`, *statement1* is executed; otherwise it is not.

Example 6.2

```
if (condition)
    statement1;
else
    statement2;
```

If *condition* evaluates to `true`, *statement1* is executed; otherwise *statement2* is executed.

Example 6.3

```
if (condition1)
    statement1;
else if (condition2)
    statement2;
else
    statement3;
```

If *condition1* evaluates to `true`, *statement1* is executed; otherwise *condition2* is checked. If *condition2* evaluates to `true`, *statement2* is executed; otherwise *statement3* is executed. Example 6.3 could be extended to include more conditions.

Each *statement* in Examples 6.1, 6.2, and 6.3 can be replaced by a block statement as described in Section 5.1 of your text.

```
if (condition)
{
    statement1;
}
else
{
    statement2;
    statement3;
}
```

It is a good idea to always use a block statement format with `if` statements. This makes your code less confusing—especially if you have nested `if` statements (one `if` statement inside another). This blocking also allows for easy insertion of statements in the event that your code is revised. This blocking is necessary if more than one statement is to be executed within the `if` branch or the `else` branch. *Quality Tip 5.1* on page 185 and *Productivity Hint 5.1* on page 186 of your text discuss the use of proper indentation and formatting of braces in your code.

6.2 Comparing Values

6.2.1 *Relational Operators*

An `if` statement performs a test. Many of these tests compare values with relational operators. There are six relational operators:

Table 6.1

Relational Operators

Relational Operator	Meaning	Relational Operator	Meaning
>	Greater than	<=	Less than or equal to
>=	Greater than or equal to	==	Equal to
<	Less than	!=	Not equal to

6.2.2 *Comparing Floating-Point Numbers*

Relational operators involving integer expressions work as you would expect but you should be very careful when comparing doubles. We talked about limited precision and roundoff errors in Chapter 5 in this guide. Because of these roundoff errors, doubles should never be compared with ==. Section 5.2.2 in your text discusses this in detail.

6.2.3 *Comparing Strings*

We also should not use == to compare strings. Strings are objects. If you compare two `String` variables with the == operator, you are testing whether they reference the same object. The Java `String` class provides methods to compare strings. These methods are `equals` and `compareTo` and are summarized in Table 6.2.

Table 6.2

`class java.lang.String implements java.lang.Comparable`

Method	Method Summary
`int compareTo(Object other)`	Compares two strings lexicographically. Returns value < 0 if this string is less than `other`. Returns 0 if this string is equal to `other`. Returns value > 0 if this string is greater than `other`.
`boolean equals(Object other)`	Compares this string to object `other`. The result is `true` if and only if `other` is not `null` and is a `String` object that represents the same sequence of characters as this object.

Strings are really sequences of characters. Each character has a unique representation that is based on the Unicode encoding scheme. The ordering of characters is such that uppercase characters come before lowercase characters (`'D'` comes before `'a'`). When two strings are compared, corresponding letters are compared until one of the strings ends or the corresponding letters differ (`"cat"` comes before `"catch"`; `"cane"` comes before `"cat"`). Strings are compared *lexicographically* (according to their Unicode values).

Example 6.4

```
String s = "Dog";
if (s.compareTo("cat") < 0)
   System.out.println("Dog comes before cat.");
else if (s.compareTo("cat") > 0)
   System.out.println("cat comes before Dog.");
else
   System.out.println("Dog equals cat.");
```

Example 6.4 prints *Dog comes before cat.* because `'D'` comes before `'c'` in the Unicode encoding scheme. *Appendix B* in your text contains the coding for the U.S. English and Western European characters. Section 5.2.3 in your text presents other examples.

Example 6.5 demonstrates the use of the `String` method `compareTo`. The task of this code segment is to examine three strings and determine and print the value of the string that lexicographically comes first.

Example 6.5

```
1      String string1 = "cat";
2      String string2 = "dog";
3      String string3 = "animal";

4      String firstInOrder = string1;
5      if (string2.compareTo(firstInOrder) < 0)
6          firstInOrder = string2;

7      if (string3.compareTo(firstInOrder) < 0)
8          firstInOrder = string3;

9      System.out.println(firstInOrder);
```

Lines 1–3 create `String` objects and assign values to these `String` objects.

Line 4 `firstInOrder` references `"cat"`.

Line 5 compares `"dog"` with `"cat"`. The expression `(string2.compareTo(firstInOrder)` `< 0)` evaluates to `false` because `"dog"` is not lexicographically before (<) `"cat"`.

Line 6 is not executed.

Line 7 compares `"animal"` with `"cat"`. The expression `(string3.compareTo` `(firstInOrder) < 0)` evaluates to `true` because `"animal"` is lexicographically before (<) `"cat"`.

Line 8 `firstInOrder` now references `"animal"`.

Line 9 prints *animal*.

Example 6.6 demonstrates the `String` method `equals` and the differences between `equals` and `==` when applied to strings.

Example 6.6

```
1      String string3 = "animal";
2      String string4 = "animal house";
3      if (string3 == string4.substring(0, 6))     // Evaluates to false
4          System.out.println("EQUAL");
5      else
6          System.out.println("NOT EQUAL");

7      if (string3.equals(string4.substring(0, 6)))  // Evaluates to true
8          System.out.println("EQUAL");
9      else
10         System.out.println("NOT EQUAL");
```

The expression in line 3 evaluates to `false` because `string3` and `string4.substring(0,6)` are not referencing the same `String` object. Line 7 evaluates to `true` because both `String` variables are referring to the same literal string `"animal"`.

Because Java treats strings differently than other objects, the result can be somewhat confusing. *Common Error 5.1* on page 190 of your text explains this in detail. It is very important to remember that the `==` operator should not be used with strings or with other objects to test whether two objects have the same contents.

6.2.4   *Comparing Objects*

If you use `==` when comparing objects, you are asking whether two object variables reference the same object. If your intention is to check whether the objects are equal in value, you need to call an `equals` method. This method is provided for Java `String` objects. With your own classes, you will need to write the `equals` method. It is not automatically provided for you. The `equals` method can be defined using any criterion that is appropriate for the class. It is always a good idea to check the class methods to be sure `equals` is included for any class whose objects you want to compare. Chapter 10 of your text covers `equals` in more detail. The implementation of `equals` is not tested on the AP Exams.

It is important to remember that strings are immutable. When concatenating two strings, a new `String` object is created. For example,

```
String stringA = "Super";
String stringB = "man";
```

creates references to `String` objects.

```
stringA =   [   "Super"   ]

stringB =   [   "man"   ]
```

The code segment

```
String stringC = stringA
stringA = stringA + stringB
```

creates a new `String` object and `stringA` now references that new object.

```
stringC =   [   "Super"   ]

stringB =   [   "man"   ]

stringA =   ["Superman"]
```

6.2.5   *Testing for* `null`

Consider the declaration

```
Car myCar;
```

After this statement is executed, no object is allocated. This declaration does not create an object. The variable `myCar` is uninitialized. The declaration simply states that the variable `myCar` may reference a `Car` object. If you attempt to execute the statement

```
System.out.println(myCar.getMileage());
```

the compiler will complain that `myCar` has not been initialized.

However, sometimes you want to indicate that an object variable *does not* reference an actual object. Then you use the `null` reference:

```
Car myCar = null;   // I don't have a car right now.
```

The `null` reference refers to no object.

If your program is organized in such a way that you sometimes initialize a variable with `null`, then you need to include a test before applying a method to such a variable:

```
if (myCar != null) mileage = myCar.getMileage();
```

A run-time error occurs when an attempt is made to invoke a method on a `null` reference. In this case, a `NullPointerException` will be thrown. Exceptions will be covered in more detail in Chapter 12 of this guide and Chapter 11 of your text.

The declaration

```
String name;
```

indicates that the variable `name` may hold a reference to a `String` object. At this point `name` is uninitialized.

```
String name = "";
```

initializes `name` with a reference to an *empty* string—a string of length 0 that has no characters. However,

```
String name = null;
```

initializes `name` with `null`. It doesn't refer to any string at all!

You use the `==` operator (not the `equals` method) to test whether an object reference is a `null` reference.

Example 6.7

```
String a;   // a not initialized
String b = null;   // b initialized to null
String c = "";   // c initialized to the empty string
System.out.println(a);   // Compile-time error
System.out.println(b);   // Prints null
System.out.println(c);   // Prints nothing
System.out.println(a.length());   // Compile-time error
System.out.println(b.length());   // Run-time error: throws
                                   // NullPointerException
System.out.println(c.length());   // Prints 0
```

Note that *instance fields* are always initialized with some value. If you don't specifically initialize an instance field whose type is a class, then it is initialized with `null`. This is a common cause of programming errors. Consider this example,

```
public class Person
{
    . . .
    private String name;
}
```

If the `Person` constructor does not set the `name` field to a specific string, then it is initialized with `null`. Calling a method on the `name` field, such as `name.length()`, causes a `Null-PointerException`. You should always initialize instance fields with appropriate values in the constructor of the class.

6.3 Multiple Alternatives

Many times we wish to solve problems that involve complex decisions. If our algorithm involves multiple alternatives, the arrangement of the conditions may determine the correctness of our result. Example 6.3 provides the basic format for multiple alternatives.

Consider the task of printing the letter grade equivalent for a given integer-valued grade. You wish to use the following grade conversions.

Numerical Grade	Letter Grade
90-100	A
80-89	B
70-79	C
60-69	D
below 60	F

Example 6.8 performs the task as intended.

Example 6.8

```
if (grade < 60)
    System.out.println('F');
else if (grade < 70)
    System.out.println('D');
else if (grade < 80)
    System.out.println('C');
else if (grade < 90)
    System.out.println('B');
else
    System.out.println('A');
```

If `grade` has the value 62, the output will be *D*. The conditions are *exclusive*. The conditions are checked until the appropriate one is determined. After this occurs, the other conditions are not checked.

Example 6.9 eliminates the `else`s in Example 6.8.

Example 6.9

```
if (grade < 60)
    System.out.println('F');
if (grade < 70)
    System.out.println('D');
if (grade < 80)
    System.out.println('C');
if (grade < 90)
    System.out.println('B');
else
    System.out.println('A');
```

This example has a very different result. If `grade` is 62, the output printed will be:

> *D*
> *C*
> *B*

This is not what was intended! The conditions in this example are not exclusive. A grade value of 62 is less than 70 and also less than 80 and also less than 90!

There can also be different results when ordering the conditions differently. You should always trace your code to ensure that you are solving the problem as intended. Section 5.3 of your text gives other examples dealing with multiple alternatives.

6.3.1   Dangling `else`

Because you can nest `if` statements (put one `if` statement inside another), the placement of braces becomes very important. Proper indentation will help you (and others) read your program more easily, but indentation does not control the flow of your program.

Example 6.10

```
int x = 9;
if (x < 7)
   if (x < 4)
      System.out.println("Hello there!");
else
   System.out.println("Have a great day!");
System.out.println("See you soon!");
```

Example 6.10 prints *See you soon!* because the `else` is paired with the *nearest* if. The indentation in Example 6.10 is very confusing and misleading. The example is rewritten with proper indentation in Example 6.11.

Example 6.11

```
int x = 9;
if (x < 7)
   if (x < 4)
      System.out.println("Hello there!");
   else
      System.out.println("Have a great day!");
System.out.println("See you soon!");
```

If the intention of Example 6.10 was to print:

Have a great day!
See you soon!

then braces must be used to clarify the pairing of the `else`. Example 6.12 illustrates this.

Example 6.12

```
int x = 9;
if (x < 7)
{
   if (x < 4)
      System.out.println("Hello there!");
}
```

```
else
    System.out.println("Have a great day!");
System.out.println("See you soon!");
```

It is always a good idea to design test cases before you begin to write your code. In this way you can think through your algorithm and plan for all possible conditions that need to be tested. *Quality Tip 5.3* on page 213 of your text and Section 6.5 in this guide discuss test cases and writing a test plan in more detail.

6.4   Using Boolean Expressions

Java has another primitive type, `boolean`. A Boolean variable has a value of `true` or `false`. These values do not convert into numbers. They are not objects. You can perform complicated tests by combining Boolean expressions using the logical operators.

Table 6.3

Logical Operators

Logical Operator	Meaning
!	not
&&	and
||	or

When working with Boolean expressions, it is sometimes helpful to review a truth table.

Table 6.4

Truth Table for Logical Operators

A	B	A && B	A || B	!A
true	true	true	true	false
true	false	false	true	false
false	true	false	true	true
false	false	false	false	true

If a legal grade is defined as a grade between 0 and 100 inclusive, an expression that checks whether a grade is legal (from 0 to 100 inclusive) would be:

```
        if (0 <= grade && grade <= 100)
not
        if (0 <= grade <= 100)    // WRONG
```

The expression that checks whether a grade is NOT a legal grade is:

```
        if (!(0 <= grade && grade <= 100))
or
        if (0 > grade || grade > 100)
```

Negating a Boolean expression can be very confusing. Many errors in programming and on the AP CS Exam are due to incorrect Boolean expressions. De Morgan's Law can be used to simplify complicated Boolean expressions. You can safely expect that the AP Exam will include questions that test your understanding of complex Boolean expressions!

```
!(A && B) is the same as (!A || !B)
!(A || B) is the same as (!A && !B)
```

De Morgan's Law is discussed in *Advanced Topic 5.5* on page 209 of your text.

A method that simply returns a Boolean value based on a condition can easily be simplified. For example, the method isLegalGrade below,

```
public boolean isLegalGrade(int grade)
{
    if  (grade >= 0 && grade <= 100)
        return true;
    else
        return false;
}
```

can be simplified to

```
public boolean isLegalGrade(int grade)
{
    return (grade >= 0 && grade <= 100)
}
```

Note that the value of the Boolean expression evaluates to true or false. This value is then returned.

6.4.1   Short Circuit Evaluation

The && operator is used to combine two Boolean expressions. If the first expression evaluates to false, the second expression is not evaluated because, once it is determined that the first expression is false, the entire && expression can only evaluate to false. This is called *short circuit evaluation*. If the first expression evaluates to true, then the second expression must be evaluated. If it is true, the entire expression evaluates to true; otherwise it evaluates to false. For example, suppose the statement

```
if ((n != 0) && (a / n < minSoFar))
```

is executed when n has the value 0. Since the first Boolean expression evaluates to false, the second Boolean expression will not be evaluated so there will be no division-by-zero error. If the first expression evaluates to true (n != 0), then the entire Boolean expression will be evaluated.

Suppose the statement

```
if ((a == 0) || (b == 0))
```

is executed when a has the value 0. Since the first Boolean expression evaluates to true, the entire expression will evaluate to true and the second expression is not evaluated. This is another example of *short circuit evaluation*. If the first expression evaluates to false (a != 0), then the entire expression must be evaluated. Short circuit evaluation is discussed in *Advanced Topic 5.4 (Lazy Evaluation of Boolean Operators)* on page 208 of your text.

6.4.2 Using Boolean Variables

A Boolean variable can be used in a test.

> `if (found)` is equivalent to `if (found == true)`

The first method is simpler and easier to read. This is explained in Section 5.4.3 of your text. With the inclusion of relational operators, we have an expanded table of operator precedence.

Table 6.5
Expanded Operator Order of Precedence

Operator Order of Precedence					
`++`	`--`				
`*`	`/`	`%`			
`+`	`-`				
`<`	`<=`	`>`	`>=`		
`==`	`!=`				
`&&`					
`||`					
`=`	`*=`	`/=`	`%=`	`+=`	`-=`

6.5   Test Coverage

The most important testing technique is the *unit test*. This is the process of compiling and testing a class in isolation. Section 4.6 of this guide and Section 3.6 of your text discuss unit testing of classes. Performing unit testing on each method in the class is also a useful tool in testing your program. Test coverage is a measure of how many parts of a program have been tested.

Generating the appropriate test data is an important testing skill. You should test your programs using legitimate (or typical) test cases, boundary test cases, and error conditions. Legitimate test cases are the values you would expect the user to supply. Boundary test cases are values that lie on the boundary of acceptable input. You should test a value on the boundary, one that is one unit below the boundary, and one that is one unit above the boundary to ensure that your code does not contain any off-by-one errors. Error conditions are test values that the program should reject. Test these values and decide on a method of handling illegal input.

You want to make sure that each part of your program is executed at least once by one of your test cases. This ensures that all branches in all conditional statements are executed during your tests. It is always a good idea to design test cases *before* you start to code. *Quality Tip 5.4* on page 214 of your text explains this procedure.

After you have selected test data and decided on the input method, you need to determine whether the output produced by the program is correct. One way to verify the output is to calculate the values by hand.

You can also hand-trace the program. To do so, develop a set of test data. Calculate the correct results by hand so that you know what results to expect. Then simply use the test data and simulate a computer. Trace the execution of the program to see what the program will do. In order to be successful with this, you must keep track of variables (both primitive and reference) and their states.

Sometimes you run a program and you are not sure exactly where your error is located. A program trace is a procedure in which output messages are added to a program to show its path of execution. For a proper trace, messages should be added at each method entry and exit point. More messages can be added to give additional information. Of course, your program will be more difficult to read because of the additional message statements and the output may be confusing; these statements should be removed when testing is complete. That means, if you revise the program at a later time, the procedure of adding and deleting message statements has to be repeated. *Advanced Topic 5.6* on page 214 of your text explains how to use the `Logger` class for handling trace messages in your program. The `Logger` class is not in the AP subset.

■ Topics That Are Useful But Not Tested

- A sequence of statements that has several alternatives can sometimes be written using a `switch` statement instead of multiple `if` statements. This is explained in *Advanced Topic 5.2* on page 197 of your text.
- The `String` method `equalsIgnoreCase` may be useful when comparing user input. This method is discussed in Section 5.2.3 of your text.
- An enumerated type has a finite set of values. For example,

```
public enum Suit { CLUBS, DIAMONDS, HEARTS, SPADES }
Suit s = Suit.CLUBS;
if (s == Suit.CLUBS)
    System.out.println(s);
```

defines and uses an enumerated type that may be very useful if you are writing a program that simulates playing cards. It is unlikely that the AP Exams will test on enumerated types. For more information on enumerated types, see *Advanced Topic 5.3* on page 204 of your text.
- The `java.util.Logger` class is useful for analyzing the behavior of a program and is explained in *Advanced Topic 5.6* on page 214 of your text.

■ Things to Remember When Taking the AP Exam

- In Java we check if `x` is between two values by writing `if (0 < x && x < 100)`. Do not write `if (0 < x < 100)`.
- Do not use `==` with strings. Use the `String` method `equals` to check whether two `String` variables have the same value.
- Do not use `==` with objects if you want to test whether two objects have the same contents. Use the object's `equals` method for this.
- Remember that the `null` reference is not the same as an empty `String`.
- Remember that a local variable that holds `null` is not the same as an uninitialized local variable.
- When comparing strings lexicographically, use the `String` method `compareTo`. Do not use `<` or `>` with strings.

- Be careful of a dangling `else` when nesting `if` statements. Remember that the `else` is paired with the *nearest* `if`.
- Do not compare doubles with the `==` operator. Use a method similar to that explained in Section 5.2.2 of your text.
- Do not confuse `==` with `=`. The `==` operator checks equality. The `=` is used for assignment.
- Know De Morgan's Law. It may help you in writing complex Boolean expressions.
- Indent the body of `if/else` statements. Proper indentation makes your program easier to read.
- Remember that indentation does not control the flow of the program. Use braces to create a block statement to improve legibility and when necessary for flow.
- Be careful not to accidentally place a semicolon after the Boolean expression in an `if` statement.

```
if (grade < 0 || grade > 100);    // WRONG
    System.out.println("Illegal grade entry");
```

will always print *Illegal grade entry*. The interpretation of the above statement is: "If the grade is less than 0 or the grade is greater than 100, do nothing." In all cases *Illegal grade entry* will be printed. On the AP Exam, you are usually not penalized for missing semicolons. However, extra semicolons can cause logic errors and change the intention of the code, which would be penalized.

■ Key Words

You should understand the terms below. The AP CS Exam questions may include references to these terms. The citations in parentheses next to each term identify the page numbers where it is defined and/or discussed in *Java Concepts for AP Computer Science*, 5th ed.

and (206)	De Morgan's Law (209)	logical operator (206)
block statement (185)	`equals` (189)	nesting (198)
Boolean (205)	error condition (214)	`null` (192)
Boolean operators (206)	expressions (205)	or (206)
`boolean` type (205)	`if` (183)	relational operators (188)
boundary conditions (212)	`if/else` (183)	short circuit evaluation (208)
condition (182)	indentation (186)	side effects (193)
dangling `else` (202)	lexicographic (190)	program trace (214)

■ Connecting the Detailed Topic Outline to the Text

The citations in parentheses identify where information in the outline can be located in *Java Concepts for AP Computer Science*, 5th ed.

- The `if` Statement (182–187)
- Comparing Values (188–193)
  - Relational Operators (188)
  - Comparing Floating-Point Numbers (188–189)
  - Comparing Strings (189–191)

■ Practice Questions

Multiple Choice

1. Consider the following code segment.

```
x = 6;
y = 19;
z = 2;
if (x > y)
    if (z > x)
        z++;
else
    z -= 5;
y += x;
```

After this code is executed, the values of x, y, and z are:

a. x = 6, y = 25, z = -3
b. x = 6, y = 19, z = 2
c. x = 6, y = 25, z = 3
d. x = 6, y = 25, z = 2
e. x = 6, y = 19, z = 3

2. Assume the following declarations have been made.

```
String fName = "Robert";
String lName = "Roberts";
```

Which of the following code segments returns **true**?

```
I.   return (fName == lName.substring(0, fName.length()));
II.  return (fName.equals(lName.substring(0, fName.length())));
III. return (fName.equals(lName.substring(0, lName.length())));
```

a. I only
b. II only
c. III only
d. I and II only
e. II and III only

3. Consider the following code segment.

```
int x = some positive integer value
double a = x;
double c = Math.pow(Math.sqrt(a), 2);
return (a == c);
```

Which of the following statements about the code segment is **true**?

a. A compile-time error occurs because x is not a double.
b. A compile-time error occurs because a method call cannot be a parameter to a method.
c. A run-time error occurs.
d. `true` is returned.
e. `true` or `false` may be returned, depending on roundoff errors.

4. Consider the following segment of code.

```
String word = "compute";
int len = word.length();
int num = 3;
String foo = word.substring(len % num, num);
String hoo = word.substring(num + 1);
if (foo.compareTo(hoo) < 0)
{
   hoo += foo;
}
else
{
   foo += hoo;
}
```

After this code is executed, what are the values of `foo` and `hoo`?

a. foo = "om", hoo = "uteom"
b. foo = "ute", hoo = "omute"
c. foo = "ute", hoo = "uteom"
d. foo = "m", hoo = "utem"
e. foo = "ute", hoo = "mute"

5. In a simplified game of craps you roll 2 dice. If you get a 7 or an 11 on the *first* roll, you win; otherwise the game continues. Given the following declarations,

```
int diceSum;
int numRolls;
```

where `diceSum` holds the sum of the two dice rolled and `numRolls` holds the number of times the dice were rolled, which of the following code segments tests for a *win* and prints *WIN* to the screen if the condition to win, as defined above, is satisfied? Assume `diceSum` and `numRolls` are assigned their values before this code is executed.

```
I.  if (numRolls == 1 && diceSum == 7 || diceSum == 11)
       System.out.println("WIN");
    else
       // Game continues
```

```
II. if (numRolls == 1 && (diceSum == 7 || diceSum == 11))
        System.out.println("WIN");
    else
        // Game continues

III. if (numRolls != 1 || (diceSum != 7 && diceSum != 11))
        // Game continues
    else
        System.out.println("WIN");
```

a. I only
b. II only
c. III only
d. II and III only
e. I and III only

6. Consider the following code segment.

```
int sum = 200;
int n = 0;
if ((n != 0) && (sum / n > 90))
    return sum += sum;
else
    return sum;
```

What is the result when this code is executed?

a. A run-time error occurs when evaluating sum / n.
b. A compile-time error occurs when evaluating sum / n.
c. 0 is returned.
d. 200 is returned.
e. 400 is returned.

7. Consider the following code segment.

```
String string1 = "Hello";
String string2 = "World";
string2 = string1;
string1 += "There!";
```

After the code is executed, what are the values of string1 and string2?

a. string1 = "Hello", string2 = "World"
b. string1 = "HelloWorld", string2 = "World"
c. string1 = "HelloThere!", string2 = "HelloThere!"
d. string1 = "HelloThere!", string2 = "World"
e. string1 = "HelloThere!", string2 = "Hello"

Questions 8 and 9 refer to the Point class partially defined below.

```
public class Point
{
```

```java
/**
    Constructs a point.
    @param x1 the x-value of the point
    @param y1 the y-value of the point
*/
Point(int x1, int y1)
{
    x = x1;
    y = y1;
}

/**
    Sets new Point coordinates.
    @param num1 the new x-coordinate
    @param num2 the new y-coordinate
*/
public void setPoint(int num1, int num2)
{
    x = num1;
    y = num2;
}

/**
    Returns x-coordinate of Point.
    @return the x-coordinate of the point
*/
public int getX()
{
    return x;
}

/**
    Returns y-coordinate of Point.
    @return the y-coordinate of the point
*/
public int getY()
{
    return y;
}

/**
    Returns true if the x-coordinate of this point has the same
    value as its y-coordinate. Returns false otherwise.
    @return true if x and y coordinates are equal, otherwise
    returns false.
*/
public boolean hasSameXandY()
{
    // Code goes here
}

private int x;    // x-coordinate of point
private int y;    // y-coordinate of point
}
```

8. A client program needs to check to see whether two `Points` have the same *x*- and *y*-coordinates. Given that the object variables `p1` and `p2` refer to different objects that have the same *x*- and *y*- coordinates, which of the following code segments will test that equality?

    I. `if (p1.x == p2.x && p1.y == p2.y)`
          statement;

    II. `if (p1.equals(p2))`
          statement;

    III. `if (p1.getX() == p2.getX() && p1.getY() == p2.getY())`
          statement;

    a. I only
    b. II only
    c. III only
    d. I and II only
    e. II and III only

9. Which of the following code segments could replace the body of the `Point` method `hasSameXandY` so that the method returns `true` if the point's *x*-coordinate is the same value as its *y*-coordinate and returns `false` otherwise.

    I. `return (x == y);`

    II. `if ((getX()).equals(getY()))`
             `return true;`
          `else`
             `return false;`

    III. `if (getX() == getY())`
             `return true;`
          `else`
             `return false;`

    a. I only
    b. II only
    c. III only
    d. I and II only
    e. I and III only

10. The Boolean expression `!(!A && !B)` is equivalent to

    a. `(!A && !B)`
    b. `(!A || !B)`
    c. `(A || B)`
    d. `!(A || B)`
    e. `(!A || B)`

11. Which of the following is **true** about unit testing?

    a. A unit test simultaneously checks all classes that are included in a program.
    b. A unit test simultaneously checks a set of cooperating classes in a program.
    c. A unit test simultaneously checks all of the methods of one class.
    d. A unit test checks a single method or set of cooperating methods in a class.
    e. A unit test checks a single statement in a method.

Questions 12–14 refer to the following problem.

The method `weeklyPay` is to return the amount of pay an employee will receive for one week's work. The parameters for `weeklyPay` are the hours worked during the week and the hourly pay. The weekly pay is based on the following standards. If the employee worked 40 hours or less during the week, he receives his regular hourly rate times the number of hours he worked. For every hour over 40 hours, the employee receives time and a half (1.5 times his regular hourly pay). The following information and method header is given.

```
final int MAX_HOURS_IN_WEEK = 168;    // 7 * 24

/**
   Computes weekly pay.
   Assumes 0 <= hoursWorked and
   hoursWorked <= MAX_HOURS_IN_WEEK, 0 < hourlyPay
   @param hoursWorked is hours worked
   @param hourlyPay is pay per hour
*/
public static double weeklyPay(double hoursWorked,
      double hourlyPay)
```

12. Which is the best set of test values for the variable `hoursWorked`?

    a. 0, 40, 168
    b. 5, 10, 20, 30, 40, 170
    c. −1, 0, 1, 39, 40, 41, 167, 168, 169
    d. −10, 20, 30, 40, 50, 200
    e. −20, −10, 10, 20, 30, 40, 100, 200

13. Which of the following method calls would test illegal input?

    I.   `weeklyPay(0, 0)`
    II. `weeklyPay(168, 169)`
    III. `weeklyPay(0, 200)`

    a. I only
    b. II only
    c. III only
    d. I and II only
    e. I and III only

14. Which of the method calls would be good choices to test boundary conditions or branches of conditionals in the `weeklyPay` method?

    I.   `weeklyPay(0, 10)`
    II. `weeklyPay(168, 20)`
    III. `weeklyPay(40, 40)`

    a. I only
    b. II only
    c. III only
    d. I and II only
    e. I, II, and III

Free Response Questions

1. Consider the Car class, whose incomplete definition is shown below.

```
public class Car
{
    /**
       Constructs a car.
       @param miles miles per gallon that car gets
       @param milesOnCar total mileage on car
       @param gasTankHolds amount of gas the tank holds
       @param gasTankHas gas in tank now
    */
    public Car(double miles, double milesOnCar,
          double gasTankHolds, double gasTankHas)
    {
        mpg = miles;
        mileage = milesOnCar;
        tankCapacity = gasTankHolds;
        gasInTank = gasTankHas;
    }

    /**
       Returns the gas needed to drive miles (based on mpg).
       @param numMiles the number of miles to be driven
       @return gas needed to drive numMiles miles
    */
    public double gasNeeded(double numMiles)
    {
        // Code goes here
    }

    /**
       Returns true if the car has enough gas in the tank to drive
       numMiles miles, otherwise returns false.
       @param numMiles miles to be driven
       @return true if gas in tank is enough to drive numMiles
       miles; false otherwise.
    */
    public boolean enoughGas(double numMiles)
    {
        // Code goes here
    }

    /**
       Updates mileage and gasInTank to reflect numMiles
       being driven.
       @param numMiles number of miles driven
    */
    public void drive(double numMiles)
    {
        // Code goes here
    }
```

```
/**
    If tank is less than half full, fills tank and updates
    gasInTank. Otherwise does nothing.
*/
public void getGas()
{
    // Code goes here
}

/**
    Returns the current mileage on the car.
    @return mileage on car
*/
public double getMileage() {. . .}

/**
    Returns the amount of gas in the gas tank.
    @return amount of gas in tank
*/
public double getGasInTank() {. . .}

private double mpg;
private double mileage;
private double tankCapacity;
private double gasInTank;
}
```

Your solution should not reimplement the functionality provided by methods given in the problem definition, or by the methods written in the previous parts of the problem.

a. Write method `gasNeeded` that will return a `double` indicating the number of gallons of gas needed to make a trip that is `numMiles` long where `numMiles` is the explicit parameter of `gasNeeded`. Use the method header below to write `gasNeeded`.

```
public double gasNeeded(double numMiles)
```

b. Write a method `enoughGas` that is passed a double parameter `numMiles`. The method `enoughGas` will return `true` is there is enough gas in the tank to drive `numMiles` miles. If there is not enough gas in the tank, `enoughGas` will return `false`. Use the method header below to write `enoughGas`.

```
public boolean enoughGas(double numMiles)
```

c. Write the method `getGas` that will fill the gas tank of the car if it is less than half full. If the car has half of a tank of gas or more, `getGas` does nothing. Use the method header below to write `getGas`.

```
public void getGas()
```

d. Write the method `drive` whose parameter is the intended number of miles the car is to travel. However, the gas tank in the car contains a finite amount of gas. If the car has enough gas to travel the specified number of miles, the appropriate private instance variables should be updated. If the car does not have enough gas to make the requested trip, the car should travel until it runs out of gas. The appropriate private variables should be updated.

For example, suppose that a client program constructs a Car with the following statement.

```
Car myMini = new Car(25, 600, 20, 20);
```

Examples of calls to drive are listed in the table below.

Before call to *drive*		Call to *drive*	After call to *drive*	
gasInTank	*mileage*		*gasInTank*	*mileage*
20	600	myMini.drive(100)	16	700
20	600	myMini.drive(0)	20	600
20	600	myMini.drive(1000)	0	1100

Use the following method header to write your method.

```
public void drive(double numMiles)
```

2. Consider the Point class partially defined below.

```
public class Point
{
    /**
       Constructs a point.
       @param x1 the x-value of the point
       @param y1 the y-value of the point
    */
    Point(int x1, int y1)
    {
        x = x1;
        y = y1;
    }

    /**
       Sets new Point coordinates.
       @param num1 the new x-coordinate
       @param num2 the new y-coordinate
    */
    public void setPoint(int num1, int num2)
    {
        x = num1;
        y = num2;
    }

    /**
       Returns x-coordinate of Point.
       @return the x-coordinate of the point
    */
    public int getX()
    {
        return x;
    }
```

```
/**
    Returns y-coordinate of Point.
    @return the y-coordinate of the point
*/
public int getY()
{
    return y;
}

/**
    Returns the distance this point is from the point (0,0).
    @return distance this point is from origin
*/
public double getDistanceFromOrigin()
{
    // Code goes here
}

private int x;    // x-coordinate of point
private int y;    // y-coordinate of point
}
```

Your solution should not reimplement the functionality provided by methods given in the problem definition, or by the methods written in the previous parts of the problem. Recall that the distance AB between two points $A(x_1, y_1)$ and $B(x_2, y_2)$ is calculated as

$$AB = \sqrt{(x_2 - x_1)^2 + (y_2 - y_1)^2}$$

a. Write the method `getDistanceFromOrigin` that will return the distance between the `Point` and the origin (0,0). Use the following header.

    ```
    public double getDistanceFromOrigin()
    ```

b. A *client* program includes a method `findFarPoint` that accepts three points as parameters and returns the `Point` that is the farthest away from the origin (0,0). Write your method using the header below.

    ```
    public static Point findFarPoint(Point p1, Point p2, Point p3)
    ```

Assume that `getDistanceFromOrigin` works as intended regardless of what you wrote for part a. Your solution should not reimplement the functionality provided by methods given in the problem definition, or by methods written in part a of this problem.

Assume that no two points are the same distance from the point (0,0).

CHAPTER

(Covers *Java Concepts for AP Computer Science* Chapter 6)

Iteration

TOPIC OUTLINE

■ Topic Summary

7.1   while Loops

Many applications require us to execute statements (or blocks of statements) multiple times. For example, averaging grades for all of the students in a particular course, printing a calendar of twelve months, processing a payroll for many employees, and any number of other applications involve doing the same task more than once. One way to implement this type of algorithm is to use a while loop. The general form of a while loop is

```
while (condition)
{
    statement;
}
```

Example 7.1 uses a while loop to sum the positive integers less than 10.

Example 7.1

```
int sum = 0;
int x = 1;   // Initializes loop control variable x.
while (x < 10)   // Checks end condition.
{
    sum += x;
    x++;   // Loop control variable updated.
}
// At the termination of the loop, x has value 10.
```

The three important pieces of a loop are initializing the variable(s) that are involved in the condition, testing for the end condition, and advancing the value of the loop control variable(s) involved in the condition so that progress is made toward the termination of the loop. If you don't change the loop control variable value within the loop, you create an endless loop.

Example 7.2

```
int sum = 0;
int i = 1;
while (i < 10)    // Infinite loop
{
    sum += i;    // WRONG! i is not incremented.
}
```

Example 7.2 will add i to sum repeatedly but, because the value of i starts at 1 and never changes, i is always less than 10. The end condition of the loop is never satisfied. This is called an *infinite loop. Common Error 6.1* on page 232 of your text discusses infinite loop errors. When writing a while loop, be sure that some statement within the body of the loop makes progress toward the termination of the loop! Consider Example 7.3 below. Try different positive integer values for a and b. Does the body of the loop make progress toward termination? Can you figure out what the value of a represents after the loop terminates?

Example 7.3

```
int a = some positive integer;
int b = some positive integer;

while (a != b)
{
    if (a < b)
        b = b - a;
    else
        a = a - b;
}
```

As long as both a and b are positive integers, the loop terminates when a = b. The value of a (and b) after the termination of the loop is their greatest common divisor (the largest integer that divides into both a and b without remainders).

It is common to have off-by-one errors when writing loops. Example 7.4 counts the number of times an "a" occurs in the word "mathematics." This program segment accomplishes this task but there are several places where an *off-by-one* error can occur. We will loop through each letter of "mathematics". Each time an "a" is encountered, a counter will be incremented.

Example 7.4

```
1    String word = "mathematics";
2    int count = 0;    // Initialize letter counter to 0
3    String lookFor = "a";
4
5    int j = 0;    // Initialize to 0
6    while (j < word.length())    // Note: < not <=
7    {
8        String temp = word.substring(j, j + 1);
```

```
 9          if (lookFor.indexOf(temp) != -1)
10          {
11              count++;
12          }
13          j++;    // Increment outside if
14      }
```

The following decisions avoided possible off-by-one errors in Example 7.4.

- The variable used as the counter is initialized to 0, not 1. (Line 2)
- The loop variable starts at 0, not 1, because the index of the first letter in a `String` is 0. (Line 5)
- The loop test is < `word.length()` not <= `word.length()` because the last letter in a `String` has index `length() - 1`. (Line 6)

Off-by-one errors are discussed in *Common Error 6.2* on page 233 of your text.

7.2   `for` Loops

Another method for iterative control is a `for` loop. If you know exactly how many times a block is to be executed, a `for` loop is often the best choice. The general form of a `for` loop is

```
for (initialization; test; update)
{
    statement;
}
```

Examples 7.5 and 7.6 add the integers 1 to 10 inclusive. The order in which the integers are added is different but the result is the same.

Example 7.5

```
int i;
int sum = 0;

for (i = 1; i <= 10; i++)
{
    sum += i;
}
// At the termination of this loop, i has value 11.
```

Example 7.6

```
int i;
int sum = 0;

for (i = 10; i >= 1; i--)
{
    sum += i;
}
// At the termination of this loop, i has value 0.
```

The loop control variable, i, is initialized and the loop test is evaluated. The loop continues while the test is true. The variable i is updated (incremented or decremented) by 1 each time the loop executes. Example 7.7 gives the equivalent `while` loop for Example 7.6.

Example 7.7

```
int sum = 0;
int i = 10;
while (i >= 1)
{
    sum += i;
    i--;
}
```

The initialization, the test, and the update in the `for` header should be related (see Example 7.8). The code to update the loop control variable should occur in the `for` header only, not in the body of the loop (see Example 7.9).

Example 7.8

```
int j = 1;
int k = 8;
for (int i = 0; j <= 10; k = k + 2)    // BAD STYLE!
        // Variables are not related.
{
    j += 2;
    i = i + 1;
    System.out.println(i + " " + j + " " + k);
}
```

Example 7.9

```
for (int i = 0; i <= 10; i++)
{
    sum += i;
    i = i + 1;   // WRONG! Update should occur only in for header.
}
```

It is common to see the loop control variable declared in the header as it is initialized.

```
for (int i = 0; i < 10; i++)
{
    statement;
}
```

A variable declared in this manner cannot be accessed outside the loop. We say that the *scope* of the variable extends to the end of the loop. This is explained in *Advanced Topic 6.2* on page 243 of your text.

Let us again consider our program of counting the number of times "a" occurs in the word "mathematics." We will again loop through each letter of "mathematics" and each time an "a" is encountered, we will increment a counter.

Example 7.10

```
1    String word = "mathematics";
2    int count = 0;
3    String lookFor = "a";
4
5    for (int i = 0; i < word.length(); i++)
```

```
 6     {
 7         if (word.substring(i, i + 1).equals(lookFor))
 8         {
 9             count++;
10         }
11     }
```

Example 7.10 avoids possible off-by-one errors in the same ways as in Example 7.4.

- The variable used as the counter is initialized to 0, not 1. (Line 2)
- The loop variable starts at 0, not 1, because the index of the first letter in a String is 0. (Line 5)
- The loop test is < word.length() not <= word.length() because the last letter in a String has index length() - 1. (Line 5)

Think through your intended task and take care when deciding on the initialization, end, and update conditions in your loops.

A for loop should be used when a statement, or group of statements, is to be executed a *known* number of times. *Quality Tip 6.1* on page 241 of your text discusses this. Use a for loop for its intended purpose only. *How To 6.1* on page 250 of your text discusses the appropriate uses for the different types of loops and walks you through the process of implementing a loop.

7.3   Nested Loops

Loops can be nested (one loop inside another loop). One application of a nested loop is printing a table with rows and columns.

Example 7.11

```
final int MAXROW = 5;
final int MAXCOL = 4;
for (int row = 1; row <= MAXROW; row++)
{
    for (int col = 1; col <= MAXCOL; col++)
    {
        System.out.print("*");
    }
    System.out.println();
}
```

This program prints:

```
****
****
****
****
****
```

7.4   Processing Sentinel Values

Occasionally you may wish to process data input until a certain condition is met. Suppose we want to find and print the average grade for an exam given in an AP CS class. Example 7.12 is a possible solution to the problem.

Example 7.12

```
int numGrades = 0;
int total = 0;
System.out.print("Enter number of students: ");
int num = get input from user
for (int i = 1; i <= num; i++)
{
    System.out.print("Enter student grade: ");
    int grade = get input from user
    total += grade;
    numGrades++;
}
if (numGrades != 0)
    System.out.println((double) total / numGrades);
else
    System.out.println("No grades entered.");
```

Although the solution above is perfectly acceptable, it requires the user to input the number of times the loop is to be executed. Example 7.13 demonstrates one possible solution to the same problem that does not require this information.

Example 7.13

```
int numGrades = 0;
int total = 0;

System.out.print("Enter student grade. Enter -1 to Quit: ");
int grade = get input from user

while (grade != -1)
{
    total += grade;
    numGrades++;
    System.out.print("Enter student grade. Enter -1 to Quit: ");
    grade = get input from user
}
if (numGrades != 0)
    System.out.println((double) total / numGrades);
else
    System.out.println("No grades entered.");
```

The special value that signals the end of the input (–1 in this case) is called a *sentinel* value. This sentinel value must be a value that could not possibly be legal input. We also get the first value from the user before we enter the loop. There are many chances to err with this code. You must be careful when you increment numGrades and when you add the grade to total. You do not want to include the sentinel value as part of your input.

Example 7.14 uses a sentinel value and sets a Boolean variable to indicate the termination of a loop. Example 7.14 is easier to understand than Example 7.13 and doesn't have quite as many chances for errors in incrementing variables. We still have the sentinel value to worry about. This value *must* be a value that is not possible for legal input.

Example 7.14

```
System.out.println("Enter student grades. Enter -1 to Quit.");
int total = 0;
int numGrades = 0;
boolean done = false;
while (!done)
{
    int grade = get input from user
    if (grade == -1)
    {
        done = true;
    }
    else
    {
        total += grade;
        numGrades++;
    }
}
if (numGrades != 0)
    System.out.println((double) total / numGrades);
else
    System.out.println("No grades entered.");
```

Section 6.4 of your text defines a method of using a `String` value for input. The `String` input is then converted to a `double`. Although the conversion methods used are not included in the AP subsets, this method eliminates the need for choosing appropriate numeric sentinel values.

7.5   Loop Invariants (AB only)

A loop invariant is a statement that is true before a loop executes, at the start of each iteration of the loop, and after the loop terminates. Loop invariants can be used to help explain algorithms that are not completely obvious. They are also statements that can be used for proving the correctness of loops. Correctness proofs, though not part of the AP CS subset, are discussed in *Random Fact 6.2* on page 263 of your text.

Example 7.15

This code segment counts the number of letters in `word` that are vowels (a, e, i, o, or u).

```
String vowel = "aeiou";
String word = some String;
int count = 0;
// Loop invariant:
// count = number of vowels in word.substring(0, i)
for (int i = 0; i < word.length(); i++)
{
    if (vowel.indexOf(word.substring(i, i + 1) >= 0)
        count++;
```

```
   }
```

The `for` loop visits each letter of `word`. If the letter is a vowel, `indexOf` returns a value between 0 and 4 and `count` is incremented. After each execution of the loop, `count` is the number of vowels in the substring looked at so far. The loop invariant is true before the loop executes, after each iteration of the loop, and after the loop terminates. After the loop terminates, `count` is the number of vowels (a, e, i, o, u) in `word`.

A more detailed example of a loop invariant is discussed in *Advanced Topic 6.5* on page 261 of your text.

7.6   Using a Debugger

The debugging method that is most popular among professional programmers is the use of a debugger. Most modern development environments contain a special program called a debugger that allows you to follow the execution of a program in order to locate errors. Adding break-points to your programs, inspecting variables, and stepping through the program execution are a few tools included in most debuggers. The debugger and a debugging session are discussed in Sections 6.6 and 6.7 of your text. The use of a debugger is not tested on the AP Exam. For less complicated programs, the use of testing techniques is sufficient and is easier than mastering the use of a debugger.

How To 6.2 on page 273 of your text lists strategies that you can use to recognize program errors and their causes.

■ Topics That Are Useful But Not Tested

- It is sometimes useful to traverse the characters in a string using the `charAt` method of the `String` class. This method uses the primitive type `char`, which is not tested on the AP CS Exams. An example of its use is demonstrated in *How To 6.1* on page 250 of your text.
- Sometimes you may want to execute the body of a loop at least once and perform the loop test at the end of the loop. A do loop serves this purpose and is explained in *Advanced Topic 6.1* on page 234 of your text.
- Several examples in your text get user input using the `Scanner` class and print information to the screen using the method `System.out.printf`. Both of these features facilitate testing methods and classes.
- Section 6.5 of your text introduces the `java.util.Random` class and uses this class to generate random numbers. The AP subset does not include `java.util.Random`. Questions involving random numbers will use the `Math.random` method as explained in Sections 5.4 and 5.5 of this guide.

■ Things to Remember When Taking the AP Exam

- When implementing a `while` loop be sure it includes the three necessary components: initialize the variable(s) that are involved in the condition, test for the end condition, and advance the value of the variables involved in the condition so that progress is made toward the termination of the loop.

- Be careful not to put a semicolon after a `for` loop header or a `while` statement.

```
for (i = 1; i < 10; i++);   // WRONG!
while (i < 10);   // WRONG!
```

- Be sure to use braces where needed for the body of a loop. If in doubt, use the braces.
- Check the initialization and the test condition in your loops. It is common to have an off-by-one error when writing loops.
- Be careful when implementing tables with nested loops. The outer loop controls the rows of the table and the inner loop controls the columns.
- **(AB only)** Know the definition of a loop invariant. You may be asked to choose the correct loop invariant on a multiple-choice question.

■ Key Words

You should understand the terms below. The AP CS Exam questions may include references to these terms. The citations in parentheses next to each term identify the page numbers where it is defined and/or discussed in *Java Concepts for AP Computer Science*, 5th ed.

debugger (264)	loop invariants (261)	variable scope (243)
for loops (237)	**(AB only)**	while (228)
infinite loops (232)	nested loops (244–246)	

■ Connecting the Detailed Topic Outline to the Text

The citations in parentheses identify where information in the outline can be located in *Java Concepts for AP Computer Science*, 5th ed.

- while Loops (228–236)
- for Loops (237–244)
- Nested Loops (244–246)
- Processing Sentinel Values (247–255)
  - ■ Loop Invariants **(AB only)** (261–263)
- Using a Debugger (Optional) (264–275)

■ Practice Questions

Multiple Choice

1. Consider the following segment of code.

```
String word = "mathematics";
String vowels = "aeiou";
String tempWord = "";
String newWord = "";

for (int i = 0; i < word.length(); i++)
{
    tempWord = word.substring(i, i + 1);
    if (vowels.indexOf(tempWord) >= 0)
    {
        newWord += tempWord;
    }
}
```

After the loop is terminated, what is the value of `newWord`?

a. `"mathematics"`
b. `"mthmtcs"`
c. `"aeai"`
d. `"aei"`
e. the empty string

2. Consider the `Die` class as defined below.

```
public class Die
{
    // Constructs an s-sided die.
    public Die(int s) {. . .}

    // Simulates a throw of the die, returning a random integer
    // from 1 to s (the number of sides) inclusive.
    public int cast() {. . .}

    // Private stuff goes here
}
```

The following declaration is made.

```
Die d1 = new Die(6);
```

Which segment of code returns the number of rolls it takes to roll double 1s (both rolls of the die result in the value 1)?

```
I.  count = 1;
    int d1 = die.cast();
    int d2 = die.cast();
    while (!(d1 == 1 && d2 == 1))
    {
        count++;
        d1 = die.cast();
        d2 = die.cast();
```

```
    }
    return count;    // Double 1s rolled on roll #count.
II. count = 1;
    int d1 = die.cast();
    int d2 = die.cast();
    while (true)
    {
       if (d1 == 1 && d2 == 1)
       {
          return count;    // Double 1s rolled on roll #count.
       }
       count++;
       d1 = die.cast();
       d2 = die.cast();
    }
III. count = 1;
    int d1 = die.cast();
    int d2 = die.cast();
    while (d1 != 1 || d2 != 1)
    {
       count++;
       d1 = die.cast();
       d2 = die.cast();
    }
    return count;    // Double 1s rolled on roll #count.
```

a. I

b. II

c. III

d. I and III only

e. I, II, and III

3. Consider the following code segment.

```
for (int i = 0; i < 5; i++)
{
   for (int j = 0; j < 5; j++)
      System.out.print(i * j % 5);
   System.out.println();
}
```

What is the output produced?

a. *01234*
    12340
    23401
    34012
    40123

b. *12345*
    12345
    12345
    12345
    12345

c. *00000*
    01234
    23401
    34012
    40123

d. *00000*
    01234
    02413
    03142
    04321

e. *00000*
    00000
    00011
    00112
    00123

4. The following triangle design is to be printed.

    4
    33
    222
    1111

Which of the following code segments correctly prints this design?

I.
```java
for (int i = 4; i >= 1; i--)
{
    for (int j = 4 - i + 1; j >= 1; j--)
        System.out.print(i);
    System.out.println();
}
```

II.
```java
for (int i = 1; i <= 4; i++)
{
    for (int j = 1; j <= i; j++)
        System.out.print(4 - i + 1);
    System.out.println();
}
```

III.
```java
for (int i = 1; i <= 4; i++)
{
    for (int j = 4; j >= 4 - i + 1; j--)
        System.out.print(4 - i + 1);
    System.out.println();
}
```

a. I only
b. II only
c. III only
d. I and II only
e. I, II, and III

5. Consider the following code segment.

```
int n = some integer value;
int a = 0;
while (n > 0)
{
    a += n % 10;
    n /= 10;
}
System.out.println("answer is :" + a);
```

Which of the following statements best describes the result of executing this code?

a. *0* is printed.
b. The number of digits in `n` is printed.
c. The sum of the digits in `n` is printed.
d. The original value of `n` is printed.
e. An endless loop results.

6. Consider the code segment below.

```
String word = "computer";
String tempWord = "";
for (int i = word.length() - 1; i >= 0; i--)
{
    tempWord = word.substring(i, i + 1) + tempWord;
}
System.out.println(tempWord);
```

What will be printed when the code is executed?

a. *computer*
b. *retupmoc*
c. *erteutpumpomco*
d. Nothing will be printed. `tempWord` is an empty `String`.
e. An error message.

7. Consider the following code segment in which `IO.readInt()` is a call to a method that reads an integer.

```
String tempSequence = "";
int x = IO.readInt();
int y = IO.readInt();
while (y >= x)
{
    tempSequence += x;
    x = y;
    y = IO.readInt();
}
tempSequence += x;
System.out.println(tempSequence);
```

What is the output if the series of integers being input is: 1 1 2 3 5 4 7 8?

a. *1 1 2 3*
b. *1 2 3 5*
c. *1 1 2 3 5*
d. *1 2 3 5 4 7 8*
e. *1 1 2 3 5 4 7 8*

8. Consider the following code segment where `IO.readWord()` is a call to a method that reads a `String`.

```
String word = IO.readWord();
for (int i = 0; i < word.length() - 1; i++)
{
    if (word.substring(i, i + 1).equals(word.substring(
        i + 1, i + 2)))
    {
        return true;
    }
}
return false;
```

Which of the following describes its results?

a. Returns `true` if any letter in `word` is repeated, `false` otherwise.
b. Returns `true` if the first and second letters are the same, `false` otherwise.
c. Returns `true` if any two consecutive letters are the same, `false` otherwise.
d. Always returns `true`.
e. Always returns `false`.

9. Given the following declarations:

```
String vowel = "aeiou";
String word = some String value;
int count = 0;
```

Which of the following segments of code accurately counts the number of letters in `word` that are vowels (a, e, i, o, or u)?

```
I.  for (int j = 0; j < vowel.length(); j++)
    {
        String temp = vowel.substring(j, j + 1);
        if (word.indexOf(temp) != -1)
        {
            count++;
        }
    }
```

```
II. for (int j = 0; j < word.length(); j++)
    {
        String temp = word.substring(j, j + 1);
        if (vowel.indexOf(temp) != -1)
        {
            count++;
        }
    }
```

```
III. for (int i = 0; i < word.length(); i++)
     {
        for (int k = 0; k < vowel.length(); k++)
        {
           if (word.substring(i, i + 1).equals(vowel.substring(
               k, k + 1)))
           {
              count++;
           }
        }
     }
```

a. I only
b. II only
c. III only
d. I and III only
e. II and III only

10. Consider the following code segment. **(AB only)**

```
int p = 1;
int i = 1;
int n = some positive integer value;
// Loop invariant
while (i <= n)
{
   p = p * i;
   i++;
}
```

Which of the following statements is a correct loop invariant?

a. $i < n$
b. $0 < i < n$
c. $p = i!$
d. $p = (i - 1)!$
e. $p = n^i$

11. Consider the following code segment.

```
for (int i = 0; i < 5; i++)
   for (int j = i; j < 5; j++)
      System.out.print("*");
```

How many stars will be printed?

a. 5
b. 10
c. 15
d. 20
e. 25

12. Consider the following code segment.

```
int count = 0;
for (int x = 0; x < 3; x++)
    for (int y = x; y < 3; y++)
        for (int z = y; z < 3; z++)
            count++;
```

What is the value of count after the code segment is executed?

a. 81
b. 27
c. 10
d. 9
e. 6

13. Each segment of code below correctly calculates the sum of the integers from 1 to n inclusive and stores this value in the integer variable sum.

I. ```
    int sum = 0;
    for (int i = 1; i <= n; i++)
        sum += i;
    ```

II.  ```
     int sum = 0;
     int i = n;
     while (i > 0)
     {
         sum += i;
         i--;
     }
     ```

III. ```
     int sum = (n + 1) * n / 2;
     ```

Informally, execution efficiency can be viewed as the number of operations performed in a segment of code. For large values of n, which of the following statements is true about the execution efficiency of the above code segments?

a.  I is more efficient than II and III because it sums the numbers in increasing numeric order.
b.  II is more efficient than I and III because it sums the numbers beginning with the largest value.
c.  III is more efficient than I and II because there are fewer operations.
d.  I and II are more efficient than III because they are easier to understand.
e.  I, II, and III always operate with the same execution efficiency.

Questions 14 and 15 refer to the following code segment.

```
int val = some integer value;
int x = 0;

while (val > 0)
{
    val = val / 2;
    x++;
}
```
```

14. If *n* refers to the original integer value, *val*, which of the following statements is always true after the loop is terminated?

    a. $2^{x-1} >= n$
    b. $2^x \geq n$
    c. $2^x \leq n$
    d. $2 \cdot x = n$
    e. $2 \cdot n = x$

15. If *val* has the value of 32 before the loop is executed, how many times is the statement

    ```
    x++;
    ```

    executed?

    a. 2
    b. 5
    c. 6
    d. 8
    e. 16

16. Which of the following is the best description of a *debugger*?

    a. A debugger is a person hired to find the mistakes in your program.
    b. A debugger is the output from your program's test data.
    c. A debugger is a hardware component available to automatically analyze and correct run-time errors.
    d. A debugger is a program you use to execute another program and analyze its run-time behavior.
    e. A debugger is a hardware component available to automatically analyze and correct compile-time errors.

Free Response Questions

1. Consider the `Investment` class, whose incomplete definition is shown below.

    ```
    public class Investment
    {
        /**
            Constructs an Investment object from a starting balance and
            interest rate.
            @param aBalance initial balance
            @param aRate interest rate
        */
        public Investment(double aBalance, double aRate)
        {
            balance = aBalance;
            rate = aRate;
            years = 0;
        }
    ```

```
/**
    Interest is calculated and added to balance at the end of
    each year for y years.
    @param y number of years
*/
public void waitForYears(int y)
{
    // Code goes here
}

/**
    Returns the current investment balance.
    @return balance
*/
public double getBalance() {. . .}

/**
    Returns the number of years this investment has
    accumulated interest.
    @return number of years of this investment
*/
public int getYears() {. . .}

/**
    Balance is compounded n times annually for y years.
    @param y number of years of investment
    @param n times per year interest is compounded
*/
public void compoundTheInterest(int y, int n) {. . .}

    // Other methods here

    private double balance;
    private double rate;
    private int years;
}
```

a. Write the method `waitForYears` for the `Investment` class that will calculate the amount of interest earned in a given number of years. Interest is accumulated and the balance is updated at the end of each year. The table below contains sample data values and appropriate updates.

Starting Balance	Interest Rate	Years (y)	Ending Balance
100.00	5%	10	162.89
500.00	4%	20	1095.56
1000.00	5%	10	1628.89

Implement the method `waitForYears` using the following header.

```
public void waitForYears(int y)
```

b. Write the method `compoundTheInterest` for the `Investment` class that will calculate the amount of interest earned in y years compounded n times per year at an annual interest rate of r%. The method `compoundTheInterest` will update the balance appropriately. For example, if your original balance is $100.00 and you invest your money in a bank with an annual interest rate of 5% compounded quarterly (4 times a year) and you leave your money in the bank for 1 year, the interest and the ongoing balance is calculated as described below.

If your original balance is $100.00, then

> After the first quarter, your balance is $100 + (100)(.05/4) = \$101.25$.
> After the second quarter, your balance is $101.25 + (101.25)(.05/4) = \$102.52$.
> After the third quarter, your balance is $102.52 + (102.52)(.05/4) = \$103.80$.
> After the fourth quarter, your balance is $103.80 + (103.80)(.05/4) = \$105.09$.

Your balance at the end of the year is $105.09.

The private instance variable, `balance`, should be updated appropriately. The table below contains sample data values and appropriate updates.

Starting Balance	Interest Rate	Years (y)	Times Per Year (n)	Ending Balance
100.00	5%	10	12	164.70
500.00	4%	20	4	1108.36
1000.00	5%	10	4	1643.62

Use the method header below to write `compoundTheInterest`.

```
public void compoundTheInterest(int y, int n)
```

2. A modified game of roulette is played as follows. A player has a purse that contains coins. The player bets one coin (chosen randomly from the purse) on a number on the roulette wheel. This modified roulette wheel is shown below.

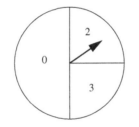

The spinner spins. If the spinner lands on "0", the player gets nothing back. If the spinner lands on "2", the player gets the wagered coin back and an additional coin of equal value. If the spinner lands on "3", the player gets 3 coins of the same value as the coin that was bet.

In this particular version of roulette, you either win big or you lose big because the spinning continues until you double the money in your purse or you have no coins left in your purse! The classes used are:
- The `Spinner` class, used to "spin" the roulette wheel
- The `Coin` class, which defines a coin
- The `Purse` class that holds the coins
- The `Game` class that simulates the roulette game

Incomplete definitions of these classes are below.

```java
/**
    The Spinner class is used to simulate the spin.
*/
public class Spinner
{
    /**
       Constructs a spinner.
       @param s number of choices on spinner
    */
    public Spinner(int s) {. . .}

    /**
       Returns an integer from 0 to the number of
       choices - 1 inclusive.
       @return a random spin in the range [0, choices)
    */
    public int spin() {. . .}

    // Private stuff here
}
```

```java
public class Coin
{
    /**
       Constructs a coin.
       @param aValue the monetary value of the coin
       @param aName the name of the coin
    */
    public Coin(double aValue, String aName) {. . .}

    /**
       Returns the coin value.
       @return coin value
    */
    public double getValue() {. . .}

    /**
       Returns the coin name.
       @return coin name
    */
    public String getName() {. . .}

    // Other methods and private stuff here
}
```

```java
public class Purse
{
    /**
       Constructs an empty purse.
    */
    public Purse() {. . .}
```

```
/**
    Adds a coin to the purse.
    @param aCoin coin to add to Purse
*/
public void add(Coin aCoin) {. . .}

/**
    Removes a coin from the purse.
    @return coin removed
*/
public Coin removeCoin() {. . .}

/**
    Returns the total value of the coins in the purse.
    @return total value in Purse
*/
public double getTotal() {. . .}

/**
    Returns the number of coins in the purse.
    @return number of coins in Purse
*/
public int coinCount() {. . .}

    // Other methods and private stuff goes here
}
```

```
public class Game
{
    /**
        Game constructor: Creates the roulette wheel by constructing
        the appropriate Spinner.
    */
    public Game()
    {
        // Code goes here
    }

    /**
        Simulates a spin returning a 0, 2, or 3 as defined by the
        roulette wheel pictured in the problem.
        @return result of spinning wheel
    */
    public int spinTheWheel()
    {
        // Code goes here
    }

    /**
        Simulates the game of roulette as follows:
        Until the purse total is twice its original value
        or there are no coins left in the purse,
        removes a coin from the purse, and updates the
        number of coins in purse according to the winnings.
        @return total value in Purse
    */
```

```
public double playRoulette(Purse myPurse)
{
    // Code goes here
}

private Spinner myWheel;
}
```

a. Write the `Game` constructor. This constructor should construct a `Spinner` that will be able to appropriately simulate the wheel shown in the problem description above. Notice that all outcomes on the wheel do not have equal probabilities. The constructor for this class simply creates a wheel with a certain number of equally likely outcomes. The probability of the outcomes and the result of a spin are not handled in the constructor.

b. Write the `Game` method `spinTheWheel` that will call `spin` to generate a random number and then return the appropriate number on the roulette wheel. Notice that all outcomes on the wheel do not have equal probabilities. Use the header below when writing `spinTheWheel`.

```
public int spinTheWheel()
```

c. Write the `Game` method `playRoulette` that will simulate the game of Roulette as follows. The following steps of the game continue until the player doubles the original amount of money in the purse or has no coins left in the purse.
    *   bet (remove a coin from the purse)
    *   spin the roulette wheel
    *   accumulate appropriate winnings by adding coins to the purse (updates the number of coins in the purse).

The method `playRoulette` will return the total value in the purse. Write `play-Roulette` using the method header below.

```
public double playRoulette(Purse myPurse)
```

CUMULATIVE REVIEW 1

Chapters 2–7

This review will check your knowledge of material in Chapters 2–7. You should consider this a mini-practice for the AP Exam. Look over the material in these chapters and read over the section *Things to Remember When Taking the AP Exam* below. Have available the Exam Reference Materials for the AP Exam that you will be taking. Because you will have reference materials available to you during the exam, you should become familiar with them now. You can download the reference materials for the Computer Science A exam at:

> http://apcentral.collegeboard.com/apc/public/repository/ap06_compsci_a_exam_appendix.pdf

and for the Computer Science AB exam at:

> http://apcentral.collegeboard.com/apc/public/repository/ap06_compsci_ab_exam_appendix.pdf

■ Things to Remember When Taking the AP Exam

General Guidelines
- Write clear, correct code in answering all free-response questions.
- Do not spend time writing comments in your free-response answers unless your solution needs to be explained or you are specifically instructed to include comments.

Variable Declaration and Initialization
- Declare all variables before you use them.
- Initialize all objects and variables before you use them.
- Do not try to reset an object by calling a constructor. You cannot invoke a constructor on an existing object.

Naming Variables, Parameters, Methods
- When deciding on a variable name, choose a name that describes the purpose of the variable.
- Do not name the variable with the same word as the class name.
- Do not give parameter variables of methods the same names as your instance fields.
- Follow the Java conventions when naming variables, classes, and methods.
- Java is case sensitive. Avoid using names that differ only by case.

Invoking Methods and Returning Values
- When calling methods from a test class (client program), include the implicit parameter in the call.

- Do not use a class name when an object name should be used.
- The `return` statement in a method returns the specified value and exits the method immediately. The type of the value you are returning must match the return type of the method.
- Include a `return` statement if your method is to return a value.

Access

- Do not attempt to access `private` data or methods from outside the class.
- Do not use *magic* numbers in your code. Magic numbers are constants that appear in your code with no explanation. Use defined constants instead.
- In mathematical and logical expressions, use parentheses as you would in algebra.
- Remember that integer divided by integer equals integer. Sometimes casting one of the operands to a `double` is required to obtain a correct result.
- Remember that the first character of a `String` is in position 0.
- The `indexOf` method of the `String` class returns `-1` if the string being searched for is not found.
- The last character of a `String` s is in position `s.length() - 1`.
- When you assign one object variable to another object variable, both object variables reference the same object.
- In Java, we check whether x is between two values by writing `if (0 < x && x < 100)`. Do not write `if (0 < x < 100)`.
- Do not compare `doubles` with the `==` operator.
- Do not confuse `==` with `=`. The `==` operator checks equality. The `=` is used for assignment.
- Do not use `==` with strings. Use the `String` method `equals` to check whether two `String` variables have the same value.
- Do not use `==` with objects if you want to test whether two objects have the same contents. Use the object's `equals` method for this.
- Remember that the `null` reference is not the same as an empty `String`.
- Remember that a local variable that holds `null` is not the same as an uninitialized local variable.
- When comparing strings lexicographically, use the `String` method `compareTo`. Do not use `<` or `>` with strings.
- Know De Morgan's Law. It may help you in writing complex Boolean expressions.
- Be careful of a dangling `else` when nesting `if` statements. Remember that the `else` is paired with the *nearest* `if`.
- Indent the body of `if/else` statements. Proper indentation makes your program easier to read.
- Remember that indentation does not control the flow of the program. Use braces to create a block statement when necessary for flow, and also to improve legibility.
- Be careful not to accidentally place a semicolon after the Boolean expression in an `if` statement or after a `for` loop header or a `while` statement.

```
if (grade < 0 || grade > 100);  // WRONG
for (i = 1; i < 10; i++);  // WRONG!
while (i < 10);  // WRONG!
```

- Be sure to initialize variables used in the loop condition before the loop begins and to adjust their values appropriately inside the loop.
- Use braces where needed for the body of a loop. If in doubt, use the braces.
- Check the initialization and the test condition in your loops. It is common to have an off-by-one error when writing loops.
- Be careful when implementing tables with nested loops. The outer loop usually controls the rows of the table and the inner loop controls the columns.
- **(AB only)** Know the definition of a loop invariant. You may be asked to choose the correct loop invariant in a multiple-choice question.
- When writing code for a free-response question, be sure to hand trace your code to ensure it works for the examples given, as well as for several of your own test cases.

■ Practice Questions

Multiple Choice

1. What output is produced by the following code segment?

    ```
    System.out.println("\"One\"");
    System.out.print(2 + "Two");
    System.out.println(" \"Three\"" + 3);
    ```

    a. *"One"*
        2Two "Three"3

    b. *One*
        2Two
        Three3

    c. *"One"*
        2"Two" "Three"3

    d. *"One"*
        2"Two"
        "Three"3

    e. Nothing is printed. There is a syntax error.

2. Consider the following output.

    ```
    *
    **
    ***
    ```

    Which of the following code segments prints the design above?

    I. ```
        System.out.println("*");
        System.out.println("**");
        System.out.println("***");
        ```

    II. ```
        System.out.print("*\n");
        System.out.print("**\n");
        System.out.print("***\n");
        ```

    III. ```
         System.out.println("*\n**\n***\n");
         ```

    a.  I only
    b.  II only
    c.  III only
    d.  I and III only
    e.  I, II, and III

3.  Which of the following is **not** a legal string?

    a.  `"//"`
    b.  `"\n\""`
    c.  `"\"\\"`
    d.  `"\n\n"`
    e.  `"\""\\"`

4.  Which of the following does **not** describe a syntax error?

    a.  a misspelled variable name
    b.  a missing semicolon
    c.  an `if` statement without parentheses around the Boolean condition
    d.  a class definition that has a class name beginning with a lower-case letter
    e.  a missing closing brace
         ```

5. An object stores its state in

    a. reference variables
    b. instance fields
    c. `double` variables
    d. a constructor
    e. a `String`

6. Consider the `BankAccount` class whose incomplete definition is shown below.

```
/**
    A bank account has a balance that can be changed by
    deposits and withdrawals.
*/
public class BankAccount
{
    /**
        Constructs a bank account with a given balance.
        @param initialBalance the initial balance of bank account
    */
    public BankAccount(double initialBalance)
    {
        balance = initialBalance;
    }

    /**
        Deposits money into the bank account.
        @param amount the amount to deposit
    */
    public void deposit(double amount)
    {
        double newBalance = balance + amount;
        balance = newBalance;
    }

    /**
        Gets the current balance of the bank account.
        @return the bank account balance
    */
    public double getBalance()
    {
        return balance;
    }

    private double balance;
}
```

Suppose the following statements were executed.

```
BankAccount b1 = new BankAccount(1000);
BankAccount b2 = new BankAccount(500);

b1.deposit(b2.getBalance());
b2.deposit(b1.getBalance());
b1.deposit(b2.getBalance());
```

What are the balances of b1 and b2 after the code is executed?

    a. b1 has balance = 1000, b2 has balance = 500.
    b. b1 has balance = 3500, b2 has balance = 500.
    c. b1 has balance = 3500, b2 has balance = 2000.
    d. b1 has balance = 1000, b2 has balance = 1000.
    e. b1 has balance = 500, b2 has balance = 1000.

7. What is the result when the following segment of code is executed?

```
for (int i = 0; i < 4; i++)
{
    for (int k = 0; k < i; k++)
    {
        System.out.print(" ");
    }

    for (int j = 4; j > i; j--)
    {
        System.out.print("$");
    }
    System.out.println();
}
```

a. $$$$
    $$$
    $$
    $

b. $$$$
       $$$
       $$
       $

c. $
    $$
    $$$
    $$$$

d. $
       $$
      $$$
     $$$$

e. $ $ $ $
     $ $ $
      $ $
       $

8. Consider the following code segment.

```
int count = 0;
for (int i = 1; i < 5; i++)
    for (int j = i; j > 0; j--)
        count++;
```

After this code segment is executed, the value of count is

a. 0
b. 1
c. 5
d. 10
e. 15

Questions 9 and 10 refer to the following information.

The Internal Revenue Service withholding tax schedule for single people earning no more than $74,200 for the 2006 tax year can be found in the following incomplete table.[1]

If TAXABLE INCOME Is Over	But Not Over	The TAX Is This Amount	Plus This %	Of the Excess Over
$0	$7,550	$0.00	10%	$0
$7,550	$30,650	$755.00	15%	$7,550
$30,650	$74,200	$4,220.00	25%	$30,650

The class Taxes, whose incomplete definition is below, is designed to calculate and return the amount of withholding tax as defined by the table above.

```java
public class Taxes
{
    /**
       Assumes money > 0.
       @param money the amount to be rounded
       @return money rounded to the nearest hundredth
    */
    public static double roundedAmount(double money)
    {
        // Code goes here
    }

    /**
       Assumes income > 0.
       @param income the income to be taxed
       @return withholding tax based on tax table
    */
    public static double calculateTaxAmount(double income)
    {
        // Code goes here
    }

    /**
       Assumes income > 74200.
       @param income the income to be taxed
       @return correct withholding tax for income
    */
    private static double more(double income) {. . .}
}
```

Assume that the method more returns the tax withheld for amounts exceeding $74,200.

9. Which of the following code segments should replace the body of method calculateTaxAmount?

```java
    I.  if (income > 0 && income <= 7550)
            return 0.10 * income;
        if (7550 < income && income <= 30650)
            return 755 + 0.15 * (income - 7550);
        if (30650 < income && income <= 74200)
            return  4220 + 0.25 * (income - 30650);
        else
            return more(income);
```

<hr>

[1] http://www.irs.gov/formspubs/article/0,,id=150856,00.html

II.
```
double tax;
    if (income > 0 && income <= 7550)
        tax = 0.10 * income;
    if (7550 < income && income <= 30650)
        tax = 755 + 0.15 * (income - 7550);
    if (30650 < income && income <= 74200)
        tax = 4220 + 0.25 * (income - 30650);
    else
        tax = more(income);
    return tax;
```

III.
```
double tax;
    if (income > 0 && income <= 7550)
        tax = 0.10 * income;
    else if (7550 < income && income <= 30650)
        tax = 755 + 0.15 * (income - 7550);
    else if (30650 < income && income <= 74200)
        tax = 4220 + 0.25 * (income - 30650);
    else
        tax = more(income);
    return tax;
```

a. I only
b. II only
c. III only
d. I and III only
e. I, II, and III

10. The method `roundedAmount` will return a `double` that is the result of rounding its `double` parameter to the nearest hundredth. For example,

Method Call	Returns
roundedAmount(7345.045)	7345.05
roundedAmount(7345.053)	7345.05
roundedAmount(7345.00)	7345.00

Which of the following code segments should replace the method body of `roundedAmount` so that the method works as intended and returns a `double` representing `money` rounded to the nearest hundredth?

a. `return (int) money * 100`
b. `return ((int) (money * 100 + .5)) / 100;`
c. `return ((int) (money * 100 - .5)) / 100;`
d. `return ((int) (money * 100 + .5)) / 100.0;`
e. `return ((int) (money * 100 - .5)) / 100.0;`

11. The first-class mail rate for letters is based on weight and is calculated to be $0.41 for the first ounce and $0.17 for each additional ounce. A partial ounce counts as an ounce. The method `postageDue` should return the cost of mailing a first-class letter given its weight in ounces as its one `double` parameter. Which of the definitions below works as intended?

I.
```
public static double postageDue(double ounces)
{
    int tempOunces = (int) ounces;
    double leftOver = ounces - tempOunces;
    if (leftOver > 0)
        tempOunces++;
    return 0.41 + (tempOunces - 1) * 0.17;
}
```

```
II.  public static double postageDue(double ounces)
     {
         int temp = 0;
         double numOunces = ounces;
         while (numOunces > 0)
         {
             temp++;
             numOunces = numOunces - 1;
         }
         return (temp - 1) * 0.17 + 0.41;
     }

III. public static double postageDue(double ounces)
     {
         double temp = ounces - 1;
         return 0.41 + (int) temp * 0.17;
     }
```

    a.   I only
    b.   II only
    c.   III only
    d.   I and II only
    e.   I, II, and III

Questions 12–14 refer to the following code segment which simulates an experiment based on the assumption that 10% of the population is left-handed.

```
double prob = 1.0 / 10.0;  // probability of being left-handed
int count;
int num = 0;
for (int g = 0; g < 500; g++)
{
    count = 0;
    for (int p = 0; p < 20; p++)
    {
        double rand = Math.random();
        if (rand < prob)
        {
            count++;
        }
    }
    if (count > 2)
    {
        num++;
    }
}
```

12. In the code segment above, how many times is a random number generated?

    a.   1
    b.   20
    c.   21
    d.   500
    e.   10,000

13. Which description below best describes the value of count after the segment is executed?

    a.   count is the approximate number of left-handed people in a population of 10,000 people.
    b.   count is the approximate number of left-handed people in a population of 500 people.
    c.   count is the approximate number of left-handed people in a population of 20 people.
    d.   count is the approximate number of right-handed people in a population of 1000 people.
    e.   count is the approximate number of right-handed people in a population of 20 people.

14. Which description below best describes the value of num after the segment is executed?

 a. num is the number of left-handed people in a population of 10,000 people.
 b. num is the number of left-handed people in a population of 20 people.
 c. num is the number of groups of 20 people that had less than 10% left-handed population.
 d. num is the number of groups of 20 people that had more than 10% left-handed population.
 e. num is the number of right-handed people in a population of 10,000 people.

15. After the code segment below is executed, what is the value of t?

```
String s = "computer";
String t = "";
int len = s.length();
for (int x = 0; x < len / 2 ; x++)
{
    t += (s.substring(len - x - 1,len - x));
}
```

 a. "computer"
 b. "retupmoc"
 c. "comp"
 d. "retu"
 e. "pmoc"

16. Consider the following code segment.

```
String s = "mathematics";
String vowels = "aeiou";
int number = 0;
for (int i = 0; i < s.length(); i++)
{
    number += s.indexOf(vowels.substring(0));
}
```

What is the value of number after the execution of the above code?

 a. 19
 b. 11
 c. 4
 d. −1
 e. −11

17. Which of the following errors is **not** classified as a compile-time error?

 a. Division by 0
 b. Missing semicolon
 c. Misspelled variable name
 d. Uninitialized local variable
 e. Mismatched parentheses

18. Assume that a class provides the following instance methods for easily reading integers from a file. The object variable input represents the file and the file is open and ready for reading.

```
// Returns true if the end-of-file was read on the previous read,
// false otherwise.
public boolean eof()

// Returns the next integer in file.
public int readInt()
```

Consider the following code segment that is intended to find the average of the integer values read from input.

```
int n, count = 0, sum = 0;
while (!input.eof())    // Testing for end-of-file
```

```
{
   n = input.readInt();    // Read integer from file
   if (!input.eof())
   {
      sum += n;
      count++;
   }
}
double avg = sum / count;
System.out.println("The average is: " + avg);
```

I.   A logic error may occur because the variable n is not initialized.
II. A run-time error will occur if the file is empty.
III. A logic error may occur because the average returned is not always the correct value.

Which statement(s) above correctly describe the errors in this code segment?

a.   I only
b.   II only
c.   III only
d.   II and III only
e.   I, II, and III

19. Consider the following method mysteryRoll that deals with rolling a 6-sided dice.

```
public static boolean mysteryRoll()
{
   int rand = (int)(Math.random() * 6 + 1);

   for (int i = 0; i < 4; i++)
   {
      int temp = (int)(Math.random() * 6 + 1);
      if (temp != rand)
      {
         return false;
      }
   }
   return true;
}
```

Which of the following is the best description of the value returned by mysteryRoll?

a.   Returns true if any two rolls of four dice have the same value, false otherwise.
b.   Returns true if the first two rolls of five dice have the same value, false otherwise.
c.   Returns true if all four rolls of four dice have the same value, false otherwise.
d.   Returns true if all five rolls of five dice have the same value, false otherwise.
e.   Always returns true.

20. Consider the following code segment.

```
int num = 0;
for (int count = 0; count < 6; count++)
{
   int roll = (int)(Math.random() * 2 + 1)
   if (roll == 1)
      num++;
}
```

Which of the following is the best description of the value of num after the code segment is executed?

a.   The number of ones rolled in the tossing of six 6-sided dice.
b.   The number of sixes rolled in the tossing of two 6-sided dice.
c.   The number of heads in the tossing of two coins.
d.   The number of heads in the tossing of six coins.
e.   The number of times a coin is tossed.

Questions 21 and 22 refer to the `FunNumber` class whose incomplete definition is below. The `FunNumber` class is intended to provide various methods that return information about the `FunNumber`.

```
/**
    Creates and manipulates a number, which is fun!
*/
public class FunNumber
{
    /**
        Constructs a FunNumber representation of the integer n.
        Assumes n > 0.
        @param n the FunNumber value
    */
    public FunNumber(int n) {. . .}

    /**
        Constructs a FunNumber representation of the String n.
        Assumes n > 0.
        @param n the string to be represented by a FunNumber
    */
    public FunNumber(String n) {. . .}

    /**
        Returns the sum of the integers less than or equal to
        this FunNumber.
    */
    // Method sumInts goes here

    // Other methods not shown

    private int myNum;
}
```

21. Which of the following statements correctly instantiates a `FunNumber`?

    I.   `FunNumber funny = new FunNumber();`
    II. `FunNumber funny = new FunNumber(123);`
    III. `FunNumber funny = new FunNumber("123");`

    a. II only
    b. III only
    c. I and II only
    d. II and III only
    e. I, II, and III

22. The method `sumInts` is intended to return the sum of the positive integers less than or equal to the number represented by this `FunNumber`. For example,

    ```
    FunNumber funny = new FunNumber(5);
    System.out.println(funny.sumInts());
    ```

    would print *15* because $1 + 2 + 3 + 4 + 5 = 15$.

    Which of the following implementations for `sumInts` would return the intended result?

    ```
    I.   public String sumInts()
         {
             String sum = "";
             for (int c = 0; c < myNum; c++)
             {
                 sum += c;
             }
             return sum;
         }
    ```

```
II.  public int sumInts()
     {
         int sum = 0;
         for (int c = 1; c <= myNum; c++)
         {
             sum += c;
         }
         return sum;
     }
III. public int sumInts()
     {
         int len = myNum.length();
         int sum = 0;
         for (int c = 0; c < len; c++)
         {
             sum += myNum.substring(c, c + 1);
         }
         return sum;
     }
```

a. I only
b. II only
c. III only
d. I and II only
e. I, II, and III

Free Response Questions

1. The FunNumber class returns interesting (or fun) information about the integer representation of itself. The FunNumber object can return the number of digits it has, the sum of its digits, whether or not it's a prime number, and whether or not it's a perfect number. An incomplete definition of the FunNumber class appears below.

```
/**
    Creates and manipulates a number, which is fun!
*/
public class FunNumber
{
    /**
        Constructs a FunNumber representation of the integer n.
        Assumes n > 0.
        @param n the FunNumber value
    */
    public FunNumber(int n) {. . .}

    /**
        Constructs a FunNumber representation of the String n.
        Assumes n > 0.
        @param n the string to be represented by this FunNumber
    */
    public FunNumber(String n) {. . .}

    /**
        Returns the number of digits in this FunNumber.
        @return the number of digits in this FunNumber
    */
    public int numDigits()
    {
        // Code goes here
    }
```

```
/**
    Returns the sum of the digits in this FunNumber.
    @return the sum of the digits in this FunNumber
*/
public int sumDigits()
{
    // Code goes here
}

/**
    Determines if this FunNumber is perfect.
    @return true if this FunNumber is perfect, false otherwise
*/
public boolean isPerfect()
{
    // Code goes here
}

/**
    Returns the FunNumber whose digits are in the reverse order of the
    digits in this FunNumber.
    @return the FunNumber that is the reverse of this FunNumber
*/
public FunNumber reverseNum()
{
    // Code goes here
}

/**
    Returns the string representation of this FunNumber.
    @return the string representation of this FunNumber
*/
public String toString() {. . .}

private int myNum;
}
```

a. Write the `FunNumber` method `numDigits` that returns the number of digits in this `FunNumber`. For example,

```
FunNumber funny = new FunNumber(12);
System.out.println(funny.numDigits());
```

would print *2* because there are two digits in 12. Use the method header below.

```
public int numDigits()
```

b. Write the `FunNumber` method `sumDigits` that returns the sum of digits in this `FunNumber`. For example,

```
FunNumber funny = new FunNumber(123);
System.out.println(funny.sumDigits());
```

would print *6* because $1 + 2 + 3 = 6$. Use the method header below.

```
public int sumDigits()
```

c. Write the `FunNumber` method `isPerfect` that returns true if this `FunNumber` is perfect, false otherwise. A number is perfect if the sum of all of its proper factors (factors that are less than the number itself) equals the number. The numbers 6, 28, and 496 are perfect numbers because their proper factors sum to equal the number itself.

$$6 = 1 + 2 + 3$$
$$28 = 1 + 2 + 4 + 7 + 14$$
$$496 = 1 + 2 + 4 + 8 + 16 + 31 + 62 + 124 + 248$$

Use the method header below.

```
public boolean isPerfect()
```

d. Write the `FunNumber` method `reverseNum` that returns a `FunNumber` that is the reverse of this `FunNumber`.

```
FunNumber funny = new FunNumber(123);
System.out.println(funny.reverseNum());    // Would print 321.
```

Use the method header below.

```
public FunNumber reverseNum()
```

2. There are many card games that are played with a deck of 52 playing cards. In this deck of 52 cards, there are 13 cards with denominations 2, 3, 4, 5, 6, 7, 8, 9, 10, Jack, Queen, King, Ace in each of four suits (Clubs, Diamonds, Hearts, and Spades). The incomplete `Card` class is below.

```
public class Card
{
    /**
        Constructs a card with given suit and denomination.
        myValue is a numerical value determined for each card.
        denom is a one-character card String for the denomination,
        i.e. "2","J","A". suit is a one character String designating
        the suit "S", "H", "D", or "C".
        @param denom the denomination of this Card
        @param suit the suit of this Card
    */
    public Card(String denom, String suit)
    {
        mySuit = suit;
        myDenom = denom;
        myValue = getValue();
    }

    /**
        Returns the card suit determined by the instance field mySuit.
        Returns "Hearts" for H, "Spades" for S, "Clubs" for C,
        or "Diamonds" for D.
        @return the suit of this Card
    */
    public String getSuit()
    {
        // Code goes here
    }

    /**
        Returns the denomination of the card, 2,3,4,5,6,7,8,9,10,
        Jack, Queen, King, or Ace.
    */
    public String getDenomination()
    {
        // Code goes here
    }

    /**
        Returns the value of the card. The value is the card number
        if the card is between 2 and 10 inclusive, 11 for "J",
        12 for "Q", 13 for "K", 14 for "A".
        @return the value of this Card
    */
    public int getValue()
    {
        // Code goes here
```

```
    }

    /**
        Returns the String representation of the card,
        i.e. "Ace of Spades" OR "4 of Hearts".
        @return the string representation of this Card
    */
    public String toString()
    {
        // Code goes here
    }

    private String mySuit;
    private String myDenom;
    private int myValue;
}
```

a. Write the `Card` method `getSuit` that returns the card suit determined by the instance field `mySuit`. The method `getSuit` returns `"Hearts"` for H, `"Spades"` for S, `"Clubs"` for C, or `"Diamonds"` for D. Use the method header below.

```
    public String getSuit()
```

b. Write the `Card` method `getDenomination` that returns the denomination of the card: 2, 3, 4, 5, 6, 7, 8, 9, 10, Jack, Queen, King, or Ace as a `String`. Use the method header below.

```
    public String getDenomination()
```

c. Write the `Card` method `getValue` that returns the value of the card. The value returned will be the card number if the card is between 2 and 10 inclusive, 11 for `"J"`, 12 for `"Q"`, 13 for `"K"`, or 14 for `"A"`. Use the method header below.

```
    public int getValue()
```

d. Write the `Card` method `toString` that returns the `String` representation of this card, i.e., `"King of Spades"`, `"5 of Diamonds"`. In writing your solution, you may include calls to methods written in other parts of this problem. Assume these methods work as intended. Use the method header below.

```
    public String toString()
```

3. In a card game, a player is dealt cards. We call a player's dealt cards a *hand*. In our simplified card game, a `SimpleHand` class will hold two `Card` objects as defined in Question 2. The incomplete definition of the `SimpleHand` class is below.

```
    public class SimpleHand
    {
        /**
            Constructs a hand of two cards.
            @param c1 a Card in this Hand
            @param c2 a Card in this Hand
        */
        public SimpleHand(Card c1, Card c2)
        {
            card1 = c1;
            card2 = c2;
        }

        /**
            Determines if this Hand contains a pair.
            @return true if both cards in the hand are the same
            denomination, false otherwise
        */
        public boolean isPair()
        {
            // Code goes here
```

```
    }

    /**
        Determines if both cards in the hand are the same suit.
        @return true if both cards in the hand are the same suit,
        false otherwise
    */
    public boolean sameSuit()
    {
        // Code goes here
    }

    /**
        Determines if both cards in the hand are the same color.
        @return true if both cards in the hand are the same color,
        false otherwise
    */
    public boolean sameColor()
    {
        // Code goes here
    }

    /**
        Gets total value of the two cards. If the card is a
        numbered card 2-10, the value of the card is that number.
        The value of an Ace is 11 and the value of a Jack,
        Queen, or King is 10.
        @return the total value of the hand
    */
    public int getTotal()
    {
        // Code goes here
    }

    private Card card1;
    private Card card2;
}
```

a. Write the `SimpleHand` method `isPair` that returns `true` if both cards in the hand are the same denomination, `false` otherwise. For example, `isPair` would return `true` if the hand consisted of two fours or two queens and would return `false` if the hand contained a four and a king. Use the method header below.

```
public boolean isPair()
```

b. Write the `SimpleHand` method `sameSuit` that returns `true` if both cards in the hand are the same suit, `false` otherwise. For example, `sameSuit` would return `true` if the hand consisted of two Clubs or two Hearts and would return `false` if the hand contained a Spade and a Club. Use the method header below.

```
public boolean sameSuit()
```

c. Write the `SimpleHand` method `sameColor` that returns `true` if both cards in the hand are the same color, `false` otherwise. Hearts and Diamonds are red and Clubs and Spades are Black. For example, `sameColor` would return `true` if the hand consisted of two Clubs or a Heart and a Diamond and would return `false` if the hand contained a Spade and a Heart. Use the method header below.

```
public boolean sameColor()
```

d. Write the `SimpleHand` method `getTotal` that returns the total value of the two cards in the hand. For this game, if the card is a numbered card 2-10, the value of the card is that number. The value of an Ace is 11 and the value of a Jack, Queen, or King is 10. Use the method header below.

```
public int getTotal()
```

CHAPTER

(Covers *Java Concepts for AP Computer Science* Chapter 7)

Arrays and Array Lists

■ Topic Summary

8.1 Arrays

It is very common for applications to require us to store a large amount of data and process that data in any number of ways. Up to now, we have dealt only with data that we were able to store in a single field as a primitive data type or as a reference to an object. We will now look at a way to store large amounts of data in a single collection that can be referred to with a single variable.

An *array* is a fixed-length sequence of values of the same type. One-dimensional arrays store linear sequences of primitive types or references to objects. When we use arrays to store data we can easily and quickly access a single element in the sequence. We can explicitly overwrite an element at a specified position in the sequence, thus changing its value. We can easily and quickly inspect the element at a specified location in the sequence.

When an array variable is declared, it must be given a length before adding elements to it.

Example 8.1

```java
private static final int MAX_ELEMENTS = 10;
int[] array1 = new int[MAX_ELEMENTS];
        // array1 is an array of 10 int values initialized to 0
for (int i = 0; i < MAX_ELEMENTS; i++)
{
    array1[i] = i;    // array1 = { 0 1 2 3 4 5 6 7 8 9 }
}
System.out.println("Printing array1");
for (int i = 0; i < array1.length; i++)
    // length is attribute of array1
    // Notice that this is NOT a method call
{
    System.out.print(array1[i] + " ");    // 0 1 2 3 4 5 6 7 8 9
}
```

Arrays can also be instantiated using initializer lists. Example 8.2 below and *Advanced Topic 7.1* on page 292 of your text give an example of initializer lists.

Example 8.2

```java
int[] array2 = { 10, 20, 30, 40, 50, 60, 70, 80 };
        // Initializer list
System.out.println("Printing array2");
for (int i = 0; i < array2.length; i++)    // array2's length is 8
{
    System.out.print(array2[i] + " ");    // 10 20 30 40 50 60 70 80
}
```

When you declare an array of a certain size, its length is fixed. What happens if you run out of room before you are done filling it? If this happens, you could create another array that is twice as large as the first, copy all of the elements from the first array to the second, and assign the reference of the first array to the second. Example 8.3 demonstrates this technique.

Example 8.3

```java
int currentLength = array1.length;
int[] copyOfarray1 = new int[2 * currentLength];
    // copyOfarray1 is twice as big as array1

for (int i = 0; i < currentLength; i++)
{
    copyOfarray1[i] = array1[i];
        // Primitive types copied (ints) and the rest of the
        // elements of copyOfarray1 are initialized to 0.
}

System.out.println("Printing copyOfarray1");
for (int i = 0; i < copyOfarray1.length; i++)
{
    System.out.print(copyOfarray1[i] + " ");
        // 0 1 2 3 4 5 6 7 8 9 0 0 0 0 0 0 0 0 0 0
```

```
    }
    array1 = copyOfarray1;      // length = 20
                                // current number of values = 10
                                // currentLength is 10
```

As you can see in Example 8.3, the number of elements you actually put into the new array may be different from the new array's `length`. Working with arrays will often require that you keep track of the number of filled elements with another variable. After the code in Example 8.3 is executed, `array1` has room for more elements (`int`s in this case). The next `int` value would be assigned to `array1[10]` because this is the first available location. The variable `currentLength` keeps track of the current number of filled elements and therefore the position to which the next element will be added. When an element is added to the new array, `currentLength` should be incremented. *Advanced Topic 7.4* on page 316 of your text discusses partially-filled arrays.

Also remember to be careful when copying elements from one array to another. If your array contains *objects*, you are dealing with references. Example 8.4 below makes a *shallow* copy of the array `coins`. This means that *references* are copied, not actual objects.

Example 8.4

```
1     final int MAX_ELEMENTS = 3;
2     Coin[] coins = new Coin[MAX_ELEMENTS];
3     coins[0] = new Coin(0.05, "nickel");
4     coins[1] = new Coin(0.10, "dime");
5     coins[2] = new Coin(0.01, "penny");
6
7     // Copies references to coin objects into money.
8     Coin[] money = new Coin[MAX_ELEMENTS];
9     for (int i = 0; i < coins.length; i++)
10    {
11        money[i] = coins[i];
12    }
```

Line 2 declares an array `coins` that will hold references to three `Coin`s.
Lines 3–5 construct `Coin` objects and assign an array reference to each `Coin` object.
Lines 8–11 loop through the `coins` array.
Line 10 assigns references.

After execution of code:

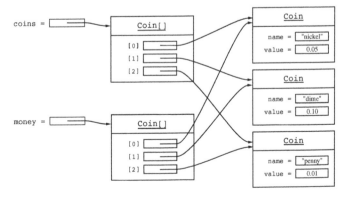

A change to the object referenced by coins [1] would also result in a change to the information referenced by money [1]. If it is your intention to actually have a copy of the array then take care to create a new object for each object that you want to copy. Example 8.5 performs a *deep* copy. This means that the actual objects are copied.

Example 8.5

```
1     final int MAX_ELEMENTS = 3;
2     Coin[] coins = new Coin[MAX_ELEMENTS];
3     coins[0] = new Coin(0.05, "nickel");
4     coins[1] = new Coin(0.10, "dime");
5     coins[2] = new Coin(0.01, "penny");
6
7     // Copies coins into money.
8     Coin[] money = new Coin[MAX_ELEMENTS];
9     for (int i = 0; i < coins.length; i++)
10    {
11        Coin temp = new Coin(coins[i].getName(), coins[i].getValue());
12        money[i] = temp;
13    }
```

Line 2 declares an array coins that will hold three Coins.

Lines 3–5 construct Coin objects and assign an array reference to each Coin object.

Lines 9–13 loop through the coins array.

Line 11 constructs a new Coin object that is a copy of the corresponding Coin object in coins.

Line 12 stores a reference to this new Coin in the corresponding position in the money array.

After execution of code:

8.1.1   A Word about Efficiency

In inserting and removing elements from an array, we must manipulate the array elements. To insert an element at the end of the array (as the last element), we must make sure the array has room. If there is enough room, we simply add the element in the first available position.

If we want to insert an element into an array in position 0, we must first make sure we have room. We do not want to replace the element in position 0, so all of the elements in the array need to be shifted before the element is added to position 0. You need to think about the order in which the shifting occurs. For example, if you want to insert newValue into arrayName in position 0, the following code segment will NOT perform the intended task!

```
// numElements is the number of filled elements in arrayName
if (numElements < arrayName.length())    // Is there room?
{
    for (int i = 1; i <= numElements; i++)
    {
        arrayName[i] = arrayName[i - 1];    // WRONG
    }
    arrayName[0] = newValue;
    numElements++;
}
```

The `for` loop above will overwrite all of the elements of the array with whatever is in the original `arrayName[0]`. That is NOT the intended result! The code segment below will accomplish the intended task if the array has room.

```
// numElements is the number of filled elements in arrayName.
if (numElements < arrayName.length())    // Is there room?
{
    for (int i = numElements; i > 0; i--)
    {
        arrayName[i] = arrayName[i - 1];    // CORRECT
    }
    arrayName[0] = newValue;
    numElements++;
}
```

When removing the last element of an array, no shifting of elements is necessary. However, if we want to maintain the original ordering of the elements in the array, removing an element in position 0 requires all of the elements in the array to be shifted! The number of filled elements, tracked by another variable (`numElements` in the above examples), will be decremented when an element is removed from the array.

8.1.2   A Formal Analysis of Array Efficiency (AB only)
The AP CS AB curriculum requires you to be able to analyze the efficiency of an algorithm in a more formal way. You should understand how algorithms perform as a data set gets larger and larger. This type of analysis uses *"big-Oh"* notation to describe the running time of an algorithm. Chapter 14 of your text and Chapter 15 of this guide look at several examples of big-Oh notation with more complicated algorithms. The algorithms dealing with inserting and removing elements of an array are relatively simple to understand, so the formal analysis of these algorithms is included here.

- When adding an element to the end of the array, no shifts are necessary. Assuming that we know the array index of the first available position in the array, we can insert this element and update the value of the variable holding the number of filled array elements if appropriate. This is done in constant time. The big-Oh analysis of this running time is $O(1)$.
- When removing the last element of an array, no shifting of elements is necessary. Assuming that we know the index of the last filled position, we simply subtract 1 from the value of the variable that keeps track of the number of elements we have in the array. Again, this is done in constant time. The analysis of the running time is $O(1)$.
- When inserting an element in position 0, we must shift all of the elements in the array to the right one index location. Only after that is done should we insert the new value in position 0 and update the value of the variable holding the number of filled elements in the array. If there are n elements in our array, this requires approximately n operations. The analysis of the running time is therefore $O(n)$.

- When removing an element from position 0, we must shift all of the elements in the array to the left one index location and update the value of the variable holding the number of filled elements in the array. If there are *n* elements in our array, this requires approximately *n* operations. The analysis of the running time is $O(n)$.

8.2　Array Lists

An array list is a sequence of objects that grows and shrinks as needed. Unlike the array, the array list does not have to be given a size when it is instantiated. This Java construct provides us with a means to easily deal with large amounts of data. The ArrayList class is part of the java.util package of the Java standard class library. There are many advantages to using array lists to store data, including

- Each element in the sequence can be accessed separately.
- We can explicitly overwrite an object at a specified location in the sequence, thus changing its value.
- We can inspect the object at a specified location in the sequence.
- We can add an object to a specified location in the sequence.
- We can add an object to the end of the sequence.
- We can remove an object from a specified location in the sequence.

Although the ArrayList class has many methods, only those listed in Table 8.1 are included in the AP Java subset to be tested on the AP CS Exam. Example 8.6 demonstrates ArrayList methods.

Table 8.1

`class java.util.ArrayList<E>`

Method	Method Summary
`boolean add(E x)`	Adds x to the end of the list and adjusts the size of the array list.
`void add(int index, E x)`	Inserts x at position index, sliding elements at position index and higher to the right (adds 1 to their indices), and adjusts size.
`E get(int index)`	Returns the element at index.
`E remove(int index)`	Removes and returns the element at position index, sliding elements at position index + 1 and higher to the left (subtracts 1 from their indices), and adjusts size.
`E set(int index, Object x)`	Replaces the element at index with x and returns the element formerly at the specified position.
`int size()`	Returns the number of elements in this list.
`Iterator<E> iterator() (AB only)`	Returns an iterator over the elements in this list in proper sequence.

It is important to remember that an array list contains references to *objects*. The ArrayList class is a generic class. This means that we specify the type of objects our array list will reference.

We will examine array list methods by looking at a simple example. As you read through the following array list example, think about the order in which the array list is being built.

Example 8.6

```
1      import java.util.ArrayList;
2
3      public class ArrayListTester
4      {
5         public static void main(String[] args)
6         {
7            ArrayList<String> students = new ArrayList<String>();
8
9            students.add("Mary");
10           students.add("James");
11           students.add("Kevin");
12
13           students.add(1, "Tanya");
14
15           String temp = students.get(3);
16
17           System.out.println(temp);
18           students.remove(2);
19
20           students.set(1, "John");
21           System.out.println(students.size());
22        }
23     }
```

Line 1 imports the `Arraylist` class contained in the `java.util` package.

Line 7 constructs an `ArrayList` that will hold `String` objects. This `ArrayList` is empty.

Lines 9, 10, and 11 add `String` objects to the `ArrayList`, each at the end of the list. At this point, `students` contains [Mary, James, Kevin].

Line 13 inserts "Tanya" into position 1 of `students`.

- The first position in an `ArrayList` has index 0. At this point, `students` contains [Mary, Tanya, James, Kevin].

Line 15 accesses the object in position 3 and assigns this to the `String` variable `temp`.

Line 17 prints *Kevin*.

Line 18 removes "James" from `students`. At this point, `students` contains [Mary, Tanya, Kevin].

Line 20 overwrites the object in position 1 thus changing "Tanya" to "John". At this point, `students` contains [Mary, John, Kevin].

Line 21 prints *3*.

Although Example 8.6 deals with `String` objects, array lists can contain references to any type of objects. Section 7.2 of your text uses `BankAccount` objects to demonstrate these same methods with the generic `ArrayList` class.

8.2.1   *Another Word about Efficiency*

To add a student into a specific position in the array list requires one call to the `ArrayList` method `add`. From Example 8.6,

```
students.add(1, "Tanya"); // Adds Tanya to position 1 of students.
```

or, more generally

```
students.add(p, name);    // Adds name to position p of students.
```

The "hidden" implementation of this operation requires much more work than is visible to us with that one simple call! When the add method is called with two parameters, the elements in the ArrayList starting at position p (specified by first parameter) are each shifted "up" one index position so that the new object can be inserted in the requested position. Of course, the "hidden" implementation takes care of making room for our addition and shifting the elements (adjusting the indices) correctly.

The remove method of the ArrayList class also requires more work than is evident to us. In Example 8.6, the call

```
students.remove(2);    // Removes Object in position 2 of students.
```

or, more generally

```
students.remove(p);    // Removes Object in position p of students.
```

removes the object in position p and shifts elements with indices greater than p "down" one.

```
students.remove(2);

┌─────────┐          ┌─────────┐
│  Mary   │          │  Mary   │
├─────────┤          ├─────────┤
│  Tanya  │          │  Tanya  │
├─────────┤          ├─────────┤
│  James  │ ───────→ │  Kevin  │
├─────────┤          └─────────┘
│  Kevin  │
└─────────┘
```

The "hidden" implementation again takes care of adjusting the ArrayList size and shifting the elements (adjusting the indices) correctly so we now must be careful not to index the out-of-bounds element by calling students.get(3)!

The size, get, and set methods operate in constant time. This means that the efficiency is not dependent on the size of the array list. These operations are very efficient. The add operation's hidden implementation shifts elements. If we add an element to the end of the array list, no shifts are necessary. If we add an element to an array list in position 0, all of the elements in the array list need to be shifted. With the remove operation, removing the last element requires no shifting of elements. Removing an element in position 0 requires all of the elements in the array list to be shifted.

8.2.2   A Formal Analysis of Array List Efficiency (AB only)

The formal analysis for inserting and removing an element in an array list is the same as for the array.

- Inserting an element at the beginning of an array list is $O(n)$.
- Inserting an element at the end of an array list is $O(1)$.
- Removing an element from the beginning of an array list is $O(n)$.
- Removing an element from the end of an array list is $O(1)$.

Although we only include one statement to accomplish each of the tasks above, the hidden implementation may require much more work.

8.3   Wrappers and Auto-boxing

One of the advantages of using array lists is that an array list grows dynamically. The size of the array list is not fixed. But array lists must contain references to objects. Numbers are not objects. In order to store doubles or integers in array lists you must use *wrapper* classes. These wrapper classes wrap numbers into objects. You can then store references to these objects in array lists.

The methods of the `Integer` wrapper class that are tested on the AP CS Exam are listed in Table 8.2.

Table 8.2
class java.lang.Integer implements java.lang.Comparable

Method	*Method Summary*
`Integer(int value)`	Constructs an object that represents the specified `int` value.
`int intValue()`	Returns the value of this `Integer` as an `int`.
`boolean equals(Object other)`	Compares this object to `other`. The result is `true` if and only if the argument is not `null` and is an `Integer` object that contains the same `int` value as this object.
`String toString()`	Returns a `String` object representing this `Integer`'s value.
`int compareTo(Object other)`	Compares this `Integer` object to `other`. If the object is an `Integer`, returns the value `0` if the argument is an `Integer` numerically equal to this `Integer`; a value less than `0` if `other` is an `Integer` numerically greater than this `Integer`; and a value greater than `0` if `other` is an `Integer` numerically less than this `Integer`. If the object is not an `Integer`, it throws a `ClassCastException` (because `Integer` objects are only comparable to other `Integer` objects).

Conversion between primitive types and their corresponding wrapper classes is automatic.

```
Integer n = new Integer(123);
int num = n;   // Auto-unboxing
```

These conversion details are explained in Section 7.3 of your text.

8.4   The Enhanced `for` Loop

You should be familiar with the simple array list algorithms that are discussed in Section 7.5 of your text. These algorithms include searching for a specific item in an array list, counting occurrences of some value in the list, and finding the minimum value or maximum value in the list. In many of these algorithms, an array list is traversed. We can do this with a simple `for` loop.

Example 8.7

```java
for (int i = 0; i < students.size(); i++)
{
    String temp = students.get(i);
    // Process temp
}
```

Java also provides the enhanced `for` loop ("for-each" loop). This is a shortcut method used to visit each element in the array or array list. Example 8.8 demonstrates the enhanced `for` loop. Notice that you do not specify the number of elements in the array list.

Example 8.8

```java
ArrayList<Student> mathClass = new ArrayList<Student>();
. . . // ArrayList filled here

for (Student s : mathClass)
{
    System.out.println(s.getId());
}
```

The enhanced for loop is only used when you want to visit all of the elements in an array or array list. The enhanced for loop is discussed in Section 7.4 of your text and included in the AP subset.

8.5   Simple Array Algorithms

Suppose we wish to write a program that generates some random number of random integers. These integers will be stored in an array list. The contents of the array list will be printed to the screen and the largest number in the array list will be found and printed to the screen. Let's look at a few methods that might help us accomplish these tasks.

Example 8.9   Filling the List

```java
public static ArrayList<Integer>
generateRandomIntegers(ArrayList<Integer> nums)
{
    final int UPLIMIT = some positive integer value;
    final int TOPNUM = some positive integer value;

    int rnum;
        // Generates the number of numbers that nums will have.
        // 0 <= numberOfNums < UPLIMIT
    int numberOfNums = (int) (Math.random() * UPLIMIT)
    for (int i = 0; i < numberOfNums; i++)
    {
        rnum = (int) (Math.random() * TOPNUM); // A random int,
                                               // 0 <= rnum < TOPNUM
        nums.add(new Integer(rnum));   // Wrapped in Integer
    }
    return nums;
}
```

Example 8.10   Printing the List

```java
public static void printArrayList(ArrayList<Integer> nums)
{
    for (int i = 0; i < nums.size(); i++)
    {
        System.out.print(nums.get(i) + " ");
    }
    System.out.println();
}
```

Notice that `nums.get(i)` returns an `Integer`. When included in the `System.out.print` statement, the `toString` method of the `Integer` class is called. This results in the intended output of the integers. We will discuss this call to the `toString` method in more detail in Chapters 10 and 11 in this guide.

Example 8.11 prints the contents of an `ArrayList` of `Integers` using the enhanced `for` loop ("for each" loop).

Example 8.11   Printing the List (enhanced for)

```java
public static void printArrayList(ArrayList<Integer> nums)
{
    for (int i : nums)    // Each element in nums is visited.
    {
        System.out.print(i + " ");    // The toString method of each
                                      // element in nums is invoked.
    }
    System.out.println();
}
```

The next example demonstrates finding the largest number in an `ArrayList` of `Integers`. This example uses the enhanced `for` loop as well as the *auto-boxing/unboxing* feature. This feature automatically *unboxes* the wrapper class object to a primitive type. Auto-boxing is explained in Section 7.3 of your text and is not tested on the AP Exam.

Example 8.12   Finding the Largest Number in the List

```java
public static int findLargest(ArrayList<Integer> nums)
{
    int large = nums.get(0);    // Initializes large to
                                // first element (unboxes)
    for (Integer i : nums)
    {
        if (i > large)    // Compares each element to large
        {
            large = i;    // Assigns value to large if larger
                          // value found (unboxes)
        }
    }
    return large;    // Returns the int value of large
}
```

An alternate method for finding the largest value in an array list can be found in Section 7.5.3 of your text. You should understand that storing wrapped numbers is inefficient. If possible, arrays should be used to store primitive types.

You are also responsible for the `Double` wrapper class. The `Double` wrapper class is very similar to the `Integer` wrapper class. The methods tested on the AP CS Exam are listed in Table 8.3.

Table 8.3

class java.lang.Double implements java.lang.Comparable

Method	Method Summary
`Double(double value)`	Constructs an object that represents the specified `double` value.
`double doubleValue()`	Returns the value of this `Double` as a `double`.
`boolean equals(Object other)`	Compares this object to `other`. The result is `true` if and only if the argument is not `null` and is a `Double` object that contains the same `double` value as this object.
`String toString()`	Returns a `String` object representing this `Double`'s value.
`int compareTo(Object other)`	Compares this `Double` object to `other`. If the object is a `Double`, returns the value 0 if the argument is a `Double` numerically equal to this `Double`; a value less than 0 if `other` is a `Double` numerically greater than this `Double`; and a value greater than 0 if `other` is a `Double` numerically less than this `Double`. If the object is not a `Double`, it throws a `ClassCastException` (because `Double` objects are only comparable to other `Double` objects).

8.6   Two-Dimensional Arrays *(AB only)*

Occasionally we want to store data in the form of a table consisting of rows and columns. Examples include airline or movie theater seating, survey results, or even a tic-tac-toe game (really, any board game). To construct such a two-dimensional array (*matrix*) we need to specify the number of rows and columns that we have.

```
final int ROWS = 3;
final int COLUMNS = 4;
int[][] table = new int[ROWS][COLUMNS];
```

This declaration results in a table with 12 `ints`.

table[0][0]	table[0][1]	table[0][2]	table[0][3]
table[1][0]	table[1][1]	table[1][2]	table[1][3]
table[2][0]	table[2][1]	table[2][2]	table[2][3]

`table.length` = 3 is the number of rows.
`table[0].length` = 4 is the number of columns.

You can also use initializer lists to instantiate two-dimensional arrays.

```
int[][] table2 = {{1, 2, 3, 4}, {5, 6, 7, 8}, {9, 10, 11, 12}};
```

would result in the following 2-dimensional array being created.

1	2	3	4
5	6	7	8
9	10	11	12

Many of the problems involving two-dimensional arrays deal with visiting all of the elements in the table. We usually do this with nested loops, where the outer loop traverses the rows and the inner loop traverses the columns. Example 8.13 prints the contents of `table2` in the order shown in the table above.

Example 8.13

```
1     int[][] table2 = {{1, 2, 3, 4}, {5, 6, 7, 8}, {9, 10, 11, 12}};
2     for (int row = 0; row < table2.length; row++)
3     {
4        for (int col = 0; col < table2[0].length; col++)
5        {
6           System.out.print(table2[row][col] + "\t");
7                 // \t tabs between columns
8        }
9        System.out.println();    // Advance to next line for next row.
10    }
```

Line 1 instantiates `table2` using an initializer list.

Line 2 loops through the rows of `table2`. Note that `table2.length` is the number of rows in `table2`.

Line 4 loops through the columns of `table2`. Note that `table2[0].length` is the number of columns.

Although Java allows for two-dimensional arrays where each row has a different number of columns (ragged arrays), this will not be tested on the AP CS Exam.

■ Expanded Coverage of Material That is Not Found in the Text

ArrayList Iterators (AB only)

The AB Exam may also include questions on traversing an `ArrayList` using an `Iterator`. The Java `ArrayList` class implements the `Iterator` interface. An `ArrayList` iterator works very much like the `ListIterator` described for linked lists in Chapter 15 of your text. The methods of the `Iterator` interface that will be tested on the AP CS AB Exam are listed in Table 8.4.

Table 8.4

interface java.util.Iterator

Method	*Method Summary*
`boolean hasNext()`	Returns `true` if the iteration has more elements.
`Object next()`	Returns the next element in the iteration.
`void remove()`	Removes the last element returned by `next`.

A `for` loop that traverses an `ArrayList` can be replaced by the code in Example 8.14 that implements the use of an `Iterator`.

Example 8.14

```
Iterator<String> it = students.iterator();
while (it.hasNext())
{
   String temp = it.next();
   // Process temp
}
```

or

```
for (Iterator<String> it = students.iterator(); it.hasNext();)
{
   String temp = it.next();
   // Process temp
}
```

Example 8.15 demonstrates the movement of an `Iterator` in an `ArrayList` of `String` objects. It uses iterators to demonstrate the same operations that Example 8.6 demonstrated. The initial position of the `Iterator` is before the first element of the `ArrayList`. The `next` method advances the `Iterator`. The `remove` method removes and returns the element that was last referenced by the `next` method. Be careful not to call `remove` more than once after a call to `next` because the first `remove` removes the object that was last referenced by the `next` method. The second `remove` will try to remove an item that's no longer there and will cause an exception to be thrown!

Example 8.15

```
import java.util.ArrayList;
import java.util.Iterator;    // Need to import class here.

public class IteratorTester
{
   public static void main(String[] args)
   {
      ArrayList<String> students = new ArrayList<String>();
      students.add("Mary");
      students.add("James");
      students.add("Kevin");
      students.add("Tanya");    // Mary, James, Kevin, Tanya (MJKT)

      // The symbol '#' indicates position of iterator
      Iterator<String> it = students.iterator();    // #MJKT

      it.next();    // M#JKT
      it.next();    // MJ#KT
      it.remove();    // M#KT
      // Another it.remove statement here would throw an
      // IllegalStateException.
      it = students.iterator();    // Resets iterator: #MKT
      while (it.hasNext())
      {
         System.out.println(it.next());    // Mary, Kevin, Tanya
      }
   }
}
```

The iterator class is also a generic type. An `Iterator<String>` iterates through an `ArrayList` of strings; an `Iterator<Student>` visits the elements in an `ArrayList<Student>`. If you do not indicate a type for the `Iterator`, the `next` method will return an `Object`. This may require you to cast to an appropriate type.

■ Topics That Are Useful But Not Tested

- Copying arrays can be done using the static `System.arraycopy` method. This is explained in Section 7.7 of your text.
- Auto-boxing and unboxing is a process that automatically converts between primitive types and their corresponding wrapper types. This eliminates some of the overhead with using wrapper classes. Auto-boxing is explained in Section 7.3 of your text.
- Regression testing is a classification given to particular testing procedure. This testing method is described in Section 7.8 of your text. The AP CS Exam will not require you to know this vocabulary or this specific testing procedure, but the concept of testing programs is included in the AP CS subset.

■ Things to Remember When Taking the AP Exam

- The generic `ArrayList` class allows us to specify the type of objects the array list will reference.
- When using iterators with the generic `ArrayList` class, you should use a generic iterator and match the iterator type to the type of objects in the `ArrayList`. Example 8.15 demonstrates this concept.
- The enhanced `for` loop is a shortcut for a loop that traverses through an array or an `ArrayList`. The enhanced `for` loop is included in the AP CS subset. The syntax for this loop is explained in Section 7.4 of your text.
- Remember that the first element of both an `ArrayList` and an array has index 0.
- The single most common loop error that occurs when dealing with arrays is an out-of-bounds error while the list is being traversed. The tests

```
while (index <= arrayName.length)    // WRONG
```

and

```
while (index <= arrayListName.size())    // WRONG
```

both try to access an out-of-bounds element. The test should be <, not <=. Remember that the last element in an array has index `arrayName.length - 1` and the last element in an `ArrayList` has index `arrayListName.size() - 1`. Think carefully about loop bounds when accessing array and `ArrayList` elements.
- Do not confuse `.length` with `.size()`. Remember that `arrayName.length` is an instance variable that holds the length of an array (not necessarily the number of filled elements in the array) and `arrayListName.size()` is a method that returns the number of elements in an `ArrayList`.
- To access the sixth element of an array we write `arrayName[5]`. To access the sixth element of an `ArrayList`, we write `arrayListName.get(5)`.

- Using `equals` with two `ArrayLists` returns `true` if the two `ArrayLists` contain the same elements in the same order, `false` otherwise. In other words, using `equals` with two `ArrayLists` returns `true` if the two `ArrayLists` have the same size, and all corresponding pairs of elements in the two lists are *equal* (Two elements `e1` and `e2` are equal if they are both `null` or `e1.equals(e2)`). Otherwise, `false` will be returned.
- Using `==` with `ArrayLists` compares references: `arrayList1 == arrayList2` is asking if `arrayList1` and `arrayList2` reference the same `ArrayList`.
- When you use `equals` with arrays, you are comparing references. `array1.equals(array2)` is asking if `array1` and `array2` reference the same array. Using `==` with arrays also compares references: `array1 == (array2)` is asking if `array1` and `array2` reference the same array.
- **(AB only)** When visiting elements in a two-dimensional array, do not confuse rows and columns. This is a common mistake made on the AP Exam.
- When shifting elements in an array, be careful not to overwrite values of other array elements. It is rare that this is an intended task! Think about the order in which the elements are being shifted.
- Iterators are included in the AB subset only. However, many problems are simplified if an array list is traversed using an iterator rather than looping through the array list with an index. If you are a student in AP CS A, you may want to cover iterators.

■ Key Words

You should understand the terms below. The AP CS Exam questions may include references to these terms. The citations in parentheses next to each term identify the page numbers where it is defined and/or discussed in *Java Concepts for AP Computer Science*, 5th ed.

array (288)
array initialization (292)
array length (290)
ArrayList (292)
auto-boxing (298)
bounds error (290)

cast (297)
counting (301)
Double (298)
index (289)
Integer (298)

Object (297)
size (293)
two-dimensional array (306)
wrapper class (298)

■ Connecting the Detailed Topic Outline to the Text

The citations in parentheses identify where information in the outline can be located in *Java Concepts for AP Computer Science*, 5th ed.

- Arrays (288–292)
- Array Lists (292–297)
- Wrappers and Auto-boxing (298–299)
- The Enhanced `for` Loop (300–301)
- Simple Array Algorithms (301–306)
- Two-Dimensional Arrays (306–310)

■ Practice Questions

Multiple Choice

1. Consider the following declaration.

   ```
   int[] A = new int[10];
   ```

   Which of the following choices describes the state of array A after this statement is executed?

   a. The elements A[1]...A[10] are not yet initialized and contain unknown int values.
   b. The elements A[1]...A[10] are initialized to 0.
   c. The elements A[0]...A[9] are not yet initialized and contain unknown int values.
   d. The elements A[0]...A[9] are initialized to 0.
   e. The elements A[0]...A[10] are initialized to 0.

Questions 2 and 3 refer to the Coin class whose incomplete definition is below.

```
public class Coin
{
    /**
        Constructs a Coin.
        @param aValue the value of the coin
        @param aName coin name
    */
    public Coin(double aValue, String aName) {. . .}

    /**
        Gets the coin's value.
        @return coin value
    */
    public double getValue() {. . .}

    /**
        Gets the coin's name.
        @return coin name
    */
    public String getName() {. . .}

    /**
        Determines whether this and other have same values.
        @param other coin which is being compared
        @return true if two coins have equal values;
        false otherwise
    */
    public boolean equals(Object other) {. . .}

    private double value;
    private String name;
}
```

2. Assume that the variable money has been initialized as follows.

   ```
   ArrayList<Coin> money = new ArrayList<Coin>();
   ```

   and that 10 Coins were added to money.

Which of the following statements or pair of statements would print the name of the sixth Coin in money?

a. ```
String temp = money[5].getName()
System.out.println(temp);
```

b. ```
System.out.println(money[5].getName());
```

c. ```
Coin temp = money.get(5);
System.out.println(temp);
```

d. ```
Coin temp = money.get(5);
System.out.println(temp.getName());
```

e. ```
String temp = money.get(5);
System.out.println(temp);
```

3. Assume that the variable money has been initialized as follows.

```
ArrayList<Coin> money = new ArrayList<Coin>();
```

and that several Coins were added to money. The following segment of code is intended to find the total value of the Coins in money.

```
1      public double getTotal()
2      {
3         double total = 0;
4         int i = 0;
5         while (i < money.size())
6         {
7            Coin tempCoin = money.get(i);
8            total += tempCoin.getValue();
9            i++;
10        }
11        return total;
12     }
```

Which of the following statements about this method is **true**?

a. There will be a compile-time error because there is a type mismatch.
b. There will be an indexOutOfBoundsException thrown during runtime because line 7 will try to access an element not in bounds of money.
c. The method will compile and run but the total returned will be incorrect.
d. There will be a run-time error when money contains no Coins, otherwise the method works as intended.
e. This method will execute as intended.

4. Consider the method doTask defined below.

```
public static int doTask(int[] a)
{
   int index = 0;
   int soFar = 1;
   int count = 1;
   for (int k = 1; k < a.length; k++)
   {
      if (a[k] == a[k - 1])
      {
         count++;
```
```

```
          if (count > soFar)
          {
              soFar = count;
              index = k;
          }
       }
       else
       {
          count = 1;
       }
    }
    return a[index];
}
```

When the following code segment is executed,

```
               0   1   2  3  4  5   6  7  8  9  10  11  12  13 14  15  16
int[] arr = { 1,  2,  3, 3, 3, 3,  4, 2, 2, 2,  2,  2,  2,  2, 5,  6,  6,
             6, 6, 6, 6, 4, 7, 8 };
             17 18 19 20 21 22 23
System.out.println(doTask(arr));
```

what is printed to the screen?

a. *1*
b. *2*
c. *6*
d. *7*
e. *24*

5. Assume that the following declarations have been made.

```
int[] A = { 1, 2, 3, 4, 5, 6, 7, 8 };
int[] B = { 4, 5, 6, 7, 8 };
```

Also assume that the method printContents is defined with the following header and works as specified in the comment.

```
// Prints the contents of array arr to the screen.
public static void printContents(int[] arr)
```

If the following segment of code is executed, what will be printed to the screen?

```
B = A;
B[3] = 0;
printContents(A);
printContents(B);
```

a. *1 2 3 4 5 6 7 8*
   4 5 6 0 8

b. *1 2 3 0 5 6 7 8*
   1 2 3 0 5 6 7 8

c. *4 5 6 0 8*
   4 5 6 0 8

d. *1 2 3 0 5 6 7 8*
   4 5 6 7 8

e. *1 2 3 4 5 6 7 8*
   4 5 6 7 8

6. Which of the following statements about arrays and `ArrayLists` is **not** true?

   a. A method can change the length of an array that is passed as a parameter.
   b. A method can change the length of an `ArrayList` that is passed as a parameter.
   c. A method can reverse the order of elements in its array parameter.
   d. A method can reverse the order of elements in its `ArrayList` parameter.
   e. A method can remove all of the elements in an `ArrayList`.

7. Consider the following method `doTask`.

   ```
   public static boolean doTask(int[] arr)
   {
      boolean found = true;
      for (int i = 0; i < arr.length; i++)
      {
         found = found && (arr[i] % 2 == 1);
      }
      return found;
   }
   ```

   Which of the following statements is **true** about method `doTask`?

   a. Method `doTask` returns `true` if all elements in its array parameter `arr` are even, `false` otherwise.
   b. Method `doTask` returns `true` if all elements in its array parameter `arr` are odd, `false` otherwise.
   c. Method `doTask` returns `true` if all elements in its array parameter `arr` are positive, `false` otherwise.
   d. Method `doTask` returns `true` if all elements in its array parameter `arr` are equal to 1, `false` otherwise.
   e. Method `doTask` will always return `true`.

8. Consider the following method definitions intended to find the smallest integer value in the `ArrayList` parameter. You may assume that the array list contains at least one value.

   I.
   ```
   public static int findSmallest(ArrayList<Integer> nums)
   {
      Integer small = nums.get(0);
      for (int i = 1; i < nums.size(); i++)
      {
         Integer tempSmall = nums.get(i);
         if (tempSmall.compareTo(small) < 0)
         {
            small = tempSmall;
         }
      }
      return small.intValue();
   }
   ```

   II.
   ```
   public static int findSmallest(ArrayList<Integer> nums)
   {
      Integer small = nums.get(0);
      for (int i = 1; i < nums.size(); i++)
      {
         Integer tempSmall = nums.get(i);
   ```

```
        if (tempSmall.intValue() < small.intValue())
        {
            small = tempSmall;
        }
    }
    return small.intValue();
}
```

III. ```
public static int findSmallest(ArrayList<Integer> nums)
{
    int small = (nums.get(0)).intValue();
    for (int i = 1; i < nums.size(); i++)
    {
        int tempSmall = (nums.get(i)).intValue();
        if (tempSmall < small)
        {
            small = tempSmall;
        }
    }
    return small;
}
```

Which of the method definitions above will work as intended?

a. I only
b. II only
c. I and II only
d. II and III only
e. I, II, and III

9. Consider the following method definitions intended to determine whether the two ArrayList parameters are equal (have the same number of elements in the same order). Assume the equals method for Student works as intended.

I. ```
public static boolean isTheSame(ArrayList<Student> A,
        ArrayList<Student> B)
{
    if (A.size() != B.size())
        return false;
    return (A == B);
}
```

II. ```
public static boolean isTheSame(ArrayList<Student> A,
        ArrayList<Student> B)
{
    if (A.size() != B.size())
        return false;
    for (int i = 0; i < A.size(); i++)
    {
        if (!(A.get(i)).equals(B.get(i)))
        {
            return false;
        }
    }
    return true;
}
```
```

```
III. public static boolean isTheSame(ArrayList<Student> A,
         ArrayList<Student> B)
    {
       if (A.size() != B.size())
         return false;
       return (A.equals(B));
    }
```

Which of the method definitions above will work as intended?

a. I only
b. II only
c. I and II only
d. II and III only
e. I, II, and III

10. Consider the following operations on an array. Insertions and deletions are done so that the original order of the array elements is not changed.

I.   Inserting an element at position 0 of an array.
II. Inserting an element at the end of an array.
III. Removing an element from the beginning of an array.
IV. Removing an element from the end of an array.

Which of the following statements about the efficiency of these operations is **true**?

a. If the array is large, I and II are more efficient than III and IV.
b. If the array is large, I and III are more efficient than II and IV.
c. If the array is large, III and IV are more efficient than I and II.
d. If the array is large, II and IV are more efficient than I and III.
e. All methods have the same efficiency. No method requires more work than any other.

11. Consider the following operations with an `ArrayList`.

I.   Inserting an element at position 0 of an `ArrayList`.
II. Inserting an element at the end of an `ArrayList`.
III. Removing an element from the beginning of an `ArrayList`.
IV. Removing an element from the end of an `ArrayList`.

Which of the following statements about the efficiency of these operations is **true**?

a. If the `ArrayList` is large, I and II are more efficient than III and IV.
b. If the `ArrayList` is large, I and III are more efficient than II and IV.
c. If the `ArrayList` is large, III and IV are more efficient than I and II.
d. If the `ArrayList` is large, II and IV are more efficient than I and III.
e. All methods have the same efficiency. No method requires more work than any other.

12. An experiment consists of tossing ten 6-sided dice and counting the number of 1's that appear on one toss of ten dice. There are 11 possibilities (0–10).

This experiment is to be repeated 500 times. The results of the 500 experiments are to be printed in a frequency table for occurrences of 1's tossed. The table will show the number of the 500 experiments that resulted in 0 ones, the number that resulted in 1 one, the number that resulted in 2 ones, and so on.

Which of the following data structures is the best choice to hold the necessary information?

a. An array of length 6.
b. An array of length 11.
c. An array of length 500.
d. An `ArrayList` of size 100.
e. An `ArrayList` of size 500.

(AB only) Questions 13 and 14 refer to the `Person` class and the array list `people` below.

```java
public class Person
{
    // Constructor.
    public Person(String aName, int howOld)
    {
        name = aName;
        age = howOld;
    }

    // Returns name of person.
    public String getName() {. . .}

    // Returns age of person.
    public int getAge() {. . .}

    //  Other methods here

    private int age;
    private String name;
}

ArrayList<Person> people = new ArrayList<Person>();
```

13. Which of the code segments below will correctly print the names of the `Person` objects in `people`?

    I.
    ```java
    for (Iterator<Person> it = people.iterator(); it.hasNext();)
    {
        Person temp = it.next();
        System.out.println(temp.getName());
    }
    ```

    II.
    ```java
    for (Iterator<Person> it = people.get(0); it.hasNext();)
    {
        Person temp = it.next();
        System.out.println(temp.getName());
    }
    ```

    III.
    ```java
    Iterator<Person> it = people.iterator();
    while (it.hasNext())
    {
        Person temp = it.next();
        System.out.println(temp.getName());
    }
    ```

    a. I only

    b. II only

    c. III only

    d. I and III only

    e. I, II, and III

14. The following segment of code is executed.

```
people.add(new Person("Anna", 23));
people.add(new Person("Thomas", 17));
people.add(new Person("Lara", 19));
people.add(new Person("David", 34));
people.add(new Person("Karen", 22));

Iterator<Person> it = people.iterator();
it.next();
it.next();
Person temp = it.next();
it.remove();
temp = it.next();
System.out.println(temp.getName());
```

What will be printed to the screen?

    a. *Anna*

    b. *Thomas*

    c. *Lara*

    d. *David*

    e. *Karen*

15. **(AB only)** Consider the following code segment that is intended to fill and print a two-dimensional array.

```
int x = 3; int y = 4; int z = 2;
int[][] tbl = new int[x][y];

for (int r = 0; r < x; r++)
{
   for (int c = 0; c < y; c++)
   {
      if (r != c)
         tbl[r][c] = y;
      else
         tbl[r][c] = z;
   }
}
for (int r = 0; r < x; r++)
{
   for (int c = 0; c < y; c++)
   {
      System.out.print(tbl[r][c]);
   }
   System.out.println();
}
```

Which of the following is the 2-dimensional array that is printed?

a. *422*
    242
    224

b. *2444*
    4244
    4424
    2222

c. *2444*
    4244
    4424

d. *4222*
    2422
    2242

e. *3222*
    2322
    2232

Free Response Questions

1. A `FooList` is a class that defines a list of strings and a string length. All strings in a `FooList` have the same length. There is no preset number of strings that a `FooList` can hold. For example,

    The `FooList` list1 may contain the strings aa, bb, cc, and dd (all strings of length 2).

    The `FooList` list2 may contain the strings cat, dog, pig, fox, bat, and eel (all strings of length 3).

    An incomplete implementation of the `FooList` class appears below.

```
public class FooList
{
    /**
        Constructor implementation initializes
        fooLength (the length of the strings in FooList's list) and
        possibleFoos (FooList's list of strings).
    */
    // Constructor code goes here

    /**
        Returns true if the string, key, is found in
        the FooList's list of strings, false otherwise.
        @param key the string we are searching for
        @return true if key is found in FooList; false otherwise
    */
    public boolean found(String key)
    {
        // Code goes here
    }
}
```

```
/**
    Adds the string, entry, to FooList's list implementation if
    it is the correct length and not already in the list. If the
    string is already in the list or if the string is not the
    correct length, it is not added.
    @param entry string to add to FooList
*/
public void addFoo(String entry)
{
    // Code goes here
}

/**
    Removes and returns a random string entry from FooList's
    list of strings.
    @return a random string from FooList
*/
public String removeRandomFoo()
{
    // Code goes here
}

/**
    Returns the string in position i of FooList's list
    implementation. The first string is in position 0.
    @return the ith entry in FooList
*/
public String getFoo(int i) {. . .}

/**
    Gets the length of a string in FooList.
    @return length of the individual strings in FooList
*/
public int getFooLength() {. . .}

/**
    Fills FooList's list with strings input by the user.
*/
public void fillFooList() {. . .}

private int fooLength;
private ArrayList<String> possibleFoos;
}
```

a. You are to implement the `FooList` constructor. This constructor will have one parameter that will indicate the length of each string in `FooList`'s list. The constructor will initialize `fooLength` with this value and will initialize `FooList`'s list of strings, `possibleFoos`, to have 0 entries.

b. You are to implement the `FooList` method `found`. The method `found` returns `true` if its `String` parameter `key` is found in the list of strings, `false` otherwise. Use the header below when writing `found`.

```
public boolean found(String key)
```

c. You are to implement the method `addFoo` as specified in the method comment shown above. Use the following header in writing `addFoo`. You may call method `found` that is specified in part b of this problem. Assume that `found` works as intended regardless of what you wrote for part b.

```
public void addFoo(String entry)
```

d. You are to implement the method `removeRandomFoo` that will remove and return a random string entry from `FooList`'s list of strings. Use the following header in writing `removeRandomFoo`.

```
public String removeRandomFoo()
```

2. Concentration is a game in which tiles are placed face-down in rows on a "concentration board". Each tile contains an image. For each tile, there is exactly one other tile with the same image. The player is to pick a tile, see which image it has, and try to find its match from the remaining face-down tiles. If the player fails to turn over its match, both tiles are turned face-down and the player attempts to pick a matching pair again. The game is over when all tiles on the board are turned face-up.

In this implementation of a simplified version of concentration,
   • Images will be strings chosen from a `FooList`. Assume that all `FooList` methods specified in Question 1 work as intended regardless of what you wrote.
   • The concentration board will contain an even number of `Tiles`.
   • The `Board` will be implemented as a one-dimensional array of `Tiles`.

For example, if the size of the concentration board is requested to be 4, the board will have 16 `Tiles`. The one-dimensional array, `gameboard`, can be viewed as a 4-by-4 concentration board as follows:

gameboard[0]	gameboard[1]	gameboard[2]	gameboard[3]
gameboard[4]	gameboard[5]	gameboard[6]	gameboard[7]
gameboard[8]	gameboard[9]	gameboard[10]	gameboard[11]
gameboard[12]	gameboard[13]	gameboard[14]	gameboard[15]

An incomplete implementation of the `Tile` class and an incomplete implementation of the `Board` class appear below.

```
public class Tile
{
    /**
        Constructs a Tile whose faceUp shows word.
        @param word is the string on the Tile
    */
    public Tile(String word)
    {
        image = word;
        faceUp = false;
    }

    /**
        Shows image on face-up Tile.
        @return image if Tile is face-up; otherwise
        return the empty string
    */
    public String showFace() {. . .}
```

```java
/**
    Checks whether Tile is face-up.
    @return true if Tile is face-up, false otherwise
*/
public boolean isFaceUp() {. . .}

/**
    Compares images on Tiles.
    @param other image to be compared to image on this tile
    @return true if the image on other is the same as this
    image; false otherwise
*/
public boolean equals(Object other) {. . .}

/**
    Turns Tile face-up.
    Postcondition: Tile is turned face-up.
*/
public void turnFaceUp() {. . .}

/**
    Turns Tile face-down.
    Postcondition: Tile is turned face-down.
*/
public void turnFaceDown() {. . .}

private String image;
private boolean faceUp;
}
```

```java
public class Board
{
    /**
        Constructs n by n concentration board of Tiles whose image
        values are chosen from the already filled FooList list.
        Precondition: n is the length of a side of the board,
        n is an even positive integer.
        FooList contains at least n * n / 2 strings.
        @param n is length of the side of the concentration board
        (an even number)
        @param list the FooList from which the values for the tiles
        are chosen
    */
    public Board(int n, FooList list)
    {
        gameBoard = new Tile[n * n];   // Concentration board
        size = gameBoard.length;   // Board size
        numberOfTilesFaceUp = 0;   // Number of Tiles face-up
        rowLength = n;   // Number of Tiles in a row
        possibleTileValues = list;   // Possible tile images
        fillBoard();   // Calls method to fill board with Tiles
    }
```

```
/**
    Randomly fills this concentration board with tiles. The
    number of distinct tiles used on the board is size / 2.
    Any one tile image appears exactly twice.
    Precondition: number of positions on board is even,
    possibleTileValues contains at least size / 2 elements.
*/
private void fillBoard()
{
    // Code goes here
}


/**
    PreCondition: 0 <= p < gameBoard.length.
    PreCondition: Tile in position p is face-down.
    PostCondition: After execution, Tile in position p
    is face-up.
    @param p the index of the tile to turn face-up
*/
public void lookAtTile(int p)
{
    // Code goes here
}


/**
    Checks whether the Tiles in pos1 and pos2 have the same
    image. If they do, the Tiles are turned face-up. If not, the
    Tiles are turned face-down.
    Precondition: gameBoard[pos1] is face-up,
    gameBoard[pos2] is face-up.
    @param pos1 index in gameBoard, 0 <= pos1 < gameBoard.length
    @param pos2 index in gameBoard, 0 <= pos2 < gameBoard.length
*/
public void checkMatch(int pos1, int pos2)
{
    // Code goes here
}


/**
    Board is printed for the player. If the Tile is turned
    face-up, the image is printed. If the Tile is turned
    face-down, the Tile position is printed.
*/
public void printBoard()
{
    // Code goes here
}

/**
    Returns Tile in position pos.
    Precondition: 0 <= pos < gameBoard.length.
    @param pos is index in gameBoard
    @return tile in position pos
*/
public Tile pickTile(int pos) {. . .}
```

```
/**
   Right-justifies a number to a given number of places.
   @param number an integer to be formatted
   @param p total number of characters in returned string
   @return right-justified number with p places as a string
*/
public String format(int number, int p) {. . .}

/**
   Right-justifies a word to a given number of places.
   @param word a string to be formatted
   @param p total number of characters in returned string
   @return right-justified word with p places
*/
public String format(String word, int p) {. . .}

/**
   Checks whether all tiles are face-up.
   @return true if all tiles are face-up, false
   otherwise
*/
public boolean allTilesUp() {. . .}

private Tile[] gameBoard;    // Concentration board of Tiles
private int size;    // Number of Tiles on board
private int rowLength;    // Number of Tiles printed in a row
private int numberOfTilesFaceUp;    // Number of Tiles face-up
private FooList possibleTileValues;    // Possible Tile images
}
```

a. Write the implementation for the Board method fillBoard. The method fillBoard will randomly fill the concentration Board with Tiles whose images are randomly chosen from strings contained in the FooList possibleTileValues. A tile image that appears on the board appears exactly twice on the board. Use the header below to write fillBoard.

```
private void fillBoard()
```

b. Write the implementation for the Board method lookAtTile. This method will call the appropriate method of the Tile class to turn the Tile face-up. Assume that the method you wrote for part a and the other methods whose headers and comments are given in the problem specification work as intended. Use the header below to write lookAtTile.

```
public void lookAtTile(int p)
```

c. Write the implementation for the Board's method checkMatch. This method will check whether the tiles in its two integer parameter positions on gameBoard have the same image. If they do, the tiles will remain face-up. If they have different images, the tiles will be turned face-down. Assume that the methods you wrote for parts a and b and the other methods whose headers and comments were given in the problem specification work as intended. Use the header below to write checkMatch.

```
public void checkMatch(int pos1, int pos2)
```

d. Complete the implementation for printBoard so that the concentration board is printed as described in the comment above and illustrated below. You should call the Board method `format` to right-justify the printing of the `Tile` image or the printing of the `Tile` position. For example, if `MAXPLACES = 5`,

```
System.out.print(format("go", MAXPLACES));
        // Will print ["   go"]

i = 4;
System.out.print(format(i, MAXPLACES));
        // Will print ["    4"]
```

Complete the implementation of `printBoard` that appears below.

```
public void printBoard()
{
    final int PADDING = 3;    // Spacing of tiles
    int spacing = possibleTileValues.getFooLength() + PADDING;
    for (int i = 0; i < size; i++)
    {
        // Code goes here
    }
}
```

An example of `printBoard` for a 4 by 4 concentration board that is partially solved is shown below after 4 matches have been found. The `FooList` passed as a parameter to the `Board` constructor contains strings of length 3.

fox	*fox*	*dog*	*dog*
cow	*5*	*6*	*7*
cow	*cat*	*10*	*11*
12	*13*	*14*	*cat*

3. **(AB only)** Suppose that the implementation of the concentration board constructed a two-dimensional array as an alternative to the one-dimensional array used in Question 2.

Board constructor

```
/**
    Constructs n by n concentration board of Tiles whose image
    values are chosen from the already filled FooList list.
    Precondition: n is the length of a side of the board,
    n is an even positive integer.
    FooList contains at least n * n / 2 strings.
    @param n is length of the side of the concentration board
    (an even number)
    @param list the FooList from which the values for the tiles
    are chosen
*/
public Board(int n, FooList list)
{
    gameBoard = new Tile[n][n];    // Concentration board

    size = n * n;    // Number of Tiles on Board
    numberOfTilesFaceUp = 0;    // Number of Tiles face-up
    rowLength = n;    // Number of Tiles in a row

    possibleTileValues = list;    // Possible Tile images
    fillBoard();    // Calls method to fill board with Tiles
}
```

Private instance fields

```
private Tile[][] gameBoard;    // Concentration board of Tiles
private int size;    // Number of Tiles on board
private int rowLength;    // Number of Tiles printed in a row
int numberOfTilesFaceUp;    // Number of Tiles face-up
private FooList possibleTileValues;    // Possible Tile values
```

a. Implement the Board method fillBoard using this two-dimensional array implementation. Use the header below to write fillBoard.

```
private void fillBoard()
```

b. Implement the Board method printBoard using this two-dimensional array implementation. Use the header below to write printBoard.

```
public void printBoard()
```

CHAPTER

(Covers *Java Concepts for AP Computer Science* Chapter 8)

Designing Classes

■ Topic Summary

9.1   Choosing Classes

Object-oriented programming is a major focus of AP Computer Science. The center of this programming paradigm in Java is a *class*. Both the AP CS A and AB Exams may test your ability to design and implement a class. The AP CS AB Exam may also test your ability to decompose a problem into classes and to define the relationships and responsibilities of those classes. A class should represent a single concept from the problem description. Some examples of classes that we have studied so far include `Rectangle`, `Student`, `BankAccount`, and `Car`. The properties of these classes were relatively easy to understand. The names of these classes are nouns that clearly identify the class. When you choose a class to implement, it should represent a single concept and should be named with a noun that easily identifies the class.

One particular category of classes is called an *actor* class. This type of class does work for you. The `Scanner` class, discussed in Chapter 4 of your text, is an actor class. We also have *utility* classes, such as `Math`, that have no objects. These types of classes are explained in Section 8.1 of your text. The AP subsets do not require you to classify classes as actor or utility classes.

9.2 Cohesion and Coupling

A class should represent one concept. All of the class responsibilities (interface features) should be closely related to the concept that the class represents. If they are, we say the class is *cohesive* or has a high degree of cohesion. Sometimes a class needs other classes so that it can do its job. A Purse class needs the Coin class because a purse contains coins. A roulette Game class needs the Spinner class to create and spin the roulette wheel. If many classes in a program depend on each other, we say that there is a high degree of *coupling*. It is a good programming practice to have high cohesion and low coupling. If a high degree of coupling exists, then modifying one class may affect many other classes. Figure 2 in Section 8.2 of your text illustrates high and low class coupling. When designing a class, you should be able to list the class's responsibilities and collaborators (the classes that it uses or depends on). Doing so will help you see the amount of cohesion and coupling in your class design.

Let's look at an example of class responsibilities and collaborators.

Consider a state lottery game. Each evening the lottery is televised and we observe the following. There is a *container* that holds the numbered *balls* such that no two balls have the same number. There is a *popper* that "pops" a random ball. It is this popped ball's number that is one of the lottery number choices.

Classes:
- Container has a collection of Balls. If asked for a Ball, the Container will remove a Ball at random from the set of Balls it contains and return it.
  - Responsibilities
    - hold Objects (Balls)
    - remove and return an Object (Ball)
  - Collaborators (other classes the Container needs or uses)
    - Ball
- Ball has a number on it. It can return its number to whoever wants to know it.
  - Responsibilities
    - return its number
  - Collaborators (other classes the Ball needs or uses)
    - none
- Popper will ask the Container for a Ball and display the number on the Ball.
  - Responsibilities
    - ask Container for Ball
    - ask Ball for its number
    - display number on Ball
  - Collaborators (other classes the Popper needs or uses)
    - Ball
    - Container

We see that there is some degree of coupling in this example because classes collaborate with other classes. We also see that the Ball's cohesion allows it to be used in other games: billiards (add a color to the "ball"), croquet, Scrabble (add a letter to the "ball" and view it as a "tile"), and any game that has a game "piece" with a number on it.

9.3   Accessors, Mutators, and Immutable Classes

A class defines the behavior of its objects by supplying methods. These methods either change the state of the object or they do not. Methods that change the state of an object are called *mutator* methods, or *modifiers,* and usually have a `void` return type. Examples of modifiers include `deposit` and `withdraw` in the `BankAccount` class. Both of these methods change the state of the `BankAccount` object by modifying its `balance`. The methods `drive` and `fillTank` in the `Car` class change the state of a `Car` object by modifying its `mileage` and `gasInTank`. *Accessor* methods do not change the state of the object. The method `getBalance` returns the balance of a `BankAccount` object without changing the state of the object. The method `getMileage` returns the total mileage of a `Car` object without changing the state of the object.

A class with no modifiers is an *immutable* class. The `String` class is immutable. After a string has been constructed, its contents cannot change. The methods of the `String` class do not change the state of the `String` object.

```
String s1 = "Hello";
String s2 = s1;
String s3 = "World";

s1 += s3;   // s1 is now HelloWorld. A new string was created.
            // s2 is still Hello.
            // s3 is World.
```

As you recall from Chapter 6 in this guide, string concatenation does not actually *add to* a string. A new string is created.

9.3.1   *Parameter Passing*

In Java, a method can never change the values of its parameters. A method with a parameter whose value is an object reference can change the state of the object referred to, but cannot replace the parameter reference with another. Example 9.1 demonstrates these very important concepts.

Example 9.1

```
public class Point
{
   Point(int x1, int y1)
   {
      x = x1;
      y = y1;
   }

   public void setPoint(int xCoordinate, int yCoordinate)
   {
      x = xCoordinate;
      y = yCoordinate;
   }

   public int getX()
   {
      return x;
   }
```

```java
    public int getY()
    {
        return y;
    }

    public String toString()
    {
        String s = "(" + x + "," + y + ")";
        return s;
    }

    private int x;
    private int y;
}
```

```java
public class ParamsTester
{
    public static void main(String[] args)
    {
        // Trying to change primitive parameters
        int a = 10;
        int b = 11;
        System.out.println("Before call to change:");
        System.out.println("a = " + a + " b = " + b);
            // a = 10 b = 11
        change(a, b);
        System.out.println("After call to change:");
        System.out.println("a = " + a + " b = " + b);
            // a = 10 b = 11
        System.out.println();

        // Trying to change object references
        Point p1 = new Point(1, 2);
        Point p2 = new Point(3, 4);
        System.out.println("Before call to changePoints:");
        System.out.println("p1 = " + p1);    // p1 = (1, 2)
        System.out.println("p2 = " + p2);    // p2 = (3, 4)
        changePoints(p1, p2);
        System.out.println("After call to changePoints:");
        System.out.println("p1 = " + p1);    // p1 = (1, 2)
        System.out.println("p2 = " + p2);    // p2 = (3, 4)
        System.out.println();

        // Changing the state of an object
        System.out.println("Before call to changeState:");
        System.out.println("p1 = " + p1);    // p1 = (1, 2)
        System.out.println("p2 = " + p2);    // p2 = (3, 4)
        changeState(p1, p2);
        System.out.println("After call to changeState:");
        System.out.println("p1 = " + p1);    // p1 = (3, 4)
        System.out.println("p2 = " + p2);    // p2 = (3, 4)
        System.out.println();
    }

    public static void change(int x, int y)
    {
```

```
        x = 123;
        y = 789;
    }

    public static void changePoints(Point first, Point second)
    {
        Point anotherPoint = new Point(9, 9);
        first = anotherPoint;
        second = first;
    }

    public static void changeState(Point first, Point second)
    {
        first.setPoint(second.getX(), second.getY());
    }
}
```

Output of ParamsTester
_____

Before call to change:
a = 10 b = 11
After call to change:
a = 10 b = 11

Before call to changePoints:
p1 = (1, 2)
p2 = (3, 4)
After call to changePoints:
p1 = (1, 2)
p2 = (3, 4)

Before call to changeState:
p1 = (1, 2)
p2 = (3, 4)
After call to changeState:
p1 = (3, 4)
p2 = (3, 4)

_____

Example 9.1 shows that all argument values are copied into the parameter variables when a method starts. You may see this described as "primitive parameters are passed by value". With objects, the object *reference* is passed by value, not the object. *Common Error 8.1* on page 343 of your text discusses primitive type parameters. *Advanced Topic 8.1* on page 346 of your text discusses "call by value" in more detail.

9.4   Side Effects

Every method should be designed to do one task. A *side effect* of a method is any externally observable behavior outside the object on which the method is invoked. Your text explains different types of side effects dealing with the `BankAccount` class and the possible consequences of these side effects. You should minimize side effects. Do not add `System.out.println` statements to indicate that a method has been completed. The `System.out.println` statement is extraneous code that manipulates the `System.out` object. Unwanted side effects such as this will result in a deduction of points on the free-response portion of the AP CS Exam. *Quality Tip 8.2* on page 345 of your text discusses side effects and classifies method behavior.

9.5   Preconditions and Postconditions

Preconditions and postconditions are statements that document the intended behavior of the method. They should appear in the method documentation. A *precondition* is a statement that describes the requirements that must be met in order for the method to complete its intended task correctly. If the precondition is not met, no promise about the method's behavior is made. It is the responsibility of the calling method to satisfy the precondition. If the precondition is not satisfied, how should the method behave? One way of handling a violation of the precondition is to throw an *exception* to indicate that the method was called inappropriately. Exceptions are introduced in *Productivity Hint 4.2* on page 160 of your text and discussed more thoroughly in Chapter 11. We will look at exceptions in more detail in Chapter 12 of this guide.

A *postcondition* is a promise that the value returned by the method is computed correctly or that the object is in a certain state. A postcondition's promise is valid only if the precondition is satisfied. Example 9.2 contains information about a `Product` class. The class contains the name and the number of available products with this name. The method `buyProduct` shows a pre- and postcondition and throws an appropriate exception when the precondition is not met.

Example 9.2

```
/**
    Product contains information about products in a store.
    Class invariant: getNumAvailable() >= 0 (AB only)
*/
public class Product
{
    /**
        Constructs a product with given name and number available.
        Precondition: number >= 0
        @param nm the name of a product
        @param number the product quantity available
    */
    public Product(String nm, int number)
    {
        numAvailable = number;
        name = nm;
    }

    /**
        Gets quantity available of product.
        @return number of product available
    */
    public int getNumAvailable()
    {
        return numAvailable;
    }

    /**
        Precondition: numWanted <= numAvailable
        Postcondition: numAvailable is updated accounting for the
        number of items bought
```

```
        @param numWanted the number of product to buy
    */
    public void buyProduct(int numWanted)
    {
        if (numWanted > numAvailable)
            throw new IllegalArgumentException();
        numAvailable -= numWanted;
    }

    // Other methods here

    private int numAvailable;
    private String name;
    // Other private stuff
}
```

If you supply a method that only works correctly under certain conditions, be sure to use preconditions to document this fact. If you supply a method that is guaranteed to have a certain effect, use postconditions to document this fact. When you are using other classes in your programs, be sure to read the pre- and postconditions carefully. Remember that the calling method is responsible for satisfying the preconditions.

Reading and understanding pre- and postconditions is important. Many times an algorithm for solving a free-response question is given in the documentation.

An *assertion* is a logical condition in a program that is believed to be true. When the statement

```
        numAvailable -= numWanted; // Assertion: numAvailable >= numWanted
```

is executed, the number of available products, numAvailable, should be greater than or equal to the number of products desired, numWanted.

9.5.1   *Class Invariants (AB Only)*
In addition to pre- and postconditions, a *class invariant* was also included in Example 9.2. A class invariant is a statement that is true about an object after every constructor and that is preserved by every modifier provided that the preconditions were met. Class invariants are discussed in *Advanced Topic 8.2* on page 351 of your text.

9.6   Static Methods

Up to now, the methods we have included in our classes have been *instance* methods. These methods belong to the object and operate on the object that is instantiated. A *static* method belongs to the *class*, not to an object, and is sometimes referred to as a *class* method. A static method has no implicit parameter. Static methods must be invoked through a class, not an object (i.e., Class.methodName(), not obj.methodName()) and cannot refer to instance fields or call instance methods. In the Car class shown in Example 9.3, the class variable numCarsMade keeps a count of the number of Car objects that have been instantiated. Each time a Car object is created, numCarsMade is incremented by 1. The class method getNumCarsMade returns that number to the calling method.

9.7 Static Fields

The class variable, numCarsMade, is a static field of the Car class. The initialization of numCarsMade is done only once, when the Car constructor is called the first time. The statement

```
System.out.println(Car.getNumCarsMade());
```

will print the value of numCarsMade, which is the number of Car objects constructed.

Example 9.3

```java
public class Car
{
    /**
        Default constructor initializes instance variables.
    */
    public Car()
    {
        // Private instance variables initialized here
        numCarsMade++;    // Number of cars manufactured so far
    }

    // Other public methods here

    /**
        Gets number of cars manufactured so far.
        @return number of cars made
    */
    public static int getNumCarsMade()
    {
        return numCarsMade;
    }

    // Counts cars instantiated
    private static int numCarsMade = 0; // Initializes static field
}
```

Static fields should be declared as private to ensure that methods of other classes do not change their values. Static *constants* can be declared as public or private. If your constant will be called only by methods within your class, then you should declare it as private. If you wish to allow the client programs or other classes access to your constants, then you would declare them as public. Static constants are initialized when they are declared. Static constants are discussed in Section 8.7 of your text.

9.8 Scope

The word *scope* is used to describe the part of a program in which a variable is accessible. We have already discussed instance variables, local variables of methods, parameter variables, and variables declared in the initialization of for loops. The issue of variable scope is an important reason to choose variable names wisely. It is bad programming technique to give instance variables the same names as the parameter or local variables. If you do, the scope issues become complicated. The constructors in Examples 9.4 and 9.5 illustrate errors involving instance fields that are commonly made by students.

Example 9.4

```java
public class Student
{
    /**
        Constructs a Student with the given information.
        @param first the student's first name
        @param last the student's last name
        @param idNumber the student identification number
    */
    public Student(String first, String last, String idNumber)
    {
        String firstName = first;   // WRONG. A local variable is
                                    // being initialized, NOT the
                                    // the instance field!

        lastName = last;
        id = idNumber;
        sumOfGrades = 0.0;
        numberOfGrades = 0;
    }

    // Other code here

    private String firstName;
    private String lastName;
    private String id;
    private double sumOfGrades;
    private int numberOfGrades;
}
```

The statements

```java
Student csStudent = new Student("Jay", "Delmonti", "333");
System.out.println(csStudent.getFirstName() + " " +
    csStudent.getLastName());
```

would result in

null Delmonti

being printed. The programmer of this class constructor *accidentally* created a local variable
firstName with the same name as the instance field. The type String should be eliminated in
the constructor body. The private instance field types are given when they are declared.

Example 9.5

```java
public class Student
{
    public Student(String first, String last, String id)
    {
        firstName = first;
        lastName = last;
        id = id;   // WRONG. private instance field NOT
                   // initialized to parameter value.
                   // private instance field id = null;
        // More code here
    }
```

```
public String getId()
{
    return id;
}

private String firstName;
private String lastName;
private String id;
}
```

If a client program constructed a student with the statement

```
Student someStudent = new Student("Joe", "Smith", "213534")
```

the private instance variable `id` would not be initialized as intended ("213534") and would have the value `null`. The statement

```
System.out.println(someStudent.getId());
```

would result in `null` being printed.

The programmer of this class constructor *accidentally* created a parameter variable `id` with the same name as the instance field. The statement

```
id = id;
```

results in the parameter value "213534" being assigned to the parameter variable `id`. The private instance field `id` is assigned `null`. Do not name parameter variables with the same name as your instance fields.

9.8.1 Scope of Local Variables

The scope of a local variable extends from the point of its declaration to the end of the block that encloses it. If a variable is declared in the loop initialization, it is accessible only within the loop. If a variable is declared at the start of a method, it is accessible in that method. Parameter variables in a method header are accessible only within that method. If you try to give two local variables with overlapping scopes the same name, the compiler will complain. You can have local variables with the same name if their scopes do not overlap. Example 9.6 illustrates these concepts.

Example 9.6

```
1    Student csStudent = new Student("Jay", "Delmonico", "333");
2
3    ArrayList<Student> apClass = new ArrayList<Student>();
4    for (int i = 0; i < 5; i++)
5    {
6        String tempId = "11" + i;
7        Student csStudent = new Student("name1", "name2", tempId);
8        apClass.add(csStudent);
9    }
10   System.out.println(i);
11   for (int i = 0; i < 5; i++)
12   {
13       System.out.println((apClass.get(i)).getId());
14   }
```

Line 1 declares and initializes variable csStudent.

Line 7 will cause the compiler to complain because there is an attempt to declare and initialize a variable with the same name that would overlap the scope of the first csStudent variable.

Line 10 would cause the compiler to complain because the scope of i is restricted to the loop.

Line 11 uses the name i as the loop control variable name again. This is OK because the scope of the two variables named i do not overlap.

To avoid confusion with scope, use different names for different variables and never change the values of parameter variables.

9.8.2   Scope of Class Members

Within an instance method of a class, you can access all other methods and all fields of that class by their simple names (without an object name prefix). If you are using a method outside the object, you must qualify it by prefixing the method name with the object name (for an instance method) or by the class name (for a class method). Whenever you see an instance method call without an implicit parameter (object name prefix), the method is called on the this parameter. Several examples of referencing variables with different scopes are given in Sections 8.8.2 and 8.8.3 of your text. *Common Error 8.2* on page 361 of your text discusses the pitfalls of declaring a local variable with the same name as an instance field.

9.8.3   Initializing Variables

The methods for initializing variables depend on the type of variable. The initialization of different variable types is summarized below:

- Local variables belong to an individual method. A local variable can be accessed only from within that method and must be initialized before you use it. Failure to initialize will cause the compiler to complain.
- Parameter variables also belong to an individual method. Parameter variables are initialized with the values that are supplied by the calling method.
- Instance fields belong to an object and can be used by all methods of its class. Instance fields should be initialized in the constructor of the class. If instance fields are not initialized explicitly, default values are assigned. Numbers are initialized to 0, objects to null, and boolean values to false. Even though these default values are assigned to instance fields, it is good programming practice to initialize instance variables in the constructors. The AP CS Exam will expect you to implement constructors that initialize all instance variables.
- Static fields are initialized when the class is loaded. This should be done by an explicit initializer. However, if no initialization is done explicitly, default values are assigned. Numbers are initialized to 0, objects to null, and boolean values to false.
- Static constants are initialized with a value provided by the programmer. Static constants are initialized when they are declared.

The AP Exam will not test default initializations. You should initialize instance variables in constructors and you should include explicit initializers for static fields.

9.9   Packages

A package is a set of related classes. Several common packages used in Java are listed in Table 1 on page 364 of your text. If you are using classes that belong to any of these packages (except java.lang), you must import the package. The import directive allows you to refer to the class of the package without fully qualifying the class name with the package prefix each time you use it.

```
import java.awt.Rectangle
// Other stuff here

Rectangle = new Rectangle(5, 10, 15, 20);
```

is much easier to read and understand than

```
java.awt.Rectangle = new java.awt.Rectangle(5, 10, 15, 20);
```

You are expected to have a basic understanding of packages and a reading knowledge of import statements. *Common Error 8.3* on page 368 of your text discusses Java naming conventions that can help you avoid confusion when looking at names with many connecting dots!

You will not be required to create packages on the AP Exam.

■ Topics That Are Useful But Not Tested

- You can sometimes avoid code duplication when writing multiple constructors for a class by calling one constructor from another. An example of this is given in *Advanced Topic 3.1* on page 110 of your text.
- Overlapping scope (Section 8.8.3) and shadowing (*Common Error 8.2* on page 361 of your text) will not be tested but reading these sections in your text will give you a more thorough understanding of variable scope.
- More information on creating packages and choosing package names is given in Section 8.9 of your text. This section also explains how classes are located by the compiler.
- Section 8.5 of your text discusses Java's assert statement. This feature helps us check assertions in our program. You are required to understand the meaning of *assertion* but you will not be tested on the assert statement.
- Unit test frameworks simplify the task of writing classes that contain many test cases. Your text describes the JUnit framework and demonstrates how it is used in testing classes. Testing is an important part of good programming. The JUnit framework is widely used in testing classes. The JUnit philosophy is to run all tests whenever you change your code.

■ Things to Remember When Taking the AP Exam

- Do not put extraneous System.out.println statements in free-response answers to indicate that the method is done or to print the answer before returning its value. This is a side effect and will result in a deduction of points on free-response questions.
    - Do not print error messages in methods unless specifically instructed to do so. This is a side effect and will result in a deduction of points on free-response questions.
- On the AP Exam, you do not need to check that the precondition of the method is satisfied unless explicitly told to do so. A method should not be called unless its precondition is satisfied.

- ▪ Remember that you cannot modify parameters of a primitive type. A Java method can never modify numbers that are passed to it. Do not try to replace an object reference parameter with another reference. You can change the state of an object reference parameter but you cannot replace the object reference with another.
- ▪ Remember that you cannot change the contents of parameter variables within methods by reassigning values to them or by getting new values for them from input. Do not use parameter variables as temporary variables. This is discussed in *Quality Tip 8.3* on page 345 of your text.
- Carefully read the pre- and postconditions given in problems, especially in the free-response questions. Many times an algorithm for solving the problem is given in the problem documentation. Read the documentation carefully!
- Unless specifically asked to write pre- and postconditions on the AP Exam, do not spend time doing this.

▪ Key Words

You should understand the terms below. The AP CS Exam questions may include references to these terms. The citations in parentheses next to each term identify the page numbers where it is defined and/or discussed in *Java Concepts for AP Computer Science*, 5th ed.

assertion (348)	`import` (365)	scope (358)
assessor method (341)	mutator method (341)	side effect (342)
class invariant (351)	package (363)	static method (352)
cohesion (338)	postcondition (349)	static field (354)
coupling (339)	precondition (347)	utility class (337)
immutable (341)		

▪ Connecting the Detailed Topic Outline to the Text

The citations in parentheses identify where information in the outline can be located in *Java Concepts for AP Computer Science*, 5th ed.

- Choosing Classes (336–337)
- Cohesion and Coupling (338–340)
- Accessors, Mutators, and Immutable Classes (341)
- Side Effects (341–345)
- Preconditions and Postconditions (347–350)
  - ▪ Class Invariants **(AB only)** (351–352)
- Static Methods (352–353)
- Static Fields (354–356)
- Scope (358–361)
  - ▪ Scope of Local Variables (358)
  - ▪ Scope of Class Members (359)
  - ▪ Initializing Variables (360)
- Packages (363–367)

■ Practice Questions

Multiple Choice

1. A class is being designed to represent an athlete. Which of the following public methods would **not** be a good choice for a cohesive public interface for this class?

   a. getName()
   b. getSport()
   c. getFavoriteSong()
   d. setPointsPerGame()
   e. getTotalGamesPlayed()

2. Which of the following statements is **true** about designing programs involving multiple classes?

   a. It is a good practice to have high degree of cohesion and a high degree of coupling.
   b. It is a good practice to have low degree of cohesion and a low degree of coupling.
   c. It is a good practice to have high degree of cohesion and a low degree of coupling.
   d. It is a good practice to have low degree of cohesion and a high degree of coupling.
   e. It is a good practice to have neither class cohesion nor coupling with a program involving multiple classes.

3. An immutable class in Java is

   a. a class that has no private methods.
   b. a class that has no accessor methods.
   c. a class that has no instance fields.
   d. a class that has no modifier methods.
   e. a class that has only modifier methods.

4. Consider the problem of modeling a Point class. A Point object represents a point in the rectangular coordinate system. A Point object has an *x*-coordinate and a *y*-coordinate. Which of the following methods would **not** be a good choice for a cohesive public interface for this class?

   a. getX();
   b. setY(int newY);
   c. distancefromOrigin();
   d. distanceFrom(Point a);
   e. perimeter(Point a, Point b, Point c);

5. **(AB)** A CashDrawer class contains a method giveChange that accepts two parameters: cost and tendered, where cost is a double representing the price of an item and tendered is a double representing the amount tendered by the purchaser. The method has the following header, precondition, and postcondition:

   ```
   /**
      Precondition: Money tendered >= cost and cost > 0
      @param tendered the amount of money tendered
      @param cost the price of item
      @return the change
   */
   public double giveChange(double tendered, double cost)
   ```

To ensure that the precondition is met, which of the following code segments is the best choice for the method body?

a.
```
if (tendered < cost || cost <= 0)
{
    System.out.println("WRONG! Your values to this
        function are not correct!");
    return 0;
}
else return (tendered - cost)
```

b.
```
if (tendered < cost || cost <= 0)
{
    System.out.println("WRONG! Your values to this
        function are not correct!");
    return 0;
}
else return (cost - tendered)
```

c.
```
if (tendered < cost || cost <= 0)
{
    cost = tendered;
}
else return 0;
```

d.
```
if (tendered < cost || cost <= 0)
{
    throw new IllegalArgumentException();
}
else return (tendered - cost);
```

e.
```
if (tendered < cost || cost <= 0)
{
    throw new IllegalArgumentException();
}
else
{
    tendered = tendered - cost;
}
```

6. Which statement below is **true** about preconditions?

   a. It is the method's responsibility to check that its precondition is satisfied.
   b. A precondition describes what is returned by the method.
   c. A precondition describes the parameters and their restrictions in order for the method to function as intended.
   d. A precondition describes how a method is implemented.
   e. If a precondition is not satisfied, the compiler will automatically throw an exception.

Questions 7 and 8 refer to the Student class whose incomplete definition is below.

```
public class Student
{
    public Student()
    {
        firstName = "";
        lastName = "";
```

```
        id = "";
        gpa = 0.0;
    }

    public Student(String first, String last,
           String idNumber, double gradePointAvg)
    {
        firstName = first;
        lastName = last;
        id = idNumber;
        gpa = gradePointAvg;
    }

    public double getGpa()
    {
        return gpa;
    }

    public void setGpa(double newGpa)
    {
        gpa = newGpa;
    }

    private String firstName;
    private String lastName;
    private String id;
    private double gpa;
}
```

7. Consider a client program of the `Student` class that includes the following methods.

```
    public static void change1(Student stdt1, Student stdt2)
    {
        stdt1 = stdt2;
    }

    public static void change2(Student stdt1, Student stdt2)
    {
        stdt1.setGpa(stdt2.getGpa());
    }
```

After the code segment below is executed,

```
    Student student1 = new Student();
    Student student2 = new Student("Joe", "Smith", "111", 3.86);
    Student student3 = new Student("Marie", "Jones", "222", 3.52);
    change1(student1, student2);
    change2(student3, student1);
```

what are the gpas of `student1`, `student2`, and `student3`?

a. `student1.gpa = 0.0, student2.gpa = 3.86, student3.gpa = 0.0`
b. `student1.gpa = 0.0, student2.gpa = 3.86, student3.gpa = 3.52`
c. `student1.gpa = 3.86, student2.gpa = 3.86, student3.gpa = 3.86`
d. `student1.gpa = 3.52, student2.gpa = 3.52, student3.gpa = 3.52`
e. `student1.gpa = 3.52, student2.gpa = 3.86, student3.gpa = 3.52`

8. For the Student class defined above, which of the following statements is **true** regarding constructors, accessor methods, and mutator methods?

    a.   The Student class has 1 constructor and 3 accessor methods.
    b.   The Student class has 1 constructor and 3 mutator methods.
    c.   The Student class has 2 constructors and 2 accessor methods.
    d.   The Student class has 2 constructors and 2 mutator methods.
    e.   The Student class has 2 constructors, 1 accessor method, and 1 mutator method.

9. Consider the following program description: A user inserts coins into a vending machine to purchase candy. Which is the best choice of classes to be implemented for this program?

    I.   A VendingMachine class that defines private instance variables to hold coin values and product items.
    II. A VendingMachine class that defines private instance variables to hold product information and uses coins from a Coin class.
    III. A VendingMachine class that uses coins from a Coin class and products from a Product class.

    a.   Method I is the best choice because there is a high degree of cohesion with this method.
    b.   Method II is the best choice because products are a part of the vending machine's structure but coins are not.
    c.   Method III is the best choice because the different vending machines can be implemented using different products and the products and coins can be used in other applications.
    d.   None of the above methods. The coins and products should be part of a utility class because they are used by the VendingMachine class and they will not be instantiated.
    e.   All methods are equally good.

10. Consider the following code segment.

```java
public class TriangleTester
{
    public static void main(String[] args)
    {
        printTriangle(5);
        // scopeCheck1
    }

    public static void printTriangle(int maxStars)
    {
        int count = 0;
        for (int r = 1; r <= maxStars; r++)
        {
            for (int c = 1; c <= r; c++)
            {
                System.out.print("*");
                count++;
                // scopeCheck2
            }
            System.out.println();
        }
        // scopeCheck3
    }
}
```

Which of the following statements is **true** about variable scope?

a. At `scopeCheck1`, variables `maxStars`, `r`, `c`, and `count` are accessible.
b. At `scopeCheck1`, only variables `r`, `c`, and `count` are accessible.
c. At `scopeCheck2`, variables `maxStars`, `r`, `c`, and `count` are accessible.
d. At `scopeCheck2`, only variables `maxStars`, `c` and `count` are accessible.
e. At `scopeCheck3`, variables `maxStars`, `r`, `c`, and `count` are accessible.

Free Response Questions

1. Consider the problem of modeling book information for a small bookstore. A book has these attributes:
   - The book title.
   - The author's name.
   - An identification number that is unique to each book title. The identification numbers are positive integers assigned in increasing numerical order as the `Book` objects are created.
   - The price of the book (a floating-point number).

   When a new `Book` object is created, it must be assigned an identification number that will be the next consecutive identification number available. The new book is created with a title, an author's name, and a price. The only operations valid for a `Book` object are:
   - Retrieve the identification number for the book.
   - Retrieve the author's name.
   - Set the price of the book (in the event that the price of the book is to be changed). The price of the book will always be a positive number.
   - Retrieve the price of the book.

   The class described above will be called `Book`.

   a. Write the public interface for the `Book` class as it would appear in a `Book.java` file. In writing this, you should write the headers for the constructor and the public methods. You must:
      - Choose appropriate variable and method names.
      - Provide the preconditions and postconditions where necessary.
      - Provide appropriate data representation for the specifications above.
      - Be consistent with information-hiding principles.

      DO NOT WRITE THE IMPLEMENTATIONS OF THE METHODS.

      Use the following class declaration to write your interface.

      ```
      public class Book
      {
          // Your interface goes here
      }
      ```

   b. Write the declarations for the private instance fields and private class fields that will be needed in the `Book` class.

   c. Implement the `Book` class constructor. (**AB Students**: If appropriate, include exception handling to ensure that the precondition is satisfied.)

d. Describe two alternative actions that the programmer of a method can take if a precondition of the method is not satisfied. Give an advantage and/or disadvantage for each alternative.

2. Get Lean Fitness (GLF) is a company dedicated to improving the fitness level of its clients. GLF has several weight reduction plans. Each plan is an instance of a class `WeightCalculator` that has the following public interface.

```
public class WeightCalculator
{
    // Constructor(s) here

    /**
        @param sex the gender of the person
        @param howTall height of the person
        @return the ideal weight for a person
        with the given height and gender
    */
    public int getIdealWeight(String sex, int howTall) {. . .}

    /**
        @param sex the gender of the person
        @param howTall height of the person
        @return recommended calorie intake for a
        person with the given height and gender
    */
    public int getCalorieIntake(String sex, int howTall) {. . .}

    // Private implementation here
}
```

The company keeps a record on each client. This client record includes the person's name, height, initial weight, and gender (all attributes of the client). The client record also includes the client's suggested daily calorie intake.

Consider the problem of modeling the client information for Get Lean Fitness in a class called `Client`.
- When a new `Client` object is created, it is created with the name, gender, height, and weight of the client.

The operations available on a `Client` object are:
- Retrieve the client's name.
- Retrieve the client's gender.
- Retrieve the client's height.
- Retrieve the client's weight.
- Set the client's recommended calorie intake per day.
- Retrieve the client's recommended calorie intake per day.

a. Write the public interface for the `Client` class as it would appear in the `Client.java` file (except for the `setRecommendedCalories` method). The `setRecommended-Calories` method will be described in part c. In writing the interface, you should write the headers for the constructor and the public methods.

You should:
- Choose appropriate variable and method names.
- Provide the preconditions and postconditions where necessary.
- Provide appropriate data representation for the specifications above.
- Be consistent with information-hiding principles.

DO NOT WRITE THE IMPLEMENTATIONS OF THE METHODS.

Use the following class declaration to write your interface.

```
public class Client
{
    //  Your interface goes here
}
```

b. Write the declarations for the private instance fields that will be needed in the `Client` class.

c. A client's ideal weight is based on gender and height and is found by giving the required information to the appropriate method of a `WeightCalculator`. Implement the `Client` method that sets the suggested number of calories to be consumed per day. An instance of the `WeightCalculator` is a parameter of the client's `setRecommendedCalories` method. The algorithm used to determine daily calorie intake is as follows.
- If the client's weight is less than or equal to the client's ideal weight, the calorie intake per day is the value that is returned by the `WeightCalculator`'s `getCalorieIntake` method.
- If the client's weight is more than the client's ideal weight, the calorie intake per day is the value that is returned by the `WeightCalculator`'s `getCalorieIntake` method minus the constant 500.

Use the following method header.

```
public void setRecommendedCalories(WeightCalculator plan)
```

Interfaces and Polymorphism

TOPIC OUTLINE

■ Topic Summary

10.1 Using Interfaces for Code Reuse

A Java interface declares methods that classes are expected to implement. It encapsulates a set of associated behaviors that can be used by dissimilar classes. Interfaces contain no instance fields and cannot be instantiated (you cannot construct an object of an interface type). A class implements an interface by providing the implementation for all of the methods in the interface. An interface can be implemented by many classes and a class can implement multiple interfaces. To implement an interface, a class must express its intention to implement it by means of its header, and then must provide implementations of all of the methods dictated by the interface. Consider the following trivial but illustrative example. A `Flier` is one that flies.

Figure 10.1

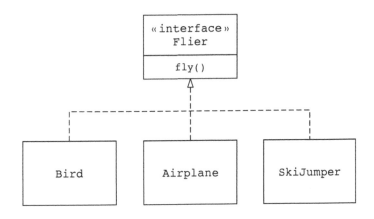

Figure 10.1 is a UML diagram. Although UML diagrams will not be tested on the AP CS Exam, you will see them throughout your text as they are commonly used to illustrate relationships among classes.

It is clear that the three classes `Bird`, `Airplane`, and `SkiJumper` are three dissimilar classes. Each of these classes defines the method `fly` in a very different way. The interface for this trivial descriptive example would be

```
public interface Flier
{
    void fly();
}
```

Notice that the `public` visibility modifier is not included for the `fly` method. The methods declared in an interface are public by default. The classes that implement this interface might include the following implementations for the `fly` method.

Example 10.1

```
public class Bird implements Flier
{
    public void fly()
    {
        System.out.println("Using my wings to fly.");
    }
}
```

```
public class Airplane implements Flier
{
    public void fly()
    {
        System.out.println("Using my jet engines to fly.");
    }
}
```

```
public class SkiJumper implements Flier
{
    public void fly()
    {
        System.out.println("Using skis to take me into the air.");
    }
}
```

The class headers of `Bird`, `Airplane`, and `SkiJumper` each indicate an intention to implement the `Flier` interface and thus promise to provide the implementation for the method `fly`.

Example 10.2 creates an `ArrayList` of `Fliers`. Since `SkiJumper` and `Airplane` both implement the `Flier` interface, both can be added to this `ArrayList`.

Example 10.2

```
ArrayList<Flier> airborne = new ArrayList<Flier>();
airborne.add(new SkiJumper("Jumper", "One"));
airborne.add(new SkiJumper("Jumper", "Two"));
airborne.add(new Airplane());
```

Now, let's be more specific about our SkiJumper. An athlete is one that competes. A SkiJumper is an Athlete. An athlete trains for hours to perfect performance in a particular sport. Most of us would agree that neither a Bird nor an Airplane is an Athlete. Therefore, if Athlete were an interface, a SkiJumper might implement Athlete as well as Flier.

Figure 10.2

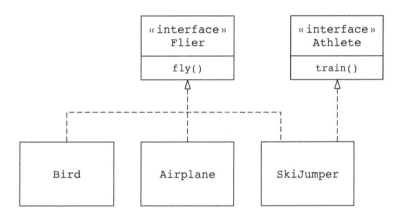

Example 10.3

```
public interface Athlete
{
    void train(double hours);
}
```

```
public class SkiJumper implements Flier, Athlete
{
    // Constructor
    public SkiJumper(String firstName, String lastName)
    {
        myFirstName = firstName;
        myLastName = lastName;
        myNumberOfJumps = 0;
        myHoursTraining = 0;
    }

    public void fly()
    {
        System.out.println("Using skis to take " + myFirstName + " "
                + myLastName + " into the air.");
        myNumberOfJumps++;
    }
```

```
        public void train(double hours)
        {
            System.out.println("I am on the slopes " + hours
                + " hours today.");
            myHoursTraining += hours;
        }

        public double getHoursTrained()
        {
            return myHoursTraining;
        }

        public int getJumps()
        {
            return myNumberOfJumps;
        }

        private String myFirstName;
        private String myLastName;
        private double myHoursTraining;
        private int myNumberOfJumps;
    }
```

Now that you have an intuitive understanding of an interface and how it works, look at two examples that might be a bit more useful.

Section 9.1 in your text defines the Measurable interface. The Measurable interface is implemented by Coin and BankAccount, two dissimilar classes. The only method declared in this interface is getMeasure. This method simply returns a double. In the text example, either a coin's value or a bank account's balance is returned. The DataSet class in Section 9.1 of your text becomes usable in different circumstances by implementing a method add whose parameter implements the Measurable interface. The variable x refers to a class object that implements Measurable.

```
        public void add(Measurable x)
```

This method will add Coin values or BankAccount balances (or any other object instantiated by a class that implements Measurable) and will keep track of the largest Coin value or BankAccount balance in the private instance field maximum.

Example 10.4

```
1      public class DataSet
2      {
3          // More code here

4          public void add(Measurable x)
5          {
6              sum = sum + x.getMeasure();
7              if (count == 0 || maximum.getMeasure() < x.getMeasure())
8                  maximum = x;
9              count++;
10         }
```

```
11          public Measurable getMaximum()
12          {
13             return maximum;
14          }

15          // Other variables here
16          private Measurable maximum;
17          private int count;
18          private double sum;
19       }
```

Line 4: The parameter x is of any type that implements the Measurable interface. If the declaration were

```
DataSet bankData = new DataSet();
```

the call to this method might be

```
bankData.add(new BankAccount(100));
```

If the declaration were

```
DataSet coinData = new DataSet();
```

the call to this method might be

```
coinData.add(new Coin(0.25, "quarter"));
```

Line 6: Adds values as defined in the getMeasure method of the individual class. If x were instantiated from the BankAccount class, we would be adding balances. If x were instantiated from the Coin class, we would be adding Coin values.

Lines 7–8: Checks for a new largest object based on the comparison of double values and resets present value of maximum if necessary. Notice that maximum is of a type that implements the Measurable interface. For the BankAccount class, maximum will store a BankAccount object. For the Coin class, maximum will store a Coin object.

Line 13: getMaximum will return the object with the largest measure.

Line 16: The private instance field is of type Measurable. This field can refer to any class that implements the Measurable interface.

Nothing prevents mixing Coin objects, BankAccount objects, or any other type of objects in this DataSet. However, this would not be a very good program design!

Our third example of an interface is one that we have already used with the String class.

```
class java.lang.String implements java.lang.Comparable
```

The Comparable interface has one method declared, compareTo. The String class implements this method so that it can compare two strings lexicographically.

Table 10.1

`class java.lang.String implements java.lang.Comparable`

Method	Method Summary
`int compareTo(Object other)`	Compares two strings lexicographically. Returns value < 0 if this `String` is less than `other`. Returns 0 if this `String` is equal to `other`. Returns value > 0 if this `String` is greater than `other`.

Table 10.2

`interface java.lang.Comparable`

Method	Method Summary
`int compareTo(Object other)`	Returns a value < 0 if `this` is less than `other`. Returns 0 if `this` is equal to `other`. Returns a value > 0 if `this` is greater than `other`.

When a class implements an interface, the class makes a contract to provide the implementation for the methods of the interface as they are declared in the interface. Therefore, the method definition in the class must have the same exact parameter types as it does in the interface. Note that the type of the `compareTo` method's parameter is `Object`.

We might want a `Student` class to allow for the ordering of students, perhaps by the student GPA, or the student ID number. If a `Student` class implemented `Comparable`, we would add our preferred definition of `compareTo` to the `Student` class implementation. The `Comparable` interface can be implemented by the `Coin` class, the `Student` class, and any class that may want to provide an ordering for objects instantiated from the class. `Coin` objects may be compared based on their value. In a `Car` class, `Car` objects may be compared based on their mileage or their price.

Because the parameter type of the method is `Object`, in order to effectively define `compareTo` for our class, we will need to cast `Object` to the correct class type. This is explained in more detail in the next section and is illustrated in the `compareTo` implementations of the `Car` class and the `Coin` class below.

A `Car` class might implement `compareTo` in the following way.

```
public int compareTo(Object obj)
{
   Car temp = (Car) obj;
   if (mileage < temp.mileage)
      return -1;
   if (mileage > temp.mileage)
      return 1;
   return 0;
}
```

The `Coin` class could implement `compareTo` in the following way:

```
public class Coin
{
   public Coin(double aValue, String aName) {...}

   public double getValue() {...}
```

```
        public String getName() {...}

        public int compareTo(Object obj)
        {
            Coin tempMoney = (Coin) obj;
            if (value < tempMoney.value)
                return -1;
            else if (value > tempMoney.value)
                return 1;
            else
                return 0;
        }

        private double value;
        private String name;
    }
```

The `Comparable` interface included in the AP subset is the non-generic `Comparable` interface explained above. Java offers a generic `Comparable` interface that is covered in *Advanced Topic 14.4* on page 656 of your text. The generic `Comparable` interface is not tested on the AP Exam.

The methods in an interface are *abstract*. That is, they are not implemented in the interface. Because all methods in an interface are public by default, the access modifier *public* doesn't need to be included in the method headers in the interface. When a class defines a method of an interface that it implements, the method must be declared as `public`.

An interface should not grow. Many classes implement an interface. If the interface is modified, all classes that implement the interface will be affected.

10.1.1 Constants in Interfaces
An interface can also declare constants. Because all variables declared in an interface are `public static final`, those keywords can be omitted when defining the constants. *Advanced Topic 9.1* on page 394 of your text and Example 10.5 below demonstrate this.

Example 10.5

```
    public interface Flier
    {
        int MAX_ALTITUDE = 10000;
        void fly();
    }
```

```
    public class SkiJumper implements Flier
    {
        public void fly()
        {
            System.out.println("Using skis to take me into the air.");
            System.out.println("Will not go higher than "
                + Flier.MAX_ALTITUDE + " feet.");
        }
    }
```

Notice that the constant is called by specifying the interface name before the constant name (`Flier.MAX_ALTITUDE`).

10.2 Converting Between Class and Interface Types

Example 10.4 defined the `DataSet` method `add`. A call to `add` could be

```
bankData.add(new BankAccount(100));
```
or
```
coinData.add(new Coin(0.25, "quarter"));
```

Any object whose class implements `Measurable` can be passed as a parameter to `add`. In this case, since a `Coin` is `Measurable`, it can be passed to a parameter that is of type `Measurable`. This type conversion from the class to the interface is legal. Section 9.2 of your text explains this example in detail.

When converting from an interface type to a class type, you must cast to the appropriate class type. The example that is explained in your text casts `Measurable` to `Coin`.

```
Measurable max = coinData.getMaximum();
String name = ((Coin) max).getName();   // Notice parentheses!
```

Parentheses are necessary because of the order of precedence of the operators in this statement. In Java, the access class feature (.) has higher precedence than the (cast). Without parentheses we would have

```
(Coin) max.getName()
```

where `max` is of type `Measurable` and `getName` is not defined for `Measurable`. Without the parentheses, a compile-time error will result. It is a common error to forget these needed parentheses! Table 10.3 contains a summary of operator precedence.

Table 10.3

Operator Order of	Description	Associativity
.	Access class feature	Left to Right
[]	Array subscript	Left to Right
()	Method call	Left to Right
++ --	Increment, decrement	Right to Left
!	Boolean not	Right to Left
+ (unary) - (unary)	Unary operators	Right to Left
(*TypeName*)	Cast	Right to Left
new	Object allocation	Right to Left
* / %	Arithmetic operators	Left to Right
+ -	Arithmetic operators	Left to Right
< <= > >=	Relational operators	Left to Right
== !=	Equals, not equals	Left to Right
&&	And	Left to Right
||	Or	Left to Right
= *= /= %= += -=	Assignment with	Right to Left

We demonstrated casting when converting from an interface type to a class type in the implementations of `compareTo` for the `Car` and `Coin` classes.

10.3 Polymorphism

Polymorphism means having many shapes or many forms. When the interface name is used to declare an object reference variable, the variable can refer to any object that is instantiated from a class that implements the interface. In the declaration

```
Flier skyReacher;    // skyReacher is an object variable.
                     // The interface CANNOT be instantiated.
```

skyReacher can refer to objects of different types if those types implement the Flier interface.

```
    skyReacher = new Airplane();
```
or
```
    skyReacher = new Bird();
```
or
```
    skyReacher = new SkiJumper("Joe", "Smith");
```

The actual type of the object skyReacher is determined at runtime.

Consider the statement

```
    skyReacher.fly();
```

The actual type of the object determines the method to be called. This principle is called *polymorphism*. The program has to run before the object to which skyReacher refers is determined. The virtual machine selects the appropriate method, not the compiler. This is referred to as late, or *dynamic*, binding.

Example 10.6
___

```
    Flier skyReacher;
    skyReacher = new SkiJumper("Joe", "Smith");
    skyReacher.fly();
```

This segment of code will bind skyReacher to a SkiJumper object and the method call to fly will print *Using skis to take Joe Smith into the air.*

___

Early binding takes place at compile time. This type of binding occurs with method overloading. Your text explains this difference in Section 9.3.

■ Topics That Are Useful But Not Tested

- Using interfaces for callbacks describes a method for improving code reusability and is explained in Section 9.4 of your text.
- An inner class is a class that is declared inside another class. Inner classes are commonly used for tactical classes that are not visible elsewhere in the program. They are explained in Section 9.5 of your text.
- UML diagrams are useful for illustrating class relationships and dependencies. The UML notation for showing dependency and interface realization is explained in Section 9.1 of your text.
- User-interface events are useful for programming graphical applications and are explained in Sections 9.6–9.10 of your text.

■ Things to Remember When Taking the AP Exam

- Early binding (overloading) of methods occurs if the *compiler* selects a method from several possible candidates before the program is run. Late binding (polymorphism) occurs if the method selection takes place when the program runs. This is an important distinction.
- All methods in an interface are public. The methods in the interface are not declared as public because they are public by default. When implementing the methods of the interface in a class, remember to include the keyword `public`.
- An interface does not have any instance variables but can have constant declarations (variable declarations that are `static` and `final`).
- An interface does not implement any methods.
- You can convert from a class type to an interface type without casting if the class implements the interface, but you need a cast to convert from an interface type to a class type.
- For both the A and the AB Exams, you should be able to read the definitions of interfaces and be able to design your own interfaces.
- An interface does not have constructors and cannot be instantiated, but you can assign an object created from a class that implements the interface. For example,
  - ```
    Flier f = new Flier();   // WRONG!
    ```
  - ```
    Flier f = new Airplane();   // OK
    ```

■ Key Words

You should understand the terms below. The AP CS Exam questions may include references to these terms. The citations in parentheses next to each term identify the page numbers where it is defined and/or discussed in *Java Concepts for AP Computer Science*, 5th ed.

abstract (390)   early binding (398)   late (dynamic) binding (398)
cast (396)   implements (390)   polymorphism (397)
constants (394)   interface (388)

■ Connecting the Detailed Topic Outline to the Text

The citations in parentheses identify where information in the outline can be located in *Java Concepts for AP Computer Science*, 5th ed.

- Using Interfaces for Code Reuse (388–394)
  - Constants in Interfaces (394)
- Converting Between Class and Interface Types (395–396)
- Polymorphism (396–398)

■ Practice Questions

Multiple Choice

1. Which of the following choices might serve as an interface for the other choices listed?

   a. `Piano`
   b. `Drum`
   c. `Guitar`
   d. `Instrument`
   e. `FrenchHorn`

Questions 2–5 refer to the `Flier` and `Athlete` interfaces and the `Airplane` and `SkiJumper` classes whose incomplete definitions are given below.

```
public interface Flier
{
    void fly();
}
```

```
public interface Athlete
{
    void train(double hours);
}
```

```
public class Airplane implements Flier
{
    public void fly()
    {
        System.out.println("Using my jet engines to fly.");
    }
}
```

```
public class SkiJumper implements Flier, Athlete
{
    public SkiJumper(String firstName, String lastName)
    {
        myFirstName = firstName;
        myLastName = lastName;
        myNumberOfJumps = 0;
        myHoursTraining = 0;
    }

    public void fly()
    {
        System.out.println("Using skis to take " + myFirstName + " "
                + myLastName + " into the air.");
        myNumberOfJumps++;
    }
```

```
        public void train(double hours)
        {
            System.out.println("I am on the slopes for " + hours
                    + "hours per day.");
            myHoursTraining += hours;
        }

        public double getHoursTrained()
        {
            return myHoursTraining;
        }

        public int getJumps()
        {
            return myNumberOfJumps;
        }

        private String myFirstName;
        private String myLastName;
        private double myHoursTraining;
        private int myNumberOfJumps;
    }
```

2. Which of the following code segments causes a compile-time error?

   a. `Airplane boeing707 = new Airplane();`
   b. `Flier boeing707 = new Flier();`
   c. `Flier boeing707 = new Airplane();`
   d. `Airplane boeing707 = new Airplane();`
      `Flier airTraveler = boeing707;`
   e. `Airplane boeing707 = new Airplane();`
      `Flier airTraveler;`
      `airTraveler = (Airplane) boeing707;`

3. Consider the following code segment.

```
1       Airplane skyRider = new Airplane();
2       Flier skyRider2 = skyRider;
3       Athlete skyRider3 = (Athlete) skyRider2;
4       Airplane skyRider4 = (Airplane) skyRider2;
5       Flier skyRider5 = skyRider4;
```

   Which statement above will cause a run-time error and throw an exception?

   a. Statement 1
   b. Statement 2
   c. Statement 3
   d. Statement 4
   e. Statement 5

Questions 4 and 5 refer to the following declarations.

```
Airplane c = new Airplane();
Flier f = new Airplane();
Athlete a = new SkiJumper("Ann", "Smith");
SkiJumper s = new SkiJumper("John", "Doe");
```

4. Which of the following statements is **not** legal?

    a. `c.fly();`
    b. `f.fly();`
    c. `a.train(3);`
    d. `s.train(3);`
    e. `a.fly();`

5. Which of the following statements needs a cast?

    I.   `f = c;`
    II. `a = s;`
    III. `s = a;`

    a. I only
    b. II only
    c. III only
    d. I and II only
    e. I and III only

6. Suppose a class `C` implements an interface `I` by implementing all of the methods of `I` and no further methods. Then which of the following *must* be **true**?

    a. All instance variables of `C` are public.
    b. All methods of `C` are abstract.
    c. All methods of `C` are public.
    d. All constants of `C` are public.
    e. All instance variables of `C` are private.

7. Which of the following statements is **true** about casting?

    a. You must cast to convert from an interface type to a class type.
    b. You must cast to convert from a class type to an interface type.
    c. You cannot cast to convert an interface type to a class type.
    d. You cannot cast from a class type to an interface type.
    e. Both a and b above are true.

8. Which of the following statements is **true** about dynamic binding?

    a. Dynamic binding occurs during compile time.
    b. Dynamic binding occurs when the appropriate overloaded method is selected.
    c. Dynamic binding is another name for early binding.
    d. In dynamic binding, the virtual machine selects the appropriate method.
    e. Dynamic binding occurs only when an interface declares `public static final` constants.

9. Which of the following statements about interfaces is **not** true?

   a. An interface can specify constants that can be used by all classes that implement the interface.
   b. An interface can specify variables that can be used by all classes that implement the interface.
   c. An interface can specify methods that must be defined by all classes that implement the interface.
   d. An interface name cannot be instantiated.
   e. The interface contains declarations but not implementations.

10. Suppose foo is an object of class C, and C implements the interface type I. Which of the following statements *must* be **true**?

   a. foo was constructed with the constructor of I.
   b. C assigns values to all constants declared in the interface I.
   c. C supplies an implementation for all methods of the interface I.
   d. foo must be declared as

      ```
      I foo = new C();
      ```

   e. All methods of I are declared as private.

Free Response Questions

1. The SkiJumper class is to implement the Comparable interface. The present definition of SkiJumper is defined below.

```java
public class SkiJumper implements Flier, Athlete
{
   /**
      Constructs a default ski jumper.
      @param firstName first name of ski jumper
      @param lastName last name of ski jumper
   */
   public SkiJumper(String firstName, String lastName)
   {
      myFirstName = firstName;
      myLastName = lastName;
      myNumberOfJumps = 0;
      myHoursTraining = 0;
   }

   /**
      Simulates a ski jumper flying.
   */
   public void fly()
   {
      System.out.println("Using skis to take " + myFirstName
            + " " + myLastName + " into the air.");
      myNumberOfJumps++;
   }
```

```java
/**
    Adds hours to total training time.
    Precondition: hours > 0
    Postcondition: myHoursTraining modified to include hours
    trained
    @param hours the number of hours to add
*/
public void train(double hours)
{
    System.out.println("I am on the slopes " + hours
        + " hours today.");
    myHoursTraining += hours;
}

/**
    Gets hours the ski jumper has trained.
    @return hours of training
*/
public double getHoursTrained()
{
    return myHoursTraining;
}

/**
    Gets number of jumps made.
    @return total jumps made
*/
public int getJumps()
{
    return myNumberOfJumps;
}

private String myFirstName;
private String myLastName;
private double myHoursTraining;
private int myNumberOfJumps;
}
```

a. Adjust the class header so that the `Comparable` interface is implemented by `SkiJumper`.

b. Implement the necessary methods so that the `Comparable` interface is implemented by the `SkiJumper` class. `SkiJumper` objects are compared by the number of jumps completed.

2. Modify the `Purse` class defined below to implement the `Comparable` interface. Purses are compared by the total value of money contained in the purse.

```java
public class Purse implements Comparable
{
    /**
        Constructs an empty purse.
    */
    public Purse()
    {
```

```
         nickels = 0;
         dimes = 0;
         quarters = 0;
      }

      /**
         Adds nickels to the purse.
         @param count the number of nickels to add
      */
      public void addNickels(int count)
      {
         nickels += count;
      }

      /**
         Adds dimes to the purse.
         @param count the number of dimes to add
      */
      public void addDimes(int count)
      {
         dimes += count;
      }

      /**
         Adds quarters to the purse.
         @param count the number of quarters to add
      */
      public void addQuarters(int count)
      {
         quarters += count;
      }

      /**
         Gets the total value of the coins in the purse.
         @return the sum of all coin values in purse
      */
      public double getTotal()
      {
         return nickels * NICKEL_VALUE
               + dimes * DIME_VALUE + quarters * QUARTER_VALUE;
      }

      private static final double NICKEL_VALUE = 0.05;
      private static final double DIME_VALUE = 0.1;
      private static final double QUARTER_VALUE = 0.25;

      private int nickels;
      private int dimes;
      private int quarters;
   }
```

3.   Consider the partial hierarchy of orchestra instruments given below.

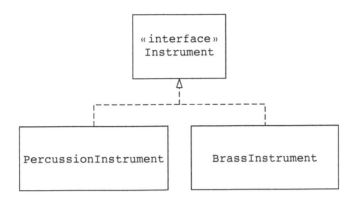

The following functionality is defined for all orchestra instruments.

*   A specific instrument (BrassInstrument or PercussionInstrument) has one piece of information, an orchestra seat assignment, which is passed as a String to its one-parameter constructor. This seat assignment can be publicly accessed and can be changed after the instrument is created.

*   All instruments *tune* but they tune in very different ways. Percussion instruments may adjust the tension of the drumhead while brass instruments may tune a middle G first.

Because a PercussionInstrument is a kind of Instrument and a BrassInstrument is a kind of Instrument, BrassInstrument and PercussionInstrument implement the Instrument interface.

a.   Write the Instrument interface that abstracts this functionality.

b.   Write the complete class definition for BrassInstrument. In writing your class, you should
*   choose appropriate method and variable names.
*   provide the functionality specified above.

Comments are not required, but may be used as desired to clarify what you write.

CHAPTER 11

(Covers *Java Concepts for AP Computer Science* Chapter 10)

Inheritance

TOPIC OUTLINE
11.1 Introduction to Inheritance
11.2 Inheritance Hierarchies
11.3 Inheriting Instance Fields and Methods
11.4 Subclass Construction
11.5 Converting Between Subclass and
     Superclass Types

11.6 Abstract Classes
11.7 Access Control
11.8 `Object`: The Cosmic Superclass
     11.8.1 Inheritance and the `toString` Method
     11.8.2 Inheritance and the `equals` Method

■ Topic Summary

11.1 Introduction to Inheritance

Inheritance is used to extend classes that already exist. By extending existing classes, you can create new, more specific classes *and* take advantage of code that is already written. Chapter 10 of your text revisits the `BankAccount` class to illustrate the key concepts of inheritance. We will revisit our `SkiJumper` class and redefine `Athlete` to illustrate these same concepts and to provide you with another example. In this example, `Athlete` will now be a class, not an interface. All methods in the `Athlete` interface are now implemented in the `Athlete` class.

We will make some basic assumptions:
* All athletes have a name and a sport in which they participate.
* An athlete keeps track of the number of hours of training done.
* All athletes train for the sport in which they participate.
* An athlete participates in only one sport.
* Athletes participating in different sports may train in different ways.

Figure 11.1

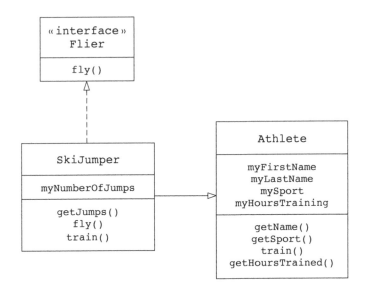

Figure 11.1 shows our SkiJumper class *implementing* the Flier interface and *extending* the Athlete class. SkiJumper is a *subclass* of Athlete. Athlete is a *superclass* of SkiJumper. SkiJumper *inherits* the instance fields myFirstName, myLastName, mySport, and myHoursTraining and defines an additional instance field, myNumberOfJumps that is specific to SkiJumper and not particularly applicable to other athletes. SkiJumper will implement the methods fly (as promised when implementing the Flier interface) and getJumps. SkiJumper will also *override* the method train by implementing the train method in a particular way that differs from the training routine of other athletes. Inheriting from Athlete differs from implementing Flier. Flier is an interface and cannot be instantiated. Flier does not have state or behavior. Athlete is a class. Athlete defines state and behavior and can be instantiated. Example 11.1 adds code to our visual interpretation.

Example 11.1

```
/**
    Describes any class whose objects can fly.
*/
public interface Flier
{
    void fly();
}
```

```
/**
    Defines an athlete.
*/
public class Athlete
{
    /**
        Constructs an athlete; myHoursTraining is initialized to 0.
        @param firstName first name of athlete
```

```java
      @param lastName last name of athlete
      @param sportPlayed sport in which athlete participates
   */
   public Athlete(String firstName, String lastName,
         String sportPlayed)
   {
      myFirstName = firstName;
      myLastName = lastName;
      mySport = sportPlayed;
      myHoursTraining = 0;
   }

   /**
      Updates myHoursTraining.
      @param hours number of hours athlete trained
   */
   public void train(double hours)
   {
      System.out.println("Athlete training for "
            + hours + " hours.");
      myHoursTraining += hours;
   }

   /**
      Gets athlete name.
      @return name of athlete
   */
   public String getName()
   {
      return (myFirstName + " " + myLastName);
   }

   /**
      Gets sport of athlete.
      @return sport participated in
   */
   public String getSport()
   {
      return mySport;
   }

   /**
      Gets hours trained by athlete.
      @return myHoursTraining
   */
   public double getHoursTrained()
   {
      return myHoursTraining;
   }

   private String myFirstName;
   private String myLastName;
   private String mySport;
   private double myHoursTraining;
}
```

```
public class SkiJumper extends Athlete implements Flier
{
    /**
        Constructs a SkiJumper object.
        Sport is ski jumping.
        Number of jumps is initialized to 0.
        @param first the first name
        @param last the last name
    */
    public SkiJumper(String first, String last)
    {
        super(first, last, "Ski Jumping");  // Call to super must be
                                            // first executable
                                            // statement in
                                            // constructor.
        myNumberOfJumps = 0;
    }

    /**
        Increments myNumberOfJumps, simulates flying.
    */
    public void fly()
    {
        System.out.println("Using skis to take " + getName()
                + " into the air.");
        myNumberOfJumps++;
    }

    /**
        Simulates training.
        @param hours hours of training
    */
    public void train(double hours)
    {
        System.out.println("I am on the slopes " + hours
                + " hours today.");
        super.train(hours);
    }

    /**
        Gets the current number of jumps of the SkiJumper.
        @return current myNumberOfJumps
    */
    public int getJumps()
    {
        return myNumberOfJumps;
    }

    private int myNumberOfJumps;
}
```

The SkiJumper class extends Athlete and implements Flier. A class can extend only one superclass but can implement many interfaces.

11.2 Inheritance Hierarchies

When the hierarchy in Section 11.1 was designed, the features and behaviors common to all athletes were collected in the Athlete superclass. All athletes have a first name, a last name, and a sport. It is therefore useful to include public methods that can return the name and sport of the athlete. All athletes train and it may be useful to return the number of hours of training for any athlete. Figure 11.2 adds a Runner to our hierarchy and Example 11.2 implements the Runner. A Runner races. A Runner keeps track of the number of races run and the number of miles raced. A Runner does not fly.

Figure 11.2

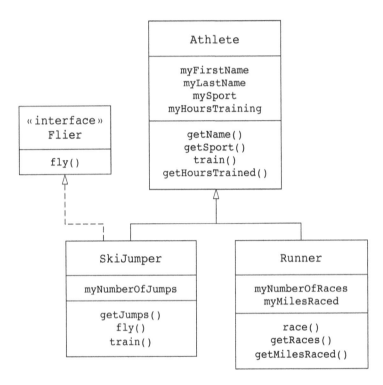

Example 11.2

```
public class Runner extends Athlete
{
    /**
        Constructs a Runner with a specified name.
        Sport is running.
        Number of races is initialized to 0.
        Miles raced is initialized to 0.
        @param first the first name
        @param last the last name
    */
    public Runner(String first, String last)
    {
        super(first, last, "Running");    // Call to super must be
                                          // first executable
                                          // statement in
                                          // constructor.
```

```
         myNumberOfRaces = 0;
         myMilesRaced = 0;
     }

     /**
         Increments number of races and updates miles raced.
         Simulates running a race.
     */
     public void race(double raceLength)
     {
         System.out.println(getName() + " is racing in a "
             + raceLength + " mile race.");
         myNumberOfRaces++;
         myMilesRaced += raceLength;
     }

     /**
         Gets the current number of races run by the runner.
         @return current numberOfRaces
     */
     public int getRaces()
     {
         return myNumberOfRaces;
     }

     /**
         Gets the current miles raced by the runner.
         @return current milesRaced
     */
     public double getMilesRaced()
     {
         return myMilesRaced;
     }

     private int myNumberOfRaces;
     private double myMilesRaced;
}
```

Notice that the Runner does not override train. The runner trains as a generic athlete trains but, in addition to hours of training, a Runner keeps track of hours racing and number of races run. The behavior and state of a Runner differ from those of the SkiJumper.

11.3   Inheriting Instance Fields and Methods

The methods getName, getSport, and getHoursTrained are inherited by the SkiJumper and the Runner.

The subclass SkiJumper of the Athlete class specifies the additional getJumps method and the Runner specifies the additional methods race, getRaces, and getMilesRaced.

The instance fields myFirstName, myLastName, mySport, and myHoursTraining are inherited by SkiJumper and Runner. The subclass SkiJumper of the Athlete class specifies the additional instance field myNumberOfJumps and the Runner specifies the additional instance fields myNumberOfRaces and myMilesRaced.

Although the subclass inherits the private instance fields of the superclass, the subclass has no access to the private fields of the superclass. *Private* means that only the class in which the instance field or method is defined has direct access. A class can allow access to private instance fields by providing public (or protected) mutator methods that modify the values of the instance fields. In our examples, we update the private instance field myHoursTraining of the superclass when the Runner trains and when the SkiJumper trains. This is done by invoking the public method train of the superclass, thus preserving encapsulation. Each subclass does this in a different way.

- The Runner subclass does not have a train method defined. The train method that is invoked by Runner is the train method inherited from Athlete. Athlete's train method updates Athlete's own private instance variable myHoursTraining that is inherited by the Runner.
- The SkiJumper subclass implements a method train with the same signature as the method train of its superclass, Athlete. The SkiJumper's train method overrides the Athlete's train method. In order to update the inherited private instance field myHoursTraining, the SkiJumper's train method invokes the superclass train method with the call super.train(...). The super keyword is used to call a method of the superclass that is overridden by a subclass.

We will discuss protected access in Section 11.7.

Subclasses should not attempt to override instance fields. Subclasses can inherit instance fields and define new instance fields but should not attempt to override existing instance fields. The consequences of attempting to overriding instance fields are explained in Section 10.3 and *Common Error 10.2* on page 449 of your text.

11.4 Subclass Construction

The constructor for Athlete has three String parameters: a first name, a last name, and a sport. The Athlete constructor initializes the appropriate instance fields with the values of these parameters and initializes myHoursTraining to 0.

When the Runner or SkiJumper constructor is called, two String parameters are passed, the first and last names of the athlete. For example,

```
Runner racer1 = new Runner("Joe", "Thomas");
SkiJumper jumper = new SkiJumper("Jane", "Smith");
```

The Runner constructor invokes the Athlete constructor passing these two parameters and the String "Running" (the sport name) to the superclass constructor.

```
public Runner(String first, String last)
{
    super(first, last, "Running");   // Call to super must be
                                     // first executable
                                     // statement in constructor.
    myNumberOfRaces = 0;
    myMilesRaced = 0;
}
```

The SkiJumper constructor invokes the Athlete constructor passing these two parameters and the String "Ski Jumping" (the sport name) to the superclass constructor.

```
public SkiJumper(String first, String last)
{
    super(first, last, "Ski Jumping");
    myNumberOfJumps = 0;
}
```

The call to the superclass constructor ensures that all inherited instance fields are properly initialized. When the superclass constructor is called from the subclass, it must be the first statement in the subclass constructor. If the subclass constructor does not include the call to the superclass constructor, the default constructor for the superclass will automatically be called. However, if there is no default constructor (as with `Athlete`), an error will be reported.

The instance fields that are not inherited are initialized in the subclass constructor. Any attempt to change the inherited instance fields, which are private, will result in an error. You should avoid creating instance fields in a subclass with the same names as the superclass instance fields.

11.5   Converting Between Subclass and Superclass Types

If we wanted to have the ability to compare ski jumpers based on the number of jumps completed, the `SkiJumper` class would implement the `Comparable` interface (as illustrated in Figure 11.3),

```
public class SkiJumper extends Athlete implements Flier,
        Comparable
```

and implement the `compareTo` method.

```
public int compareTo(Object other)
{
    SkiJumper temp = (SkiJumper) other;
    if (getJumps < temp.getJumps()) return -1;
    if (getJumps() > temp.getJumps()) return 1;
    return 0;
}
```

Because we want to compare the number of jumps of two `SkiJumpers`, we cast the `Object` parameter to a `SkiJumper`.

Figure 11.3

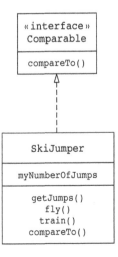

Suppose the following declarations were made.

```
SkiJumper jumper1 = new SkiJumper("John", "Miller");
SkiJumper jumper2 = new SkiJumper("Jane", "Dole");
Athlete jumper3 = new SkiJumper("Mark", "Morris");
Runner racer1 = new Runner("Mary", "Smith");
```

The following calls to `compareTo` are legal.

```
if (jumper1.compareTo(jumper2) > 0)
    // Code here
if (jumper2.compareTo(jumper1) > 0)
    // Code here
if (jumper1.compareTo(jumper3) > 0)
    // Code here
```

However, the statement

```
if (jumper3.compareTo(jumper1) > 0)    // WRONG!
    // Code here
```

will not compile. The variable `jumper3` is an `Athlete` and `compareTo` is not defined in the `Athlete` class.

The statement

```
if (jumper1.compareTo(racer1) > 0)
    // Code here
```

will compile but will throw a `ClassCastException` at runtime because the `compareTo` method of the `SkiJumper` class tries to cast a `Runner` to a `SkiJumper` in the first statement.

The statements

```
jumper3.fly();
racer1.fly();
```

will cause compile-time errors because `fly` is not defined for `Athlete` or for `Runner`.

The statement

```
jumper3.train(2);
```

is a legal statement because `train` is defined for `Athlete`. The `train` method of the `SkiJumper` class is invoked. Method calls are always determined by the type of the actual object (`SkiJumper`), not the type of the object reference (`Athlete`). This is an example of late (dynamic) binding.

The assignment

```
jumper3 = jumper1;    // OK because SkiJumper is a subclass of
                      // Athlete.
```

is legal. An object reference of a subclass can be assigned to an object of its superclass without casting.

The assignment

```
jumper1 = (SkiJumper) jumper3    // OK, cast necessary
```

is legal. An object reference of a superclass can be assigned to an object reference of its subclass with proper casting (and if the reference actually refers to an object of the subclass).

Example 11.3 is a sample client program to test these concepts.

Example 11.3

```java
public class InheritanceTester
{
    public static void main(String[] args)
    {
        SkiJumper jumper1 = new SkiJumper("John", "Miller");
        SkiJumper jumper2 = new SkiJumper("Jane", "Dole");
        Athlete jumper3 = new SkiJumper("Mark", "Morris");

        jumper1.fly();
        jumper1.fly();
        jumper2.fly();
        jumper2.fly();
        jumper2.fly();

        if (jumper1.compareTo(jumper2) > 0)
        {
            System.out.println(jumper1.getName() + " is better than "
                + jumper2.getName() + ".");
        }
        else if (jumper1.compareTo(jumper2) < 0)
        {
            System.out.println(jumper2.getName() + " is better than "
                + jumper1.getName() + ".");
        }
        else
        {
            System.out.println("The jumpers have completed an equal
                number of jumps!");
        }
        jumper3.train(2);
    }
}
```

The results of program execution are:

Using skis to take John Miller into the air.
Using skis to take John Miller into the air.
Using skis to take Jane Dole into the air.
Using skis to take Jane Dole into the air.
Using skis to take Jane Dole into the air.
Jane Dole is better than John Miller.
I am on the slopes 2.0 hours today.
Athlete training for 2.0 hours.

The statement

```java
jumper3.train(2);
```

first invokes the `train` method of `SkiJumper` class which prints "*I am on the slopes 2.0 hours today.*" After that statement is printed, a call to `super.train(2)` is made. This call invokes the train method of the superclass, Athlete. It is the Athlete train method that causes *"Athlete training for 2.0 hours."* to be printed.

11.6   Abstract Classes

An *abstract method* is a method whose implementation is not specified. An *abstract class* (see *Advanced Topic 10.1* on page 460 of your text) is a class that contains one or more abstract methods. Abstract classes cannot be instantiated. Abstract classes can be used if you want to force programmers to define a method. Let's redefine our Athlete class one more time to demonstrate an abstract class. In the following example, Athlete is an abstract class, which means it cannot be instantiated.

Example 11.4

```
public abstract class Athlete
{
    public Athlete(String firstName, String lastName,
        String sportPlayed)
    {
        myFirstName = firstName;
        myLastName = lastName;
        mySport = sportPlayed;
        myHoursTraining = 0;
    }

    //  Other methods defined here

    public abstract String getEquipment();
    //  More code here
    //  Private instance fields here
}
```

Example 11.4 mandates that any subclass of Athlete must implement the method getEquipment. If the subclass does not define this abstract method, the subclass cannot be instantiated and must be declared as abstract itself. Runner might define getEquipment in the following way.

```
public String getEquipment()
{
    return "Running shoes";
}
```

An abstract class differs from an interface because an abstract class can have instance variables, concrete (implemented) methods, and constructors that are inherited by subclasses. Although you cannot instantiate an abstract class, you can still have an object reference whose type is an abstract class. For example, the following assignment is legal.

```
Athlete jumper3 = new SkiJumper("Mark", "Morris");  // This is OK.
```

11.7 Access Control

Java has four levels of access to fields, methods, and classes.
- public
- private
- protected
- package

The AP CS Java subset does not include `protected` and package visibilities.

The `protected` level of visibility allows for access by all subclasses and all classes in the same package. This method of access control is explained in *Advanced Topic 10.3* on page 464 of your text. In our `Athlete` example, if we declared `myHoursTraining` as `protected`, then the `Runner` and the `SkiJumper` would be able to access and update this instance field of `Athlete` directly. In our example, the `Athlete`'s `train` method is called to update this variable because the variable is private. It is a good habit to declare all instance fields as private. If you want subclasses to be able to modify inherited instance fields, provide `protected` mutator methods that do this. If you want the world to have the ability to modify the values of the instance fields, provide `public` mutator methods to do this.

11.8 `Object`: The Cosmic Superclass

In Java, all classes inherit from the `Object` class. The methods of the `Object` class included in the AP CS subset are listed in Table 11.1.

Table 11.1
`class java.lang.Object`

Method	Method Summary
`String toString()`	Returns `String` representation of the object.
`boolean equals(Object other)`	Indicates whether the object `other` is "equal to" this one.
`int hashCode()` (AB)	Returns a hash code value for the object.

11.8.1 Inheritance and the `toString` Method
The `toString` method is automatically called by `System.out.println`. If our `InheritanceTester` client program invokes the statement

```
System.out.println(jumper1);
```

`Object`'s `toString` method is called and a cryptic message about `SkiJumper` is printed to the screen. However, we may wish to print a meaningful message about `SkiJumper` that includes values of the instance variables. This will allow us to inspect the object for possible errors in our program. In order to do this, `SkiJumper` must override the `Object` `toString` method.

```
public String toString()
{
    return "SkiJumper number of jumps = " + myNumberOfJumps;
}
```

The statement

```
System.out.println(jumper1);
```

will now print *SkiJumper number of jumps = 2.*

It may be more useful to provide a `toString` method that prints the values of all instance fields. This can be a very good way to test your programs. A `toString` method for `Athlete` might be:

```
public String toString()
{
    return ("class Athlete: \nname = " + myFirstName + " "
            + myLastName + "\nsport = " + mySport
            + "\nhours training = " + myHoursTraining);
}
```

and the more inclusive `toString` method for `SkiJumper` would be:

```
public String toString()
{
    String s = super.toString();
    return (s + "\nclass SkiJumper:\nnumber of jumps = "
            + myNumberOfJumps);
}
```

The statement

```
System.out.println(jumper2);
```

would print

> *class Athlete:*
> *name = Jane Dole*
> *sport = Ski Jumping*
> *hours training = 0.0*
> *class SkiJumper:*
> *number of jumps = 3*

You can include whatever meaningful information you need when you override `Object`'s `toString` method. It is a good programming habit to supply a `toString` method in the classes that you write. Example 11.5 visits our `Athlete`, `SkiJumper`, and `Runner` classes one more time. Each of these classes overrides `Object`'s `toString` method.

Example 11.5

```
public abstract class Athlete
{
    public Athlete(String firstName, String lastName,
            String sportPlayed)
    {
        // Instance fields initialized here
    }

    public String toString ()
    {
        return("class Athlete: \nname = " + myFirstName + " "
                + myLastName + "\nsport = " + mySport
                + "\nhours training = " + myHoursTraining);
    }
```

```
    // Other methods here
    // Private declarations here
}
```

```
public class SkiJumper extends Athlete implements Flier
{
    public SkiJumper(String firstName, String lastName)
    {
        super(firstName, lastName, "Ski Jumping");
        // Instance fields initialized here
    }

    public String toString()
    {
        String s = super.toString();
        return (s + "\nclass SkiJumper:\nnumber of jumps = "
                + myNumberOfJumps);
    }

    // Other methods here
    // Private instance fields here
}
```

```
public class Runner extends Athlete
{
    public Runner(String firstName, String lastName)
    {
        super(firstName, lastName, "Running");
        // Instance fields initialized here
    }

    public String toString()
    {
        String s = super.toString();
        return (s + "\n" + getName() + " is a runner.");
    }

    // Other methods here
    // Private instance fields here
}
```

Example 11.6 demonstrates adding `Athletes` to an `ArrayList`, then printing the contents of the `ArrayList` by calling `System.out.println` for each element of the `ArrayList`. The `println` method of the `PrintStream` class invokes the `toString` method of each object it is requested to print. Example 11.6 is implemented using the generic `ArrayList` and enhanced `for` loop.

Example 11.6

```
ArrayList<Athlete> teamMembers = new ArrayList<Athlete>();
teamMembers.add(new SkiJumper("SkiJumper", "One"));
teamMembers.add(new SkiJumper("SkiJumper", "Two"));
teamMembers.add(new Runner("Runner", "One"));
teamMembers.add(new Runner("Runner", "Two"));
```

```
for (Athlete i : teamMembers)
{
    System.out.println(i);
}
```

Example 11.6 prints:

> *class Athlete:*
> *name = SkiJumper One*
> *sport = Ski Jumping*
> *hours training = 0.0*
> *class SkiJumper:*
> *number of jumps = 0*
> *class Athlete:*
> *name = SkiJumper Two*
> *sport = Ski Jumping*
> *hours training = 0.0*
> *class SkiJumper:*
> *number of jumps = 0*
> *class Athlete:*
> *name = Runner One*
> *sport = Running*
> *hours training = 0.0*
> *Runner One is a runner.*
> *class Athlete:*
> *name = Runner Two*
> *sport = Running*
> *hours training = 0.0*
> *Runner Two is a runner.*

11.8.2 Inheritance and the `equals` Method

If you wish to test whether two objects have equal states (have the same contents), you need to override `Object`'s equals method. An equals method for `Athlete` would be:

```
public boolean equals(Object other)
{
    Athlete temp = (Athlete) other;
    return ((myFirstName.equals(temp.myFirstName))
        && (myLastName.equals(temp.myLastName))
        && (mySport.equals(temp.mySport))
        && (myHoursTraining == temp.myHoursTraining));
}
```

The parameter `other` needs to be cast to `Athlete`. Since three of the instance fields are objects (`Strings`), they need to be compared using the `String` equals method. The myHoursTraining instance field is a number. Numbers are compared using the `==` operator. Objects are compared using `equals`.

If a class implements `Comparable` and has defined `compareTo`, the best implementation for that class's equals method would be:

```
public boolean equals(Object other)
{
    return compareTo(other) == 0;
}
```

or

```
public boolean equals(Object other)
{
    return this.compareTo(other) == 0;
}
```

This ensures that comparison of two objects of the same class is consistent (`equals` and `compareTo` compare the same way).

Although the implementation of the `equals` method is not tested on the AP CS Exam, you do need to understand the difference between object equality (`equals`) and identity (`==`).

■ Expanded Coverage of Material That Is Not Found in the Text

- The inheritance relationship between a subclass and its superclass is an *is-a* relationship. The subclass is more specific than the superclass. For example,
  - A `SkiJumper` **is-a** `Athlete`
  - A `Runner` **is-a** `Athlete`

  Not all athletes are runners. Not all athletes are ski jumpers. A good check for subclass selection is to apply this *is-a* phrase. Ask yourself if your *is-a* statement is true. Chapter 12 of your text covers *is-a* relationships in more detail. When determining if an assignment statement is legal, read from right to left with *is-a*. If `SkiJumper` implements `Athlete` and the following instantiation is made,
  - `SkiJumper s = new SkiJumper("John", "Bates");`

  then
  - `Athlete a = new SkiJumper("Mary", "Williams");`   is OK because a `SkiJumper` *is-a* `Athlete`.
  - `a = s;`   is OK because a `SkiJumper` *is-a* `Athlete`.
  - `s = a;`   is WRONG because an `Athlete` is NOT always a `SkiJumper`.
- An object can be composed of other objects. For example, an `Athlete` has a first name, a last name, and a sport. All three of these instance fields are `String` objects. This situation is an example of a *has-a* relationship. *Has-a* relationships are used when a class is composed of other types of objects. This is often referred to as composition. For example,
  - A `SkiJumper` **has-a** name (`String`).
  - A `DeckOfPlayingCards` **has-a** `Card`.
  - An `Airplane` **has-a** `Engine`.

  Chapter 12 of your text covers *has-a* relationships in more detail.

■ Topics That Are Useful But Not Tested

- `protected` features can be accessed by all subclasses and all classes in the same package. `protected` access is explained in *Advanced Topic 10.3* on page 464 of your text.
- The `getClass().getName()` call can be used to print the class name in a `toString` method. This is explained in *Advanced Topic 10.4* on page 467 of your text.
- The `getClass` method can also be used to test if two objects belong to the same class. This is explained in *Advanced Topic 10.5* on page 470 of your text.

■ Things to Remember When Taking the AP Exam

- The `instanceof` operator tests whether an object belongs to a particular type. This is explained in Section 10.5 of your text. Although the `instanceof` operator is listed in the subset as potentially relevant but not tested, it is used in the GridWorld case study and you are responsible for understanding `instanceof` in the context of the case study.
- A subclass inherits the behavior and state of its superclass.
- Do not give an instance field of a subclass the same name as an instance field of its superclass. This "shadowing of instance fields" is explained in *Common Error 10.2* on page 449 of your text.
- A subclass has no direct access to the private fields or private methods of its superclass.
- The call to a superclass constructor, if included, must be the first statement in a subclass constructor. Otherwise, the superclass must have a default constructor, and that default constructor will be called.
- An object reference of a subclass can be assigned to an object reference of its superclass.
- An object reference of a superclass can be assigned to an object reference of its subclass with the appropriate casting (and if the reference actually refers to an object of the subclass).
- For both the A and AB Exams you should be able to extend existing code using inheritance. For the AP CS A Exam, you should be able to modify subclass implementations. For the AP CS AB Exam, you should be able to design and implement subclasses.
- An abstract class is a class containing one or more abstract methods. For the AP CS A Exam, you should understand the concepts of abstract classes and be able to use them. For the AP CS AB Exam, you should be able to design and implement abstract classes.
- An abstract class cannot be instantiated even though it usually has one or more constructors.
- Implementing the `equals` method is not part of the AP CS subset, but you do need to understand the difference between object equality (`equals`) and identity (`==`).

■ Key Words

You should understand the terms below. The AP CS Exam questions may include references to these terms. The citations in parentheses next to each term identify the page numbers where it is defined and/or discussed in *Java Concepts for AP Computer Science*, 5th ed.

abstract class (460)	inheritance (438)	`super` (448)
abstract method (460)	`Object` (439)	subclass (439)
access control (462)	object reference (452)	superclass (439)
code reuse (440)	override (445)	`toString` (466)
equals (465)	`private` (447)	
extends (439)	`public` (447)	

■ Connecting the Detailed Topic Outline to the Text

The citations in parentheses identify where information in the outline can be located in *Java Concepts for AP Computer Science*, 5th ed.

- An Introduction to Inheritance (438–442)
- Inheritance Hierarchies (443–445)
- Inheriting Instance Fields and Methods (445–450)

■ Practice Questions

Multiple Choice

1. A programmer notices that a method of a subclass has the same signature as a method in its superclass. Which of the following statements best characterizes this situation?

   a. The superclass method is overloaded.
   b. The superclass method shadows the subclass method.
   c. The subclass method overrides the superclass method.
   d. The superclass method overrides the subclass method.
   e. The program will not compile because methods of two classes in the same inheritance hierarchy cannot have the same name.

2. Which of the following statements is **true** about abstract classes?

   a. Instance fields declared in abstract classes are automatically `public`.
   b. Instance fields cannot be declared in abstract classes.
   c. A subclass that extends an abstract class must override instance variables declared in the abstract class.
   d. A subclass that extends an abstract class inherits the instance variables in the abstract class.
   e. The instance fields declared in an abstract class are automatically `static final`.

3. Which of the following statements is **not** true about subclass methods?

   a. A subclass can override methods in a superclass.
   b. A subclass can define new methods that are not in the superclass.
   c. A subclass can inherit methods in a superclass.
   d. A subclass can access private methods in a superclass.
   e. A subclass can access public methods of its superclass.

Questions 4, 5, and 6 refer to the `Employee`, `Manager`, and `Programmer` classes incompletely defined below.

```
public class Employee
{
    // Constructors and other methods here

    public void work()
    {
        System.out.println("Employee working.");
```

```
        }

        // Instance fields here
    }
```

```
    public class Manager extends Employee
    {
        // Constructors and other methods here

        public void work()
        {
            System.out.println("Manager working.");
        }

        // Instance fields here
    }
```

```
    public class Programmer extends Employee
    {
        // Constructors and other methods here

        public void work()
        {
            System.out.println("Programmer working.");
        }

        // Instance fields here
    }
```

4. Which of the following declarations will cause a compile-time error?

    a. `Employee employA = new Employee();`
    b. `Employee employB = new Manager();`
    c. `Manager employC = new Manager();`
    d. `Manager employD = new Employee();`
    e. `Programmer employE = new Programmer();`

5. Consider the following declarations.

    ```
    Employee employ1 = new Employee();
    Manager employ2 = new Manager();
    Employee employ3 = new Manager();
    ```

    Which of the following assignments is legal?

    I.   `employ1 = employ2;`
    II. `employ2 = (Manager) employ3;`
    III. `employ1 = (Manager) employ2;`

    a. I only
    b. II only
    c. III only
    d. I and II only
    e. I, II, and III

6. Consider the following declarations.

    ```
    Employee employ1 = new Employee();
    Manager employ2 = new Manager();
    Employee employ3 = new Manager();
    ```

    What will be printed if the code segment below is executed?

    ```
    employ1 = employ2;
    employ1.work();
    employ3.work();
    ```

    a. *Manager working.*
        Manager working.

    b. *Employee working.*
        Employee working.

    c. *Employee working.*
        Manager working.

    d. *Manager working.*
        Employee working.

    e. Nothing is printed. A `ClassCastException` occurs.

7. You implement three classes: `Person`, `Student`, and `Instructor`. A `Person` has a name
    and a year of birth. A `Student` has a major, and an `Instructor` has a salary. Which of the
    following would be the best design for this situation?

    a. `Person` should be an interface. `Student` and `Instructor` should implement `Person`.
    b. `Person` should be an abstract class that includes declarations for four abstract methods:
        `getName`, `getYearOfBirth`, `getMajor`, `getSalary`.
    c. `Person` should be an abstract class that includes declarations for two abstract methods:
        `getName` and `getYearOfBirth`.
    d. `Person` should be a superclass that includes implementations for four methods:
        `getName`, `getYearOfBirth`, `getMajor`, `getSalary`. `Student` and `Instructor` will
        be subclasses of `Person`.
    e. `Person` should be a superclass that includes implementations for two methods:
        `getName`, `getYearOfBirth`. The `Student` class and the `Instructor` class will be
        subclasses of `Person`.

Questions 8 and 9 refer to the following scenario.

A Barbershop Quartet is a group of four singers: a lead, a tenor, a bass, and a baritone. These four
singers harmonize to produce a purely American form of music developed in the 19th century.
Consider the incomplete class definitions below.

```
public class BarberShopQuartet
{
    public BarberShopQuartet()
    {
        Tenor highSinger = new Tenor();
        Baritone bari = new Baritone();
        Lead melody = new Lead();
        Bass lowSinger = new Bass();
        System.out.println("Quartet created.");
```

```
      }
   }
```

```
public class Singer
{
   public Singer()
   {
      System.out.println("Singing...");
   }
}
```

```
public class Tenor extends Singer
{
   public Tenor()
   {
      System.out.println("Singing...the high notes");
   }
}
```

```
public class Baritone extends Singer
{
   public Baritone()
   {
      System.out.println("Singing...harmonizing with the lead");
   }
}
```

```
public class Lead extends Singer
{
   public Lead()
   {
      System.out.println("Singing...the melody and providing the
            emotion");
   }
}
```

```
public class Bass extends Singer
{
   public Bass()
   {
      System.out.println("Singing...the very low notes");
   }
}
```

8. What output would be produced if the following code was executed?

```
BarberShopQuartet fourSingers = new BarberShopQuartet();
System.out.println("This quartet is on stage!");
```

   a. *Quartet created.*
      This quartet is on stage!

   b. *This quartet is on stage!*

  c. *Singing ... the high notes*
     Singing ... harmonizing with the lead
     Singing ... the melody and providing the emotion
     Singing ... the very low notes
     This quartet is on stage!

  d. *Singing ... the high notes*
     Singing ... harmonizing with the lead
     Singing ... the melody and providing the emotion
     Singing ... the very low notes
     Quartet created.
     This quartet is on stage!

  e. *Singing ...*
     Singing ... the high notes
     Singing ...
     Singing ... harmonizing with the lead
     Singing ...
     Singing ... the melody and providing the emotion
     Singing ...
     Singing ... the very low notes
     Quartet created.
     This quartet is on stage!

9. Which of the following *is-a, has-a* relationships is **true**?

  a. A `BarberShopQuartet` is-a `Singer`.
  b. A `Tenor` is-a `Singer`.
  c. A `Baritone` has-a `BarberShopQuartet`.
  d. A `Singer` has-a `BarberShopQuartet`.
  e. A `Singer` has-a `Lead`.

10. Which of the following statements about inheritance is **not** true?

  a. A class can be both a subclass and a superclass at the same time.
  b. Every class is a subclass of the `Object` class.
  c. Common features should be located as high in the inheritance hierarchy as possible.
  d. The `toString` and `equals` methods are inherited by all classes.
  e. The type of the reference, not the type of the object, is used to determine which version of an overridden method is invoked.

Free Response Questions

1. Consider the following detailed inheritance hierarchy diagram.

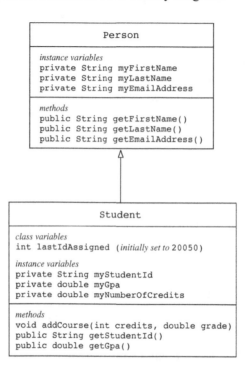

a. The `Person` constructor has two `String` parameters: a first name and a last name. The constructor initializes the e-mail address to the first letter of the first name followed by the first five letters of the last name followed by @jc.com. If the last name has fewer than five letters, the e-mail address will be the first letter of the first name followed by the entire last name followed by @jc.com. Examples:

Name	Email address
Jane Smith	JSmith@jc.com
John Morris	JMorri@jc.com
Mary Key	MKey@jc.com

Implement the `Person` constructor.

b. Override `Object`'s `toString` method for the `Person` class. The `toString` method should return the present state of the object. Assume that the constructor written for the previous part of this problem works as intended.

c. Write the `Student` class header so that `Student` is a subclass of `Person` and implements the `Comparable` interface.

d. The `Student` constructor will be called with two `String` parameters, the first name and the last name of the student. When the `Student` is constructed, the inherited fields `myFirstName`, `myLastName`, and `myEmailAddress` will be properly initialized, the student's GPA (`myGpa`) and number of credits (`myNumberOfCredits`) will be set to 0. The variable `lastIdAssigned` will be properly incremented each time a `Student` is constructed and the student ID (`myStudentId`) will be set to the next available ID number as tracked by the class variable, `lastIdAssigned`. Implement the `Student` constructor. Assume that the constructor written for part a of this problem works as intended.

e. Override `Object`'s `toString` method for the `Student` class. The `toString` method should return the present state of the object. Assume that all methods and constructors written for the previous parts of this problem work as intended.

f. Students are compared to each other by comparing GPAs. Implement the `compareTo` method for the `Student` class.

2. Refer to the `Athlete` class and the `Runner` class below.

```java
public class Athlete
{
    public Athlete(String firstName, String lastName,
            String sportPlayed)
    {
        myFirstName = firstName;
        myLastName = lastName;
        mySport = sportPlayed;
        myHoursTraining = 0;
    }

    public void train(double hours)
    {
        System.out.println("Athlete training for " + hours
                + " hours.");
        myHoursTraining += hours;
    }

    public String getName()
    {
        return (myFirstName + " " + myLastName);
    }

    public String getSport()
    {
        return mySport;
    }

    public double getHoursTrained()    {
        return myHoursTraining;
    }

    private String myFirstName;
    private String myLastName;
    private String mySport;
    private double myHoursTraining;
}
```

```java
public class Runner extends Athlete
{
    public Runner(String firstName, String lastName)
    {
```

```
            super(firstName, lastName, "Running");
            myNumberOfRaces = 0;
            myMilesRaced = 0;
        }

        public void race(double raceLength)
        {
            System.out.println(getName() + " is racing in a "
                    + raceLength + " mile race.");
            myNumberOfRaces++;
            myMilesRaced += raceLength;
        }

        public int getRaces()
        {
            return myNumberOfRaces;
        }

        public double getMilesRaced()
        {
            return myMilesRaced;
        }

        private int myNumberOfRaces;
        private double myMilesRaced;
    }
```

A `Marathoner` is a long distance `Runner`. Write the `Marathoner` class according to the following specifications.

The `Marathoner` is a subclass of the `Runner` class. The `Marathoner`'s sport is "Running". However, in order for a race to "count" as a race for the `Marathoner`, the race must be at least 10 miles in length. If it is shorter than 10 miles, the race counts as a training run and the training time credited to `myHoursTraining` is 8 1/2 minutes for each mile run. The variable `myNumberOfRaces` is not incremented, nor is `myMilesRaced` increased if the race is shorter than 10 miles in length. The `Marathoner` class will override the `Runner`'s race method so that these specifications are met.

3. Consider the following list of classes.

Person	Object
Course	Employee
Teacher	ClassRoster
HomeAddress	Secretary
MathDepartmentChairperson	Nurse
Student	

a. List the *has-a* relationships that exist in the list of classes above. Keep the inheritance relation in mind when you answer this question. For example, suppose `Name` was in the list above. If `Person` *has-a* `Name` and `Teacher` *is-a* `Person`, then you need only write `Person` *has-a* `Name` (`Teacher` inherits that from `Person`).

b. Sketch a class hierarchy illustrating the *is-a* relationships that exist for the classes above.

Exception Handling

TOPIC OUTLINE

■ Topic Summary

12.1 Introduction to Exceptions

You plan a vacation to the Florida Keys to do some SCUBA diving. On the morning of your first day of diving, you arrive at the boat dock, prepared with all the appropriate equipment. Before launching the boat, the skipper listens to the weather report. The skipper finds out that the sea is far too rough, cancels the dive, and gives you a memo confirming cancellation. This is akin to *throwing an exception.* An exceptional situation causes abrupt termination of the normal processing (the SCUBA dive). Note that throwing an exception doesn't tell you how to *recover* from the exceptional situation. An example of recovery would be if the manager, upon seeing the cancellation memo, buys everyone breakfast or refunds the dive trip costs. In Java, a *catch clause* is responsible for recovering from an exceptional condition.

Java provides an exception mechanism for handling *exceptional,* or abnormal, conditions in your programs. These problematic conditions prevent the continuation of the method execution. Exceptions in Java are represented by objects. These objects store information that includes the type of exception and where the exception was created. In the example, the cancellation memo confirmed this type of information about our SCUBA trip.

As we have seen in many of our programs, when we encounter run-time errors, a message on the screen describes the reason for that error. For example, the statements below are included in a program that compiles without error.

```
int[] numbers = new int[2];
numbers[0] = 54;
numbers[1] = 12;
numbers[2] = 14;
```

When the program is executed, the following message is printed.

> *Exception in thread "main" java.lang.ArrayIndexOutOfBoundsException*
> *at ArrayTester.main(ArrayTester.java:12)*

The segment of code *throws an exception* to indicate an error condition. The Java exception handling mechanism terminates the program with an error message. The information given includes the exception type (`ArrayIndexOutOfBoundsException`) and the location at which the exception was created (line 12 of the `main` method of the `ArrayTester` class in the file `ArrayTester.java`).

You can handle abnormal or problematic situations by including exception handling code in your program. For example, if a person tries to withdraw more money than a bank account has, you may wish to have the program terminated and indicate the reason rather than to alter the balance and cause unpredictable results later. The `throw` statement is used to invoke the exception handling mechanism. To throw an exception, you create an exception object with `new` and then throw it, using the `throw` keyword. The current flow of the method execution is terminated and the exception handler takes over.

12.1.1 Understanding Exceptions

You are responsible for understanding the exceptions that are commonly generated in your Java programs. Table 12.1 lists some common exceptions and their meaning.

Table 12.1

Common Run-time (Unchecked) Exceptions

Exception	Exception Summary
ArithmeticException	Thrown when an illegal arithmetic operation has occurred. For example, an integer "divide by zero" throws an instance of this class.
ArrayIndexOutOfBoundsException	Thrown when there is an attempt to access an array index that is either negative or greater than or equal to the size of the array. This class is a subclass of the IndexOutOfBoundsException class.
ClassCastException	Thrown when there is an attempt to cast an object to a class of which it is not an instance.
IllegalArgumentException	Thrown when a method is passed an illegal or inappropriate argument.
IllegalStateException	Signals that a method has been invoked at an illegal or inappropriate time.
IndexOutOfBoundsException	Thrown when an index is out of range. ArrayIndexOutOfBoundsException and StringIndexOutOfBoundsException are subclasses of this class.
NoSuchElementException	Thrown when an attempt to access a nonexistent element is made.

`NullPointerException`	Thrown when there is an attempt to use `null` where an object is required.
`NumberFormatException`	Thrown when an attempt to convert a string to one of the numeric types is made when the string does not have the appropriate format. This class is a subclass of `IllegalArgumentException`.
`StringIndexOutOfBoundsException`	Thrown when an index is either negative or greater than the size of the string. This class is a subclass of the `IndexOutOfBoundsException` class.

Examples of various exceptions are given below.

ArithmeticException
If the following code were executed,

```
int num = some integer value;
int count = 0;
System.out.println(num / count);    // ArithmeticException
```

An `ArithmeticException` (division by 0) would occur in the `System.out.println` statement.

ClassCastException
`Manager` is a subclass of the `Employee` class.

```
Employee worker1 = new Employee();
System.out.println((Manager) worker1);    // ClassCastException
```

`worker1` is an `Employee`, not a `Manager`.

IndexOutOfBoundsException
Consider the following code segment.

```
int[] anArray = new int[10];
anArray[11] = 0;    // ArrayIndexOutOfBoundsException

ArrayList aList = new ArrayList();
aList.add("Ann");
System.out.println(aList.get(1)); // IndexOutOfBoundsException

String s = "aString";
System.out.println(s.substring(0, 8));
        // StringIndexOutOfBoundsException
```

The exceptions that are thrown are subclasses of the `IndexOutOfBoundsException` class.

NoSuchElementException
Consider the following code segment.

```
ArrayList friends = new ArrayList();

Iterator it2;
for (it2 = friends.iterator(); it2.hasNext();)
{
```

```
        String temp2 = (String) it2.next();
        System.out.println(temp2);
    }
    System.out.println(it2.next());    // NoSuchElementException
```

Assuming that the `ArrayList` friends is declared, the `for` loop has the iterator traverse the entire array. In the second `println` statement, the iterator `it2` tries to access an element after the last one has been accessed. Iterators are part of the AP CS AB subset.

NullPointerException

```
    Manager worker1 = null;
    String temp = worker1.getName();    // NullPointerException
```

We cannot access an instance method of a `null` object.

NumberFormatException

```
    int units = Integer.parseInt("1234a");
    System.out.println(units + 1);
```

Although `parseInt` is not required in the AP CS subsets, it can be useful when getting input from the user. It can also lead to `NumberFormatExceptions`. In the above example, `"1234a"` is not a valid number so a `NumberFormatException` occurs. If `"1234a"` were replaced by `"12345"`, *12346* would be printed.

12.2   Throwing Exceptions (AB only)

Throwing exceptions allows you to ensure that certain conditions exist when your programs are executed. Although it is the responsibility of the calling procedure to meet the preconditions of a called method, it can be useful to check that the preconditions of your own methods are met. To do this, you can have your methods throw the appropriate exception if the precondition is not met. For example, the `Runner` class (Example 11.2 in this guide) has a method `race` that requires a `double` parameter. This parameter indicates the length of a race in miles. The length of a race should be a positive number. If the user passes a non-positive value to this method, you may choose to throw an exception.

IllegalArgumentException

```
    /**
        Adds raceLength miles to myMilesRaced.
        @param raceLength number of miles to add
        @throws IllegalArgumentException if raceLength is <= 0
    */
    public void race(double raceLength)
    {
        if (raceLength <= 0)
        {
            throw new IllegalArgumentException("Race length must be
                    greater than 0.");
        }
        System.out.println(getName() + " is racing in a " + raceLength
                + " mile race.");
```

```
        myNumberOfRaces++;
        myMilesRaced += raceLength;
    }
```

When the exception is thrown, the method terminates immediately. Execution is transferred to the exception handler. You can pass whatever `String` makes sense for the error condition you are checking or you can call the default constructor by not passing any parameter. Of course, it is more meaningful to pass a `String` parameter that adequately identifies the specific error.

IllegalStateException

An `IllegalStateException` might be thrown if a class invariant is violated. For example, a `BankAccount` is constructed with a non-negative balance. If an attempt is made to construct a `BankAccount` with a negative balance, an `IllegalStateException` could be thrown.

```
    /**
        Constructs a BankAccount object with balance = initialBalance.
        @param initialBalance the starting balance for this BankAccount
        @throws IllegalStateException if initialBalance < 0
    */
    public BankAccount(double initialBalance)
    {
        if (initialBalance < 0)
        {
            throw new IllegalStateException("Initial balance must be
                non-negative.");
        }
        balance = initialBalance;
    }
```

AB students are expected to be able to throw the `IllegalStateException` and `NoSuchElementException` exceptions in their own methods.

12.3   Checked and Unchecked Exceptions

There are two types of exceptions: checked exceptions and unchecked exceptions. Checked exceptions are compiler-enforced exceptions. This means that when you call a method that throws a *checked* exception, you *must* tell the compiler what you are going to do about the exception if it is thrown. Checked exceptions are due to external circumstances that the programmer cannot prevent. They are subclasses of the `Exception` class but are *not* subclasses of `RuntimeException`. Figure 1 in Section 11.2 of your text illustrates the inheritance hierarchy for exceptions. Checked exceptions are not part of the AP CS Java subset but they are discussed in Section 11.3 of your text.

Unchecked exceptions are subclasses of `RuntimeException`. In the programming of a method, an unchecked exception is thrown to indicate an exceptional or problematic situation. We have already been exposed to several unchecked exceptions, which are listed in Table 12.1 above. To reiterate, these are errors such as division by 0 which are not checked by the compiler (in fact they can't be), but that you may encounter.

■ Topics That Are Useful But Not Tested

- Checked exceptions are due to external circumstances that the programmer cannot prevent. The compiler checks that your program handles these exceptions. Checked exceptions are explained in Section 11.3 of your text.
- The throws specifier is used to indicate that a method may throw a checked exception. The throws specifier is discussed in Section 11.3 of your text.
- Designing your own exceptions can help to more accurately describe the exceptional situation. Designing your own exceptions is discussed in Section 11.6 of your text.
- Every exception should be handled somewhere in your program. The exceptions discussed in this chapter cause your program to terminate. The try block, catch clause, and finally clause describe a more professional way to handle exceptions. These topics are explained in Sections 11.4–11.5 of your text.
- The Scanner class can be used to read information from and to write information to text files. Storing information in text files is a very common way to get user input for your programs. Using text files is discussed in Section 11.1 of your text.

■ Things to Remember When Taking the AP Exam

- Know the conditions under which the common exceptions listed in this chapter are thrown.
- Understand javadoc comments containing @throws. Examples of @throws are in Section 12.2 of this guide.
- AB students should be able to throw the unchecked IllegalStateException and NoSuchElementException exceptions in their own methods.

■ Key Words

You should understand the terms below. The AP CS Exam questions may include references to these terms. The citations in parentheses next to each term identify the page numbers where it is defined and/or discussed in *Java Concepts for AP Computer Science*, 5th ed.

argument (503)	RuntimeException (506)
checked exception (506)	throws (506)
exception handler (506)	unchecked exception (506)
IllegalArgumentException (503)	

■ Connecting the Detailed Topic Outline to the Text

The citations in parentheses identify where information in the outline can be located in *Java Concepts for AP Computer Science*, 5th ed.

- Throwing Exceptions **(AB only)** (503–505)
- Checked and Unchecked Exceptions **(AB only)** (506–507)

■ Practice Questions

Multiple Choice

1. Which of the following statements about checked and unchecked exceptions is **true**?

    a. Checked exceptions are subclasses of `RuntimeException`.
    b. Unchecked exceptions are subclasses of `RuntimeException`.
    c. Checked and unchecked exceptions generate compile-time errors.
    d. Unchecked exceptions are checked by the compiler and will not terminate your program.
    e. In order for an unchecked exception to be generated, you must include a `throws` clause in your method.

2. Which of the following exceptions will be generated when the code segment below is executed?

    ```
    int numerator = 10;
    int denominator = 0;
    int wholePart = numerator / denominator;
    ```

    a. `ArithmeticException`
    b. `IllegalArgumentException`
    c. `NumberFormatException`
    d. `IndexOutOfBoundsException`
    e. `IllegalStateException`

Questions 3 and 4 refer to the `Person` constructor below. The `Person` constructor has two `String` parameters, a first name and a last name. The constructor initializes the e-mail address to the first letter of the first name followed by the first five letters of the last name followed by @jc.com. If the last name has fewer than five letters, the e-mail address will be the first letter of the first name followed by the entire last name followed by @jc.com. Examples:

Name	E-mail address
Jane Smith	JSmith@jc.com
John Morris	JMorri@jc.com
Mary Key	MKey@jc.com

```
public Person(String firstName, String lastName)
{
    myFirstName = firstName;
    myLastName = lastName;
    emailAddress = myFirstName.substring(0, 1)
            + myLastName.substring(0, 5)
            + "@jc.com";
}
```

3. Which of the following exceptions may be thrown by this constructor?

   a. `ArithmeticException`
   b. `IllegalArgumentException`
   c. `NumberFormatException`
   d. `StringIndexOutOfBoundsException`
   e. `IllegalStateException`

4. Which of the following calls to the `Person` constructor will cause the exception in Question 3 to be thrown?

   a. `Person scm1 = new Person("Marian", "Jones");`
   b. `Person scm2 = new Person("Joe", "Thomas");`
   c. `Person scm3 = new Person("Harry", "Tote");`
   d. `Person scm4 = new Person("J", "Franks");`
   e. `Person scm5 = new Person("Ellen", "Johnson");`

Questions 5 and 6 refer to the `ArrayList friends` as declared below.

```
ArrayList friends = new ArrayList();
friends.add("Mary");
friends.add("James");
friends.add("Kevin");
friends.add(1, "Tanya");
```

5. Consider the method `search` defined below.

```
public static int search(String key, ArrayList a)
{
   int count = 0;
   String temp = (String) (a.get(count));
   while (count < a.size() && !temp.equals(key))
   {
      count++;
      temp = (String) (a.get(count));
   }
   if (count < a.size())
      return count;
   else
      return -1;
}
```

   Suppose the following call to `search` was made.

```
int indexFound = search("John", friends);
```

   Which of the following statements best describes the result of this call?

   a. −1 is returned.
   b. 0 is returned.
   c. 4 is returned.
   d. An `IndexOutOfBoundsException` is thrown.
   e. A compile-time error occurs.

6. What is the result of the call

```
String s = (String) friends.get(4);
```

a. `s` is assigned the value `"Kevin"`
b. A compile-time error occurs.
c. A `ClassCastException` is thrown.
d. An `IllegalArgumentException` is thrown.
e. An `IndexOutOfBoundsException` is thrown.

Questions 7–9 refer to the `Employee` class and the `Manager` class incompletely defined below.

```
public class Employee
{
   public Employee()
   {
      myFirstName = null;
      myLastName = null;
      salary = 0;
   }

   public Employee(String firstName, String lastName,
      double money)
   {
      myFirstName = firstName;
      myLastName = lastName;
      salary = money;
   }

   public String getName()
   {
      return (myFirstName + " " + myLastName);
   }

   public void work()
   {
      System.out.println("Employee working.");
   }

   private String myFirstName;
   private String myLastName;
   private double salary;
}
```

```
public class Manager extends Employee
{
   public Manager()
   {
      super();
   }

   public Manager(String firstName, String lastName, double money)
   {
      super(firstName, lastName, money);
   }

   public void work()
   {
      System.out.println("Manager working.");
```

```
        }
    }
```

The following code is executed.

```
ArrayList<Employee> workers = new ArrayList<Employee>();
workers.add(new Manager());
workers.add(new Employee());
workers.add(new Manager("John", "Doe", 20000));
```

7. Which of the following statements results in a `ClassCastException` being thrown?

   I.   `Employee temp = (Manager) workers.get(0);`
   II. `Employee temp = (Manager) workers.get(1);`
   III. `Employee temp = (Manager) workers.get(2);`
   IV. `Employee temp = (Manager) workers.get(3);`

   a. I only
   b. II only
   c. III only
   d. IV only
   e. None of the statements above cause a `ClassCastException` to be thrown.

8. Which of the statements below execute without exceptions being thrown?

   I.   `Employee temp = (Manager) workers.get(0);`
   II. `Employee temp = (Manager) workers.get(1);`
   III. `Employee temp = (Manager) workers.get(2);`
   IV. `Employee temp = (Manager) workers.get(3);`

   a. I only
   b. I and II only
   c. I and III only
   d. I, II, III only
   e. I, II, III, and IV

9. The statement

   ```
   String temp = ((Manager) (workers.get(2))).getName();
   ```

   a. Compiles and executes without error.
   b. Reports a compile-time error: Incompatible types.
   c. Causes a `ClassCastException` to be thrown.
   d. Causes a `StringIndexOutOfBoundsException` to be thrown.
   e. Causes an `IllegalStateException` to be thrown.

10. Which of the following exceptions is **not** an unchecked exception?

    a. `IndexOutOfRangeException`
    b. `IOException`
    c. `IllegalArgumentException`
    d. `ArithmeticException`
    e. `NumberFormatException`

Free Response Questions

1. You are to design a `Teacher` class that is a subclass of the `Person` class whose incomplete definition is below.

```java
public class Person
{
    public Person(String firstName, String lastName)
    {
        // Constructor code goes here.
        // Private instance variables are initialized.
    }

    public String getName()
    {
        return myFirstName + " " + myLastName;
    }

    public String getEmail()
    {
        return emailAddress;
    }

    public String toString()
    {
        return ("name = " + getName() + "\n"
            + "email address = " + getEmail());
    }

    private String myFirstName;
    private String myLastName;
    private String emailAddress;
}
```

The `Teacher` class inherits instance variables and methods from `Person`. In addition, a `Teacher` has a private instance field, `salary` (of type `double`) and a public instance method `getRaise`. The method `getRaise` has a `double` parameter and will increment the `Teacher`'s salary by the amount of its parameter. You are to implement the `Teacher` class according to the specifications given. The `Teacher` has one constructor that expects three parameters: a first name (`String`), a last name (`String`), and a salary (`double`).

AB only: You should design your constructor to throw the appropriate exception if the salary passed is not a positive number. In writing `getRaise`, you should throw the appropriate exception if the parameter passed is not a positive number.

2. For a study in probability, we want to simulate the tossing of coins. A `CoinTosser` object tosses a coin a random number of times and reports on its outcomes. The `CoinTosser` constructor generates a random integer between 0 and 20 (inclusive). This generated value determines how many tosses this particular coin tosser will carry out. The constructor initializes all necessary instance fields.

It has the following public interface:

```java
public class CoinTosser
{
    /**
        CoinTosser Constructor.
        Generates a random integer in the range [0, 20] and
        initializes necessary instance fields.
    */
    public CoinTosser()
    {
        // Code goes here
    }

    /**
        Checks whether there are coin tosses remaining.
        @return true if the coin tosser has more
        coin tosses to report, false otherwise
    */
    public boolean hasMoreTosses()
    {
        // Code goes here
    }

    /**
        Randomly generates coin toss.
        @return "HEAD" or "TAIL"
    */
    public String nextToss()
    {
        // Code goes here
    }

    ...     // Private implementation
}
```

a. List the necessary private instance fields and their types.

b. Implement the `CoinTosser` constructor as described in the problem definition above.

c. Implement the `hasMoreTosses` method that returns `true` if there are tosses remaining, `false` otherwise. Use the header below.

```java
public boolean hasMoreTosses()
```

d. Write the `nextToss` method that randomly generates a 1 or a 0 and returns "HEADS" if 1 is generated and returns "TAILS" if 0 is generated. Assume `hasMoreTosses` works as defined in part c. Use the header below.

```java
public String nextToss()
```

(AB students) The `nextToss` method should throw a `NoSuchElementException` if it is called after the `hasMoreTosses` method has returned false.
(A students) The `nextToss` method should return the empty string if it is called after the `hasMoreTosses` method has returned false.

CHAPTER **13**

(Covers *Java Concepts for AP Computer Science* Chapter 12)

Object-Oriented Design

■ Topic Summary

13.1 The Software Life Cycle

The AP CS Topic Outline requires that all AP Computer Science students
- Understand encapsulation.
- Understand the *is-a* and *has-a* inheritance relationships.
- Understand and be able to implement an inheritance class hierarchy according to given specifications.
- Design and implement a class according to given specifications.
- Understand when to use an interface and be able to design an interface.
- Extend a given class with inheritance.

In addition to the above, AP Computer Science AB students should be able to
- Discover and design classes.
- Determine relationships between classes.
- Determine responsibilities of each class.
- Use object-oriented design to build a program from a set of interacting classes.

We have introduced many of these topics separately. This chapter will give you practice pulling the pieces together to design a program involving more than one class.

The five steps in the software life cycle are listed and defined in Table 13.1.

Table 13.1

Process	Process Description
Analysis	The *analysis* phase is the time when you determine what your software system is intended to accomplish.
Design	The *design* phase is when you develop a plan to implement your system.
Implementation	The *implementation* phase is when you write the code according to the specifications made in the design phase.
Testing	During the *testing* phase you verify that the system works as intended.
Deployment	The *deployment* phase is when the intended user of the system installs and uses it.

Section 12.1 of your text explains this life cycle in detail.

13.2   Discovering Classes

In the design phase, you need to be able to describe a set of classes that can be used to implement the task(s) your software system is intended to accomplish. Look for *nouns*.

- Task: Print an invoice
  - Candidate classes: `Invoice, Item, Customer`
- Task: Publish a book
  - Candidate classes: `Book, Page, Binding`
- Task: Organize a 5-mile race
  - Candidate classes: `Race, Runner, VolunteerWorker`
- Task: Play the lottery
  - Candidate classes: `Ball, BallPicker, BallShaker`
- Task: Build a house
  - Candidate classes: `Wall, Window, Roof`

Some of these classes may consist of objects defined by other classes. For example, a customer has a name (`String` object), a customer identification number (an `int`), an address (perhaps an object instantiating an `Address` class composed of a street address, a city, and a state).

13.3   Relationships Between Classes

It is sometimes useful to classify relationships between classes. There are several different types of class relationships. The AP CS Topic Outline includes the following two relationships:
- *is-a* relationships
- *has-a* relationships

Using some of the examples already presented, we have:
- A `Bank` *has-a* `Customer`.
- A `Customer` *has-a* `BankAccount`.
- A `SavingsAccount` *is-a* `BankAccount`.

- A `Car` *is-a* `Vehicle`.
- A `Car` *has-a* `Tire`.

- A `Race` *has-a* `Runner`.
- A `Marathoner` *is-a* `Runner`.

- A `Purse` *has-a* `Coin`.

A class is *associated* with another class if the class has an instance field whose type is another class. Your textbook covers another relationship, the *uses-a* relationship or *dependency*. A class *depends* on another class if it *uses* an object of the other class. The original version of `Purse` *uses* a `Coin`. The `Purse` did not have a private instance field of type `Coin`, nor did it have an `ArrayList` that collected `Coin` objects. The distinction between *association* and *dependency* is not part of the AP CS subsets, but understanding this concept can help you in designing your software systems.

Remember, if many classes in a program depend on each other, there is high coupling. If all of the features in a class are related to the concept the class represents, there is high cohesion. In designing system software, one should strive for low coupling and high cohesion.

Once the set of classes has been identified, you need to define the responsibilities (behaviors) of each class. When you look for these behaviors, look for *verbs* in the task description. The verbs will define the candidate methods.
- Task: Print an invoice
    - Candidate classes: `Invoice`, `Item`, `Customer`
    - Example candidate methods:
        - `Invoice` has method `computeAmountDue`.
        - `Item` has method `getPrice`.
        - `Customer` has method `getName`.
- Task: Organize a 5-mile race
    - Candidate classes: `Race`, `Runner`, `VolunteerWorker`
    - Example candidate methods:
        - `Race` has methods `addRunner`, `getNumberOfRunners`.
        - `Runner` has methods `getRaceNumber`, `setFinishTime`.
        - `VolunteerWorker` has methods `getName`, `setJob`.

When designing a class, it is also useful to list the attributes (usually instance fields) that a class might have.
- A `Runner` has a `name`, a `raceNumber`, a `finishTime`.
- A `Race` has a *list* (probably an array list) of `Runners`, a `raceDistance`, a *list* of `VolunteerWorkers`.

When trying to decide which class has what responsibilities, start by listing the tasks that your system needs to accomplish and assign each task to the class that is responsible for carrying out that task. If an action modifies the state (the private instance fields or attributes) of the object, it is the responsibility of the object itself. One way to ensure this is to keep the attributes of the object private.

One popular way to illustrate class relationships is with the use of CRC cards. CRC stands for "classes", "responsibilities", and "collaborators". CRC cards are discussed in Section 12.2 of your text. *How To 12.1* on page 541 of your text lists the steps in the design process that will help you discover class interactions and responsibilities.

You may also need to provide a data representation for your software design. So far, we have studied arrays and array lists. You will need to choose a data representation consistent with the specifications given in the problem description.

Consider a state lottery game. Each evening the lottery is televised and we observe the following. There is a *container* that holds the numbered *balls* such that no two balls have the same number. There is a *popper* that "pops" a random ball. It is this popped ball's number that is one of the lottery number choices.

Classes:
- Container has a collection of Balls. If asked for a Ball, the Container will remove a Ball at random from the set of Balls it contains and return it.
- Ball has a number on it. It can return its number to whoever wants to know it.
- Popper will ask the Container for a Ball and display the number on the Ball.

The Container is a collection of Ball objects. A data representation that is consistent with the problem requirements needs to be chosen in order to implement the lottery game. Example 13.1 contains one such data representation in an incomplete implementation of the Container class.

Example 13.1

```java
public class Container
{
    /**
        Balls in this container are numbered in the range
        [1, numberOfBalls].
    */
    public Container(int numberOfBalls)
    {
        for (int i = 1; i <= numberOfBalls; i++)
            lotteryBalls.add(new Ball(i));
    }

    // Other methods

    private ArrayList<Ball> lotteryBalls = new ArrayList<Ball>();
}
```

The data representation chosen in Example 13.1 is an array list. Array lists contain objects. In this problem, Ball objects need to be added to and removed from the Container. An array list is a reasonable choice for the following reasons:
- add and remove methods are defined for the ArrayList.
- The Popper will ask the Container for a ball.
- The Container will return a random ball to the Popper. The Popper will ask the Ball for its number and display that number.

■ Topics That Are Useful But Not Tested

- Using CRC (classes-responsibilities-collaborators) cards is an excellent way to discover class responsibilities and class collaborators. CRC cards are described in Section 12.2 of your text.
- UML diagrams can be used to illustrate class relationships. Section 12.3 of your text discusses the use of UML diagrams for illustrating relationships between classes and interfaces.
- The aggregation (*has-a*) relationship and the dependency (*uses*) relationship are discussed in detail in Section 12.3 and *Advanced Topic 12.3* on page 543 of your text.
- Extreme Programming is a development methodology that strives for simplicity by removing formal structure and focusing on best practices. Extreme programming has become very popular and is discussed in Section 12.1 of your text.

■ Things to Remember When Taking the AP Exam

- Read the free-response questions very carefully. Hints to the answer may appear in the way the question is worded.
- Look for key words: "extends", "is a", "is a kind of". These phrases indicate an inheritance relationship.
- Look for key words: "has a", "has", "is made from", "uses". These phrases indicate an aggregation or dependency relationship.
- Modifying the state of an object is the responsibility of the object itself.

■ Key Words

You should understand the terms below. The AP CS Exam questions may include references to these terms. The citation within parentheses next to each term identifies the page number where it is defined and/or discussed in *Java Concepts for AP Computer Science*, 5th ed.

analysis (530)
candidate classes (536)
collaborators (537)
CRC cards (537)
dependency (540)

deployment (531)
design (531)
has-a relationship (539)
implementation (530)

is-a relationship (539)
software life cycle (530)
testing (531)
uses (540)

■ Connecting the Detailed Topic Outline to the Text

The citations in parentheses identify where information in the outline can be located in *Java Concepts for AP Computer Science*, 5th ed.

- The Software Life Cycle (530–534)
- Discovering Classes (536–538)
- Relationships Between Classes (539–541)

■ Practice Questions

Multiple Choice

1. Which of the following choices gives the correct order of the software development processes for a complex program?

   a. Analysis, Design, Implementation, Testing, Deployment
   b. Design, Analysis, Implementation, Testing, Deployment
   c. Design, Implementation, Testing, Analysis, Deployment
   d. Design, Implementation, Testing, Deployment, Analysis
   e. Analysis, Design, Implementation, Deployment, Testing

2. Which of the following pairs is **not** an inheritance (*is-a*) relationship?

   a. Violin, Instrument
   b. Car, Vehicle
   c. Tire, Car
   d. Student, Person
   e. Sedan, Car

3. Which of the following is a *has-a* relationship?

   a. Camera, Lens
   b. Student, Person
   c. Truck, Vehicle
   d. Student, Freshman
   e. Fruit, Apple

4. You are to design a program that simulates a vending machine. Your design might include all of the following except

   a. `Product`
   b. `Coin`
   c. `VendingMachine`
   d. `Customer`
   e. `ChangeMachine`

5. In designing a software system, you should:

   I. Look for nouns in the system description to identify candidate classes.
   II. Look for verbs in the system description to identify class responsibilities.
   III. Describe relationships among the candidate classes.

   a. I only
   b. II only
   c. III only
   d. I and II only
   e. I, II, and III

Questions 6 and 7 refer to the following design problem.

You are to create a software design that simulates a fast food restaurant. You will have food items (hamburgers, hot dogs, chicken sandwiches) and drink items (Coke, Sprite, root beer). The drinks come in various sizes given in ounces (for example: 12, 24, 48). Food items will be assigned a price when they are created but this price can be changed by the employee taking the order if the customer requests "extras" such as bacon, cheese, tomato, etc. The price for drink items will be assigned according to the size of the drink.

6. Which of the following would be the best choice for the design of this system?

    a. The design should include the following classes: `Hamburger`, `HotDog`, `Chicken`, `Coke`, `Sprite`, and `RootBeer`.
    b. The design should include the following classes: `FoodItem` with `Hamburger`, `HotDog`, and `Chicken` extending `FoodItem` and `DrinkItem` with `Coke`, `Sprite`, and `RootBeer` extending `DrinkItem`.
    c. The design should include the following classes: `Item` with `FoodItem` and `DrinkItem` extending `Item`; `Hamburger`, `HotDog`, and `Chicken` extending `FoodItem`; and `DrinkItem` with `Coke`, `Sprite`, and `RootBeer` extending `DrinkItem`.
    d. The design should include the following classes: `FoodItem` and `DrinkItem`. The individual types of food and drink are only descriptions of the food or drink and should not be separate classes.
    e. The design should include the following classes: `Item` with `FoodItem` and `DrinkItem` extending `Item`. The individual types of food and drink are objects that are instances of these classes, not separate classes.

7. The fast food restaurant also offers value meals. A value meal is a drink and a food item purchased at the same time. A 10% discount off the full price of purchasing each separately is applied to the price of a value meal. A deluxe value meal costs $0.50 more than a value meal and includes apple pie for dessert. Which of the following is the best choice for this system design?

    a. `DeluxeValueMeal` should be a subclass of `ValueMeal`.
    b. `ValueMeal` should be a subclass of `DeluxeValueMeal`.
    c. Both `DeluxeValueMeal` and `ValueMeal` should be separate classes that have no inheritance relationship.
    d. `ValueMeal` has an association (*has-a*) relationship with `DeluxeValueMeal`.
    e. `ValueMeal` and `DeluxeValueMeal` both have an instance field of type `Meal` which is a superclass of both `ValueMeal` and `DeluxeValueMeal`.

Questions 8–10 refer to the problem stated below.

Your task is to automate the booking system of a travel agency. Some customers of the travel agency only purchase a single ticket, but others purchase whole trips consisting of multiple airline, boat, or train tickets, hotel stays, and car rentals.

8. Consider these statements about a possible system design:

    I.   A class `Ticket` has subclasses `AirlineTicket`, `BoatTicket`, `TrainTicket`.
    II. A class `Trip` *has-a* collection of `Ticket` objects, describing all tickets needed for the trip.
    III. To facilitate travelers who only buy a single ticket, we use inheritance so that a `Ticket` *is-a* `Trip`.

    Which of the choices above describe suitable design decision(s) for the travel agency's booking system?

   a. I only
   b. II only
   c. III only
   d. I and II only
   e. I, II, and III

9. A good travel agent is expected to check that a customer does not accidentally end up with mismatched reservations, such as a flight from New York to Rome and a hotel reservation in Karachi on the same night. Thus, there is a need to implement the responsibility "check trip" that flags itineraries with mismatched reservations. These flagged itineraries require special attention. Consider these statements about the assignment of this responsibility:

   I. The `Ticket` and `HotelReservation` class are jointly responsible for carrying out the "check trip" responsibility.
   II. The "check trip" responsibility must lie with the `Trip` class.
   III. It is useless to implement this responsibility because some customers might get a rental car and drive to an unknown destination.

   Which of the choices above describe suitable design decision(s) for the travel agency's itinerary system?

   a. I only
   b. II only
   c. III only
   d. I and II only
   e. I, II, and III

10. Consider these statements about the implementation of the `Trip` class:

   I. The `Trip` class can use an `ArrayList` of `Ticket` objects to store a variable number of tickets.
   II. The `Trip` class should have an instance field of type `CarRental`.
   III. The `Trip` class must contain a field of type `String[]` to store hotel names.

   Which of the choices above describe suitable implementation decision(s) for the `Trip` class?

   a. I only
   b. II only
   c. III only
   d. I and II only
   e. I, II, and III

Free Response Questions

1. A used car lot contains cars of various makes and models. The size of a car lot is fixed. The owner of the car lot wants to inventory the cars he has available. For the inventory, he needs the following information about each car:

Make (Toyota, Ford, etc.)
Year (1997, 2001, etc.)
Mileage (120734.6, 23555.2, etc.)
Cost (20000.00, 24500.00, etc.)

When a new car is created, the make, the car year, and the mileage are given. The cars are occasionally taken for test rides. A test ride alters the mileage of the car. The price of the car is set by the owner of the car lot. The car dealer will eventually need to print all of the information about each car in the lot. It will also be necessary for the car dealer to request and print a list of all cars with a specified year and make.

a.   Implement the Car class. In implementing the class, you should:
  • Choose appropriate variable names, parameter names, and method names.
  • Properly identify access modifiers (private, public) of each method and instance field.
  • Include a toString method that will print the information about a car.

Consider the CarLot class partially implemented below.

```java
public class CarLot
{
    /**
       Constructs a CarLot (array of cars).
    */
    public CarLot()
    {
        lot = new Car[MAX_CARS];
    }

    /**
       Adds a car to car lot.
       Precondition: numberOfCars < MAX_CARS
       @param aNewCar a car to be added to this car lot
    */
    public void addCar(Car aNewCar)
    {
        // Code goes here
    }

    /**
       Prints the information about the cars in the car lot.
    */
    public void printCarsInLot()
    {
        // Code goes here
    }

    /**
       Fills the array list with cars in the car lot that have the
       same year and make as the parameters passed to the method.
       @param year the year to search for
       @param make the make of car to search for
    */
    private ArrayList<Car> findMatchingCars(int year, String make)
    {
        // Code goes here
    }
```

```
/**
    Prints the year, make, mileage, and price of each car in the
    lot that has the same year and make as the method
    parameters.
    @param year the year to search for
    @param make the make of car to search for
*/
public void printMatchingCars(int year, String make)
{
    // Code goes here
}

private static final int MAX_CARS = 100;
private static int numberOfCars = 0;
private Car[] lot;
}
```

b. Write the `CarLot` method, `addCar`, that will add a `Car` to the car lot in the next available place. (**AB students:** If there are no more spaces available, throw an appropriate exception.) Use the method header below.

```
public void addCar(Car aNewCar)
```

c. Write the `CarLot` method, `printCarsInLot`, that will print the information about each car in the lot. Use the method header below.

```
public void printCarsInLot()
```

d. Write the `CarLot` method `findMatchingCars`, that will return an `ArrayList` of cars that match the year and make passed as the parameters to the method. Use the method header below.

```
private ArrayList findMatchingCars(int year, String make)
```

e. Write the `CarLot` method, `printMatchingCars`, that will print the year, make, mileage, and price of each car in the lot that matches the year and make passed as parameters to the method. If there are no cars with the requested specifications, an appropriate statement should be printed. Use the method header below.

```
public void printMatchingCars(int year, String make)
```

2. Consider the task of modeling record keeping for a real estate company. The company keeps records on each of its real estate agent employees. Each employee's record contains the following information:
   - The employee first name
   - The employee last name
   - The employee identification number (integer)
   - The total value of real estate property sold by the employee (floating-point number)

When a new employee record is created, it is created with the employee's first name and last name. The next available employee identification number is assigned to the employee and the total real estate property sold is initialized to 0.

The company keeps a list of employees that is constantly updated so that newly hired employees are added to the list and employees that quit or are fired are removed from the list. A newly created real estate company has no employees.

Among the many tasks that need to be completed are:
- Create a new employee record given the first and last name of the employee.
- Add the value of real estate property sold to an employee record given the property value.
- Get commission earned to date for an employee. Commission earned is 6% of the total value of real estate property sold by the employee.
- Create a new real estate company.
- Add an employee to the company list of employees.
- Get a list of current company employees.
- Remove an employee from the list of employees given the employee identification number.
- Retrieve the employee who sold the highest value of real estate.

a. **(AB only)** Design each class that is needed in the real estate system described above. The class design should include:
   - Class name
   - Constructor header for each constructor
   - Method signatures (include parameters) and return type for each method
   - Instance fields
   - Static variables

   In completing each class design, you should:
   - Choose appropriate variable names, parameter names, and method names.
   - Properly identify access modifiers (private, public) for each method, instance field, and static variable.

b. Write the class header, declare and initialize any static and instance variables, and write the constructor(s) for the class that creates a new employee record. Follow the specifications given in the problem description.

c. Write the class header, declare and initialize any static and instance variables, and write the constructor(s) for the class that creates a new real estate company. Follow the specifications given in the problem description.

3. The game of Nim is a well-known game with a number of variants. We will consider the following variant, which has an interesting winning strategy. Two players alternately take marbles from a pile. In each move, a player chooses how many marbles to take. The player must take at least one but at most half of the marbles. Then the other player takes a turn. The player who takes the last marble loses.

You will design a program in which the computer plays against a human opponent. Nim specifications include:
- The initial size of the pile will be a random integer generated between two values passed to the constructor of NimGame by the calling method.
- The decision of who goes first, the computer or the human, is determined by generating a random number so that each has an equal chance to go first.
- The decision whether the computer plays smart or stupid is determined by generating a random number so that both possibilities are equally likely. A computer then knows if it is smart or stupid.
- A player that is not smart simply takes a random legal value (between 1 and $n/2$) from the pile whenever it has a turn, where n is the number of marbles in the pile.

- A smart player takes off enough marbles to make the size of the pile a power of two minus 1 that is, 3, 7, 15, 31, 63, etc. That is always a legal move, except if the size of the pile is currently one less than a power of two. In that case, the smart player makes a random legal move.
- A human player has a name that is given when asked. A human player is asked how many marbles s/he wishes to take.
- The computer's name is "ROBO COMPUTER".

You will note that a smart player cannot be beaten when it has the first move, unless the pile size happens to be 1 less than a power of 2. Of course, a human player who has the first turn and knows the winning strategy can win against the computer.

In implementing this game, choose the following classes:

```
NimGame
NimPile
Player
HumanPlayer
SmartPlayer
```

The following methods are available to you in a `Utilities` class:

```
getRandNumber
largestPowerOfTwoMinusOneBelow
isPowerOfTwoMinusOne
readInt
readWord
```

The public interface for the `Utilities` class is below.

```
public class Utilities
{
    /**
        Generates random integer in [low, high].
        Precondition: low < high
        @param low the lower limit of the range of random values
        @param high the higher limit of the range of random values
        @return a random integer in [low, high]
    */
    public static int getRandNumber(int low, int high) {. . .}

    /**
        Tests whether n has the form pow(2, k) - 1.
        Precondition: n > 0
        @param n a positive integer to test
        @return true if n is a power of two minus
        one, false otherwise.
    */
    public static boolean isPowerOfTwoMinusOne(int n) {. . .}
```

```
/**
   Precondition: n > 0
   @param n a number
   @return the largest power of two minus one that is
   below a given number (the largest pow(2, k) - 1 < n).
*/
public static int largestPowerOfTwoMinusOneBelow(int n) {. . .}

/**
   Reads an integer from the keyboard.
   @return the integer entered by user
*/
public static int readInt();

/**
   Reads a string from the keyboard.
   @return the string entered by user
*/
public static String readWord();
}
```

The main method that invokes the game of Nim is:

```
public static void main(String[] args)
{
   NimGame nim = new NimGame(10, 100);
      // The pile will have a random number of marbles between
      // 10 and 100 inclusive.
   nim.playNim();
}
```

a. Find and list the *has-a* and *is-a* relationships between the following classes.
   - `NimGame`
   - `NimPile`
   - `Player`
   - `HumanPlayer`
   - `SmartPlayer`

b. Find the responsibilities of each of the classes in part a, and provide the following for each class.
   - Class name
   - Constructor headers for each constructor
   - Method signatures (including parameters) and return type for each method
   - Instance fields

c. Implement the methods that you determined in the preceding step.

Note: It is highly improbable that the AP Exam will ask you to implement an entire program such as Nim. Consider part c a "just for fun" activity!

CUMULATIVE REVIEW 2

Chapters 8–13

This review will check your knowledge of material in Chapters 8–13. You should consider this a mini-practice for the AP Exam. Look over the material in these chapters and read over the section *Things to Remember When Taking the AP Exam* below. Have available the Exam Reference Materials for the AP Exam that you will be taking. Because you will have reference materials available to you during the exam, you should become familiar with them now.

■ Things to Remember When Taking the AP Exam

General Guidelines
- Do not put extraneous `System.out.println` statements in free-response answers to indicate that the method is done, to print an error message, or to print the answer before returning its value. This is a side effect and will result in a deduction of points.
- Unless specifically asked to write pre- and postconditions, do not spend time doing this.
- You do not need to check that the precondition of the method is satisfied unless explicitly told to do so. A method should not be called unless its precondition is satisfied.
- Do not try to modify parameters of a method by reassigning values to these variables.
- Carefully read the pre- and postconditions given in problems, especially in the free-response questions. Many times an algorithm for solving the problem is given in the problem documentation. Read the documentation carefully!
- Understand the differences among compile-time errors, run-time errors, and logic errors.
- If asked to choose test data for a situation, remember to include legitimate test cases as well as degenerate test cases (cases that check error conditions).
- Check the code you write for free-response questions by hand tracing your code for the examples given and for your own additional examples.
- Know the conditions under which the common exceptions are thrown.
- **(AB only)** You should be able to throw the unchecked `IllegalStateException` and `NoSuchElementException` in your own methods.

Arrays and Array Lists
- Remember that the first element of both an array list and an array has index `0`.

- The single most common loop error that occurs when dealing with arrays is an out-of-bounds error while the list is being traversed. The tests

    ```
    while (index <= arrayName.length)    // WRONG
    ```

    and

    ```
    while (index <= arrayListName.size()    // WRONG
    ```

    both try to access an out-of-bounds element. The test should be `<`, not `<=`. Remember that the last element in an array has index `arrayName.length - 1` and the last element in an `ArrayList` has index `arrayListName.size() - 1`. Think carefully about loop bounds when accessing array and `ArrayList` elements.
- Do not confuse `.length` with `.size()`. Remember that `arrayName.length` is an instance variable that holds the length of an array (not necessarily the number of filled elements in the array) and `arrayListName.size()` is a method that returns the number of elements in an `ArrayList`.
- To access the sixth element of an array we write `arrayName[5]`. To access the sixth element of an `ArrayList`, we write `arrayListName.get(5)`.
- Using `equals` with two `ArrayLists` returns `true` if the two `ArrayLists` contain the same elements in the same order, `false` otherwise.
- When you use `equals` with arrays, you are comparing references. `array1.equals(array2)` is asking if `array1` and `array2` reference the same array. The result of comparing two arrays with `==` is identical to the result using `equals`.
- Using an enhanced `for` loop to traverse an array or array list eliminates the chance of off-by-one errors. If you are traversing an array or array list and not changing its contents, use an enhanced `for` loop. Do not use an enhanced for loop if you are removing elements or changing contents of an array or array list.
- **(AB only)** When visiting elements in a two-dimensional array, do not confuse rows and columns.
- When shifting elements in an array, be careful not to overwrite values of other array elements. It is rare that this is an intended task! Think about the order in which the elements are being shifted.
- Iterators are included in the AB subset only. However, many problems are simplified if an iterator is used to traverse the array list instead of a `while` loop or a `for` loop. If you are a student in AP CS A, you may want to learn to use iterators.

Polymorphism and Inheritance

- Early binding (overloading) of methods occurs if the *compiler* selects a method from several possible candidates. Late binding (overriding) occurs if the method selection takes place when the program runs. This is an important distinction.
- All methods in an interface are public. The methods in the interface are not declared as public because they are public by default. When implementing the methods of the interface in a class, remember to include the keyword `public`.
- An interface does not have any instance variables or constructors.
- An interface does not implement any methods.
- An interface cannot be instantiated.
- You can assign an object reference from a class type to an interface type if the class implements the interface, but you need to cast to assign an object reference from an interface type to a class type.
- For both the A and the AB Exams, you should be able to read the definitions of interfaces. For the AB exam, you should be able to define your own interfaces.
- An interface does not have constructors and cannot be instantiated, but you can convert from a class type to an interface type if the class implements the interface. For example, recall that `Flier` is an interface and `Airplane` is a class that implements `Flier`, so

    - ```
      Flier f = new Flier();    // WRONG!
      ```
    - ```
      Flier f = new Airplane();    // OK
      ```

    The object created (`Airplane`) is converted to an interface type (`Flier`).

- A subclass inherits the behavior and state of its superclass.
- Do not name an instance field of a subclass the same name as an instance field of its superclass (shadowing).
- Do not give variables a name that differs only in case from the class name (i.e. `Fish fish = new Fish();`).
- A subclass has no direct access to the private fields of its superclass.
- The call to a superclass constructor must be the first statement in the subclass constructor.
- An object of a subclass can be assigned to an object of its superclass.
- An object of a superclass can be assigned to an object of its subclass with the appropriate casting.
- An abstract class cannot be instantiated.
- An abstract class can have instance variables.
- An abstract class will have methods that are implemented and at least one which is not.
- An abstract class always has at least one class that extends it.
- You can convert from a class type to an abstract class type if the class extends the abstract class, but you need a cast to convert from an abstract class type to a class type.
- The AP CS Java subset specifies that all classes should be designated public and all instance variables should be designated private. The AP CS Java subset does not use `protected` and package (default) visibility.
- Look for key words: "extends", "is a", "is a kind of". These phrases indicate an inheritance relationship.
- Look for key words: "has a", "has", "is made from", "uses". These phrases indicate a class association.
- Modifying the state of an object is the responsibility of the object itself.

■ Practice Questions

Multiple Choice

1. Consider the following segment of code.

```
ArrayList<String> names = new ArrayList<String>();
names.add("Joe");
names.add("Mary");
names.add("Ann");
names.add("David");
names.add("Harry");
names.add("Rob");
names.add("Lance");

int i = 1;
while (i < names.size())
{
    names.remove(i - 1);
    i += 2;
}
```

What will the `ArrayList names` contain as a result of executing this code?

a. [Joe, Mary, Ann, David, Harry, Rob, Lance]
b. [Joe, Ann, Harry, Lance]
c. [Mary, David, Rob]
d. [Mary, Ann, Harry, Rob, Lance]
e. [Mary, Ann, Harry, Rob]

Questions 2 and 3 refer to the following problem description.

Suppose it is known that 10% of the population is left-handed. You are asked to simulate this statistic in a Java program by generating handedness values for 500 random samples of 30 people each. You must record your results from each random sample in such a way as to be able to answer questions similar to, "In how many of the 500 samples were there exactly 3 left-handed people?" or "In how many of the 500 samples were there more than 5 left-handed people?"

2. Which of the following is the best choice to store your information so that you can efficiently answer the questions posed above?

    a. an array of size 500
    b. an array of size 30
    c. an array list of size 500
    d. an array list of size 30
    e. an array of size 31

3. Which of the following code segments will correctly allow you to simulate a left-handed person?

    a. ```
        double probOfLefty = 1.0 / 10.0;
        if (Math.random() < probOfLefty) . . .
        ```

    b.  ```
        double probOfLefty = 1.0 / 10.0;
        if (Math.random() > probOfLefty) . . .
        ```

    c. ```
        double probOfLefty = 1.0 / 30.0;
        if (Math.random() < probOfLefty) . . .
        ```

    d.  ```
        double probOfLefty = 10.0 / 30.0;
        if (Math.random() < probOfLefty) . . .
        ```

    e. ```
        double probOfLefty = 1.0 / 10.0;
        if (Math.random(1, 10)) < probOfLefty) . . .
        ```

4.  Which of the following statements about arrays is **not** true?

    a.  All elements of an array are of the same type.
    b.  Array subscripts must be integers.
    c.  Arrays cannot contain string references as elements.
    d.  Arrays cannot use strings as subscripts.
    e.  A method cannot change the size of an array.

5.  The method weeklyPay is to return the amount of pay an employee will receive for one week's work. The parameters for weeklyPay are the hours worked during the week and the hourly pay. The weekly pay is based on the following standards. If the employee worked 40 hours or less during the week, he receives his regular hourly rate times the number of hours he worked. For every hour over 40 hours, the employee receives time and a half (1.5 times his regular hourly pay). The following information and method header is given.

    ```
    final int MAX_HOURS_IN_WEEK = 168;   // 7 * 24
    /**
        Precondition: 0 <= hoursWorked and
        hoursWorked <= MAX_HOURS_IN_WEEK, 0 < hourlyPay
    */
    public static double weeklyPay(double hoursWorked, double hourlyPay)
    ```

    If all preconditions are satisfied, what assertion can you make as a result of the execution of the following statement?

    ```
    myPay = weeklyPay(hours, rate);
    ```

    a. hours >= 0 and rate >=0
    b. myPay > 0
    c. myPay >= 0
    d. rate >= 0
    e. No assertion can be made.
    ```

6. Consider the following incomplete implementation of the BankAccount class.

```
public class BankAccount
{
    // Constructs a bank account with a given balance.
    // Precondition: initialBalance >= 0
    public BankAccount(double initialBalance)
    {
        balance = initialBalance;
    }

    // Returns the current balance.
    public double getBalance()
    {
        return balance;
    }

    // Deposits amount in account. Updates balance.
    // Precondition: amount >= 0
    public void deposit(double amount)
    {
        balance += amount;
        // Assertion : ???????
    }

    private double balance;
}
```

   If all preconditions are satisfied, which of the following statements should replace ??????? as an assertion after the statement

```
balance += amount;
```

   in the deposit method is executed?

   a. amount < 0
   b. balance > 0
   c. amount <= balance
   d. amount < balance
   e. amount >= balance

7. A Java program contains the following declaration and initialization of an array a.

```
int[] a = {1,2,3,4,5,6,7,8,9};
```

   It is necessary to provide a method to exchange the values of two array elements. Which of the following method implementations and calls to the method will swap the values in two specified positions in the array? For example, if the specified positions were 1 and 2, array a would have the values

```
a = {1,3,2,4,5,6,7,8,9}
```

   after the method is executed.

   I. Method implementation
   ```
   // Swaps the values in array positions b and c.
   public static void swap(int b, int c)
   {
       int  temp = b;
       b = c;
       c = temp;
   }
   Method Call: swap(a[1], a[2]);
   ```

II. Method implementation

```
// Swaps the values in array positions b and c.
public static void swap(int[] arr, int b, int c)
{
    int temp = arr[b];
    arr[b] = arr[c];
    arr[c] = temp;
}
Method Call: swap(a, 1, 2);
```

III. Method implementation

```
// Swaps the values in array positions b and c.
public static void swap(int b, int c, int[] arr)
{
    int temp = arr[b];
    arr[b] = arr[c];
    arr[c] = temp;
}
Method Call: swap(a[1], a[2], a);
```

a.   I only
b.   II only
c.   III only
d.   II and III only
e.   I, II, and III

Questions 8 and 9 refer to the following problem description.

Consider the following incomplete Point class given below.

```
public class Point
{
    /**
        Constructs the point (x1, y1).
        @param x1 the x-coordinate of this point
        @param y1 the y-coordinate of this point
    */
    Point(double x1, double y1) {. . .}

    /**
        @return the x-coordinate of this point
    */
    public double getX() {. . .}

    /**
        @return the y-coordinate of this point
    */
    public double getY() {. . .}

    /**
        Sets the x-coordinate of this point to xValue.
        @param xValue the new x-coordinate
    */
    public void setX(int xValue) { . . .}

    /**
        Sets the y-coordinate of this point to yValue.
        @param yValue the new y-coordinate
    */
    public void setY(int yValue) { . . .}
```

```
/**
    @param p a point to find distance to
    @return the distance from this point to its Point parameter
*/
public double distanceFromPoint(Point p) {. . .}

/**
    @return the string representation of this point: (x,y)
*/
public String toString() {. . .}

private double x;
private double y;
}
```

Suppose the `ArrayList<Point>` `manyPoints` contains more than two `Point` objects and all points in `manyPoints` are unique.

The incomplete code segment below is intended to find the two points that are closest in distance to each other.

```
Point a = manyPoints.get(0);
Point b = manyPoints.get(1);
int numPoints = manyPoints.size();
double minimumDistance = a.distanceFromPoint(b);

for (int i = 0; i < numPoints; i++)
{
    missing code
}
```

8. Which of the following code segments could replace *missing code* so that the segment works as intended?

   a.
```
for (int j = i + 1; j < numPoints; j++)
{
    double currentDistance =
        manyPoints.get(i).distanceFromPoint(manyPoints.get(j));
    if (currentDistance < minimumDistance)
    {
        minimumDistance = currentDistance;
        a = manyPoints.get(i);
        b = manyPoints.get(j);
    }
}
```

   b.
```
for (int j = i; j <= numPoints; j++)
{
    double currentDistance =
        manyPoints.get(i).distanceFromPoint(manyPoints.get(j));
    if (currentDistance < minimumDistance)
    {
        minimumDistance = currentDistance;
        a = manyPoints.get(i);
        b = manyPoints.get(j);
    }
}
```

   c.
```
double currentDistance =
    manyPoints.get(i).distanceFromPoint(manyPoints.get(i + 1));
if (currentDistance < minimumDistance)
{
    minimumDistance = currentDistance;
    a = manyPoints.get(i);
    b = manyPoints.get(i + 1);
}
```

   d.
```
int j = numPoints - 1;
while (j > 0)
{
   double currentDistance =
         manyPoints.get(i).distanceFromPoint(manyPoints.get(j));
   if (currentDistance < minimumDistance)
   {
      minimumDistance = currentDistance;
      a = manyPoints.get(i);
      b = manyPoints.get(j);
   }
   j--;
}
```

   e.
```
int j = i + 1;
while (j < numPoints)
{
   double currentDistance =
         manyPoints.get(i).findDistanceFromPoint(manyPoints.get(j));
   if (currentDistance < minimumDistance)
   {
      minimumDistance = currentDistance;
      a = manyPoints.get(i);
      b = manyPoints.get(j);
   }
   j = i + 1;
}
```

9. **(AB)** The correct algorithm looks at each possible pair of Point objects to determine the two points with the minimum distance between them. Mathematically, for n distinct points, this evaluates to $n(n-1)/2$ possible pairs of points. This would imply that the algorithm would have a big-Oh time efficiency of:

   a. $O(1)$
   b. $O(n)$
   c. $O(2n)$
   d. $O(n^2)$
   e. $O(n^3)$

10. Consider the following code segment.

```
ArrayList<String> names = new ArrayList<String>();
names.add("Joe");
names.add("Mary");
names.set(1, "Ann");
names.add(1, "David");
names.add("Harry");
System.out.println(names);
```

What is printed as a result of executing the code segment?

   a. [Joe, Mary, David, Ann, Harry]
   b. [Joe, Mary, Ann, David, Harry]
   c. [Joe, David, Ann, Harry]
   d. [Ann, David, Joe, Mary Harry]
   e. [Joe, Mary, David, Ann, Harry]

11. A pet adoption agency needs a program to store information about the pets available for adoption. For each pet, they want to keep track of breed, age, and whether or not the pet is friendly to other pets. Which of the following is the best design?

a. Use four unrelated classes: Pet, Breed, Age, Friend.
b. Use one class Pet that has three instance fields: String breed, int age, and boolean friendly.
c. Use a class Pet which has three subclasses: Breed, Age, and Friend.
d. Use a class Pet which has a subclass Breed; Breed has two instance fields int age, and boolean friendly.
e. Use a class Breed that has a subclass Pet that has two instance fields int age, and boolean friendly.

Questions 12–15 refer to the Person, Employee, and Manager classes defined below.

Person **Class**

```java
public class Person
{
    public Person(String theName, int birth, String sex)
    {
        name = theName;
        dob = birth;
        gender = sex;
    }

    public void work()
    {
        getWorkDetail(this);
    }

    public void getWorkDetail(Employee e)
    {
        System.out.println("This person is an Employee.");
    }

    public void getWorkDetail(Manager m)
    {
        System.out.println("This person is the boss.");
    }

    public void getWorkDetail(Person p)
    {
        System.out.println("This person is not an Employee.");
    }

    public String toString()
    {
        return name + "\nDate of Birth: " + dob  + "\n";
    }

    private String name;
    private int dob;
    private String gender;
}
```

Employee **Class**

```java
public class Employee extends Person
{
    public Employee(String theName, int birth, String sex,
            String jobAssignment)
    {
        super(theName, birth, sex);
        department = jobAssignment;
        salary = 30000;
```

```java
    }

    public Employee(String theName, int birth, String sex)
    {
       super(theName, birth, sex);
       department = "Not Assigned";
       salary = 30000;
    }

    public void setSalary(double moneyEarned)
    {
       salary = moneyEarned;
    }

    public double getSalary()
    {
       return salary;
    }

    public void printSalary(Employee e)
    {
       System.out.println("Salary has not changed.");
    }

    public String toString()
    {
       String s = super.toString();
       s += "Department: " + department + "\nSalary = " + getSalary()+ "\n";
       return s;
    }

    String department;
    double salary;
}
```

Manager **Class**

```java
public class Manager extends Employee
{
    public Manager(String theName, int birth, String sex)
    {
       super(theName, birth, sex, "Manager");
       double oldSalary = getSalary();
       double newSalary = 0.20 * oldSalary + oldSalary;
       setSalary(newSalary);
    }

    public void printSalary(Manager m)
    {
       System.out.println("More money.");
    }

    public void printSalary(Employee e)
    {
       System.out.println("Regular pay.");
    }
}
```

12. Which of the following declarations is **not** legal?

    a. `Person p1 = new Person("Person1", 1988, "Male");`
    b. `Employee e1 = new Employee("Employee1", 1980, "Female", "Foods");`
    c. `Employee e2 = new Manager("Employee1", 1981, "Female");`
    d. `Person e3 = new Manager("Person2", 1987, "Male");`
    e. `Manager m1 = new Employee("Employee1", 1980, "Female", "Art");`

13. What is printed as a result of executing the following code segment in a client program?

    ```
    Employee e1 = new Manager("Manager1", 1976, "Female");
    System.out.println(e1);
    Person p3 = new Employee("Person3", 1980, "Male", "Operations");
    System.out.println(p3);
    ```

    a. ```
    Manager1
    Date of Birth: 1976
    Department: Not Assigned
    Salary = 36000.0

    Person3
    Date of Birth: 1980
    Department: Operations
    Salary = 30000.0
    ```

    b. ```
    Manager1
    Date of Birth: 1976
    Department: Not Assigned
    Salary = 30000.0

    Person3
    Date of Birth: 1980
    Department: Operations
    Salary = 30000.0
    ```

    c. ```
    Manager1
    Date of Birth: 1976
    Department: Manager
    Salary = 36000.0

    Person3
    Date of Birth: 1980
    Department: Operations
    Salary = 30000.0
    ```

    d. ```
    Manager1
    Date of Birth: 1976
    Department: Not Assigned
    Salary = 30000.0

    Person3
    Date of Birth: 1980
    ```

    e. An error message would be printed because `Manager` does not define a `toString` method.

14. What is printed as a result of the following code segment in a client program?

    ```
    Employee e1 = new Employee("Manager1", 1976, "Female");
    e1.work();
    ```

    a. *This person is an employee.*
    b. *This person is the boss.*
    c. *This person is not an employee.*
    d. Nothing would be printed. A `ClassCastException` would be thrown.
    e. Nothing would be printed. A compile-time error would occur.

15. What is printed as the result of the following code in a client program?

```
Employee e1 = new Employee("Employee1", 1972, "Female");
Employee e2 = new Manager("Employee2", 1976, "Female");
Manager m1 = new Manager("Manager1", 1980, "Male");

e2.printSalary(e2);
e1.printSalary(e1);
m1.printSalary(m1);
e1.printSalary(m1);
```

   a.   Regular pay.
       Salary has not changed.
       More money.
       Salary has not changed.

   b.   Regular pay.
       Regular pay.
       More money.
       Regular pay.

   c.   Salary has not changed.
       Salary has not changed.
       More money.
       Salary has not changed.

   d.   Regular pay.
       Regular pay.
       More money.
       More money.

   e.   Salary has not changed.
       Salary has not changed.
       More money.
       More money.

16. Consider the following declaration and initializations.

```
int[] a = new int[20];
```

What is the outcome of the following code segment?

```
for (int k = 0; k < 20; k++)
{
    int r = (int)(Math.random() * 100 + 1);
    int j = k;
    while (j >= 0 && r != a[j])
        j--;
    if (j < 0)
        a[k] = r;
    else
        k--;
}
```

   a.   Array a contains 20 random integers in the range of 1 to 100 inclusive in ascending order.
   b.   Array a contains 20 random integers in the range of 1 to 100 inclusive in descending order.
   c.   Array a contains 20 copies of one random integer in the range of 0 to 100 inclusive.
   d.   Array a contains 20 non-duplicated random integers in the range of 1 to 100 inclusive.
   e.   Array a contains 20 non-duplicated random integers in the range of 0 to 100 inclusive.

17. **(AB)** Consider the following code segment.

```java
public int mystery(int[] a, int value)
{
    int current = 0;
    // Invariant
    while (current < a.length)
    {
        if (a[current] == value)
            return current;
        else
            current++;
    }
    return -1;
}
```

What is the loop invariant of the `while` loop above?

a. `current <= a.length` and `value` was not found in `a[0]...a[current]`
b. `current < a.length` and `value` was not found in `a[0]...a[current - 1]`
c. `current <= a.length` and `value` was not found in `a[0]...a[current - 1]`
d. `value` is found in `a[current]` or `value = -1`
e. `value` was not found in `a` or `value = a[current - 1]`

18. The method `noDuplicates` is intended to return an array of 20 non-duplicated random integers in the range of 1 to 100 inclusive. Which of the algorithms below successfully completes this task?

I.
```java
public static int[] noDuplicates()
{
    int[] a = new int[20];
    int[] b = new int[101];
    int n = 100;
    for (int i = 0; i < b.length; i++)
        b[i] = i;
    for (int k = 0; k < 20; k++)
    {
        int r = (int)(Math.random() * n + 1);
        a[k] = b[r];
        b[r] = b[n];
        n--;
    }
    return a;
}
```

II.
```java
public static int[] noDuplicates()
{
    int[] a = new int[20];
    int[] b = new int[100];
    int n = 100;
    for (int i = 0; i < b.length; i++)
        b[i] = i + 1;
    for (int k = 0; k < 20; k++)
    {
        int r = (int)(Math.random() * 100);
        int temp = b[r];
        b[r] = b[k];
        b[k] = temp;
    }
    for (int i = 0; i < 20; i++)
        a[i] = b[i];
    return a;
}
```

```
III. public static int[] noDuplicates()
     {
         int[] a = new int[20];
         ArrayList<Integer> b = new ArrayList<Integer>(); // Generic
         for (int i = 0; i < 100; i++)
             b.add(i + 1); // Auto-boxing
         for (int k = 0; k < 20; k++)
         {
             int r = (int)(Math.random() * b.size());
             a[k] = b.get(r); // Auto-unboxing
             b.remove(r);
         }
         return a;
     }
```

    a. I only
    b. II only
    c. III only
    d. I and III only
    e. I, II, and III

Questions 19 and 20 refer to the following interface and classes.

```
interface SampleInterface
{
    void someMethod();
}
```

```
class SampleClassA implements SampleInterface
{
    public void someMethod()
    {
        System.out.println("test in A");
    }
}
```

```
class SampleClassB extends SampleClassA
{
    public void someMethod()
    {
        System.out.println("test in B");
    }
}
```

19. Which of the following declarations are legal?

    I.   `SampleClassA a = new SampleClassB();`
    II. `SampleInterface s1 = new SampleClassA();`
    III. `SampleInterface s2 = new SampleInterface();`

    a. I only
    b. II only
    c. III only
    d. I and II only
    e. I, II, and III

20. Consider the following incompletely defined method in a client program.

    ```
    public static void testInClient(SampleInterface s) {. . .}
    ```

    Which of the following statements is **true** concerning this method?

    a. The method header is illegal because the parameter type cannot be an interface type.
    b. The method header is legal and an object of any class that extends `SampleInterface` can be passed as a parameter to the method.
    c. The method header is legal but only a variable that is declared as `SampleInterface` type can be passed as a parameter to the method.
    d. The method header is legal and an object of any class that implements `SampleInterface` can be passed as a parameter to the method.
    e. The method header is legal but only objects of type `SampleInterface` and subclasses of `SampleInterface` can be passed as a parameter to the method.

Free Response

1. There are many card games that are played with a deck of 52 playing cards. In this deck of 52 cards, there are 13 cards with denominations 2, 3, 4, 5, 6, 7, 8, 9, 10, Jack, Queen, King, and Ace in each of four suits (Clubs, Diamonds, Hearts, and Spades). The incomplete `Card` class is below.

`Card` **Class**

```java
public class Card implements Comparable
{
    /**
        Constructs a card with given suit and denomination. Value is the card
        number if the card is between 2 and 10 inclusive, 11 for "J", 12 for
        "Q", 13 for "K", 14 for "A".
        @param denom a String representing the card denomination, i.e., "2",
        "Jack", "Ace"
        @param suit "Hearts", "Diamonds", "Clubs", or "Spades"
    */
    public Card(String denom, String suit)
    {
        mySuit = suit;
        myDenom = denom;
        myValue = getValue();
    }

    /**
        Gets the card's suit.
        @return the suit
    */
    public String getSuit() {. . .}

    /**
        Gets the card's denomination.
        @return the String representation of the denomination of the
        card: 2,3,4,5,6,7,8,9,10, Jack, Queen, King, or Ace
    */
    public String getDenomination(){. . .}

    /**
        Gets the card's value.
        @return the value of the card. The value is the card number
        if the card is between 2 and 10 inclusive, 11 for "J",
        12 for "Q", 13 for "K", 14 for "A"
    */
    public int getValue(){. . .}
```

```
    /**
        @return the String representation of the card
    */
    public String toString()
    {
        return getDenomination() + " of " + getSuit();
    }

    public int compareTo(Object other)
    {
        Card c = (Card) other;
        return myValue - c.myValue;
    }

    public boolean equals(Object other)
    {
        return compareTo(other) == 0;
    }

    private String mySuit;
    private String myDenom;
    private int myValue;
}
```

Many card games require that the player is dealt a *hand* of cards. The number of cards in a hand is dependent on the card game being played. The incomplete Hand class is below.

Hand Class

```
public class Hand
{
    /**
        Constructs new hand with capacity for numCards cards.
        @param numCards number of cards in card hand
    */
    public Hand(int numCards)
    {
        // Code goes here
    }

    /**
        If possible, adds a card to this hand.
        @param c the card to add
    */
    public void addCard(Card c)
    {
        // Code goes here
    }

    /**
        Tests whether the hand is full.
        @return true if hand is full (cardsInHand = myHand.length),
        false otherwise
    */
    public boolean isHandFull() {. . .}

    /**
        Reorders cards in ascending order.
    */
    public void sortCards()
```

```
/**
    Gets a copy of myHand.
    @return a copy of the array of Cards in myHand
*/
public Card[] getHand()
{
    Card[] cards = new Card[myHand.length];
    for (int i = 0; i < myHand.length; i++)
        cards[i] = new Card(myHand[i].getDenomination(),
                myHand[i].getSuit());
    return cards;
}

/**
    Prints the Cards in Hand to screen.
*/
public void printHand()
{
    // Code goes here
}

private Card[] myHand;
private int cardsInHand;
    // Actual number of cards in myHand at a particular time
}
```

Poker is a card game requiring a Hand of 5 Cards. The value of a poker hand is based on the combination of denominations and suits of the individual cards in the hand. These combinations are identified in the incomplete definition of the PokerHand class below and are explained in the individual method comments.

PokerHand **Class**

```
public class PokerHand extends Hand
{
    /**
        Constructs an empty poker hand.
    */
    public PokerHand()
    {
        super(MAX_CARDS);
    }

    /**
        Precondition: isHandFull() returns true
        @return true if all cards in this hand are the same suit;
        otherwise return false
    */
    public boolean isFlush()
    {
        // Code goes here
    }

    /**
        Precondition: isHandFull() returns true
        @return true if the cards in this hand are of consecutive
        values when ordered; otherwise return false
    */
    public boolean isStraight()
    {
        // Code goes here
    }
```

```
/**
    Precondition: isHandFull() returns true
    @return true if the cards in this hand are consecutive values when
    ordered and all cards are the same suit; otherwise, return false
*/
public boolean isStraightFlush()
{
    // Code goes here
}


/**
    Precondition: isHandFull() returns true
    @return true if the cards in this hand are consecutive values
    with the largest value being 14 when ordered and all cards are
    the same suit; otherwise, return false
*/
public boolean isRoyalFlush()
{
    // Code goes here
}


/**
    Precondition: isHandFull() returns true
    @return true if the hand consists of three cards of one value
    and 2 cards of another value; otherwise, return false
*/
public boolean isFullHouse()
{
    // Code goes here
}

private static final int MAX_CARDS = 5;
}
```

In writing solutions to the following problems, assume that methods provided in the classes above work as specified. Also assume that the methods you write in parts previous to the question you are working on work as specified, regardless of what you wrote. Solutions that reimplement functionality provided, rather than invoking the appropriate method, will not receive full credit.

a. Write the `Hand` constructor that constructs an empty card hand with capacity for `numCards` cards, where `numCards` is the constructor's one `int` parameter. Use the header below.

```
public Hand(int numCards)
```

b. The `Hand` method `addCard` adds a card to this `Hand` if the hand has fewer than `cardsInHand` cards (the maximum number of cards in the hand). Use the following header in writing `addCard`.

```
public void addCard(Card c)
```

c. Write the `Hand` method `printHand` that prints the `String` representations of the cards in the hand. Use the following header in writing `printHand`.

```
public void printHand()
```

d. Write the `PokerHand` method `isFlush` that returns `true` if all cards in hand are the same suit, otherwise returns `false`. For example, `isFlush` would return `true` for the poker hand composed of the five cards 10 of Clubs, 2 of Clubs, 6 of Clubs, 9 of Clubs, and Ace of Clubs. Use the following header in writing `isFlush`.

```
public boolean isFlush()
```

e. Write the `PokerHand` method `isStraight` that returns `true` if the cards in this hand have consecutive values when ordered, otherwise returns `false`. For example, `isStraight` would return `true` for the poker hand composed of the five cards 10 of Clubs, Jack of Clubs, 8 of Hearts, 7 of Diamonds, and 9 of Spades. Use the following header in writing `isStraight`.

```
public boolean isStraight()
```

f. Write the `PokerHand` method `isStraightFlush` that returns `true` if the cards in this hand are all the same suit and have consecutive values when ordered, otherwise returns `false`. For example, `isStraightFlush` would return `true` for the poker hand composed of the five cards 3 of Clubs, 5 of Clubs, 6 of Clubs, 4 of Clubs, and 7 of Clubs. Use the following header.

```
public boolean isStraightFlush()
```

g. Write the `PokerHand` method `isRoyalFlush` that returns `true` if the cards in this hand are all the same suit, have consecutive values when ordered, and the highest card value is 14 (Ace); otherwise returns `false`. For example, `isRoyalFlush` would return `true` for the poker hand composed of the five cards 10 of Clubs, Jack of Clubs, Queen of Clubs, King of Clubs, and Ace of Clubs. Use the following header in writing `isRoyalFlush`.

```
public boolean isRoyalFlush()
```

h. Write the `PokerHand` method `isFullHouse` that returns `true` if there are 3 cards of one denomination and 2 cards of a second denomination, otherwise returns `false`. For example, `isFullHouse` would return `true` for the poker hand composed of the five cards 10 of Clubs, 3 of Clubs, 10 of Diamonds, 10 of Spades, and 3 of Diamonds. Use the following header.

```
public boolean isFullHouse()
```

2. The need to use descriptive statistics in many areas has grown enormously in the past 50 or so years. Your task is to complete the utility class `Stats` that includes methods to calculate the most commonly used statistical measurements. The incomplete `Stats` class appears below.

`Stats` **Class**

```
public class Stats
{
    /**
       @param sampleData an array of the data
       @return an array with the values of sampleData sorted in
       increasing numerical order
    */
    private static int[] sortValues(int[] sampleData){. . .}

    /**
       Precondition: sampleData.length > 0
       @param sampleData an array of the data
       @return the average of the values in sampleData
    */
    public static double mean(int[] sampleData)
    {
        // Code goes here
    }

    /**
       Precondition: sampleData.length > 0
       @param sampleData an array of the data
       @return the variance of the values in sampleData
    */
    public static double variance(int[] sampleData)
    {
        // Code goes here
    }
```

```
/**
    Precondition: sampleData.length > 0
    @param sampleData an array of the data
    @return the standard deviation of the values in sampleData
*/
public static double standardDeviation(int[] sampleData)
{
    // Code goes here
}


/**
    Precondition: sampleData.length > 0
    @param sampleData an array of the data
    @return the mode of the values in sampleData. If there is more than
    one mode, returns the smallest mode value
*/
public static int mode(int[] sampleData)
{
    // Code goes here
}


/**
    Precondition: sampleData.length > 0
    @param sampleData an array of the data
    @return the median of the values in sampleData
*/
public static double median(int[] sampleData)
{
    // Code goes here
}


/**
    Prints a stem and leaf plot representing the values in sampleData.
    Precondition: sampleData.length > 0; for all j such that
    0 <= j < sampleData.length, sampleData[j] <= 100.
    @param sampleData an array of the data
*/
public static void stemAndLeafPlot(int[] sampleData)
{
    // Code goes here
}
}
```

In writing solutions to the following problems, assume that the method `sortValues` provided in the class above works as specified. Also assume that the methods you write in parts previous to the question you are working on work as specified, regardless of what you wrote. Solutions that reimplement functionality provided, rather than invoking the appropriate method, will not receive full credit.

a. Write the `Stats` method `mean` that will return the average of the values in `sampleData`. The mean of n numbers is their sum divided by n. Use the header below in writing `mean`.

```
public static double mean(int[] sampleData)
```

b. One of the most useful statistical measures is the standard deviation. This is a measure of data variation from the mean. To calculate the standard deviation, find the difference between each value in the data set and the mean of the data set. Sum the squares of these differences. Divide this sum by $n - 1$ and take the square root of this number. Therefore, the standard deviation of a set of values, denoted by s, is calculated as

$$s = \sqrt{\frac{\sum (X - \overline{X})^2}{n - 1}}$$

and its square, the *variance*, is

$$s^2 = \frac{\sum (X - \overline{X})^2}{n - 1}$$

where $\overline{X}$ is the mean of the values in the set of data.

Write the `Stats` method `variance` that will return the variance of the values in `sampleData`. The variance is found by dividing the sum of the squared deviations from the mean by $n - 1$ where n is the number of items in `sampleData`. The formula to calculate the variance is given above. Use the header below in writing `variance`.

```
public static double variance(int[] sampleData)
```

c. Write the `Stats` method `standardDeviation` that will return the standard deviation of the values in `sampleData`. The standard deviation is found using the formula for s above. Use the header below.

```
public static double standardDeviation(int[] sampleData)
```

d. Write the `Stats` method `mode` that will return the *mode* of the values in `sampleData`. The *mode* is the value that occurs with the most frequency in the set of values. If there is more than one mode, the smallest mode value will be returned. Use the header below in writing `mode`.

```
public static int mode(int[] sampleData)
```

e. Write the `Stats` method `median` that will return the median of the values in `sampleData`. If `sampleData` contains n items arranged in increasing order, the *median* is defined to be the value of the middle item if n is odd and the mean of the two middle items if n is even. Use the header below.

```
public static double median(int[] sampleData)
```

f. Write the `Stats` method `stemAndLeafPlot` that will illustrate the values in `sampleData` graphically. A stem-and-leaf plot displays the data by breaking each number into two parts: `number / 10` (informally called the tens digit) and `number % 10` (informally called the units digit), grouping together the values that share the same tens digit. The tens digit is aligned vertically and the units digits is displayed to the right. The value 67 is represented as 6 | 7. Single digit numbers are assumed to have a "tens digit" of 0. The numbers 100 – 109 would be assumed to have a "tens digit" of 10. For example, if

```
sampleData = { 14, 23, 24, 25, 35, 36, 40, 42, 42, 43, 43, 45, 58,
        67, 68, 82, 88, 91, 94, 95 }
```

the stem-and-leaf display would be:

```
 0  |
 1  | 4
 2  | 3 4 5
 3  | 5 6
 4  | 0 2 2 3 3 5
 5  | 8
 6  | 7 8
 7  |
 8  | 2 8
 9  | 1 4 5
10  |
```

Use the header below in writing `stemAndLeafPlot`. and assume that the maximum stem value is 10.

```
/**
   Precondition: for all i such that 0 <= i < sampleData.length, 0 <
   sampleData[i] <= 109
*/
public static void stemAndLeafPlot(int[] sampleData)
```

3.   In order to satisfy national certification requirements, an Emergency Medical Technician (EMT) is required to stay current by completing continuing education courses. Each continuing education course is designated as *required* or *elective* and is worth a designated number of continuing education units (CEUs). An EMT is required to complete at least 48 required credits and at least 48 elective credits.

You are to design and implement classes to represent an Emergency Medical Technician and a Continuing Education Course.

The information about an Emergency Medical Technician includes a name (String), a social security number (String), and a record of all courses completed by the EMT. It is possible to retrieve all of this information about an EMT. Courses are added to the EMT's record but not deleted.

The course information includes a course name, the number of continuing education credits the course is worth, and a designation indicating whether this course is a required course or not.

An EMT's record is periodically reviewed to see if the EMT has satisfied the requirements of completing a minimum of 48 required credits and a minimum of 48 elective credits.

CHAPTER **14**

(Covers *Java Concepts for AP Computer Science* Chapter 13)

Recursion

TOPIC OUTLINE
14.1 Thinking Recursively
14.2 Permutations

14.3 Tracing Through Recursive Methods
14.4 The Efficiency of Recursion

■ Topic Summary

14.1   Thinking Recursively

In Chapter 7 we discussed iterative control structures (the `for` loop and the `while` loop). In this chapter we look at another method of repetition, recursion. A recursive computation solves a problem by calling itself to solve a smaller piece of the problem. There are three basic rules for developing recursive algorithms.

• Know how to take one step.
• Break each problem down into one step plus a smaller problem.
• Know how and when to stop.

Here is the method for converting and printing the decimal number 100 to a binary number (base 2) that was presented in Chapter 5 of this guide.

    100 / 2 = 50 remainder 0
    50 / 2 = 25 remainder 0
    25 / 2 = 12 remainder 1
    12 / 2 = 6 remainder 0
    6 / 2 = 3 remainder 0
    3 / 2 = 1 remainder 1
    1 / 2 = 0 remainder 1

Reading the remainders in reverse order, we have 1100100 which is the binary representation for the decimal number 100.

Now let's look at this same problem recursively.

- First, know how to take one step: A step seems to be "Divide by 2; Note the quotient and the remainder."
- Second, break each problem down into one step plus a smaller problem:
  - The quotient is smaller than the original number.
  - The above process can be applied to the quotient.
  - Therefore you have a smaller problem.
- Know how and when to stop: Stop when the quotient is 0. Actually, the recursion stops when the quotient <= 0. Print out the remainders when you reach a quotient of 0. Remember that in the original example from *Advanced Topic 4.2* on page 137 of your textbook, the remainders were read "from bottom up". The last remainder must be printed first.

Now let's look at code.

Example 14.1

```java
/**
    Precondition: decimalNum >= 0
    @param the decimal number to be converted to binary
*/
public static void convertToBinary(int decimalNum)
{
    if (decimalNum < 0)
        throw new IllegalArgumentException("number must be >= 0");

    int quotient = decimalNum / 2;
    int remainder = decimalNum % 2;

    if (quotient > 0)
    {
        convertToBinary(quotient);    // Smaller problem
    }

    System.out.print(remainder);    // After all recursive calls
                                    // have been made, last
                                    // remainder printed first

}
```

Divide the decimal number by 2 and remember the remainder. Keep repeating this process with a smaller decimal number (quotient) until the quotient <= 0. Then, print out the remainder for each call. As long as the quotient is > 0, another recursive call is made (no printing occurs yet). When the quotient is <= 0, the `if` statement is not executed and the algorithm continues by executing the `System.out.print` statement. This statement is executed for each recursive call that was made beginning with the last. The "stack" of recursive calls is "unstacked." Thus, the remainders will be printed in the "correct" order. That is, the result on the screen will be the binary representation of the decimal number we started with.

Do you think this solution would work to convert decimal numbers to octal numbers? To hexadecimal numbers?

Section 13.1 in your text presents another simple example using recursion with triangle numbers. This example again demonstrates that a recursive solution solves a problem by using the solution of the same problem with simpler values.

14.2   Permutations

Many gas pumps have displays that spin digits (either analog or digital) while the gas is being pumped into your car's gas tank. The display's digits change to indicate the amount of gas in the tank and the current price.

We'll look at one of these displays and recursively generate the spinning of the digits. Our GasPumpDisplay class will allow us to create a "gas pump" display with a specified number of display places and will allow us to specify the highest digit in use. We will simplify a gas pump display by using a smaller display of only three digits where the digits are in the limited range of 0–4 inclusive.

Example 14.2

```java
// Permutation generator
public class GasPumpDisplay
{
   /**
      Constructs a display of digits.
      @param numberOfPositions the number of positions displayed
   */
   public GasPumpDisplay(int numberOfPositions)
   {
      digits = numberOfPositions;
      if (digits > 1)
         tail = new GasPumpDisplay(digits - 1);
      else
         tail = null;
      currentDigit = 0;
   }

   /**
      Gets the next permutation display
      @return the next permutation display
   */
   public String nextElement()
   {
```

```
            String r = null;
            if (digits == 1)   // filling last position in string
            {
               r = currentDigit + "";
               currentDigit++;
               return r;
            }

            // Permutation not yet complete
            r = currentDigit + tail.nextElement();
            if (!tail.hasMoreElements())
            {
               currentDigit++;
               tail = new GasPumpDisplay(digits - 1);
            }
            return r;
         }

         /**
            Returns true if there are more elements.
            @return true if there are more elements, false otherwise
         */
         public boolean hasMoreElements()
         {
            return currentDigit <= MAX_DIGIT;
         }

         private int digits;
         private GasPumpDisplay tail;
         private int currentDigit;
         private static final MAX_DIGIT = 4;
      }
```

```
      /**
         This program tests the permutation generator.
      */
      public class GasPumpTester
      {
         public static void main(String[] args)
         {
            GasPumpDisplay d = new GasPumpDisplay(3);   // 3 digits in
                                                        // display
            while (d.hasMoreElements())
               System.out.println(d.nextElement());
         }
      }
```

GasPumpTester prints the following permutations.

000 001 002 003 004 010 011 012 013 014 020 021 022 023 024 030 031 032 033 034
040 041 042 043 044 100 101 102 103 104 110 111 112 113 114 120 121 122 123 124
130 131 132 133 134 140 141 142 143 144 200 201 202 203 204 210 211 212 213 214
220 221 222 223 224 230 231 232 233 234 240 241 242 243 244 300 301 302 303 304
310 311 312 313 314 320 321 322 323 324 330 331 332 333 334 340 341 342 343 344

400 401 402 403 404 410 411 412 413 414 420 421 422 423 424 430 431 432 433 434 440 441 442 443 444

Section 13.2 of your text demonstrates a `PermutationGenerator` class that generates the permutations of a string using a similar approach.

14.3 Tracing Through Recursive Methods

The AP Exam may include multiple-choice questions that give a recursive algorithm and then ask questions about that algorithm. You need to be able to analyze the algorithm and hand-simulate (trace through) the algorithm. Consider the recursive method below.

Example 14.3

```
public class MysteryMaker
{
    /**
       Constructor.
    */
    public MysteryMaker() {. . .}

    /**
       Precondition: x > 0, y > 0
       @return ?????
    */
    public int mystery(int x, int y)
    {
        if (y == 1)
            return x;
        else
            return x * mystery(x, y - 1);
    }
    . . .
}
```

Suppose the statements

```
MysteryMaker magic = new MysteryMaker();
System.out.println(magic.mystery(2, 5));
```

were executed. Examining the method in Example 14.3, we see that our three rules of recursion are satisfied.

- Taking one step is defined in the general case (the `else` clause).
- `y` starts with a positive integer value and each recursive call is made with a smaller `y` (a smaller problem).
- The end condition (base case) occurs when `y == 1`.

Tracing through the program requires us to write down the work done for each recursive call. When the end condition is reached, work backwards, substituting values into the recursive calls.

Figure 14.2

```
mystery(2, 5) = 2 * mystery(2, 4);                          2 * 16 = 32
                      ↓                                          ↑
                2 * mystery(2, 3);                          2 * 8 = 16
                      ↓                                          ↑
                  2 * mystery(2, 2);                        2 * 4 = 8
                        ↓                                        ↑
                    2 * mystery(2, 1);                      2 * 2 = 4
                          ↓                                      ↑
                          2 ─────────────────────────────→ 2
```

From Figure 14.2, we can conclude the following:

- The statement `System.out.println(mystery(2, 5))` would print *32*.
- The number of times the call to `mystery` was made, including the original call, is 5.
- `mystery(x, y)` returns x^y.

14.4   The Efficiency of Recursion

Although recursion is always fun, it's not always the most efficient way to solve a problem. The example of finding the nth Fibonacci number, which is illustrated in Section 13.4 of your text, certainly demonstrates this!

One of the best known recursive functions, Ackerman's Function, is not very useful, but it is very interesting. For *lots* of practice with tracing a recursive function, try tracing this algorithm to evaluate `acker(2, 3)` (or any other call with small numbers). This function grows very fast! By tracing Ackerman's function, you can see that the same method call is executed multiple times.

$$
acker(x, y) = \begin{cases} y + 1 & \text{when } x = 0 \\ acker(x - 1, 1) & \text{when } x \ != 0, \ y = 0 \\ acker(x - 1, acker(x, y - 1)) & \text{when } x \ != 0, \ y \ != 0 \end{cases}
$$

After you try this by hand, test it out by writing a recursive method to solve the problem. If you try to evaluate this function for large values your program will report a "stack fault". *Common Error 13.1* on page 592 of your text discusses stack faults. Although your method may not be infinitely recursive, after some number of calls, all the computer memory that is available is used, and a stack fault occurs.

■ Topics That Are Useful But Not Tested

- Section 13.3 of your text demonstrates the use of helper methods to simplify recursive solutions. Section 13.5 discusses mutual recursion. Neither of these topics is specifically listed in the AP CS Topic Outline but both are extensions of recursive solutions. You should read through the examples presented in your text.

■ Things to Remember When Taking the AP Exam

- Recursion is a topic for both AP CS A and AP CS AB. The programming exercises at the end of Chapter 13 in your text provide great practice in writing recursive methods.
- It is a common error to use a `while` statement when an `if` statement should be used to check for the base case in a recursive function. Check your work!
- A recursive solution is not necessarily more efficient than an iterative solution to the same problem.
- Remember to include an end condition for recursive solutions. Infinite recursions are undesirable!
- Write recursive solutions when the problem statement is defined recursively or when explicitly instructed to do so. Do not use recursion as a substitute for iteration.

■ Key Words

You should understand the terms below. The AP CS Exam questions may include references to these terms. The citations in parentheses next to each term identify the page numbers where it is defined and/or discussed in *Java Concepts for AP Computer Science*, 5th ed.

infinite recursion (592) permutation (592) recursive solution (589)

■ Connecting the Detailed Topic Outline to the Text

The citations in parentheses identify where information in the outline can be located in *Java Concepts for AP Computer Science*, 5th ed.

- Thinking Recursively (597–600)
- Permutations (592–596)
- Tracing through Recursive Methods (596)
- The Efficiency of Recursion (602–608)

■ Practice Questions

Multiple Choice

Questions 1 and 2 refer to the following three code segments.

```
I.  public static void mysteryPrint(int n)
    {
        if (n > 0)
        {
            mysteryPrint(n - 1);
        }
        System.out.println(n);
    }
```

```
II. public static void mysteryPrint(int n)
    {
        if (n > 0)
        {
            mysteryPrint(n - 1);
            System.out.println(n);
        }
    }

III. public static void mysteryPrint(int n)
    {
        if (n > 0)
        {
            mysteryPrint(n - 1);
        }
        else
        {
            System.out.println(n);
        }
    }
```

1. Assuming that the method `mysteryPrint` is called with a positive integer parameter, which statement about methods I, II, and III above is **true**?

    a. All three methods produce the same output.
    b. Methods I and II produce the same output that is different from the output produced by Method III.
    c. Methods I and III produce the same output that is different from the output produced by Method II.
    d. Methods II and III produce the same output that is different from the output produced by Method I.
    e. All three methods produce different outputs.

2. If the statement

    ```
    mysteryPrint(5);
    ```

    were executed, what output would be produced by code segment II ?

a. 0	b. 1	c. 5	d. 5	e. 0
1	2	4	4	
2	3	3	3	
3	4	2	2	
4	5	1	1	
5		0		

3. Which of the following statements is **true** about recursive methods?

    a. Iterative methods are always easier to write than recursive methods.
    b. Recursive solutions to methods are always more efficient than iterative solutions.
    c. For recursion to terminate there must be a special non-recursive case for simple inputs.
    d. If a problem is solved both iteratively and recursively, the solutions will always have the same efficiency.
    e. Recursion is the most elegant and appropriate way to solve all problems.

4. Consider the recursive method whose definition appears below.

```
public static String mysteryString(String s)
{
    if (s.length() == 1)
        return s;
    else
        return s.substring(s.length() - 1)
                + mysteryString(s.substring(0, s.length() - 1));
}
```

What is the result of the following call?

```
System.out.println(mysteryString("computer"));
```

a. *computer* is printed to the screen.
b. *retupmoc* is printed to the screen.
c. *c* is printed to the screen.
d. A stack fault occurs.
e. A `StringIndexOutOfBoundsException` is thrown.

Questions 5 and 6 refer to the following recursive method definition.

```
public static int foo(int n)
{
    if (n < 10)
        return 1;
    else
        return 1 + foo(n / 10);
}
```

5. Which of the following statements best describes the value returned by method `foo`?

a. `foo` returns the sum of the digits in its positive integer parameter.
b. `foo` returns the sum of the digits in its integer parameter.
c. `foo` returns the number of digits in its positive integer parameter.
d. `foo` returns the number of digits in its integer parameter.
e. `foo` returns the number of 1's in its integer parameter.

6. If the following statement is executed,

```
int n = foo(1234);
```

what is the total number of times the method `foo` is called (including the original call)?

a. 1
b. 2
c. 3
d. 4
e. 5

Questions 7–9 refer to the `ArraySearcher` class incompletely defined below.

```
public class ArraySearcher
{
    public ArraySearcher(int[] anArray)
    {
        a = anArray;
```

```
        }

        public int searchFor(int n)
        {
            int low = 0;
            int high = a.length - 1;
            return search(low, high, n);
        }

        /**
            @param low lowest index to search
            @param high highest index to search
            @param key int being searched for
            @return the index in the array a where key
            occurs or -1 if key is not found in a.
        */
        public int search(int low, int high, int key)
        {
            if (low > high)
                return -1;
            else
            {
                int mid = (low + high) / 2;
                if (key == a[mid])
                    return mid;
                else if (key < a[mid])
                    return search(low, mid - 1, key);
                else
                    return search(mid + 1, high, key);
            }
        }

        private int[] a;
    }
```

The recursive method search is intended to locate the value key in array a. The method is to return the index of the first location of key in a and return -1 if key is not found in a.

7. Under which conditions will this work as intended?

    a. search will work as intended only if key is not found in a.
    b. search will work as intended only if key is in position 0.
    c. search will work as intended only if array a is sorted in ascending order.
    d. search will work as intended only if array a is sorted in descending order.
    e. search will never work as intended.

8. Assume that a client program included the following declarations and method calls,

```
    int[] a = {1, 21, 32, 45, 58, 61, 72, 80, 99, 100, 101};
    ArraySearcher searcher = new ArraySearcher(a);
    int pos = searcher.searchFor(58);
```

How many times is the method `search` called before a value is returned?

a. 1
b. 2
c. 3
d. 4
e. 5

9. Assume that a client program included the following declarations and method calls,

```
int[] a = {6, 5, 4, 3, 2, 1};
ArraySearcher searcher = new ArraySearcher(a);
int pos = searcher.searchFor(5);
```

What value would be assigned to `pos`?

a. −1
b. 0
c. 1
d. No value would be assigned. There would be a compile-time error.
e. No value would be assigned. This would result in infinite recursion.

10. Consider the `Triangle` class defined below.

```
public class Triangle
{
    public Triangle(int aWidth)
    {
        width = aWidth;
    }

    public int getArea()
    {
        if (width <= 0) return 0;
        if (width == 1) return 1;
        Triangle smallerTriangle = new Triangle(width - 1);
        int smallerArea = smallerTriangle.getArea();
        return smallerArea + width;
    }

    private int width;
}
```

Suppose a client program included the following code segment.

```
Triangle t = new Triangle(4);
int area = t.getArea();
```

What value would be assigned to `area`?

a. 1
b. 4
c. 5
d. 10
e. 15

Free Response Questions

1. Euclid's Algorithm can be used to find the greatest common divisor (gcd) of two integers. The algorithm works recursively as illustrated in the example below.

Method Call		Recursive Method Call
gcd(3388, 436)	3388 = 7 * 436 + 336	gcd(3388, 436) = gcd(436, 336)
gcd(436, 336)	436 = 1 * 336 + 100	gcd(436, 336) = gcd(336, 100)
gcd(336, 100)	336 = 3 * 100 + 36	gcd(336, 100) = gcd(100, 36)
gcd(100, 36)	100 = 2 * 36 + 28	gcd(100, 36) = gcd(36, 28)
gcd(36, 28)	36 = 1 * 28 + 8	gcd(36, 28) = gcd(28, 8)
gcd(28, 8)	28 = 3 * 8 + 4	gcd(28, 8) = gcd(8, 4)
gcd(8, 4)	8 = 2 * 4 + 0	gcd(8, 4) = gcd(4, 0)
gcd(4, 0) = 4		

Therefore, gcd(3388, 436) = 4.

You are to implement the recursive method for Euclid's Algorithm. Write your method using the method header below.

```
/**
    Precondition: num1 >= 0, num2 >= 0
    Returns the greatest common divisor of num1 and num2
*/
public static int gcd(int num1, int num2)
```

2. The area of a triangle with corner points $(x1, y1)$, $(x2, y2)$, and $(x3, y3)$ can be computed as:

$$A = \frac{|x1 * y2 + x2 * y3 + x3 * y1 - y1 * x2 - y2 * x3 - y3 * x1|}{2}$$

a. Write the method `triangleArea` that computes the area of its three `Point` parameters using the above formula. The `triangleArea` method can be static because a `Polygon` object does not need to be created to determine the area of a triangle formed by the three points that are passed as parameters. The incomplete `Point` class implementation appears below.

```
public class Point
{
    /**
        Constructs a point.
        @param x1 the x-coordinate of the point
        @param y1 the y-coordinate of the point
    */
    Point(double x1, double y1)
    {
        x = x1;
        y = y1;
    }
```

```
/**
    @return the x-coordinate of this point
*/
public double getX() {. . .}

/**
    @return the y-coordinate of this point
*/
public double getY() {. . .}

    private double x;
    private double y;
}
```

Write your method `triangleArea` using the method header below.

```
public static double triangleArea(Point p1, Point p2, Point p3)
```

b. To compute the area of a polygon with more than three corner points, you can chop off a triangle and recursively compute the area of the remaining polygon (which has one corner point less than the original).

Refer to the incomplete `Polygon` class below.

```
import java.util.ArrayList;

/**
    A polygon with a number of Point corners.
*/
public class Polygon
{
    /**
        Constructs a Polygon object with no corners.
    */
    public Polygon()
    {
        corners = new ArrayList();
    }

    /**
        Adds a point p to the list of Polygon corners.
        Corners are added in clockwise order.
        @param p the point to be added
    */
    public void add(Point p)
    {
        corners.add(p);
    }
```

```
/**
    @param p1 a vertex of the triangle
    @param p2 a vertex of the triangle
    @param p3 a vertex of the triangle
    @return the area of the triangle with vertices p1,p2,p3
*/
public static double triangleArea(Point p1, Point p2,
     Point p3) {. . .}

/**
    Recursively computes and returns the area of a polygon.
    If this polygon has fewer than 3 vertices, return 0.
    Otherwise, return the sum of the area of a triangle
    and the area of a smaller polygon.
    @return area of polygon
*/
public double getArea()
{
    // Code goes here
}

    private ArrayList corners;
}
```

In writing the method `getArea`, you may call the method `triangleArea`. Assume `triangleArea` works as specified regardless of what you wrote for part a. Write `getArea` using the method header below.

```
public double getArea()
```

CHAPTER

(Covers *Java Concepts for AP Computer Science* Chapter 14)

Sorting and Searching

■ Topic Summary

15.1   Selection Sort

The selection sort algorithm orders array elements by inspecting all elements in the array to find the smallest element. This element is exchanged with the first entry in the array. The smallest element is now first. The next step is to inspect the elements to find the second smallest element and exchange this element with the second entry in the array. The smallest two elements in the array are now in the first two positions of the array. This procedure continues until all elements in the array are in sorted order. The complete `SelectionSorter` class can be found in Section 14.1 of your text. Example 15.1 examines three key methods used in the selection sort.

Example 15.1   `sort` Method

```
public void sort()
{
   /**
      Loop invariant: Elements a[0]...a[i - 1] are in their final
      positions.
   */
   for (int i = 0; i < a.length - 1; i++)
   {
      int minPos = minimumPosition(i);
      swap(minPos, i);
   }
}
```

The method `sort` calls the method `minimumPosition` to return the index of the smallest entry in the tail portion of the array beginning in position `i` and then calls the method `swap` to exchange the entries in these two positions of the array. This is the method that puts each element in its final position.

`minimumPosition` Method

```
private int minimumPosition(int from)
{
   int minPos = from;
   for (int i = from + 1; i < a.length; i++)
      if (a[i] < a[minPos])
         minPos = i;
   return minPos;
}
```

The method `minimumPosition` searches the array for the smallest value beginning in position `from`. The index of the element with the smallest value in this portion of the array is returned.

`swap` Method

```
private void swap(int i, int j)
{
   int temp = a[i];
   a[i] = a[j];
   a[j] = temp;
}
```

The method `swap` has two parameters that represent indices of the array. `swap` exchanges the entries in these two positions in the array.

Your text uses the `ArrayUtil` class to fill the array with random values and to print the array values to the screen. The `ArrayUtil` class is a utility class (similar to the `Math` class). A utility class has no objects but contains related static methods. These static methods are called by using the class name and passing the appropriate parameters. The statement

```
int[] a = ArrayUtil.randomIntArray(20, 100);
```

calls a static method of the `ArrayUtil` utility class to fill a 20-element array (first parameter) with integers in the range [0 – 99] (second parameter).

15.1.1 *Analyzing the Performance of the Selection Sort Algorithm*

We are sometimes asked to analyze the running time of an algorithm or to determine how many comparisons are made in a certain algorithm. Consider the following array:

13	34	1	50	21

Using the selection sort algorithm we have:

- Starting with position 0: 4 comparisons are made to determine that 1 is the smallest value in the array. 1 is swapped with 13.

1	34	13	50	21

1 is in its final position.

- Advancing to position 1: 3 comparisons are made to determine that 13 is the smallest value in the remaining part of the array. 13 is swapped with 34.

1	**13**	34	50	21

1 and **13** are in their final positions.

- Advancing to position 2: 2 comparisons are made to determine that 21 is the smallest value in the remaining part of the array. 34 is swapped with 21.

1	**13**	**21**	50	34

1, **13**, and **21** are in their final positions.

- Advancing to position 3: 1 comparison is made to determine that 34 is the smallest value in the remaining part of the array. 34 is swapped with 50.

1	**13**	**21**	**34**	**50**

All numbers are in their final positions.

The total number of comparisons made during this simulation of the selection sort is

$$4 + 3 + 2 + 1 = 10$$

For 5 elements, the number of comparisons made by the selection sort algorithm is the sum of the first 4 integers. For *n* elements, the number of comparisons would be the sum of the first $n-1$ integers:

$$(n - 1) + (n - 2) + (n - 3) + ... + 3 + 2 + 1.$$

The formula for finding the sum of the first *k* integers is: $\sum_{i=1}^{k} i = \frac{(k)(k + 1)}{2}$. In our example, the

sum of the first 4 integers is $\frac{(4)(5)}{2}$.

The original order of the array elements has no effect on the number of comparisons made by the selection sort algorithm. The nested loop executes the same number of times regardless of the original ordering of the array elements.

For the AP CS A Exam, you should be able to count comparisons (or statement executions) for a given algorithm. For the AB Exam, you need to be able to classify algorithms based on their performance efficiency (*Big Oh* efficiency).

(AB only) As explained above, the number of comparisons made to sort an array with n elements is the sum of the first $n-1$ integers. In general, for an n-element array, this computation evaluates to

$$\frac{n(n-1)}{2} = \frac{n^2}{2} - \frac{n}{2}$$

We classify the selection sort as a *quadratic* sort because it has complexity of the form $y = an^2$, where n is the number of elements being sorted and y is the run-time complexity (in our case, the number of comparisons), and a is some constant. We use the expression $O(n^2)$ (read as "big-Oh of n squared") to represent the complexity of this algorithm. We are generally concerned with what happens to a sorting algorithm's behavior and efficiency as the number of elements, n, gets very large. The curves $y = n^2$, $y = \frac{n^2}{2}$ and $y = \frac{n^2}{2} - \frac{n}{2}$ have the same basic shape and are all classified as $O(n^2)$.

15.2 Insertion Sort

The insertion sort algorithm takes each element of the array and inserts it into an already sorted portion of the array. For each element we look at, the elements to its left are sorted. We look at the first element in the unsorted part of the array. The elements in the sorted part of the array are shifted to make room for this element to be inserted. Insertion sort is outlined below and covered in *Advanced Topic 14.1* on page 637 of your text.

To sort our original array using insertion sort, position 0 is already sorted.

| 13 | 34 | 1 | 50 | 21 |

- Starting with position 1: Ready to insert 34.

| 13 | 34 | 1 | 50 | 21 |

34 is compared to 13. Since 13 is not greater than 34, it is not shifted.
34 is inserted into position 1.

| 13 | 34 | 1 | 50 | 21 |

- Advancing to position 2: Ready to insert 1.

| 13 | 34 | 1 | 50 | 21 |

1 is compared to 34. Since 34 is greater than 1, 34 is shifted.

1 is compared to 13. Since 13 is greater than 1, 13 is shifted.

1 is inserted into position 0.

- Advancing to position 3: Ready to insert 50.

50 is compared to 34. Since 34 is not greater than 50, no entry is shifted.
50 is inserted into position 3.

- Advancing to position 4: Ready to insert 21.

21 is compared to 50. Since 50 is greater than 21, 50 is shifted.

21 is compared to 34. Since 34 is greater than 21, 34 is shifted.

21 is compared to 13. Since 13 is not greater than 21, no other entries are shifted.
21 is inserted into position 2.

The array is now sorted. Example 15.2 shows the sort method of the InsertionSorter class.

Example 15.2

```
public void sort()
{
    for (int i = 1; i < a.length; i++)
    {
        int temp = a[i];
        int pos = i;
        while (0 < pos && temp < a[pos - 1])
        {
            a[pos] = a[pos - 1];
            pos--;
        }
        a[pos] = temp
    }
}
```

15.2.1   *Analyzing the Performance of the Insertion Sort Algorithm*

Using insertion sort, we saw that the number of comparisons and the number of shifts made were dependent on the original order of the array. The insertion sort algorithm only compares terms until the correct position of the element to insert is determined. If the original array were in increasing order, there would be only one comparison (and no shifts) for each element we insert. Many more comparisons and shifts are needed if the original array is in decreasing order.

There are different implementations for the insertion sort algorithm but you should recognize the insertion sort regardless of the implementation.

(**AB only**) For the insertion sort algorithm, the number of comparisons made to sort an array with n elements in the worst case (when the array is in reverse order) will take $(n - 1) + (n - 2) + ... + 2 + 1$ comparisons (and shifts). This is

$$\frac{n(n - 1)}{2} = \frac{n^2}{2} - \frac{n}{2}$$

We see that the insertion sort is also an $O(n^2)$ sorting algorithm. Of course if we start with a sorted array, the complexity is $O(n)$ because only one comparison is made for each of the $n-1$ elements visited. Wouldn't it be nice if all of the arrays we had to sort were already sorted!

15.3   Merge Sort

The merge sort algorithm sorts an array by cutting the array in half, recursively sorting each half, and then merging the sorted halves. Section 14.4 of your text shows the MergeSorter class. Let's look at the basic parts of the merge sort algorithm.

Example 15.3   sort Method

```
public void sort()
{
    if (a.length <= 1) return;
    int[] first = new int[a.length / 2];
    int[] second = new int[a.length - first.length];
```

```
   // System.arraycopy(a, 0, first, 0, first.length);
   int j = 0;
   for (int i = 0; i < first.length; i++)
   {
      first[j] = a[i];
      j++;
   }

   // System.arraycopy(a, first.length, second, 0, second.length);
   j = 0;
   for (int i = first.length; i < second.length + first.length;
         i++)
   {
      second[j] = a[i];
      j++;
   }

   MergeSorter firstSorter = new MergeSorter(first);
   MergeSorter secondSorter = new MergeSorter(second);
   firstSorter.sort();    // Recursive call on first half
   secondSorter.sort();   // Recursive call on second half
   merge(first, second);  // Merge two sorted halves
}
```

This `sort` method contains 2 recursive calls, each calling itself with a smaller array. This process continues with each of the smaller arrays until the array has 1 or 0 elements. Since `System.arraycopy` is not part of the AP subset, the calls to `System.arraycopy` have been commented out and replaced by `for` loops that perform the same task.

Let's look at the merge sort algorithm with a sample array containing 8 elements. One call to `sort` is made to sort 8 elements

`sort` now makes 2 recursive calls to sort 2 smaller arrays, each with 8/2 or 4 elements.

And now, 4 recursive calls are made to sort 4 smaller arrays, each with 8/4 or 2 elements.

Finally, 8 recursive calls are made to sort 8 arrays, each of size 1.

12 34 7 2 63 45 17 20

Then the method `merge` is called to merge two adjacent sorted arrays.

Example 15.4 `merge` Method

```
private void merge(int[] first, int[] second)
{
    // Merge both halves into the temporary array
    int iFirst = 0;    // Next element in first half to look at
    int iSecond = 0;    // Next element in second half to look at
    int j = 0;    // Next open position in a

    // Merging the 2 arrays
    while (iFirst < first.length && iSecond < second.length)
    {
        if (first[iFirst] < second[iSecond])
        {
            a[j] = first[iFirst];
            iFirst++;
        }
        else
        {
            a[j] = second[iSecond];
            iSecond++;
        }
        j++;
    }

    // Exactly one of the two following loops will be executed.

    // Copy any remaining entries of the first half
    for (int i = iFirst; i < first.length; i++)
    {
        a[j] = first[i];
        j++;
    }

    // Copy any remaining entries of the second half
    for (int i = iSecond; i < second.length; i++)
    {
        a[j] = second[i];
        j++;
    }
}
```

The `System.arraycopy` statements have again been replaced by equivalent `for` loops.

After recursive calls to `sort` we have

| 12 | 34 | 7 | 2 | 63 | 45 | 17 | 20 |

Now, the `merge` method is called to merge two adjacent sorted arrays.

| 12 | 34 | | 2 | 7 | | 45 | 63 | | 17 | 20 |

We merge two adjacent sorted arrays again,

And again.

15.3.1 Analyzing the Performance of the Merge Sort Algorithm

In almost all cases, merge sort is more efficient than insertion sort and in all cases merge sort is more efficient than selection sort.

(AB only) Suppose that the original size of our array is n where $n = 2^m$. The recursive calls to `sort` create m levels that we must merge.

Each level merges n elements so the complexity of the merge sort algorithm can be informally classified as $O(nm)$. If we apply our rules for logarithms, since $n = 2^m$ we have $m = \log_2(n)$. The shape of logarithm curves is the same regardless of the base. Substituting $\log_2(n)$ for m, we have $O(n \log_2(n))$ and we classify merge sort as an $O(n \log(n))$ algorithm. A more formal analysis of merge sort is in Section 14.5 of your text.

15.4   Quicksort (AB only)

Another $O(n \log(n))$ sort is quicksort. Unlike merge sort, quicksort does not need temporary arrays. The algorithm chooses an element from the array (pivot) and then partitions the array into two smaller arrays so that those elements to the left of the partition are less than or equal to `pivot` and those elements to the right of the partition are greater than or equal to `pivot`. Example 15.5 shows the recursive quicksort `sort` method and the `partition` method.

Example 15.5   `sort` Method

```
public void sort(int from, int to)
{
    if (from >= to) return;   // There are no elements to sort.

    int p = partition(from, to);   // Array partitioned.
    // So that the elements a[from]...a[p] (left partition) are
    // less than or equal to the elements a[p + 1]...a[to]
    // (right partition)

    sort(from, p);   // Sort left partition
    sort(p + 1, to);   // Sort right partition
}
```

`sort` calls `partition` to divide the array into two partitions such that all elements in the left partition are less than or equal to `pivot` and those elements in the right partition are greater than or equal to `pivot`. The method `sort` then recursively calls itself to do the same on the left partition and the right partition.

partition Method

```
private int partition(int from, int to)
{
    int pivot = a[from];
    int i = from - 1;
    int j = to + 1;
    while (i < j)
    {
        i++;
        while (a[i] < pivot)
            i++;
        j--;
        while (a[j] > pivot)
            j--;
        if (i < j) swap(i, j);
    }
    return j;
}
```

partition returns an index, j, in the array such that the elements a[from]...a[j] are less than or equal to the elements a[j + 1]...a[to].

Consider the array: a = {7 9 1 6 4 8 2 5}

The partition method chooses the first element in the array (7) as pivot.

After the call to partition, the array is partitioned into two smaller arrays.

{5 2 1 6 4}   {8 9 7}

The elements in the left partition are all less than or equal to 7 and the elements in the right partition are all greater than or equal to 7. Then sort is called with each smaller array and each smaller array is partitioned. You are encouraged to trace through this code for the example presented so that you can understand how the partition method and the quicksort algorithm work. *Advanced Topic 14.3* on page 645 of your text discusses the quicksort algorithm.

15.4.1 Analyzing the Performance of the Quicksort Algorithm (AB only)

The most efficient behavior of quicksort occurs when the partition is always found to be in the center of the array (approximately the same number of elements to the left of the partition as there are to the right of the partition). Assume that the number of elements, n, is a power of 2. Then $n = 2^m$. Assume also that the position of the partition is in the exact middle of the subarray.

After dividing m times, there are n partitions of size 1.

$$\text{Total comparisons} = n + 2\left(\frac{n}{2}\right) + 4\left(\frac{n}{4}\right) + 8\left(\frac{n}{8}\right) + \cdots + n\left(\frac{n}{n}\right)$$

$$= n + n + n + \cdots + n \ \{m \text{ times}\}$$

$$= nm$$

But, if $n = 2^m$, then $m = \log_2(n)$, so substituting, we have

Total comparisons = $n \log_2(n)$, which classifies the quicksort algorithm as $O(n \log(n))$.

Table 15.1   Quicksort Comparisons

Number of subarrays	Number of elements in each subarray	Number of comparisons in each subarray	Total number of comparisons
1	n	$n - 1 \approx n$	$1(n)$
2	$\dfrac{n}{2}$	$\dfrac{n}{2} - 1 \approx \dfrac{n}{2}$	$2\left(\dfrac{n}{2}\right)$
4	$\dfrac{n}{4}$	$\dfrac{n}{4} - 1 \approx \dfrac{n}{4}$	$4\left(\dfrac{n}{4}\right)$
8	$\dfrac{n}{8}$	$\dfrac{n}{8} - 1 \approx \dfrac{n}{8}$	$8\left(\dfrac{n}{8}\right)$
...	...	...	...
...	...	...	$n + 2\left(\dfrac{n}{2}\right) + 4\left(\dfrac{n}{4}\right) + \cdots + n\left(\dfrac{n}{n}\right)$

The efficiency of the Quicksort algorithm can go to $O(n^2)$ if the selection of a pivot doesn't partition the array evenly. If the data was ordered and you chose your pivot to be the first element, the efficiency would be $O(n^2)$. However, if the data was ordered, and you chose your pivot to be the *middle* element of the array, the algorithm would be $O(n \log(n))$.

Remember that there are different implementations for the sort algorithms that we present but you should recognize an algorithm regardless of the implementation.

15.5   Comparing $O(n^2)$ and $O(n \log(n))$ (AB only)

We are generally concerned with what happens to a sorting algorithm's behavior and efficiency as the number of elements, n, gets very large. The curves $y = n^2$, $y = n \log(n)$, and $y = n$ are graphed in Figure 15.1 for values of n ranging from 1 to 20. This graph shows that $y = n^2$ increases in value much faster than $y = n \log(n)$.

Figure 15.1   Comparing $y = n^2$, $y = n \log(n)$, and $y = n$

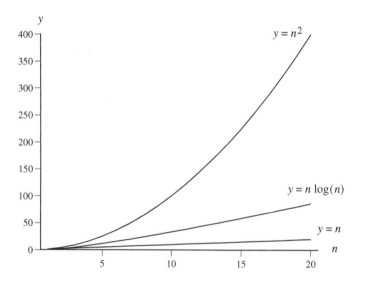

If you look at Table 15.2, you can see that the difference in running times is more pronounced when the number of elements is very large.

Table 15.2   Comparing $O(n^2)$ with $O(n \log(n))$

n	n^2	$n \log(n)$
100	10,000	664
300	90,000	2,468
500	250,000	4,482
800	640,000	7,715
1,000	1,000,000	9,965
10,000	100,000,000	132,877
100,000	10,000,000,000	1,660,964

Table 15.2 uses $\log_2$. Remember that $\log_2(x) = \log_{10}(x) / \log_{10}(2)$. You can calculate the values in Table 15.2 using your calculator and this $\log_2$ relationship.

15.6   Sequential Search

A sequential (or linear) search examines each element in the array until the required match is found or the end of the array is reached. In the best case, the element is found in the first position of the array. In the worst case, the element is not found in the array, so all of the elements in the array are visited. Generally, the sequential search does not depend on any particular ordering of the array elements. If the elements are sorted in increasing order, a sequential search will examine the array elements until the required match is found or until the element being examined is greater than the value being sought (which indicates the required match is not in this sorted array).

15.6.1   Analyzing the Performance of the Sequential Search Algorithm (AB only)
In the worst case, the sequential search is $O(n)$. If you are lucky enough to find the element in position 0 of the array, then the search is $O(1)$. The average number of elements examined with the sequential search is $n/2$ and therefore, the sequential search is classified as an $O(n)$ algorithm.

15.7   Binary Search

The binary search algorithm is used to search a sorted array. Binary search locates a value in a sorted array by determining whether the value occurs in the first half or the second half of the array. This process is repeated in the half where it is expected to be found.

The game of *High-Low* is a game where one person thinks of a number between 1 and 100. The other person is to guess that number. The first person responds "Correct!", "Too high!", or "Too low!" for each guess. What would be your first guess? If you are familiar with the binary search, you can guess the number with no more than 7 tries! A person who attempts to play this game using a sequential search may make 100 guesses before being successful.

15.7.1 Analyzing the Performance of the Binary Search Algorithm

The formal analysis of the binary search is explained in Section 14.7 of your text. Informally, let's assume an array has 8 elements whose values are 11–18. Suppose you are searching for the value 13.

$$a = \{11 \quad 12 \quad 13 \quad 14 \quad 15 \quad 16 \quad 17 \quad 18\}$$

You know how to play this game. You guess 14. The answer is "Too high." You guess 12. The answer is "Too low." You guess 13. If there is no case of "cheating," you will guess the correct value in at most 3 guesses. Notice that $2^3 = 8$.

The maximum number of guesses for *High-Low* is the smallest power of 2 that results in a value greater than or equal to the number of numbers from which we are guessing. For our 1–100 *High-Low* game, the maximum number of guesses is 7 (if you know how to play the game efficiently) because $2^7 > 100$. 7 is the smallest power of 2 that results in a value greater than or equal to 100.

The `BinarySearcher` class is shown in Section 14.7 of your text. Example 15.6 shows the `search` method from `BinarySearcher`. The `search` method returns the index of the value `v` in the array. If `v` is not found in the array, `-1` is returned.

Example 15.6

```java
public int search(int v)
{
   int low = 0;
   int high = a.length - 1;
   while (low <= high)
   {
      int mid = (low + high) / 2;
      int diff = a[mid] - v;

      if (diff == 0)    // a[mid] == v
         return mid;
      else if (diff < 0)    // a[mid] < v
         low = mid + 1;
      else
         high = mid - 1;
   }
   return -1;
}
```

(AB only) If there are n elements in a sorted array, and $n = 2^m$, then $m = \log_2(n)$. The maximum number of visits in the array is $\log(n)$. The binary search is an $O(\log(n))$ algorithm.

15.8 Comparing $O(n)$ and $O(\log(n))$ (AB only)

We are again primarily concerned with what happens to an algorithm's behavior and efficiency as the number of elements, n, gets very large. The curve $y = n$ and $y = \log(n)$ are graphed below for values ranging from 1 to 20. You can see in Figure 15.2 that $y = n$ increases in value much faster than $y = \log(n)$.

Figure 15.2   Comparing $O(n)$ and $O(\log(n))$

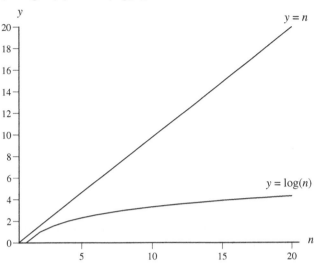

In Table 15.3, you can see that the difference between n and $\log(n)$ is again more pronounced when the number of elements, n, is very large.

Table 15.3

n	$\log(n)$
100	6.64
300	8.22
500	8.97
800	9.64
1000	9.97
10,000	13.28
100,000	16.61

Using a binary search with 100,000 elements will require no more than 17 visits but a sequential search may require 100,000! However, the binary search requires that the array be sorted.

An interesting relationship to remember is that the truncated value of $\log_{10}(n) + 1$ is the number of decimal digits of n, and the truncated value of $\log_2(n) + 1$ is the number of binary digits of n. Thus, $\log_2(n)$ is approximately $(10/3) * \log_{10}(n)$.

■ Topics That Are Useful But Not Tested

- The Java `Arrays` class contains a static `sort` method for sorting arrays of integers and floating-point numbers. This is discussed in Section 14.5 of your text.

- Defining a class that implements the Comparator interface is one way to sort objects of a class that we do not own and that does not implement the Comparable interface. The Comparator interface can also be used to sort objects in a way other than that which is defined in the class. This is explained in *Advanced Topic 14.5* on page 657 of your text.
- The Collections class contains sort methods that can sort array lists. This is presented in Section 14.8 of your text.

■ Things to Remember When Taking the AP Exam

- When given a particular algorithm, you should be able to count the number of times a specific statement is executed.
- The merge sort is almost always more efficient than the insertion sort and always more efficient than the selection sort but the merge sort does requires a temporary array.
- When writing a sorting algorithm, there are many places where off-by-one errors can occur. Be careful when choosing between 0 and 1, < and <=, and a.length and a.length − 1 for loop initializations. Walk through your code carefully.
- When given an algorithm similar to the binary search algorithm and an algorithm similar to the sequential search algorithm, you should be able to choose the algorithm that is more efficient for a specific set of data.
- Remember that an array has to be sorted in order to use binary search.
- Binary search generally is more efficient than sequential search if the array is sorted.
- (**AB only**) Merge sort and quicksort are $O(n \log(n))$ algorithms. Insertion and selection sorts are $O(n^2)$.
- (**AB only**) The worst case for the quicksort algorithm is when the original array is in order or in reverse order and the pivot is at the first (or last) position in the array. This makes the quicksort running time $O(n^2)$.
- (**AB only**) Algorithms that are $O(n \log(n))$ are more efficient than algorithms that are $O(n^2)$.
- (**AB only**) When given an algorithm, you should be able to classify it as $O(1)$, $O(n)$, $O(\log(n))$, $O(n^2)$, or $O(n \log(n))$.
- (**AB only**) Do not classify an algorithm as $O(2n)$, $O(3)$, or $O(n^2 + 2n + 1)$. These are $O(n)$, $O(1)$, and $O(n^2)$ respectively.
- (**AB only**) Do not simply count loops when determining the big-Oh running time. Consecutive loop algorithms are most often $O(n)$. Nested loop algorithms tend to be $O(n^2)$.

■ Key Words

You should understand the terms below. The AP CS Exam questions may include references to these terms. The citations in parentheses next to each term identify the page numbers where it is defined and/or discussed in *Java Concepts for AP Computer Science*, 5th ed.

big-Oh notation (636)	merge sort (639)	sorting algorithm (628)
binary search (651)	quicksort (645)	worst-case runtime
insertion sort (637)	selection sort (628)	behavior (647)
linear search (649)	sequential search (649)	

■ Connecting the Detailed Topic Outline to the Text

The citations in parentheses identify where information in the outline can be located in *Java Concepts for AP Computer Science*, 5th ed.

- Selection Sort (628–636)
  - ■ Analyzing the Performance of the Selection Sort Algorithm (631–636)
- Insertion Sort (637–638)
  - ■ Analyzing the Performance of the Insertion Sort Algorithm (638)
- Merge Sort (639–645)
  - ■ Analyzing the Performance of the Merge Sort Algorithm (642–645)
- Quicksort (645–647)
  - ■ Analyzing the Performance of the Quicksort Algorithm (647)
- Sequential Search (649–651)
  - ■ Analyzing the Performance of the Sequential Search Algorithm (649)
- Binary Search (651–654)
  - ■ Analyzing the Performance of the Binary Search Algorithm (653–654)

■ Practice Questions

Multiple Choice

Questions 1 and 2 refer to the incomplete definition of the `SelectionSorter` class below.

```java
public class SelectionSorter
{
    public SelectionSorter(int[] anArray)
    {
        a = anArray;
    }

    public void sort()
    {
        for (int i = 0; i < a.length - 1; i++)
        {
            int minPos = minimumPosition(i);
            swap(minPos, i);
        }
    }

    // Returns the position of the smallest element
    // in a[from]...a[a.length - 1]
    private int minimumPosition(int from){. . .}

    // Exchanges a[i] with a[j]
    swap(int i, int j) {. . .}

    private int[] a;
}
```

The following segment of code is executed.

```
SelectionSorter sorter = new SelectionSorter(a);
sorter.sort();
```

Consider arrays initialized with the values below.

   I.   {2, 3, 4, 5, 6}
  II. {6, 5, 4, 3, 2}
III. {2, 6, 1, 5, 4}

1. Which of the following statements regarding the number of comparisons made to sort the array is **true**?

   a. I takes fewer comparisons than both II and III.
   b. II takes fewer comparisons than both I and III.
   c. III takes fewer comparisons than both I and II.
   d. I and II require the same number of comparisons, which is different from the number of comparisons required to sort III.
   e. I, II, and III require the same number of comparisons.

2. Consider the `SelectionSorter` method `sort`. Which of the following statements is **true** at the beginning of each iteration of the loop?

   I.   For all `j`, such that `0 <= j < i`, `0 <= a[j] <= a[i]`.
   II. For all `j`, such that `0 <= j < i`, `a[j]` is in its final position in the sorted array.
   III. For all `j`, such that `0 <= j < i`, `a[0]...a[j]` is sorted.

   a. I only
   b. II only
   c. III only
   d. II and III only
   e. I, II, and III

3. **(AB only)** Consider the following algorithms to accomplish the task of removing duplicates from an array list `list`.

   I. For each element in `list` (x_i), look at x_i. Now look at each element in `list` and count how many times x_i occurs in `list`. If the count is larger than 1, remove x_i.

   II. Sort the array list with an efficient sort algorithm. For each x_i in `list`, look at its next neighbor to decide whether it is present more than once. If it is, remove x_i.

   III. Sort the array list, `list`, with an efficient algorithm. Traverse the array list looking at each x_i in `list`. Whenever the element after x_i (if there is one) is strictly larger than x_i, append x_i to a second (initially empty) array list, `list2`. Append the last element to `list2`. Find the difference, `diff`, in the sizes of `list` and `list2`. Beginning with the last element of `list`, delete `diff` elements from `list`. Then, copy the elements of `list2` back into `list`.

   Of the following, which best describes the running time of these algorithms?

a. I, II, and III are all $O(n^2)$.
b. I and II are $O(n^2)$, III is $O(n \log(n))$.
c. I is $O(n^2)$, II and III are $O(n \log(n))$.
d. I and III are $O(n^2)$, II is $O(n \log(n))$.
e. I, II, and III are $O(n \log(n))$.

4. The method `removeDupes` is intended to remove duplicates from array a, returning n, the number of elements in a after duplicates have been removed. For example, if array a has the values

    {4, 7, 11, 4, 9, 5, 11, 7, 3, 5}

    before `removeDupes` is called, then after duplicates are removed,
    a will be {4, 7, 11, 5, 9, 3} and 6 will be returned.

    ```
    public static int removeDupes(int[] a)
    {
        int n = a.length;
        for (int i = 0; i < n; i++)
        {
            int current = a[i];
            int j = i + 1;
            while (j < n)
            {
                if (current == a[j])
                {
                    a[j] = a[n - 1];
                    n--;
                }
                else
                    j++;
            }
        }
        return n;
    }
    ```

    How many times is the comparison

    ```
    (current == a[j])
    ```

    executed in `removeDupes`?

    a. 45
    b. 42
    c. 36
    d. 25
    e. 21

5. The method `removeDupes` is intended to remove duplicates from array a, returning n, the number of elements in a after duplicates have been removed. For example, if array a has the values

    {4, 7, 11, 4, 9, 5, 11, 7, 3, 5}

    before `removeDupes` is called, then after duplicates are removed,
    a will be {4, 7, 11, 5, 9, 3} and 6 will be returned.

Consider the following three implementations of removeDupes.

```
I.  public static int removeDupes(int[] a)
    {
        int n = a.length;
        for (int i = 0; i < n; i++)
        {
            int current = a[i];
            int j = i + 1;
            while (j < n)
            {
                if (current == a[j])
                {
                    a[j] = a[n - 1];
                    n--;
                }
                else
                    j++;
            }
        }
        return n;
    }

II. public static int removeDupes(int[] a)
    {
        int n = a.length;
        for (int i = 0; i < n; i++)
        {
            int current = a[i];
            for (int j = 0; j < n; j++)
            {
                if (i != j && current == a[j])
                {
                    a[j] = a[n - 1];
                    n--;
                }
            }
        }
        return n;
    }

III. public static int removeDupes(int[] a)
    {
        int n = a.length;
        int count = 0;
        int i = 0;
        while (i < n)
        {
            int j = i + 1;
            boolean found = false;
            while (!found && j < n)
            {
                if (a[i] == a[j])
                {
                    a[j] = a[n - 1];
                    n--;
                    found = true;
                }
```

```
            j++;
        }
        if (!found)
            i++;
    }
    return n;
}
```

Which of the code segments above requires the fewest number of operations?

a. I
b. II
c. III
d. All choices require the same number of operations.
e. It is impossible to determine which segment requires the fewest operations.

6. Which of the following statements about searching is **not** true?

a. The sequential search examines all values in an array until it finds a match or until it reaches the end.
b. A binary search is generally more efficient than a sequential search.
c. A binary search can only be used to search for an item in a sorted array.
d. A sequential search generally takes more comparisons than a binary search.
e. A binary search is always faster than a sequential search.

7. (**AB only**) The quicksort algorithm is to be used to sort an array of integers in decreasing order. Which of the cases below describes the worst case for the quicksort algorithm when the first element is used as the pivot?

I. The original array is in increasing order.
II. The original array is in decreasing order.
III. The original array is in random order.

a. I only
b. II only
c. III only
d. I and II only
e. I, II, and III all take the same number of comparisons.

8. Consider the `search` method (of some class) below which is intended to return the index of the position in array a where `key` is found. If `key` is not in the array a, `-1` is returned.

```
public int search(int key)
{
    int low = 0;
    int high = a.length - 1;
    while (low <= high)
    {
        int mid = (low + high) / 2;
        int diff = a[mid] - key;

        if (diff == 0)    // a[mid] == key
            return mid;
        else if (diff < 0)    // a[mid] < key
            low = mid + 1;
        else
```

```
            high = mid - 1;
      }
      return -1;
   }
   private int[] a;
```

Suppose:

```
   a = {8, 10, 1, 5, 7, 9, 6, 2}
```

What value will search(2) return?

a. 8
b. 4
c. 3
d. −1
e. No value will be returned. An ArrayIndexOutOfBoundsException is thrown.

9. What is the maximum number of elements that will be visited by the binary search algorithm when searching a sorted 45-element array?

a. 1
b. 6
c. 7
d. 22
e. 45

10. An array, a, is initialized to contain the following values.

```
   a = {1, 23, 44, 56, 77, 81, 88, 90, 99}
```

The following search algorithm is provided.

```
public int search(int v, int high)
{
   int low = 0;
   while (low <= high)
   {
      int mid = (low + high) / 2;
      int diff = a[mid] - v;

      if (diff == 0)
         return mid;
      else if (diff < 0)
         low = mid + 1;
      else
         high = mid - 1;
   }
   return -low - 1;
}
```

When the call search(60, 9) is invoked, what is returned by this method call?

a. −1
b. −4
c. −5
d. 3
e. 7

Free Response Questions

1. Two words are anagrams if one of the words is made by transposing the letters of the other word. For example, "stop" and "tops" are anagrams. This problem involves reading a dictionary of words, storing the words in a list, and then generating and printing all words in the dictionary that are anagrams of a given word. The problem uses the `Word` and `AnagramList` classes whose incomplete implementations are below.

Word **Class**

```
/**
    Holds words in two forms: the original word and the word with
    its letters in sorted order.
*/
public class Word
{
    /**
        Constructs a word.
        @param theWord the word to hold with its sorted version
    */
    public Word(String theWord)
    {
        originalWord = theWord;
        sortedWord = sortWord();
    }

    /**
        Sorts the letters of the word.
        Example: if originalWord = "apple", "aelpp" is returned.
        @return the sorted word
    */
    private String sortWord()
    {
        // Code goes here
    }

    /**
        @return the original word
    */
    public String getWord() {. . .}

    /**
        @return the sorted word
    */
    public String getSortedWord() {. . .}

    private String originalWord;
    private String sortedWord;
}
```

AnagramList **Class**

```
/**
    Holds a list of Words.
*/
public class AnagramList
{
```

```
/**
    Constructs an empty list.
*/
public AnagramList()
{
    wordList = new ArrayList<Word>();
}

/**
    Adds a Word to wordList.
    @param newString the word to add to wordList
*/
public void addWord(String newString){. . .}

/**
    @param aWord a word to check for anagram property
    @param anotherWord a word to check for anagram property
    @return true if aWord and anotherWord have original
    strings that are anagrams (words composed of the same
    letters); otherwise returns false
*/
public boolean checkAnagram(Word aWord, Word anotherWord)
{
    // Code goes here
}

/**
    Prints original words of all Words in wordList that
    are anagrams of key.
*/
public void printAnagrams(String key)
{
    // Code goes here
}

    private ArrayList<Word> wordList;
}
```

a. One way to check whether two words are anagrams is to sort the letters of each word and compare the sorted words. If the sorted words contain the same sequence of letters and are the same length, the original words are anagrams.

You are to write the `sortWord` method of the `Word` class. `sortWord` will return a string that contains the letters of `originalWord` in sorted order. For example,

originalWord	sortWord *returns*
cat	act
apple	aelpp
table	abelt

Use the method header below to write `sortWord`.

```
private String sortWord()
```

b. Write the `AnagramList` method `checkAnagram`. `checkAnagram` returns `true` if its two `Word` parameters have original words that are anagrams. If not, `checkAnagram` returns `false`. Use the method header below to write `checkAnagram`. Assume that all `Word` methods work as intended regardless of what you wrote for part a.

```
public boolean checkAnagram(Word aWord, Word anotherWord)
```

c. Write the `AnagramList` method `printAnagrams`. `printAnagrams` prints the original words of all `Words` in `wordList` that are anagrams of `key`. Use the method header below to write `printAnagrams`. Assume that all `Word` methods work as intended regardless of what you wrote for part a. You may call `checkAnagram` in writing `printAnagrams`. Assume that `checkAnagram` works as intended regardless of what you wrote in part b. Use the method header below to write `printAnagrams`.

```
public void printAnagrams(String key)
```

2. An `AddressBook` contains an unknown number of entries. Each entry contains a person's first and last names and an e-mail address. The `Person` class, whose incomplete definition is below, is used to represent an entry.

```java
public class Person implements Comparable
{
    /**
        Constructs a person.
        @param fName the first name of this Person
        @param lName the last name of this Person
    */
    public Person(String fName, String lName)
    {
        firstName = fName;
        lastName = lName;
        emailAddress = makeEmailAddress();
    }

    /**
        Creates an e-mail address for the person based on a
        person's name.
        @return the e-mail address
    */
    private String makeEmailAddress() {. . .}

    /**
        Gets the person's name.
        @return name of person in the form 'last, first'
    */
    public String getName() {. . .}

    /**
        Gets the person's e-mail address.
        @return the e-mail address of person
    */
    public String getEmailAddress() {. . .}
```

```
/**
    Compares two persons by the alphabetical ordering of
    name (lastName, firstName).
*/
public int compareTo(Object obj)
{
    // Code goes here
}

private String firstName;
private String lastName;
private String emailAddress;
}
```

Some useful public methods in the `AddressBook` class include:

```
addEntry    // Adds entry of type Person to address book.
printEntries    // Prints information in address book.
sortByLastName    // Sorts the information by last name.
sortByEmailAddress    // Sorts the information by e-mail
                        // address.
search    // Returns the e-mail address given the person's name.
```

The incomplete `AddressBook` class appears below.

```
public class AddressBook
{
    /**
        Creates an empty address book of Persons.
    */
    public AddressBook()
    {
        list = new ArrayList<Person>();
    }

    /**
        Adds an entry to the address book.
        @param p the Person entry to add to address book
    */
    public void addEntry(Person p) {. . .}

    /**
        Prints the entries in the address book.
    */
    public void printEntries() {. . .}

    /**
        Uses selection sort algorithm to sort the
        address book entries by name (last, first).
    */
    public void sortByLastName()
    {
        for (int i = 0; i < list.size() - 1; i++)
        {
            int minPos = minimumPosition(i);
            swap(minPos, i);
        }
    }
```

```
/**
    Finds smallest element in a tail range of the ArrayList.
    @param from the position to start search from
    @return the index of smallest element in tail range
*/
private int minimumPosition(int from)
{
    // Code goes here
}

/**
    Sorts the address book entries by e-mail address.
*/
public void sortByEmailAddress()
{
    for (int i = 0; i < list.size() - 1; i++)
    {
        int minPos = minimumEmailPosition(i);
        swap(minPos, i);
    }
}

/**
    Finds smallest e-mail address in a tail range of the list.
    @param from the position to start search from
    @return the index of the element with an e-mail address
    alphabetically less than other e-mail addresses in range
*/
private int minimumEmailPosition(int from)
{
    // Code goes here
}

/**
    Swaps the entry in the ith position of the address
    book with the entry in the jth position of the
    address book.
    @param i index of element to swap
    @param j index of element to swap
*/
private void swap(int i, int j){. . .}

private ArrayList<Person> list;
}
```

a. Person implements Comparable. You are to write the method compareTo for the Person class. compareTo for the Person class compares two Person objects by the alphabetical ordering of their names (last, first). You may call Person's method getName in writing compareTo. Assume getName works as intended.

compareTo	Summary
int compareTo(Object other)	Returns a value < 0 if this Person is less than other. Returns 0 if this Person is equal to other. Returns a value > 0 if this Person is greater than other.

Use the method header below to write `compareTo`.

```
public int compareTo(Object obj)
```

b. The `AddressBook` class has a method `sortByLastName` that uses the selection sort algorithm to sort the address book entries by last name. `sortByLastName` calls the method `minimumPosition` that returns the index of the `AddressBook` entry that has the minimum value (the entry whose name (last, first) comes alphabetically before other names in a portion of the `AddressBook`). You are to write the method `minimumPosition`. You may (and should) use the `Person` method `compareTo` when writing your solution. Assume `compareTo` works as specified regardless of what you wrote in part a.

```
private int minimumPosition(int from)
```

c. In order to be able to sort by e-mail address as well as by name, a `Comparator` is used. The `PersonComparator` class is defined below. **(Note: The Comparator interface is not part of the AP subset.)**

```
public class PersonComparator implements Comparator
{
   public int compare(Object first, Object second)
   {
      Person firstPerson = (Person) first;
      Person secondPerson = (Person) second;
      String firstEmail = firstPerson.getEmailAddress();
      String secondEmail = secondPerson.getEmailAddress();
      return firstEmail.compareTo(secondEmail);
   }
}
```

The `AddressBook` class uses this `PersonComparator` class to sort entries alphabetically by e-mail address. The `AddressBook` class has a method `sortByEmailAddress` that uses the selection sort algorithm to sort the address book entries alphabetically by e-mail addresses. `sortByEmailAddress` calls the method `minimumEmailPosition` that returns the index of the `AddressBook` entry that has the minimum e-mail value (the entry whose e-mail comes alphabetically before other entries in a portion of the `AddressBook`). You are to complete the method `minimumEmailPosition`. You may (and should) use the `PersonComparator` method `compare` (defined above) when writing your solution.

```
private int minimumEmailPosition(int from)
{
   int minPos = from;
   Comparator comp = new PersonComparator();

   // Code goes here

   return minPos;
}
```

CHAPTER 16

(Covers *Java Concepts for AP Computer Science* Chapter 15)

An Introduction to Data Structures
(AB only)

TOPIC OUTLINE

■ Topic Summary

16.1 Using Linked Lists

A linked list is a sequence of elements. Each element stores an object and a reference to the next element.

Figure 16.1

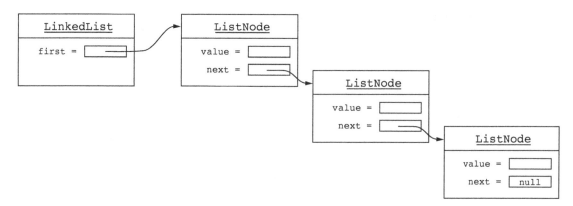

The figures in Section 15.1 of your text illustrate this concept in detail. The Java library provides a LinkedList class in the java.util package. LinkedList implements java.util.List<E> and java.util.Queue<E>.

The LinkedList class in the java.util package is a generic (typed) class, just like the generic ArrayList class.

311

Table 16.1 lists the `List` methods that are currently included in the AP subset.

Table 16.1

`interface java.util.List<E>`

Method	Method Summary
`boolean add(E elt)`	Appends the element `elt` to the end of this list.
`void add(int index, E elt)`	Inserts `elt` at position `index`, sliding elements at position `index` and higher to the right (adds 1 to their indices) and adjusts size.
`E get(int index)`	Returns the element at position `index` in this list.
`Iterator<E> iterator()`	Returns an iterator for the elements in this list.
`ListIterator<E> listIterator()`	Returns a list iterator for the elements in this list.
`E set(int index, E elt)`	Replaces the element at position `index` in this list with the specified element.
`E remove(int index)`	Removes element from position `index`, sliding the elements at position `index + 1` and higher to the left (subtracts 1 from their indices) and adjusts size; returns the element formerly at the specified position.
`int size()`	Returns the number of elements in the list.

Both the `ArrayList` and the `LinkedList` implement the `List` interface. Example 16.1 illustrates this.

Example 16.1

```
1      import java.util.List;
2      import java.util.ArrayList;
3      // import java.util.LinkedList;
4      import java.util.Iterator;

5      public class ArrayListTester
6      {
7         public static void main(String[] args)
8         {
9            ArrayList<String> staff = new ArrayList<String>();
10               // Construct an empty ArrayList
11           // LinkedList<String>  staff = new LinkedList<String> ();
12               // Construct an empty LinkedList
13           staff.add("Dick");    // Objects added to end of list
14           staff.add("Harry");
15           staff.add("Romeo");
16           staff.add("Tom");
17           printList(staff);    // Dick Harry Romeo Tom
18           System.out.println(staff.get(2));    // Romeo
19           staff.set(2, "Karen");   // Dick Harry Karen Tom
20           staff.add(2, "Ann");     //Dick Harry Ann Karen Tom
21           staff.remove(3);     // Dick Harry Ann Tom
22           printList(staff);    // Dick Harry Ann Tom
23        }

24        public static void printList(List staff)
25        {
```

```
26              System.out.println();
27              Iterator iter = staff.iterator();
28              while (iter.hasNext())
29                  System.out.println(iter.next());
30          }
31      }
```

Because `ArrayList` and `LinkedList` both implement `List`, the implementation used in Example 16.1 can be changed from an `ArrayList` implementation to a `LinkedList` implementation with two modifications:
- The import statement (Replace line 2 with line 3).
- The declaration (Replace line 9 with line 11).

The `printList` method (line 24) takes a `List` parameter so no changes are necessary.

As we will discuss in more detail later, some of these `List` methods are extremely inefficient when used with a `LinkedList` implementation.

The `java.util.LinkedList` class includes the `List` methods as well as some additional methods. The additional methods that are included in the AP subset are listed in Table 16.2.

Table 16.2

`class java.util.LinkedList<E> implements java.util.List<E>,`
`java.util.Queue<E>`

Method	Method Summary
`void addFirst(E elt)`	Inserts `elt` to the beginning of this list.
`void addLast(E elt)`	Appends `elt` to the end of this list.
`E getFirst()`	Returns the first element in this list.
`E getLast()`	Returns the last element in this list.
`E removeFirst()`	Removes and returns the first element from this list.
`E removeLast()`	Removes and returns the last element from this list.

The `java.util.LinkedList` also implements the `java.util.Queue` interface. Queues are discussed in Section 15.4 of your text and Section 16.4 of this guide.

To access elements in a `LinkedList`, you can use an iterator. Table 16.3 shows the iterator methods that are included in the AP subset. The iterator works in the same way as the `ArrayList` iterator introduced in Chapter 8 of this guide.

Table 16.3

`interface java.util.Iterator<E>`

Method	Method Summary
`boolean hasNext()`	Returns `true` if this iterator has more elements when traversing the list in the forward direction.
`E next()`	Moves the iterator past the next element and returns the traversed element.
`void remove()`	Removes from the list the last element that was returned by `next`.

In addition to the operations `hasNext`, `next`, and `remove` that the `Iterator` interface provides, the `List` interface provides a special iterator, called a `ListIterator` (extending `Iterator`), that allows for element insertion and replacement. The `LinkedList` class provides a method to obtain a list iterator. The statement

```
ListIterator<String> iter = staff.listIterator();
```

calls this method for the `LinkedList` staff. Table 16.4 shows the additional `ListIterator` methods that are included in the AP subset.

Table 16.4

interface java.util.ListIterator<E> extends java.util.Iterator<E>

Method	Method Summary
void add(E elt)	Inserts the specified element into the list before the current iterator position and moves the iterator past the inserted element.
void set(E elt)	Replaces the last element returned by next with elt.

Example 16.2 demonstrates the `LinkedList` and `ListIterator` methods included in the AP testable subset. Remember that the iterator position is *between* two list elements.

Example 16.2

```java
import java.util.LinkedList;
import java.util.ListIterator;
/**
    A program that demonstrates the LinkedList methods and
    ListIterator methods in AP subset.
*/
public class LinkedListTester
{
    public static void main(String[] args)
    {
        // Demonstrating LinkedList methods
        LinkedList<String> staff = new LinkedList<String>();
            // Construct empty list.
        staff.addFirst("Dave");    // Add to front of list, D
        staff.addFirst("Harry");    // H D
        staff.addFirst("Romeo");    // R H D
        staff.addFirst("Tom");    // T R H D
        staff.addLast("Mary");    // Add to end of list, T R H D M
        staff.addLast("Sue");    // T R H D M S
        System.out.println(staff.getFirst());    // Tom
        System.out.println(staff.getLast());    // Sue

        staff.removeFirst();    // R H D M S
        staff.removeLast();    // R H D M
        staff.add("George");    // R H D M G

        System.out.println(staff.size());    // 5
        System.out.println(staff.get(2));    // Dave
        staff.set(2, "Kevin");    // R H K M G

        // Demonstrating additional ListIterator methods
        // # indicates iterator position
```

```
ListIterator<String> iter = staff.listIterator();
    // # R H K M G

iter.next();    // R # H K M G
iter.next();    // R H # K M G
iter.remove();    // R # K M G
iter.next();    // R K # M G
iter = staff.listIterator();    // Resets iterator # R K M G
iter.next();    //R # K M G

iter.set("Cathy");    // C # K M G

iter = staff.listIterator(); // Resets iterator
iter.next();    // C # K M G
iter.remove();    // # K M G
iter.add("Nina");    // N # K M G

iter = staff.listIterator();    // Resets iterator
while(iter.hasNext())
{
    System.out.print(iter.next() + " ");
        // Nina Kevin Mary George
}
    }
}
```

The `ListIterator` method `remove` removes the last element returned by the iterator. This method can be called only once after a call to `next`.

Example 16.2 includes calls to the methods `get` and `set` because `java.util.LinkedList<E>` implements `java.util.List<E>` and the `List` class includes these methods. However, the `List` methods `get` and `set` are primarily used with the `ArrayList` implementation and *not* with a `LinkedList` implementation. Because array lists allow for random access, the call

```
System.out.println(arrayListName.get(x));
```

gives immediate access to the object whose index is x. This operation is $O(1)$. With a linked list, the list must be traversed to arrive at the element in position x. This operation is $O(n)$. That is, in Example 16.2, Romeo and Harry were visited before Dave with execution of the statement

```
System.out.println(staff.get(2));    // Dave
```

Think about the consequences of the `printList` method when a linked list is passed as the parameter!

```
public static void printList(List staff)
{
    for (int i = 0; i < staff.size(); i++)
        System.out.println(staff.get(i));
}
```

Each call to `get` traverses the list. The method `printList` (as implemented above) is $O(n^2)$. We can see why iterating over the elements in a linked list with an iterator is typically preferable to accessing the elements by indexing through the list!

The same is true for the `List` method `set`. The statement

```
staff.set(2, "Kevin");
```

must traverse the list to arrive at position 2 in order to set the object to "Kevin" (an $O(n)$ operation). In an `ArrayList`, the statement

```
arrayListName.set(2, "Kevin");
```

provides immediate access to the element in position 2 (an $O(1)$ operation).

An iterator should be used to access the elements of a `LinkedList`. Do not use `get` and `set` with linked lists.

Example 16.2 resets the iterator to traverse through the list more than once. You should not use two iterators on the same list at the same time. Resetting the iterator is preferred.

Example 16.3 illustrates the use of an enhanced `for` loop (for-each loop) to print the list elements. The enhanced `for` loop is a convenient way to traverse a list and is equivalent to using an iterator. Behind the scenes the enhanced `for` loop actually uses an iterator to traverse the list. Printing the list using either an iterator or an enhanced `for` loop is an $O(n)$ operation.

Example 16.3

```
            // Demonstrating LinkedList of strings
            LinkedList<String> staff = new LinkedList<String>();
                  // Construct empty list.

            staff.addFirst("Dave");     // Add to front of list, D
            staff.addFirst("Harry");    // H D
            staff.addFirst("Romeo");    // R H D
            staff.addFirst("Tom");      // T R H D
            staff.addLast("Mary");      // Add to end of list, T R H D M

            // Enhanced for loop to print items in list
            for (String name : staff)
            {
                System.out.print(name + " ");
            }
            System.out.println();    // Tom Romeo Harry Dave Mary
```

16.2   Implementing Linked Lists

Because the implementation of a linked list is a part of the AB course, we will look at pieces of this implementation and discuss how the elements of a linked list are manipulated.

Elements in a linked list are called *nodes*. Nodes are visited in sequential order. Unlike an array, there is no random access in a linked list. Your text uses the `Node` class to define a node. To facilitate a consistency in the exam questions, the AP Exam uses the `ListNode`[1] class shown in Example 16.4 to define a node and its methods.

---

[1] College Board's AP Computer Science AB: Implementation Classes and Interfaces

Example 16.4

```java
public class ListNode
{
    /**
        Constructs a node.
        @param initValue the value of the node
        @param initNext the next field of this node
    */
    public ListNode(Object initValue, ListNode initNext)
    {
        value = initValue;
        next = initNext;
    }

    /**
        @return the value of this node
    */
    public Object getValue()
    {
        return value;
    }

    /**
        @return the next field of this node
    */
    public ListNode getNext()
    {
        return next;
    }

    /**
        Sets the value of the list node to theNewValue.
        @param theNewValue the new value for this node
    */
    public void setValue(Object theNewValue)
    {
        value = theNewValue;
    }

    /**
        Sets this node's next field to a new reference.
        @param theNewNext the new reference for this node's
        next field
    */
    public void setNext(ListNode theNewNext)
    {
        next = theNewNext;
    }

    private Object value;
    private ListNode next;
}
```

This ListNode class (without the comments) will be given to you in the Quick Reference Guide provided during the exam.

Because the `ListNode` class does not implement `equals`, if two `ListNodes` are compared using `equals`, *references* are being compared (using the inherited `Object` `equals` method). For example, if `node1` and `node2` are references to `ListNodes`, the expression

```
node1.equals(node2)
```

evaluates to `true` only if `node1` and `node2` reference the same `ListNode`.

The AP implementation of a linked list involves the `ListNode` and the `LList` classes. Example 16.5 contains the `LList` methods that directly involve manipulating the first element in a linked list. These methods are `getFirst`, `addFirst`, and `removeFirst`. The `ListNode` class is used in this implementation. Your text uses the private inner class `Node` that implements these same methods. Inner classes are not included in the AP subset.

Example 16.5

```
public class LList
{
    /**
        Constructs an empty list.
    */
    public LList()
    {
        first = null;
    }

    /**
        @return the first object in the list if there is one
    */
    public Object getFirst()
    {
        if (first == null)
            throw new NoSuchElementException();
        return first.getValue();
    }

    /**
        Adds an object to the front of the list.
        @param obj the object to add to the list
    */
    public void addFirst(Object obj)
    {
        ListNode newNode = new ListNode(obj, first);
        first = newNode;
    }

    /**
        Removes and returns the first object in the list if there
        is one.
        @return the first object in the list if there is one
    */
    public Object removeFirst()
    {
        if (first == null)
            throw new NoSuchElementException();
        Object obj = first.getValue();
        first = first.getNext();
```

```
            return obj;
        }

        private ListNode first;
    }
```

Figures 4 and 5 in Section 15.2 of your text provide illustrations of adding to and removing from the front of a linked list.

It is also useful to be able to add and remove from the end of a linked list. The Java class library implementation of a linked list provides immediate access to the beginning and the end of the list as illustrated in Figure 16.2.

Figure 16.2

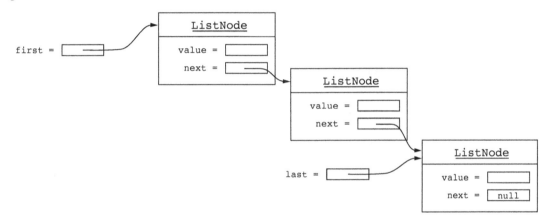

We can write our own linked list implementation with end-of-list access by adding a private instance field that keeps track of the last `ListNode` in the linked list. Example 16.6 includes the methods that directly manipulate the last element in a linked list. In Section 15.2 of your text, the `LinkedList` class defines a private inner class `LinkedListIterator` and its implementation. The iterator is used to traverse the linked list. Example 16.6 traverses the list without the use of an iterator.

Example 16.6

```
    public class LList
    {
        /**
            Constructs an empty list.
        */
        public LList()
        {
            first = null;
            last = null;
        }

        /**
            @return the last object in the list if there is one
        */
        public Object getLast()
        {
```

```java
      if (first == null)    // The list is empty.
         throw new NoSuchElementException();
      return last.getValue();
   }

   /**
      Adds an object to the end of the list.
      @param obj the object to add to the end of the list
   */
   public void addLast(Object obj)
   {
      ListNode newNode = new ListNode(obj, null);
      if (first == null)    // The list is empty.
      {
         first = newNode;
         last = newNode;
      }
      else
      {
         last.setNext(newNode);
         last = newNode;
      }
   }

   /**
      Removes and returns the last object in the list if there
      is one.
      @return the last element in the list if there is one
   */
   public Object removeLast()
   {
      if (first == null)    // The list is empty.
         throw new NoSuchElementException();
      Object obj = last.getValue();
      if (first == last)    // Only 1 node in list.
      {
         first = null;
         last = null;
         return obj;
      }
      ListNode temp = first;

      while (temp.getNext() != last)    // More than 1 node in list
      {
         temp = temp.getNext();    // Looking for the node
      }                            // before the last node.

      Object obj = last.getValue();
      temp.setNext(null);
      last = temp;
      return obj;
   }

   private ListNode first;
   private ListNode last;
}
```

Now, what happens if you don't have that private instance field, `last`? In order to implement any of the methods above, the list must be traversed. Example 16.7 demonstrates traversing the list to do the same tasks as in Example 16.6.

Example 16.7

```
public Object getLast()
{
   if (first == null)    // The list is empty.
      throw new NoSuchElementException();
   ListNode temp = first;   // Must traverse to find the end.
   while (temp.getNext() != null)
      temp = temp.getNext();
   return temp.getValue();
}

public void addLast(Object obj)
{
   ListNode newNode = new ListNode(obj, null);
   if (first == null)
   {
      first = newNode;
   }
   else
   {
      ListNode temp = first;   // Must traverse to find the end.
      while (temp.getNext() != null)
         temp = temp.getNext();
      temp.setNext(newNode);
   }
}

public Object removeLast()
{
   if (first == null)    // The list is empty.
      throw new NoSuchElementException();

   if (first.getNext() == null)   // Only 1 node in list.
   {
      Object obj = first.getValue();
      first = null;
      return obj;
   }
   ListNode temp = first;       // Must traverse to find the end
   ListNode follower = temp;    // and the node before the last.
   while (temp.getNext() != null)
   {
      follower = temp;
      temp = temp.getNext();
   }
   follower.setNext(null);
   return temp.getValue();
   }
}
```

It's a good exercise to trace the implementation above and draw pictures similar to Figure 5 in Section 15.2 of your text as you walk through the code. Try walking through the test program in Example 16.8. Go through each method implementation and sketch your `ListNode` additions and deletions.

Example 16.8

```
public static void main(String[] args)
{
   LList staff = new LList();   // Construct empty list.
   staff.addLast("Dick");      // D
   staff.addFirst("Harry");    // H D
   staff.addLast("Romeo");     // H D R
   staff.addFirst("Tom");      // T H D R
   staff.removeLast();         // T H D
   staff.printList();
   staff.removeFirst();     // H D
   System.out.println(staff.getFirst());   // Harry
   System.out.println(staff.getLast());    // Dick
}
```

Finally, what happens if we want to add to the middle of a linked list? Suppose you have a linked list that maintains its elements in order. How do you insert or delete an element from this list? Let's look at inserting a `ListNode` whose value is a string. We wish to insert the node so that the strings are in alphabetical order. We will use our linked list implementation without the `last` instance field.

Our list is initialized to be empty.

```
ListNode first = null;
```

Our new `ListNode` is created to hold the new string value (`name`).

```
ListNode newNode = new ListNode(name, null);
```

Now, let's insert. First check to see if we are inserting into an empty list.

```
if (first == null)
{
   first = newNode;
}
```

If the list is not empty, check to see if the new node should be inserted in the front of the list. Because our `ListNode` value is an `Object`, we must cast to the appropriate type (`String` in this case) to compare values.

```
String firstValue = (String) first.getValue();
String newValue = (String) newNode.getValue();
if (firstValue.compareTo(newValue) >= 0)   // New node goes first
{
   newNode.setNext(first);
   first = newNode;
}
```

If the new node isn't inserted in the front of the list, see if it belongs in the middle or at the end of the list.

```
String newValue = (String) newNode.getValue();
ListNode temp = first;
ListNode follower = temp;
// Checking for end and for order
while (temp != null &&
       newValue.compareTo((String) temp.getValue()) > 0)
{
   follower = temp;
   temp = temp.getNext();
}

// Stopped because end of list OR correct position found in middle
// Does it belong in the middle?
follower.setNext(newNode);
newNode.setNext(temp);
```

Deleting a node from our linked list of `ListNodes` follows a similar coding pattern. You should first make sure that you are not trying to delete a node from an empty list. Then check to see if you are deleting the first node. If so, `first` will have to be adjusted. And finally, consider deleting from the middle or end of the list, setting the `next` fields where required.

When using the Java Library's `LinkedList` class, inserting nodes in order follows a similar pattern. First, start with an empty list.

```
LinkedList<String> list = new LinkedList<String>();
```

Now, are you adding to an empty list?

```
if (list.size() == 0)
{
   list.addFirst(name);
}
```

If the list is not empty, does the new node belong in the front of the list?

```
String firstValue = list.getFirst();
if (name.compareTo(firstValue) <= 0)
{
   list.addFirst(name);
}
```

If the node doesn't belong in the front of the list, then check to see if it belongs in the middle or at the end of the list.

```
ListIterator<String> iter = list.listIterator();
boolean foundLarger = false;
while (!foundLarger && iter.hasNext())
{
   // Does object belong in the middle?
   if (name.compareTo(iter.next()) < 0)
   {
      foundLarger = true;
      iter.previous();   // previous is not tested on the AP Exam
      iter.add(name);
   }
}
```

```
   // Or does it belong at the end?
   if (!iter.hasNext())
      list.addLast(name);
```

The `ListIterator` has a `previous` method that allows us to traverse in reverse. `previous` is very useful when inserting or deleting from the middle or from the end of a `LinkedList`. The use of `previous` will not be tested on the AP Exam.

The preceding code inserts `String` objects into a linked list in lexicographical order. Suppose you wish to keep an ordered linked list of `Integers`, or `Coins`, or `Students`. How could we modify our code so that it can be used by any of these classes? To "order" objects of a class, what must be true of the class (what interface should the class implement)? Of course, your answer to this question is that "ordering" objects of a class requires the class to implement the `Comparable` interface!

Example 16.9 shows an implementation of a generic `ListNode` class and a simplified generic `LinkedList` implementation (includes only a method to add to the front of the list).

Example 16.9 Generic `ListNode` class

```
public class ListNode<E>
{
   public ListNode(E initValue, ListNode initNext)
   {
      value = initValue;
      next = initNext;
   }

   public E getValue()
   {
      return value;
   }

   public ListNode getNext()
   {
      return next;
   }

   public void setValue(E theNewValue)
   {
      value = theNewValue;
   }

   void setNext(ListNode theNewNext)
   {
      next = theNewNext;
   }

   private E value;
   private ListNode next;
}
```

Generic Simplified Linked List Implementation

```java
public class LList<E>
{
    public LList()
    {
        first = null;
    }

    public void addFirst(E elt)
    {
        ListNode<E> newNode = new ListNode<E>(elt, first);
        first = newNode;
    }

    public void printList()
    {
        System.out.println();
        ListNode<E> temp = first;
        while (temp != null)
        {
            System.out.println(temp.getValue());
            temp = temp.getNext();
        }
    }

    private ListNode<E> first;
}
```

Test Harness for Generic LList and ListNode Classes

```java
public class LLTester
{
    public static void main(String[] args)
    {
        LList<String> staff = new LList<String>();
        staff.addFirst("Ann");
        staff.addFirst("Bob");
        staff.addFirst("Harry");
        staff.addFirst("Dave");
        staff.addFirst("Carol");
        staff.printList();    // Carol Dave Harry Bob Ann
    }
}
```

16.2.1   Doubly Linked Lists

In addition to linked lists that have a next field referencing the next node in the list, we can have a doubly linked list. In a doubly linked list, the node contains a value, a reference to the next node in the list, and a reference to the previous node in the list.

Figure 16.3

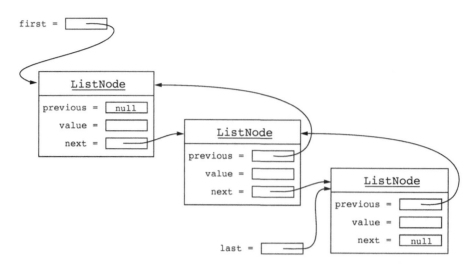

Suppose our ListNode class were modified to be a DLListNode class. Example 16.10 modifies the ListNode constructor for the DLListNode class. A doubly linked list node *is a* linked list node with another instance field.

Example 16.10

```
public DLListNode(DLListNode initPrevious,
    Object initValue, DLListNode initNext)
{
   previous = initPrevious;
   value = initValue;
   next = initNext;
}
```

When adding a node to a doubly linked list, you must make a few more node adjustments! Before writing any code, draw pictures of the intended adjustments. Example 16.11 and Figure 16.4 show adjustments necessary to add a DLListNode to the middle of a doubly linked list.

Example 16.11

```
/**
    Adding a node to middle or end of an ordered doubly linked
    list.
*/
Comparable newValue = (Comparable) newNode.getValue();
DLListNode temp = first;
while (temp.getNext() != null &&
    newValue.compareTo((Comparable) temp.getValue()) > 0)
{
   temp = temp.getNext();
}

if (newValue.compareTo((Comparable) temp.getValue()) <= 0)
{
   // Adding to middle.
   // Four references must be set.
```

```
        DLListNode hold = temp.getPrevious();
        hold.setNext(newNode);
        newNode.setNext(temp);
        newNode.setPrevious(temp.getPrevious());
        temp.setPrevious(newNode);
    }
    else
    {
        // Adding to end.
        // Two references must be set.
        temp.setNext(newNode);
        newNode.setPrevious(temp);
    }
```

Figure 16.4

To delete a node from a singly or a doubly linked list, you need to consider the same cases as you do when you insert a node into a linked list. Is the list empty? Is the node that is to be deleted the first node of the list? Is it in the middle? Is it the last node? Is the node to be deleted even in the list? If the node is not in the list, what should happen? If there is more than one node with the same value as the node to be deleted, should only the first occurrence be deleted or all nodes with that value?

To delete from the middle of a doubly linked list, you must adjust two references.

```
        DLListNode hold = temp.getPrevious();
        hold.setNext(temp.getNext());
        DLListNode hold2 = temp.getNext();
        hold2.setPrevious(temp.getPrevious());
```

Figure 16.5

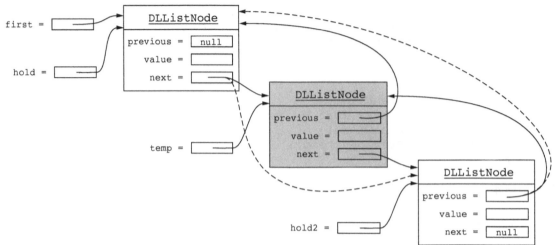

It is a good exercise to draw the nodes of a doubly linked list and write the code necessary to delete the first and last nodes of the list.

The Java LinkedList class is implemented using a doubly linked list with references to the first node and to the last node. Operations that index into the list (accessing the *i*th node) will traverse the list from the beginning or the end, whichever is closer to the specified index (*i*).

16.2.2 Circularly Linked Lists

A circularly linked list is a list whose last node references the first node. The implementation works much like the singly linked list implementation except that, when traversing the list with the temp, the last node of the list is found when

```
temp.getNext() == first
```

evaluates to true. Figure 16.6 illustrates a circularly linked list.

Figure 16.6

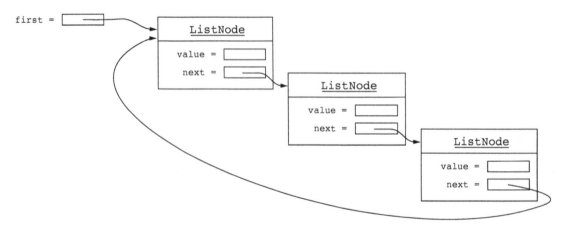

And, if you want to be challenged even more, you can implement a doubly-circularly linked list!

16.2.3 Header and Trailer Nodes

When implementing a linked list or a doubly linked list, you considered several cases: adding to the empty list, adding or removing the first node, adding or removing the last node, adding or removing a middle node. A *header* node is a node that comes before all other nodes in the list. A *trailer* node is a node that comes after all of the nodes in the list. If a list has a header node and a trailer node, most of these cases are eliminated. We are left only with adding and deleting from the middle of the list. The header and trailer nodes are not included when printing the list contents or searching the list. They can be considered "dummy" nodes.

The constructor of a linked list implementation that has a header and trailer node would create a list similar to the one illustrated in Figure 16.7. For example, if the list is designed to hold values in increasing order, the value in the header node will be a value smaller than all values in the list and the value in the trailer node will be a value larger than all values in the list.

Figure 16.7

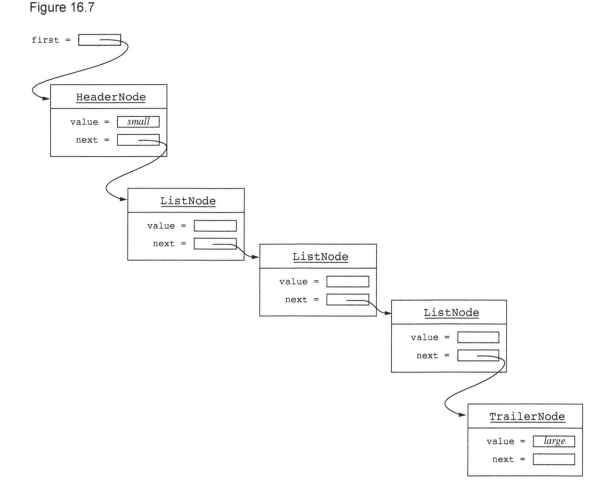

You may see these terms used on the AP Exam but, when implementing linked lists on the free-response questions on the AP Exam, do not use header and trailer nodes unless explicitly told to do so.

16.3   Abstract and Concrete Data Types

An abstract data type defines the fundamental operations on the data but does not specify the implementation. When we refer to a list, we think of an ordered sequence of elements in which an element can be inserted or removed. The concrete representation of a list may be a `LinkedList` or an `ArrayList`. Although the operations performed on both implementations appear to have the same outcome, the performance efficiency of these operations can be quite different. As we discussed in Example 16.1, the implementation of the `List` methods is quite different for the `LinkedList` and the `ArrayList`. The `ArrayList` has random access. The `LinkedList` is accessed sequentially. Figures 8 and 10 in Section 15.3 of your text illustrate the differences. Table 16.5 summarizes the efficiency of some of the more common operations on lists of elements that maintain their order.

Table 16.5

Operation	`ArrayList`	`LinkedList` *(Java library class)*
Insert at front	$O(n)$	$O(1)$
Insert at end	$O(1)$	$O(1)$
Remove from front	$O(n)$	$O(1)$
Remove from end	$O(1)$	$O(1)$
Linear Traversal	$O(n)$	$O(n)$
Random Access	$O(1)$	$O(n)$

As you can see, if random access to list elements is important and done frequently, an `ArrayList` may be a better choice than a linked list.

16.4   Stacks and Queues

A stack is an abstract data type to which elements can be added and removed at one end only. Think about a stack of dinner plates in your kitchen cabinet. Each plate you add to the stack is placed on the top of the stack. When you remove a plate, you remove the topmost plate first. A stack is a collection of items with "last in first out" (LIFO) retrieval. The stack's insert method is `push`. The remove method is `pop`. The stack can also "look at" the top element without removing it with the `peek` method. There is a `Stack` class in the Java library that implements the stack methods. Table 16.6 lists `java.util.Stack` methods that are currently included in the AP subset.

Table 16.6

`class java.util.Stack<E>`

Method	Method Summary
`E push(E elt)`	Pushes item `elt` onto the top of this stack. Returns the item pushed.
`E pop()`	Removes and returns the element at the top of this stack.
`E peek()`	Returns the object at the top of this stack without removing it from the stack.
`boolean isEmpty()`	Returns `true` if this stack is empty, `false` otherwise.

The `java.util.Stack` class inherits methods that access and manipulate elements other than the top of the stack. Such methods violate the abstract data structure definition. You should not use those methods in writing answers to free-response questions on the AP Exam. Using those methods on the AP Exam may result in a deduction of points. You may also notice that the `java.util.Stack` method to test if a stack is empty is `empty()`. You may use either `empty` (`Stack` method) or `isEmpty` (`Stack` inherited method) to test if a `Stack` is empty.

The `java.util.Stack` methods included in the AP subset are demonstrated in Example 16.12.

Example 16.12

```java
public class StackTester
{
    public static void main(String[] args)
    {
        Stack<String> s = new Stack<String>();    // Constructor call
        s.push("Dick");
        s.push("Harry");
        s.push("Romeo");
        s.push("Tom");
        System.out.println(s.peek());
        System.out.println();

        while (!(s.isEmpty()))
        {
            System.out.println(s.pop());
        }
    }
}
```

The resulting output is:

Tom

Tom
Romeo
Harry
Dick

Remember, a stack is an abstract data type. The `java.util.Stack` class uses an array to implement a stack. An `ArrayList` or a `LinkedList` can also be used to implement a stack.

Example 16.13 shows an `ArrayList` implementation of a stack holding `String` objects where the top of the stack is the element with the highest index. With this implementation `push` and `pop` are $O(1)$.

Example 16.13

```java
public class StackArrayList
{
    public StackArrayList()
    {
        stck = new ArrayList<String>();
    }

    public void push(String x)
    {
        stck.add(x);
    }

    public String pop()
    {
        return stck.remove(stck.size() - 1);
    }

    public String peek()
    {
        return stck.get(stck.size() - 1);
    }

    public boolean isEmpty()
    {
        return stck.size() == 0;
    }

    private ArrayList<String> stck;
}
```

Some applications where stacks might be useful include:
- Evaluation of postfix expressions.
- Testing the balancing of nested parentheses (symbols) in an algebraic expression. $\{a + (b - [c + d]) / e + (f - g - h)\}$
- Keeping track of variable declarations inside nested { } inside a compiler.

A queue is an abstract data type to which you add elements at one end and remove elements from the other end. Think about a queue as being a water fountain line or a cafeteria line. The first person in the line is the first person out of the line. When one is added to the line, he is added to the rear of the line. A queue is a collection of items with "first in first out" (FIFO) retrieval. The `add` method is used to *enqueue*, or add, an element to the rear of the queue. The `remove` method is used to *dequeue*, or remove, and element from the front of the queue. The queue can also "look at" the front element without removing it with the `peek` method. The Java library includes the `java.util.Queue` interface. The `java.util.Queue` interface inherits methods that allow access to elements other than the front and rear of the queue. In writing solutions to free-response questions involving queues, use only the queue methods included in the AP subset. Using methods that violate the data structure definition of a queue on the AP Exam may result in a deduction of points. Table 16.7 lists the queue methods that are part of the AP subset.

Table 16.7

`interface java.util.Queue<E>`

Method	Method Summary
`boolean add(E elt)`	Enqueues `elt` to the end of this queue. Returns `true`.
`E remove()`	Dequeues and returns the element at the front of this queue.
`E peek()`	Returns the object at the front of this queue without removing it from the queue. Returns `null` if this queue is empty.
`boolean isEmpty()`	Returns `true` if this queue is empty, `false` otherwise.

Example 16.14 demonstrates the queue methods included in the AP subset. In Section 16.1 of this guide, we mentioned that `java.util.LinkedList` implements `java.util.Queue`. In Example 16.14, our abstract data type, queue, is implemented using a `java.util.LinkedList`. Because our linked list data structure is representing a queue, we limit ourselves to the queue methods listed in Table 16.7 above.

Example 16.14

```java
import java.util.Queue;
import java.util.LinkedList;

public class QueueTester
{
    public static void main(String[] args)
    {
        Queue<String> que = new LinkedList<String>();

        que.add("Harry");
        que.add("Romeo");
        que.add("Tom");

        System.out.println(que.peek());
        System.out.println();

        while (!(que.isEmpty()))
        {
            System.out.println(que.remove());
        }
    }
}
```

The resulting output is:

Harry

Harry
Romeo
Tom

Some applications where queues might be useful include:
- A simulation of planes on a runway or customers waiting in a line at a bank.
- A printer queue (where your print requests are held while the printer is busy).

- A queue of user-interface events (button clicks, keystrokes) that need to be processed.
- Other requests, e.g., service requests for a web-based application.

■ Expanded Coverage of Material That is Not Found in the Text

- Circularly linked lists are not covered in your text but are in Section 16.2.2 of this guide.
- Header and trailer nodes are not covered in your text but are in Section 16.2.3 of this guide.

■ Topics That Are Useful But Not Tested

- The `ListIterator` includes the methods `hasPrevious` and `previous`. These methods are used to determine if there is a previous node and to move the iterator position backwards.
- Your text implements a linked list using inner classes for `Node` (a `ListNode` class) and `LinkedListIterator` (the list iterator). Inner classes are very useful here and allow for simpler implementation of the linked list methods. This is shown in Section 15.2 of your text.

■ Things to Remember When Taking the AP Exam

- Inserting and deleting from a `LinkedList` is efficient because these operations do not require shifting the other elements in the list.
- The enhanced `for` loop can be used with `java.util.LinkedList`. This is demonstrated in Example 16.3.
- If an application requires many look-ups (searches), use an implementation that provides $O(1)$ access whenever possible. Specifically, use an array when you need random access to individual elements (e.g., sorting algorithms) and use a linked list when you frequently need to insert or remove in the middle of the list (e.g., simulation of cars on a freeway with entrance/exit ramps).
- Be sure to check whether the list data structure is empty before you try to remove an item from it.
- The AB Quick Reference Guide that you will be given during the AP Exam contains the `ListNode` class but you should be familiar with this class prior to the exam.
- Be careful when implementing code that adds or removes nodes from a linked list. Ask yourself the following questions:
  - Does this code handle the empty list case?
  - Does this code handle the front of the list case?
  - Does this code handle the end of the list case?
  - Does this code handle the middle of the list case?
  - Does this code handle the list with only one node?
- Use a list iterator to access elements of a `LinkedList`. DO NOT use `get/set/insert`.
- Check for `null` pointers! Whenever calling `p.getNext()`, `p.getData()`, etc., ask yourself "Can p be empty? If so, am I checking for it? If not, why not?"
- Stacks are LIFO (last-in, first-out). Queues are FIFO (first-in, first-out).

■ Key Words

You should understand the terms below. The AP CS Exam questions may include references to these terms. The citations in parentheses next to each term identify the page numbers where it is defined and/or discussed in *Java Concepts for AP Computer Science*, 5th ed.

abstract data type (682)	LIFO (686)	pop (686)
concrete implementation (682)	linked list (666)	push (686)
	links (667)	queue (686)
doubly linked list (669)	list iterator (667)	stack (686)
FIFO (686)	node (666)	stack top (686)

■ Connecting the Detailed Topic Outline to the Text

The citations in parentheses identify where information in the outline can be located in *Java Concepts for AP Computer Science*, 5th ed.

- Using Linked Lists (666–670)
- Implementing Linked Lists (671–682)
  - Doubly Linked Lists (669)
  - Circularly Linked Lists
  - Header and Trailer Nodes
- Abstract and Concrete Data Types (682–685)
- Stacks and Queues (686–689)

■ Practice Questions

Multiple Choice

1. What is printed to the screen when the following code segment is executed?

    ```
    LinkedList<String> staff = new LinkedList<String>();
    staff.addFirst("Mary");
    staff.addFirst("Joe");
    staff.addLast("Fran");
    System.out.print(staff.removeLast() + " ");
    System.out.print(staff.removeFirst()+ " ");
    System.out.println(staff.removeFirst());
    ```

    a. *Joe Mary Fran*
    b. *Fran Joe Mary*
    c. *Mary Joe Fran*
    d. *Fran Mary Joe*
    e. *Joe Fran Mary*

2. An application is being written to simulate planes waiting to take off on an airport runway. Which of the following data structures is the best choice for this application?

    a. A fixed-length array
    b. An `ArrayList`
    c. A singly-linked list
    d. A queue
    e. A stack

3. Suppose the following code segment is executed.

    ```
    LinkedList<String> list = new LinkedList<String>();
    ListIterator<String> iter = list.listIterator();
    iter.add("David");
    iter.add("Juliet");
    iter.add("Gail");
    iter.add("Chris");
    iter = list.listIterator();
    iter.next();
    iter.remove();
    iter.add("Mom");
    ```

    What does the linked list, `list`, contain after this code segment is executed?

    a. David Mom Gail Chris
    b. Mom Gail Juliet David
    c. Chris Mom Juliet David
    d. Mom Juliet Gail Chris
    e. Mom David Gail Chris

4. For the Java library `LinkedList` class, which operations are constant time ($O(1)$) in the worst case?

    I.   `addFirst`
    II. `addLast`
    III. `getLast`

    a. I only
    b. II only
    c. III only
    d. II and III only
    e. I, II, and III

5. A client program wishes to test to see if two `ListNodes`, `node1` and `node2`, have the same `String` values in their value fields. Which of the following conditions properly checks this?

    a. `node1 == node2`
    b. `node1.equals(node2)`
    c. `node1.value == node2.value`
    d. `(node1.value).equals(node2.value)`
    e. `(node1.getValue()).equals(node2.getValue())`

6. Which of the following conditions tests whether two `ListNodes`, `node1` and `node2`, reference the same node?

   I.   `node1 == node2`
   II. `node1.equals(node2)`
   III. `node2.equals(node1)`

   a. I only
   b. II only
   c. III only
   d. II and III only
   e. I, II, and III

7. Consider a partially-filled array implementation of a stack, `stck`. Suppose the implementation uses `stck[0]` as the top of the stack and the last filled position of the array as the bottom of the stack. Which of the following statements about this implementation is **true**?

   a. `push`, `pop`, and `peekTop` are $O(n)$.
   b. `push`, `pop`, and `peekTop` are $O(1)$.
   c. `push` and `pop` are $O(1)$; `peekTop` is $O(n)$.
   d. `push` and `pop` are $O(n)$; `peekTop` is $O(1)$.
   e. `pop` and `peekTop` are $O(n)$; `push` is $O(1)$.

8. Consider a partially-filled array implementation of a stack, `stck`. Suppose the implementation uses `stck[0]` as the bottom of the stack and the last filled position of the array as the top of the stack. Which of the following statements about this implementation is **true**?

   a. `push`, `pop`, and `peekTop` are $O(n)$.
   b. `push`, `pop`, and `peekTop` are $O(1)$.
   c. `push` and `pop` are $O(1)$; `peekTop` is $O(n)$.
   d. `push` and `pop` are $O(n)$; `peekTop` is $O(1)$.
   e. `pop` and `peekTop` are $O(n)$; `push` is $O(1)$.

9. The `Integers` 1, 2, 3, 4, and 5 are added to a queue (in that order), then removed one at a time and pushed on a stack. The stack is popped three times. What element is now on the top of the stack?

   a. 1
   b. 2
   c. 3
   d. 4
   e. 5

10. Which statement is **true** about an abstract data type?

    a. An abstract data type defines the fundamental operations on the data but does not specify an implementation.
    b. An abstract data type is an abstract class. It cannot be instantiated.
    c. An abstract data type defines the implementation choices made.
    d. An abstract data type is more efficient than a concrete data type.
    e. An abstract data type is another name for an interface.

11. Suppose you need to organize a collection of phone numbers for a company. There are currently over 6,000 employees. You know the phone system can handle at most 10,000 phone numbers. You expect several hundred lookups against the collection every day. What would be the best choice for a data structure in implementing this simulation?

    a. array
    b. linked list
    c. doubly linked list
    d. stack
    e. queue

12. Assume the declarations below have been made.

```
Stack<Integer> s = new Stack<Integer>();
Queue<Integer> q = new LinkedList<Integer>();
```

Consider the following.
- Integers from 1 to 5 inclusive are added into an initially empty queue, q, in that order.
- Integers from 1 to 5 inclusive are pushed onto an initially empty stack, s, in that order.

The following code is executed.

```
for (int x = 1; x <= 5; x++)
{
    Integer y, z;
    y = q.remove();
    if (y.intValue() % 2 == 0)
        s.push(y);
    else
        q.add(y);

    z = s.pop();
    if (z.intValue() % 2 == 0)
        s.push(z);
    else
        q.add(z);
}

while (!s.isEmpty())
{
    System.out.print(s.pop() + " ");
}

while (!q.isEmpty())
{
    System.out.print(q.remove() + " ");
}
```

What will be printed while evaluating the above expression?

    a. *4 4 3 2 1 5 1 5 3 5*
    b. *1 2 3 4 2 4 1 5 3 5*
    c. *1 2 3 4 2 4 1 5 3 5*
    d. *4 2 4 3 2 1 1 5 3 5*
    e. *4 4 3 2 1 1 5 3 5 5*

13. The following implementations of the method `reverse` are intended to reverse the order of the elements in a `LinkedList`.

I.
```java
public static void reverse(LinkedList<SomeType> aList)
{
    LinkedList<SomeType> temp = new LinkedList<SomeType>();
    while (aList.size() > 0)
        temp.addLast(aList.removeFirst());
    while (temp.size() > 0)
        aList.addFirst(temp.removeFirst());
}
```

II.
```java
public static void reverse(LinkedList<SomeType> aList)
{
    Queue<SomeType> temp = new LinkedList<SomeType>();
    while (aList.size() > 0)
        temp.add(aList.removeFirst());
    while (!temp.isEmpty() )
        aList.addFirst(temp.remove());
}
```

III.
```java
public static void reverse(LinkedList<SomeType> aList)
{
    Stack<SomeType> temp = new Stack<SomeType>();
    while (aList.size() > 0)
        temp.push(aList.removeLast());
    while (!temp.isEmpty() )
        aList.addFirst(temp.pop());
}
```

Which of the choices above perform the intended task successfully?

a. I only
b. II only
c. III only
d. II and III only
e. I, II, and III

Questions 14 and 15 refer to the following problem statement.

Consider the algorithm for determining whether a sequence of parentheses is balanced (has correct nesting). The pseudocode for this algorithm appears below.

Initialize a boolean variable `validExpression` *to true.*
while (there are more symbols in the expression)
{
    look at the next `symbol`
    if `symbol` *is a {, [, or (*
        push it on the stack
    if it is a },], or)
    {
        if the stack is empty then return false
        else pop the stack
    }
    if the element popped is not the match for `symbol` *then return false*
}
if the stack is not empty then return false, else return true.

14. What is the maximum number of symbols that will appear on the stack at any one time for the sequence { [( )] [( )] [( )] }?

    a. 1
    b. 2
    c. 3
    d. 4
    e. 5

15. What sequence of elements is on the stack after processing the input { [( )] [(( ))] { [(? (The top of the stack is to the right.)

    a. { [( )] [(( ))] { [(
    b. { [([(({ [(
    c.)]))]
    d. { { [(
    e. ([{ {

Questions 16 and 17 refer to the postfix problem statement below.

We normally write algebraic expressions with an arithmetic operator between two operands (numbers). A postfix expression is an expression in which the operator is written after the operands. For example, the postfix notation for the expression 2 + 3 is 2 3 +.

The following algorithm describes the evaluation of a postfix expression using a stack. The postfix expression is evaluated from left to right. If a number is read, it is pushed on the stack. If an operator is read, two numbers are popped off the stack, the operator is applied to the two popped values and the answer is pushed on the stack. When all has been read from the expression, what's left on the stack is the answer.

16. Using the above algorithm, the postfix expression:

    3 4 + 5 * 3 4 * 6 / 8 * +

evaluates to:

    a. 0
    b. 4
    c. 19
    d. 51
    e. 192

17. What is the maximum number of numbers on the stack at any one time?

    a. 2
    b. 3
    c. 4
    d. 5
    e. 6

18. You are implementing a program for tracking appointments. You have a class `Person` and a class `Appointment`. A person can have multiple appointments. Each appointment has a start time, an end time, and a description. You keep the appointments in order sorted by start time. Which of the following statements are correct?

   I.   If appointments are frequently deleted and inserted, then a linked list of appointments is more efficient than an array.
   II. Using a linked list of appointments makes it efficient to use the binary search algorithm for finding an appointment that falls on a given time.
   III. Appointments should be kept on a stack so that the most important appointment, regardless on start time, is always on the top of the stack.

   a. I only
   b. II only
   c. III only
   d. I and II only
   e. I and III only

19. You are implementing a word processor. You need to find an appropriate data structure to store a sequence of characters. Users will frequently insert and remove characters from the middle of a document. Which of the following statements are **true**?

   I.   Storing all characters in a single array is inefficient, particularly for long documents.
   II. The characters should be stored in a stack so that the most recently inserted character can be immediately deleted when the user hits the "Backspace" key.
   III. A singly linked list of characters is not an appropriate data structure for the document because each node would need to store one character and one link, which uses a lot of storage.

   a. I only
   b. II only
   c. II and III only
   d. I and III only
   e. I, II, and III

20. Suppose we have a stack, `aStack`, implemented using an array list. The methods `push` and `pop` are implemented without causing any shifting of elements in the array list. Also suppose that 5 items are pushed onto this initially empty stack. Now, a new item is pushed onto the stack and 2 items are popped off the stack. In what position of the array list will the next item pushed be placed?

   a. 0
   b. 1
   c. 4
   d. 5
   e. 6

Free Response Questions

1. `DLListNode` *is a* `ListNode` with an additional instance field that references the previous node in a doubly linked list. Refer to the `ListNode` implementation in Example 16.4 or the `ListNode` class in the *AB Quick Reference Guide* to answer this question.

    a. To convert the `ListNode` class to a `DLListNode` class, what do we need to modify?

    b. What additional methods should be added?

    c. Given the class header for `DLListNode` below,

        ```
        public class DLListNode extends ListNode
        ```

        implement the `DLListNode` constructor.

    d. Indicate the efficiency of each operation listed in the table below for the doubly linked list of `DLListNode`s illustrated.

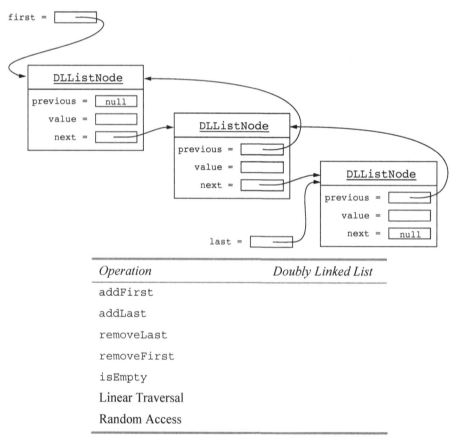

Operation	Doubly Linked List
addFirst	
addLast	
removeLast	
removeFirst	
isEmpty	
Linear Traversal	
Random Access	

Consider the doubly linked list class whose incomplete implementation appears below. This list has two private instance variables: `first` accesses the first node of the list, and `last` accesses the last node of the list. The list does not contain header or trailer nodes.

```
/**
    Invariant: All nodes in the DLList are DLListNodes.
*/
public class DLList
{
```

```java
/**
   Constructs an empty list.
*/
public DLList()
{
   first = null;
   last = null;
}

/**
   Inserts a new node containing key in the list.
   @param key the object to be inserted
*/
public void insert(Object key) {. . .}

/**
   Prints the contents of the nodes in the list.
*/
public void printList() {. . .}

/**
   Searches for node that contains key.
   @param key the object to search for
   @return a reference to the first node containing key;
   if key is not found in the list, null is returned
*/
public DLListNode search(Object key)
{
   // Code goes here
}

/**
   Removes the first node that contains key if that node
   exists.
*/
public void removeOne(Object key)
{
   // Code goes here
}

/**
   Removes all nodes in the list that contain key.
*/
public void removeAll(Object key)
{
   // Code goes here
}

private DLListNode first;
private DLListNode last;
}
```

e. Implement the method `search` that takes one parameter, `key`, and searches the doubly linked list for the first occurrence of a node whose value is the same as `key` and returns a reference to this node. If `key` is not in the list, `search` returns `null`. Assume that all `DLListNode` methods and constructors work as intended. In writing `search`, use the method header below.

```
public DLListNode search(Object key)
```

f. Implement the method `removeOne`. `removeOne` removes the first node in the list whose value is the same as its one parameter, `key`. You may call `search` in writing `removeOne`. Assume that `search` works as intended regardless of what you wrote in part e. Also assume that all `DLListNode` methods and constructors work as intended. In writing `removeOne`, use the method header below.

```
public void removeOne(Object key)
```

g. Implement the method `removeAll`. `removeAll` removes all nodes in the list whose value is the same as its parameter `key`. You may call `search` and/or `removeOne` in writing `removeAll`. Assume that all methods and constructors written in parts a–f of this problem work as intended regardless of what you wrote. In writing `removeAll`, use the header below.

```
public void removeAll(Object key)
```

2. A stack can be used to convert decimal numbers to binary numbers.

a. You are to write the method `displayBinary` that will convert a decimal number into a binary number using a stack. The pseudocode for an algorithm that converts a decimal number to a binary number is given below.

```
public static void displayBinary(int decimalNum)
{
    Stack<Integer> stck = new Stack<Integer>();
    while decimalNum not equal to 0
    {
        find remainder when decimalNum is divided by 2
        push remainder on the stack
        divide the decimalNum by 2
    }
    while stack isn't empty
        pop num off the stack and display
}
```

Use the following header in writing your method `displayBinary`.

```
/**
    Displays the binary representation of decimalNum.
    Precondition: decimalNum > 0
    @param decimalNum the number to convert to binary
*/
public static void displayBinary(int decimalNum)
```

b. Implement a method `displayOtherBase` that will convert a decimal number to a number in any base less than or equal to 16 (hexadecimal numbers). Examples of conversions are given in the table below.

Decimal number	Converted to this base	Results in
21	2	10101
100	2	1100100
64	8	100
73	8	111
74	16	4A
447	16	1BF

In writing `displayOtherBase`, use the header given below.

```
/**
    Displays the decimal number converted to base.
    Precondition: num > 0, 0 < base, and base <= 16
    @param num the decimal number to convert
    @param base the base to which num will be converted
*/
public static void displayOtherBase(int num, int base)
```

3. A graphical user interface (GUI) system (such as *Microsoft Windows, Mac OSX,* or an *X Windows* window manager in *Linux*) keeps track of all of the windows on the user's screen. One of the windows is the *top* window. It has a specially marked title bar and is displayed on top of the other windows. The GUI has an operation to *cycle* through the windows, typically with a keystroke such as ALT + TAB. That operation moves the current top window to the bottom and the other windows up by one position. It also has operations to open a new window, which now becomes the top window, and to close the top window, so that the next window under it becomes the top window.

Your task is to implement a class `WindowManager` that manages a collection of objects of type `Window`. Each `Window` has a `Rectangle` indicating its size, and a `String` indicating the message on the title bar. (Real windows would know how to draw their contents, but we will ignore that aspect in this problem.)

The `Rectangle` constructor takes four parameters: *x*- and *y*-coordinates of its top left point, its width, and its height. The `Rectangle` `toString` method returns the `String` representing the `Rectangle` object's coordinate and size values.

Operations of the `WindowManager` are:
- `add`: Adds a new `Window` as the top window.
- `remove`: Removes the top window.
- `cycle`: Moves the current top window to the bottom and the other windows up by one position.
- `print`: Prints the windows from top to bottom. The `toString` method of `Window` returns a "printable" `Window`.

The implementation of `Window` and an incomplete implementation of `WindowManager` are below.

```java
public class Window
{
    /**
        Constructs a rectangular Window with title, winTitle.
        @param winTitle the window title
        @param winBounds the window rectangle
    */
    public Window(String winTitle, Rectangle winBounds)
    {
        title = winTitle;
        bounds = winBounds;
    }

    /**
        @return the string representation of the Rectangular window
        that includes the window title and dimensions
    */
    public String toString()
    {
        return "Window[title=" + title + ", bounds=" + bounds + "]";
    }

    private String title;
    private Rectangle bounds;
}

public class WindowManager
{
    /**
        Adds window, which now becomes the new top window.
        @param w window to add
    */
    public void add(Window w)
    {
        // Code goes here
    }

    /**
        Removes the top window.
    */
    public void remove()
    {
        // Code goes here
    }

    /**
        Moves the current top window to the bottom and the other
        windows are moved up by one position.
    */
    public void cycle()
    {
        // Code goes here
    }
```

```
    /**
       Prints the windows from top to bottom.
    */
    public void print()
    {
        // Code goes here
    }

    // Private stuff here
}
```

A Sample Client Program

```java
import java.awt.Rectangle;

public class WindowManagerTester
{
    public static void main(String[] args)
    {
        WindowManager manager = new WindowManager();
        manager.add(new Window("A", new Rectangle(5, 10, 15, 20)));
        manager.add(new Window("B", new Rectangle(15, 20, 15, 20)));
        manager.add(new Window("C", new Rectangle(25, 30, 15, 20)));
        manager.print();
        manager.cycle();
        manager.print();
        manager.remove();
        manager.print();
    }
}
```

The program run is:

```
Window[title=C, bounds=java.awt.Rectangle[x=25,y=30,width=15,height=20]]
Window[title=B, bounds=java.awt.Rectangle[x=15,y=20,width=15,height=20]]
Window[title=A, bounds=java.awt.Rectangle[x=5,y=10,width=15,height=20]]

Window[title=B, bounds=java.awt.Rectangle[x=15,y=20,width=15,height=20]]
Window[title=A, bounds=java.awt.Rectangle[x=5,y=10,width=15,height=20]]
Window[title=C, bounds=java.awt.Rectangle[x=25,y=30,width=15,height=20]]

Window[title=A, bounds=java.awt.Rectangle[x=5,y=10,width=15,height=20]]
Window[title=C, bounds=java.awt.Rectangle[x=25,y=30,width=15,height=20]]
```

a. What data structure is most appropriate for storing the collection of `Window` objects? Choose from an array, a linked list, a stack, and a queue. Justify your choice.

b. Use your chosen data structure to implement the method `add`. Use the method header below when writing `add`.

```java
public void add(Window w)
```

c. Use your chosen data structure to implement the method `remove`. Use the method header below when writing `remove`.

```java
public void remove()
```

d. Given the incomplete implementation of the `WindowManager` class above, use your chosen data structure to implement the method `cycle`. Use the method header below when writing `cycle`.

```
public void cycle()
```

e. Given the incomplete implementation of the `WindowManager` class above, use your chosen data structure to implement the method `print`. `print` should print the windows from top to bottom. The `toString` method of `Window` returns a "printable" `Window`. If `w` is a `Window`,

```
System.out.println(w);
```

will print the correct `Window` information in the format displayed in the execution shown above. Use the method header below when writing `print`.

```
public void print()
```

CHAPTER

(Covers *Java Concepts for AP Computer Science* Chapter 16)

Advanced Data Structures (AB only)

■ Topic Summary

17.1 Sets

A *set* is an unordered collection of distinct elements. Unlike linked lists, stacks, and queues, sets contain no duplicate items. Elements can be added to, located in, and removed from a set. The AP subset contains the set methods listed in Table 17.1.

Table 17.1
`interface java.util.Set<E>`

Method	*Method Summary*
`boolean add(E elt)`	Adds the parameter `elt` as an element to this set if it is not already in the set and returns `true`. If the element is already in the set, returns `false`.
`boolean contains(Object obj)`	Returns `true` if this set contains the element `obj`, otherwise returns `false`.
`boolean remove(Object obj)`	Removes the element `obj` from this set and returns `true` if the `obj` is in this set; if the element is not present, returns `false`.
`int size()`	Returns the number of elements in this set.
`Iterator<E> iterator()`	Returns an `Iterator` that provides access to the elements of this set.

The elements of a set are accessed using a set iterator. Since sets are unordered, the iterator may visit the set elements in a different order from the order in which the elements were added to the set. The set iterator includes the methods listed in Table 17.2.

Table 17.2
```
interface java.util.Iterator<E>
```

Method	Method Summary
`boolean hasNext()`	Returns `true` if the iteration has more elements.
`E next()`	Returns the next element in the iteration.
`void remove()`	Removes the last element returned by `next`.

We do not use the `ListIterator` methods `add`, `set`, and `previous` with sets. The list iterator methods `previous` and `add` are dependent on iterating the elements in some order and adding an element to a specific place. This makes no sense with sets because sets are not ordered. The list iterator method `set` allows replacement of an element. Because there are no duplicates in a set, calling a method to replace an element in a set could be dangerous because the replacement may already exist in the set.

Because `Set` is an interface, we cannot instantiate a `Set`. In other words, we can't create an object of type `Set`. Java provides classes that implement the `Set` interface. The AP subset includes two of these classes, `HashSet` and `TreeSet`.

```
class java.util.HashSet<E> implements java.util.Set<E>
class java.util.TreeSet<E> implements java.util.Set<E>
```

These classes enable quick retrievals (searches). To search for a particular element in a linked list, we must search the list sequentially ($O(n)$). To search an ordered array or an ordered `ArrayList` we can use the binary search which improves the retrieval time ($O(\log(n))$). A `HashSet` can be implemented using a hash table which can search in $O(1)$ time and a `TreeSet` can be implemented for searching in $O(\log(n))$ time.

We will look at these data structures in more detail later in this chapter.

The `Set` interface, the `Map` interface, and the Java classes that implement these interfaces are generic. The examples in Section 16.1 of your text instantiate a `HashSet` of `Strings` and demonstrate the use of a generic iterator and an enhanced `for` loop to traverse the items in the `HashSet`.

17.2 Maps

A *map* is a data type that keeps associations between *keys* and *values*. Each *key* in a map is mapped to a unique *value*. But a value may be associated with more than one *key*. Some examples:

- A mapping of names to phone numbers ("Gail Thomas" maps to "212-555-1234").
- A mapping of your college friends to the university that they attend. ("Cay Horstmann" maps to "San Jose State University", "Fran Trees" maps to "Drew University").
- A mapping of animals to animal sounds ("cat" maps to "meow").
- A mapping of a coin name to its value ("Quarter" maps to 0.25).
- A mapping of a car model to its make ("4-Runner" maps to "Toyota").

- A mapping of case numbers of medical patients to the medical technician handling the case.
- A mapping of login IDs to passwords.

Each association has a *key* mapped to a *value*. Figure 3 in Section 16.2 of your text illustrates this mapping relationship. Associations can be put in, changed, and located in a map. The `Map` interface methods that will be tested on the AP CS Exam are listed in Table 17.3.

Table 17.3
`interface java.util.Map<K,V>`

Method	*Method Summary*
`V put(K key, V value)`	Associates `value` with `key` in this map so that `get(key)` returns `value`. If the map previously contained a mapping for this key, the old value is replaced by the specified value. Returns the old value or `null` if there is no value associated with `key`.
`V get(Object key)`	Returns the value associated with `key` in this map, or `null` if there is no value associated with `key`.
`V remove(Object key)`	Removes the mapping for `key` from this map if it is present. Returns the old value or `null` if there is no value associated with `key`.
`boolean containsKey(Object key)`	Returns `true` if there is a value associated with `key` in this map, otherwise returns `false`.
`int size()`	Returns the number of keys in this map.
`Set<K> keySet()`	Returns a `Set` of the keys in the map.

Because a `Map` is an interface, we cannot create an object of type `Map`. The AP CS subset includes the Java `HashMap` and `TreeMap` classes that implement `Map`.

```
class java.util.HashMap<K,V> implements java.util.Map<K,V>
class java.util.TreeMap<K,V> implements java.util.Map<K,V>
```

The `Map` interface requires that the `keySet` method be implemented. The `keySet` method produces a `Set` of keys. We can visit all of the elements of a `HashMap` or `TreeMap` by iterating through the keys in the set that the `keySet` method produces. The `Map` method `get` will return the value associated with a map key. `HashMap` and `TreeMap` differ in implementation. A `HashMap` does not keep the elements ordered. In fact, the order may not even remain the same throughout the implementation. A `TreeMap` keeps the elements in an order (according to the key) from smallest to largest. The choice as to which implementation to use for a given application depends largely on the requirements of that particular application. We will discuss this more as we look at each of the different data structures. Section 16.2 of your text illustrates a `HashMap` that associates `String` references to `Color` references.

Before we look at the details of a `HashSet` or a `HashMap`, we need to understand what *hashing* is and why it is used. Before we talk about a `TreeSet` and a `TreeMap`, we need to understand binary search trees and their implementation.

17.3   Hash Tables

Hashing is an efficient way to store data for quick insertion and retrieval. Hashing involves the use of a hash function that computes and returns an integer value. This value can be used to determine the place in the hash table where the object will be inserted or can be found. A well constructed hash table allows for quick insertion and quick look-up. Figure 6 in Section 16.3 of your text illustrates a simple example of a hash table that stores names. The hash table illustrated in this example is an array of *buckets* that hold names (String objects). Each bucket holds all the names that produce the hash code that corresponds to the index of the bucket. Figure 17.1 illustrates a small portion of this hash table in your text.

Figure 17.1

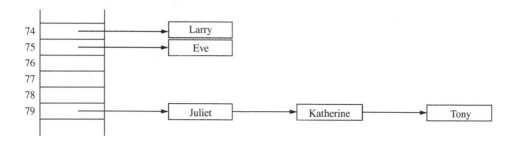

The hash code returned for the name Larry is 74. The names Juliet, Katherine, and Tony return the same hash code, 79. When two objects have the same hash code, a *collision* occurs. The goal of a good hash function is to minimize the number of collisions. If the hash function distributes the elements so that there is one element per bucket (which would be the ideal goal) then searching for a particular name is $O(1)$.

Suppose that a search for the name "Eve" is to be done. First, the hash code for "Eve" is calculated by calling the hashCode method of the String class (because the object is a String). This hash code determines the array index (bucket) in which "Eve" should be found. Searching a hash table is $O(1)$ if the hashCode method uniformly distributes the elements in the hash table. A very bad hash function would put all names in the same bucket. Retrieving an element in this worst case would then be $O(n)$. All objects in that bucket would have to be traversed.

17.3.1   Using HashSet

A hash table can be implemented using a HashSet. A hash set stores an unordered collection of objects. First, we will look at a test program that uses the Java library class HashSet. We will add names (strings) to our hash set.

Example 17.1

```
import java.util.Iterator;
import java.util.Set;
import java.util.HashSet;

/**
   This program tests the HashSet class.
*/
public class HashSetTester
{
```

```java
public static void main(String[] args)
{
    Set<String> names = new HashSet<String>();

    names.add("Mary");
    names.add("Sue");
    names.add("Art");
    names.add("Michael");
    names.add("Paul");
    System.out.println(names.size());

    Iterator<String> iter = names.iterator();

    while (iter.hasNext())
    {
        System.out.println(iter.next());
    }

    // Enhanced for loop (alternative to while loop)
    /*
        for (String i : names)
        {
            System.out.println(i);
        }
    */
}
```

The output of the above test program is:

```
5
Paul
Michael
Mary
Sue
Art
```

You can see that the iterator does not return the elements in a particular order. The iterator (or the enhanced `for` loop) traverses the hash table by visiting each bucket and sequentially traversing the elements in the bucket. The iterator and the enhanced `for` loop produce the same output. Table 17.4 lists the `HashSet` methods in the AP subset as well as two constructors that can be used to instantiate a `HashSet`. Example 17.1 invoked the `HashSet` default constructor. This created an empty hash table with initial capacity of 16 and a *load factor* of 0.75. The load factor of a hashset is a measure of how full the hash table is allowed to get before its size is automatically increased. When the table gets too full, a new table twice the size is automatically created and all the elements are inserted into the new table. The second constructor in Table 17.4 allows the initial capacity to be passed as a parameter. Research shows that the best size for a hash table is a prime number larger than the number of elements your table is expected to hold. An excess of approximately 30% is typical. This means that, if s is the number of slots in the table and e is the number of elements, then

$$s = a\ prime\ number \geq \frac{4}{3} * e$$

Table 17.4

class java.util.HashSet<E>

Method	Method Summary
HashSet<E>()	Constructs a new, empty hash table with default initial capacity of 16 and load factor of 0.75.
HashSet<E>(int initialSize)	Constructs a new, empty hash table with an initial capacity of initialSize.
boolean add(E elt)	Adds the parameter elt as an element to this set if it is not already stored in this set and returns true. If the element is already in the set, returns false.
boolean contains(Object obj)	Returns true if this set contains the element obj, otherwise returns false.
boolean remove(Object obj)	Removes the argument obj from this set and returns true if the argument is in this set; if it is not present, returns false.
int size()	Returns the number of elements in this set.
Iterator<E> iterator()	Returns an Iterator that provides access to the elements of this set.

Example 17.2 extends Example 17.1 to show calls to the other HashSet methods in Table 17.4.

Example 17.2

```
names.add("Sue");
names.remove("Mary");
System.out.println(names.size());
iter = names.iterator();
while (iter.hasNext())
    System.out.println(iter.next());
if (names.contains("Fran"))
    System.out.println("Fran found.");
else
    System.out.println("Fran NOT found.");
```

The resulting output is:

4
Paul
Michael
Sue
Art
Fran NOT found.

The objects added to and removed from the HashSet names in Examples 17.1 and 17.2 were done so using the HashSet methods add and remove. How did the method add know in which bucket to insert a given name? How did the method remove find the appropriate name to remove? HashSet add calls the hashCode method of its Object parameter. The objects in our example are String objects. The HashSet add method uses the String hashCode method and the table size to determine where to place (or where to look for) the object. Although the String hashCode method will not be tested on the AP Exam, it's important to understand how hashing works. It's not magic! Notice in Example 17.2, the name *Sue* is not added a second time. Sets contain no duplicate entries.

When you are using the HashSet class to store objects instantiated by your own classes, you need to be careful. You must define an equals method and a hashCode method for your class. For example, do you wish to store Student objects in a hash table according to the student's name, the ID number, the GPA, or a combination of these instance field values? Forgetting to define hashCode is an error that is discussed in *Common Error 16.1* on page 719 of your text. Although implementing the equals method and the hashCode method will not be tested on the AP Exam, hashing concepts will be tested.

17.3.2 Implementing *HashSet*

Section 16.3 of your text implements the HashSet as an array of Nodes using the inner classes Node and HashSetIterator. The implementation below implements the hash table as an array of ListNodes. This method of hashing is often referred to as *chaining* because a bucket contains a *chain* of ListNodes with the same hash value. Example 17.3 demonstrates this implementation.

Example 17.3

```
/**
   A hash set stores an unordered collection of objects, using
   a hash table.
*/
public class HashSet
{
   /**
      Constructs a hash table.
      @param bucketsLength the length of the buckets array
   */
   public HashSet(int bucketsLength)
   {
      buckets = new ListNode[bucketsLength];
      size = 0;
   }

   /**
      Tests for set membership.
      @param x an object to search for
      @return true if x is an element of this set, false otherwise
   */
   public boolean contains(Object x)
   {
      int h = getBucketIndex(x);

      ListNode current = buckets[h];
      while (current != null)
      {
         if ((current.getValue()).equals(x))
            return true;    // x is already in bucket
         current = current.getNext();
      }
      return false;    // x not found in this bucket
   }
```

```java
/**
   Adds an element to this set. Assumes that the hash table's
   load factor is not exceeded (there is room for the element).
   @param x an object
   @return true if x is a new object, false if x was already in
   the set
*/
public boolean add(Object x)
{
   if (contains(x))
   {
      return false;
   }
   int h = getBucketIndex(x);
   buckets[h] = new ListNode(x, buckets[h]); // Add x to bucket
   size++;
   return true;
}

/**
   Removes an object from this set.
   @param x an object
   @return true if x was removed from this set, false if x was
   not an element of this set
*/
public boolean remove(Object x)
{
   int h = getBucketIndex(x);
   ListNode current = buckets[h];
   ListNode previous = null;
   while (current != null)
   {
      if ((current.getValue()).equals(x))    // Is x in bucket?
      {
         if (previous == null) buckets[h] = current.getNext();
         else previous.setNext(current.getNext());
         size--;
         return true;   // If found, x is removed.
      }
      previous = current;
      current = current.getNext();
   }
   return false;
}

/**
   Gets the number of elements in this set.
   @return the number of elements
*/
public int size()
{
   return size;
}

/**
   Prints the contents of the HashSet.
*/
```

```java
public void printHashSet()
{
   for (int i = 0; i < buckets.length; i++)
   {
      ListNode temp = buckets[i];
      while (temp != null)
      {
         System.out.println(temp.getValue());
         temp = temp.getNext();
      }
   }
}

/**
   Determines bucket in which x belongs.
   @param x an object to find bucket for
   @return index (bucket) in which x belongs
*/
private int getBucketIndex(Object x)
{
   int h = x.hashCode();    // Calls String hashCode method
   if (h < 0) h = -h;
   h = h % buckets.length;   // Finding bucket index
   return h;
}

private ListNode[] buckets;   // Array of ListNodes
private int size;
}
```

17.3.3 *Using HashMap*

The HashMap class implements the Map interface and uses hashing as the technique to store entries. Each entry of a hash map consists of a *key* and a *value*. A HashMap stores pairs (key, value) according to the hash code determined by the key. Assuming that the hashCode method defined for the key object distributes the entries uniformly in the hash table, searching, insertion, and removal of an entry in the hash map is constant time ($O(1)$). The HashMap methods included in the AP subset are listed in Table 17.5.

Table 17.5

`class java.util.HashMap<K,V>`

Method	Method Summary
HashMap<K,V>()	Constructs an empty HashMap with default size of 16 and load factor of 0.75.
V put(K key, V value)	Associates value with key in this map so that get(key) returns value. If the map previously contained a mapping for this key, the old value is replaced by the specified value and returned; returns null otherwise.
V get(Object key)	Returns the value associated with key in this map, or null if there is no value associated with key.

V remove(Object key)	Removes the mapping for key from this map if it is present. Returns the old value or null if there is no value associated with key.
boolean containsKey(Object key)	Returns true if there is a value associated with key in this map, otherwise returns false.
int size()	Returns the number of keys in this map.
Set<K> keySet()	Returns a Set of the keys in the map.

Example 17.4 demonstrates the HashMap methods with the case number for a medical patient mapped to the name of the medical technician handling the case.

Example 17.4

```java
import java.util.Iterator;
import java.util.Map;
import java.util.HashMap;
import java.util.Set;

/**
    This program tests the HashMap class.
*/
public class HashMapTester
{
    public static void main(String[] args)
    {
        // Constructs an empty HashMap
        Map<Integer, String> names = new HashMap<Integer, String>();

        names.put(new Integer(1435), "Smith");
        names.put(new Integer(1110), "Thomas");
        names.put(new Integer(1425), "Jones");
        names.put(new Integer(987), "Evans");
        names.put(new Integer(1323), "Murray");

        System.out.println("Number of cases: " + names.size()); // 5

        Integer lookfor = new Integer(1435);
        if (names.containsKey(lookfor))
            System.out.println("Key found.");
        else
            System.out.println("Key NOT found.");

        Set<Integer> namesSet = names.keySet();
        Iterator<Integer> iter = namesSet.iterator();
        while (iter.hasNext())
        {
            Integer caseNumber = iter.next();
            System.out.println(caseNumber + " handled by "
                    + names.get(caseNumber));
        }
    }
}
```

The resulting output (the order of which is arbitrary) is:

> *Number of cases: 5*
> *Key found.*
> *987 handled by Evans*
> *1425 handled by Jones*
> *1323 handled by Murray*
> *1435 handled by Smith*
> *1110 handled by Thomas*

If the statements that insert keys and values into the HashMap were changed to:

```
names.put(new Integer(1435), "Smith");
names.put(new Integer(1110), "Thomas");
names.put(new Integer(1425), "Jones");
names.put(new Integer(987), "Evans");
names.put(new Integer(1323), "Murray");
names.put(new Integer(1323), "Duplicate");
```

The resulting output would be:

> *Number of cases: 5*
> *Key found.*
> *987 handled by Evans*
> *1425 handled by Jones*
> *1323 handled by Duplicate*
> *1435 handled by Smith*
> *1110 handled by Thomas*

Notice that case #1323 is handled by Duplicate, not by Murray. If a duplicate key entry is attempted, the original one is replaced.

17.3.4 *Implementing* **HashMap**

Our implementation of HashMap would be similar to the implementation for HashSet in Example 17.3. The differences are

- A class MapEntry is defined. MapEntry has a key field, a value field, and the appropriate constructors and accessor methods.
- The ListNode contains a reference to an object, MapEntry.
- When the hashCode method is called on a table entry, it is called on the key field of a MapEntry object.

17.4 Computing Hash Codes

A hash function should be easy and fast to compute and should scatter the data evenly throughout the hash table. Choose a table size that has more space than is actually needed and develop a function to compute the hash address. Remember that a good table size is a prime number greater than or equal to 4/3 times the expected number of elements. You can define hashCode methods for your own classes by combining the hash codes for the individual instance variables. Section 16.4 of your text describes how to do this is detail. The implementation of hashCode methods is not part of the AP subset but hashing concepts will be tested. You should understand the goal of a good hash function.

17.5 Binary Search Trees

A binary tree consists of nodes, each of which has two child nodes. One of the nodes is the root node; all non-root nodes in the tree can trace their ancestry up the tree to the root. A *leaf* of a binary tree is a node that has no children. A *complete* binary tree is binary tree where each leaf is at the same level and each non-leaf has exactly two children. A complete binary tree is illustrated in Figure 17.2.

Figure 17.2

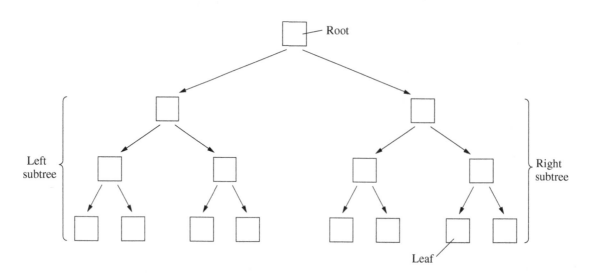

A *binary search tree (BST)* is a binary tree in which the descendants to the left of a node have smaller values than the node value field and the descendants to the right have values that are greater than or equal to the node value field. Figure 17.3 illustrates a binary search tree of `Integers`.

Figure 17.3

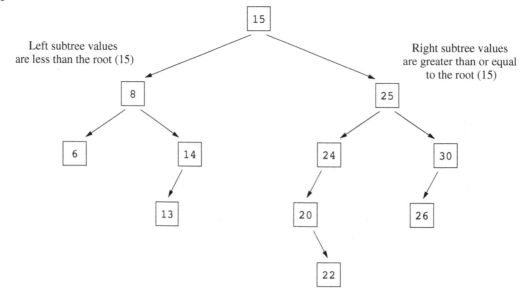

A binary tree is made up of nodes that have a data field and two reference fields. In Figure 17.3, a node is illustrated as a square containing a number (data field) and left and right arrows (reference fields). To facilitate a consistency in the exam questions, the AB exam uses the TreeNode[1] class shown in Example 17.5 to define a node and its methods.

Example 17.5

```java
public class TreeNode
{
    public TreeNode(Object initValue)
    {
        value = initValue;
        left = null;
        right = null;
    }

    public TreeNode(Object initValue,
            TreeNode initLeft, TreeNode initRight)
    {
        value = initValue;
        left = initLeft;
        right = initRight;
    }

    /**
        Gets the value of a tree node.
        @return the node's value
    */
    public Object getValue()
    {
        return value;
    }

    /**
        Gets the left field of a tree node.
        @return the node's left field
    */
    public TreeNode getLeft()
    {
        return left;
    }

    /**
        Gets the right field of a tree node.
        @return the node's right field
    */
    public TreeNode getRight()
    {
        return right;
    }
```

[1] College Board's AP Computer Science AB: Implementation Classes and Interfaces

```
/**
    Sets the value of the tree node to theNewValue.
    @param theNewValue is the new value of the tree node
*/
public void setValue(Object theNewValue)
{
    value = theNewValue;
}

/**
    Sets the tree node's left field to a new reference.
    @param theNewLeft is the new reference for the left
    field of the tree node
*/
public void setLeft(TreeNode theNewLeft)
{
    left = theNewLeft;
}

/**
    Sets the tree node's right field to a new reference.
    @param theNewRight is the new reference for the right
    field of the tree node
*/
public void setRight(TreeNode theNewRight)
{
    right = theNewRight;
}

private Object value;
private TreeNode left;
private TreeNode right;
}
```

A description of the TreeNode class will appear at the beginning of the exam booklet.

Figure 7 in Section 16.5 of your text illustrates a binary search tree. Figure 8 illustrates a binary tree that is not a binary search tree. In order to build a binary search tree, we must be able to compare the objects in the value field of the TreeNode. This means that the objects that we are inserting into the binary search tree must implement Comparable and define compareTo. To insert a node into a binary search tree we check first to see if the tree is empty. If it is, then the root of the tree references the new node.

```
public void insert(Comparable obj)
{
    TreeNode newNode = new TreeNode(obj);
    if (root == null) root = newNode;
    else root.insertNode(root, newNode);
}
```

If the tree is not empty, the new node must be inserted to the left if the new value is smaller than the present node's value, and to the right if the new node's value is greater than or equal to the value of the current node. An implementation of the binary search tree using the TreeNode class appears in Example 17.6.

Example 17.6

```java
/**
    This class implements a binary search tree whose nodes hold
    objects that implement the Comparable interface.
*/
public class Tree
{
    // Constructs an empty tree.
    public Tree()
    {
        root = null;
    }

    /**
        Inserts a new node into the tree.
        @param obj the object to insert
    */
    public void insert(Comparable obj)
    {
        TreeNode newNode = new TreeNode(obj);
        if (root == null)
            root = newNode;
        else
            insertNode(root, newNode);
    }

    // Prints the contents of the tree in sorted order.
    public void print()
    {
        if (root != null)
            printNodes(root);
    }

    /**
        Recursive helper method.
    */
    public void insertNode(TreeNode current, TreeNode newNode)
    {
        Comparable newValue = (Comparable) newNode.getValue();
        Comparable currValue = (Comparable) current.getValue();
        if (newValue.compareTo(currValue) < 0)
        {
            if (current.getLeft() == null)
                current.setLeft(newNode);
            else
                insertNode(current.getLeft(), newNode);
        }
        else
        {
            if (current.getRight() == null)
                current.setRight(newNode);
            else
                insertNode(current.getRight(), newNode);
        }
    }
```

```
/**
    Prints this TreeNode and all of its descendants
    in sorted order.
*/
public void printNodes(TreeNode current)
{
    if (current != null)
    {
        printNodes(current.getLeft());
        System.out.println(current.getValue());
        printNodes(current.getRight());
    }
}

private TreeNode root;
}
```

Example 17.7 tests this binary search tree implementation for `String` objects and for `Integer` objects.

Example 17.7

```
// This program tests the binary search tree class.
public class TreeTester
{
    public static void main(String[] args)
    {
        Tree names = new Tree();
        names.insert("Romeo");
        names.insert("Juliet");
        names.insert("Tom");
        names.insert("Dick");
        names.insert("Harry");
        names.print();    // Dick Harry Juliet Romeo Tom

        // Inserting 15 8 25 6 14 24 20 22 30 13 26
        Tree numbers = new Tree();
        numbers.insert(new Integer(15));
        numbers.insert(new Integer(8));
        numbers.insert(new Integer(25));
        numbers.insert(new Integer(6));
        numbers.insert(new Integer(14));
        numbers.insert(new Integer(24));
        numbers.insert(new Integer(20));
        numbers.insert(new Integer(22));
        numbers.insert(new Integer(30));
        numbers.insert(new Integer(13));
        numbers.insert(new Integer(26));
        numbers.print();    // 6 8 13 14 15 20 22 24 25 26 30
    }
}
```

17.5.1 Searching a Binary Search Tree

Searching a binary search tree follows the same basic algorithm as a binary search of an array. If the key is less than the current value, go left, otherwise go right.

Example 17.8

```
/**
    Searches for a key in a binary search tree.
    @param key the value to search for in tree
    @return true if key found in tree, false otherwise
*/
public boolean find(Comparable key)
{
    if (root == null)
      return false;
    else
      return findNode(root, key);
}

/**
    Recursive helper method.
    @return true if key is found in tree, false otherwise
*/
public boolean findNode(TreeNode current, Comparable key)
{
    if (current == null)
      return false;
    else
    {
      Comparable currValue = (Comparable) current.getValue();
      if (key.compareTo(currValue) == 0)
        return true;
      else if (key.compareTo(currValue) < 0)
        return findNode(current.getLeft(), key);
      else
        return findNode(current.getRight(),key);
    }
}
```

A *balanced* tree contains approximately as many children in the left subtree as in the right subtree. A binary search tree (BST) is a sorted collection of elements, and searching for a value or inserting a value in a reasonably balanced BST is $O(\log(n))$. However, if a BST were created by inserting the Integers 1-10 in that order, a very unbalanced tree would result. The tree, in fact, would be linked as a linked list. The efficiency of searching this tree is $O(n)$. Trace through the insertion algorithm for the numbers 1 to 10 and sketch your resulting tree.

17.5.2 Removing a Node from a Binary Search Tree

Removing a node from a binary search tree is not as intuitive. There are three basic situations: removing a node with no children, removing a node with one child, and removing a node with two children.

To remove a node with no children, set the appropriate field of the parent to `null`. Delete 22.

Figure 17.4

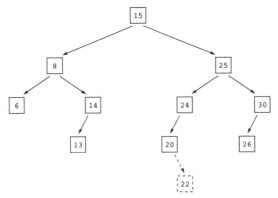

To remove a node with one child, replace the node with its child. Delete 30. The node containing 30 is replaced with the node containing 26.

Figure 17.5

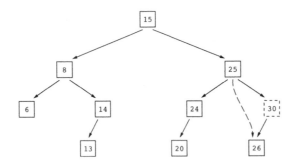

To remove a node with two children, go right once then all the way left. The smallest value in the right subtree of the node we are deleting will replace the deleted node. Delete 15. The node containing 15 is replaced by the node containing 20

Figure 17.6

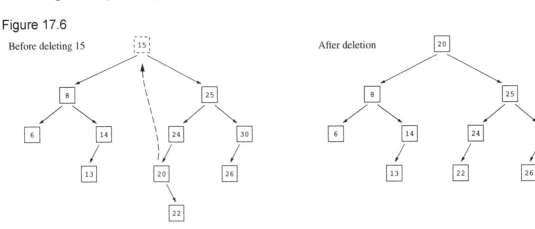

Section 16.5 of your text includes the `BinarySearchTree` class implementation. This implementation contains the `remove` method and a non-recursive `find` method using an inner class `Node`. Inner classes will not be tested on the AP Exam.

17.6 Tree Traversal

Notice that the tree node values are printed in order. The print method does an *inorder* traversal of the `TreeNodes`. This means the left subtree is printed, the root value is printed, and then the right subtree is printed. Because the `insert` algorithm inserts nodes with values less than the current node value in the left subtree and nodes with values greater than or equal to the current node value in the right subtree, the inorder traversal results in an ordered printing of the node values. *Preorder* and *postorder* traversals are explained in Section 16.6 of your text. The inorder traversal visits nodes in the order: left, root, right. Preorder traversal visits root, left, right. Postorder traversal visits left, right, root. Consider the binary search tree in Figure 17.3.

- Inorder traversal yields: 6 8 13 14 15 20 22 24 25 26 30
- Preorder traversal yields: 15 8 6 14 13 25 24 20 22 30 26
- Postorder traversal yields: 6 13 14 8 22 20 24 26 30 25 15

The postorder traversal of an expression tree gives a postfix expression. Preorder traversal of an arithmetic expression will result in Lukasiewicz notation (prefix notation). Prefix notation is discussed in *Random Fact 16.1* on page 734 of your text. The operators precede the operands. Prefix and postfix expressions do not need parentheses. Although prefix and postfix are not topics explicitly listed in the AP CS Topic Outline, they are applications involving binary trees and stacks, and questions related to these traversals and applications may be on the AP Exam.

17.7 Using Tree Sets and Tree Maps

The `TreeSet` class uses a form of a balanced binary tree that guarantees that adding and removing an element takes $O(\log(n))$ time. We know that a good hashing function can give us retrieval with efficiency $O(1)$ but if we also wanted to be able to list our data in order, a hash table would not be the appropriate choice. Binary search trees, when traversed with an inorder traversal, allow for an efficient search ($O(\log(n))$) and can also be traversed so that elements can be printed in order. The `TreeSet` class implements the `Set` interface. Table 17.6 lists the methods of `TreeSet` that may be tested on the AP Exam.

Table 17.6
`class java.util.TreeSet<E>`

Method	*Method Summary*
`TreeSet<E>()`	Constructs a new, empty tree set. `E` should implement `Comparable`.
`boolean add(E elt)`	Adds the parameter `elt` as an element if it is not already in this set and returns true. If `elt` is already in the set, returns `false`.
`boolean contains(Object obj)`	Returns `true` if this set contains the element `obj`, otherwise returns `false`.
`boolean remove(Object obj)`	Removes the argument `obj` from this set and returns `true` if the argument is in this set; if it is not present, returns `false`.
`int size()`	Returns the number of elements in this set.
`Iterator<E> iterator()`	Returns an `Iterator` that provides access to elements of this set.

A `TreeSet` requires that its elements be comparable. That means that `compareTo` is defined for the objects placed in the `TreeSet`. This is important because the elements in a tree are ordered (unlike a `HashSet`). For your own classes, you must implement the `Comparable` interface and define `compareTo` or provide a `Comparator` (explained in Section 16.7 of your text; `Comparator` is not tested on the AP Exam) in order to use the `TreeSet`. Because a `TreeSet` implements `Set`, a `TreeSet` contains no duplicates. Example 17.9 demonstrates a test program for `TreeSet`.

Example 17.9

```java
import java.util.Iterator;
import java.util.Set;
import java.util.TreeSet;

// This program tests the tree set class.
public class TreeSetTester
{
    public static void main(String[] args)
    {
        Set<String> names = new TreeSet<String>();
        names.add("Larry");
        names.add("Tony");
        names.add("Katherine");
        names.add("Eve");
        names.add("Juliet");

        System.out.println(names.size());
        Iterator<String> iter = names.iterator();
        while (iter.hasNext())
            System.out.println(iter.next());
        System.out.println();

        names.add("Tony");   // Attempting to add duplicate.
        // Duplicate is not added. (Sets do not contain duplicates.)
        names.remove("Eve");   // Removing name.
        iter = names.iterator();
        while (iter.hasNext())
            System.out.println(iter.next());
        System.out.println();
    }
}
```

The resulting output is:

```
5
Eve
Juliet
Katherine
Larry
Tony

Juliet
Katherine
Larry
Tony
```

A `TreeSet` guarantees reasonable search performance ($O(\log(n))$) and allows for visiting the elements of the tree set in order. Because traversing a `TreeSet` with an iterator visits the tree set in order, the first call to the iterator's `next` method takes $O(\log(n))$ time.

A `TreeMap` also requires that the objects belong to a class that implements the `Comparable` interface and defines `compareTo` for the keys. There is no requirement for the values. The `TreeMap` methods included in the AP subset are listed in Table 17.7 and demonstrated in Example 17.10.

Table 17.7

`class java.util.TreeMap<K,V>`

Method	Method Summary
`TreeMap<K,V>()`	Constructs a new, empty tree map. `K` should implement `Comparable`.
`V put(K key, V value)`	Associates `value` with `key` in this map so that `get(key)` returns value. If the map previously contained a mapping for this key, the old value is replaced by the specified value. Returns the value formerly associated with `key` or `null` if `key` was not present.
`V get(Object key)`	Returns the value associated with `key` in this map, or `null` if there is no value associated with `key`.
`V remove(Object key)`	Removes the mapping for `key` from this map if it is present. Returns the value associated with `key` or `null` if there is no value associated with `key`.
`boolean containsKey(Object key)`	Returns `true` if there is a value associated with `key` in this map, otherwise returns `false`.
`int size()`	Returns the number of keys in this map.
`Set<K> keySet()`	Returns a `Set` of the keys in the map.

Example 17.10

```
import java.util.Iterator;
import java.util.Map;
import java.util.TreeMap;
import java.util.Set;

// This program tests the TreeMap class.
public class TreeMapTester
{
    public static void main(String[] args)
    {
        Map<Integer,String> names = new TreeMap<Integer,String>();
        names.put(new Integer(1435), "Smith");
        names.put(new Integer(1110), "Thomas");
        names.put(new Integer(1425), "Jones");
        names.put(new Integer(987), "Evans");
        names.put(new Integer(1323), "Murray");

        System.out.println("Number of cases: " + names.size());

        Integer lookfor = new Integer(1435);
```

```
        if (names.containsKey(lookfor))
           System.out.println("Key found.");
        else
           System.out.println("Key NOT found.");

        Set<Integer> namesSet = names.keySet();
        Iterator<Integer> iter = namesSet.iterator();
        while (iter.hasNext())
        {
           Integer caseNumber = iter.next();
           System.out.println(caseNumber + " handled by "
                 + names.get(caseNumber));
        }
     }
  }
```

The resulting output is:

Number of cases: 5
Key found.
987 handled by Evans
1110 handled by Thomas
1323 handled by Murray
1425 handled by Jones
1435 handled by Smith

If the same test program were executed replacing

```
names.put(new Integer(1435), "Smith");
names.put(new Integer(1110), "Thomas");
names.put(new Integer(1425), "Jones");
names.put(new Integer(987), "Evans");
names.put(new Integer(1323), "Murray");
```

with

```
names.put("Smith", new Integer(1435));
names.put("Thomas", new Integer(1110));
names.put("Jones", new Integer(1425));
names.put("Evans", new Integer(987));
names.put("Murray", new Integer(1323));
```

and the iterator code was replaced by

```
Set<String> namesSet = names.keySet();
Iterator<String> iter = namesSet.iterator();
while (iter.hasNext())
{
   String who = iter.next();
   System.out.println(who + " handled " + names.get(who));
}
```

the resulting output would be:

Number of cases: 5
Evans handled 987
Jones handled 1425
Murray handled 1323
Smith handled 1435
Thomas handled 1110

In both executions, the nodes are visited in order according to the order dictated by the key's `compareTo` method.

The examples of binary search trees that have been discussed so far contain integer and string values. Recall that a `TreeNode` stores any comparable object. Suppose `Student` objects were to be stored in a binary search tree. The `Student` class must implement the `Comparable` interface. This means `compareTo` must be defined in the `Student` class. The decision is made to compare students by the alphabetical (really lexicographical) ordering of last name, first name, and then ID. Example 17.11 demonstrates this.

Example 17.11

```java
// A student with an ID.
public class Student implements Comparable
{
   /**
      Constructs a Student object.
      @param aFirstName the first name
      @param aLastName the last name
      @param anId the ID
   */
   public Student(String aFirstName, String aLastName, int anId)
   {
      firstName = aFirstName;
      lastName = aLastName;
      id = anId;
   }

   /**
      Gets the student's first name.
      @return firstName the first name
   */
   public String getFirstName() {. . .}

   /**
      Gets the student's last name.
      @return lastName the last name
   */
   public String getLastName() {. . .}

   /**
      Gets the student's ID.
      @return id the ID
   */
   public int getId() {. . .}

   public int compareTo(Object obj)
   {
      if (obj == null)
         return -1;
      String thisName = lastName + " " + firstName + " " + id;
      String objName = ((Student) obj).lastName + " " +
            ((Student) obj).firstName + " " + ((Student) obj).id;
      return thisName.compareTo(objName);
   }
```

```
/**
    Determines if the students are equal.
    @param otherObject the other student
    @return true if the students are equal, false otherwise
*/
public boolean equals(Object otherObject)
{
    return compareTo(otherObject) == 0;
}

/**
    Displays a string representation of the student object.
    @return a string describing the student object
*/
public String toString() {. . .}

private String firstName;
private String lastName;
private int id;
}
```

The program segment below adds students to a binary search tree and prints the students using an inorder traversal.

```
Tree drewCsiClass = new Tree();
drewCsiClass.insert(new Student("Ann", "Brown", 111));
drewCsiClass.insert(new Student("Alan", "Frazee", 122));
drewCsiClass.insert(new Student("Bob", "Brown", 132));
drewCsiClass.insert(new Student("Ann", "Bergin", 451));
drewCsiClass.insert(new Student("Tim", "Brown", 112));
drewCsiClass.insert(new Student("Tom", "Casper", 171));
drewCsiClass.print();
```

The result is:

Student[First name=Ann,Last name=Bergin,ID=451]
Student[First name=Ann,Last name=Brown,ID=111]
Student[First name=Bob,Last name=Brown,ID=132]
Student[First name=Tim,Last name=Brown,ID=112]
Student[First name=Tom,Last name=Casper,ID=171]
Student[First name=Alan,Last name=Frazee,ID=122]

Because it may also be important to list students by ID number, a Comparator is implemented for Student. Example 17.12 shows this StudentComparator implementation and a test program that stores Student objects in a TreeSet ordered by ID numbers.

Example 17.12

```
import java.util.Comparator;

public class StudentComparator implements Comparator
{
    public int compare(Object firstObject, Object secondObject)
    {
        Student first = (Student) firstObject;
        Student second = (Student) secondObject;
```

```
        if (first.getId() < second.getId())
            return -1;
        else if (first.getId() == second.getId())
            return 0;
        else
            return 1;
    }
}
```

The program segment below adds students to a `TreeSet` using the `StudentComparator` that compares student ID numbers.

```
    Comparator comp = new StudentComparator();
    Set studentsByID = new TreeSet(comp);

    studentsByID.add(new Student("Ann", "Brown", 111));
    studentsByID.add(new Student("Alan", "Frazee", 122));
    studentsByID.add(new Student("Bob", "Brown", 132));
    studentsByID.add(new Student("Ann", "Bergin", 451));
    studentsByID.add(new Student("Tim", "Brown", 112));
    studentsByID.add(new Student("Tom", "Casper", 171));

    System.out.println();
    Iterator iter = studentsByID.iterator();
    while (iter.hasNext())
        System.out.println(iter.next());
```

The result is:

Student[First name=Ann,Last name=Brown,ID=111]
Student[First name=Tim,Last name=Brown,ID=112]
Student[First name=Alan,Last name=Frazee,ID=122]
Student[First name=Bob,Last name=Brown,ID=132]
Student[First name=Tom,Last name=Casper,ID=171]
Student[First name=Ann,Last name=Bergin,ID=451]

The `Comparable` interface and the `Comparator` interface are parameterized types. *Advanced Topic 14.4* on page 656 of your text gives an example of a parameterized `compareTo` method for `Coins` and *Advanced Topic 14.5* on page 657 of your text gives an example of a `CoinComparator`. The `Comparator` interface will not be tested on the AP Exam. The AP subset uses the non-parameterized `Comparable` interface, not the `Comparable<T>` interface. The example above uses a non-parameterized `Comparator`.

17.8   Priority Queues

A priority queue is an abstract data type that has two operations: add an element and remove the element with the highest priority. When you send your job to a printer, it is placed in a queue. In some systems, some printing jobs may have a higher priority than other jobs because of their importance. If we assign each of these printing jobs a number to indicate its priority in the queue, then the smaller number is assigned to the most important job indicating that it should be handled first. The `java.util.PriorityQueue` class defines a priority queue in which the item with the smallest value is the one with the highest priority and is removed from the priority queue first (similar to the printer queue example). Table 17.8 contains the `PriorityQueue` methods in the AP subset and Example 17.13 demonstrates these methods.

Table 17.8

class java.util.PriorityQueue<E>

Method	Method Summary
`PriorityQueue<E>()`	Constructs a new, empty priority queue. `E` should implement `Comparable`.
`boolean add(E elt)`	Adds the parameter `elt` to the priority queue. Returns `true`.
`E remove()`	Removes and returns the minimal element from the priority queue.
`E peek()`	Returns the minimal element from the priority queue without removing it.
`boolean isEmpty()`	Returns `true` if the priority queue is empty, `false` otherwise.

A priority queue requires that its elements be comparable. That means that `compareTo` must be defined for the objects placed in the priority queue.

Example 17.13

```java
import java.util.PriorityQueue;

public class PriorityQueueTester
{
    public static void main(String[] args)
    {
        PriorityQueue<String> pq = new PriorityQueue<String>();
        pq.add("Harry");
        pq.add("Dick");
        pq.add("Tom");
        pq.add("Romeo");
        pq.add("Ann");

        System.out.println(pq.peek()); // prints Ann
        System.out.println();

        while (!(pq.isEmpty()))
        {
            System.out.println(pq.remove());
        }

    }
}
```

The result is:

Ann

Ann
Dick
Harry
Romeo
Tom

Remember, a priority queue is an abstract data type. The `java.util.PriorityQueue` is implemented using a *priority heap* (discussed next and in Section 16.9 of your text) but you can also implement a priority queue using other data structures. Let's consider some options for implementing a priority queue and discuss their limitations.

- An unsorted array (or `ArrayList`)
  - Adding an element is $O(1)$.
    - Elements will be added to the end of the array.
  - removeMin is $O(n)$.
    - In order to delete this element from the array, the smallest value must be found ($O(n)$) and deleted.
- A sorted array (or `ArrayList`)
  - Adding an element is $O(n)$.
    - The array must be searched for the correct place and then elements must be shifted to accommodate the insertion. We should keep the list sorted so that the element with the smallest value is last.
  - removeMin is $O(1)$ if this element is stored in last position.
- An unsorted linked list
  - Adding an element is $O(1)$.
    - Elements will be added to the front of the list.
  - removeMin is $O(n)$.
    - We must search the linked list to find the element ($O(n)$) and then delete the element.
- A sorted linked list
  - Adding an element is $O(n)$.
    - Must search for the correct place and then insert it. The list will be sorted in ascending order so that the element with the smallest value is first.
  - removeMin is $O(1)$ because we are removing the first element of the linked list.
- A tree set
  - Adding an element is $O(\log(n))$.
  - removeMin is $O(\log(n))$.

Example 17.14 is an example of a generic `TreeSet` implementation of `PriorityQueue`.

Example 17.14

```java
import java.util.TreeSet;
import java.util.Iterator;

public class TreePriorityQueue<E>
{
   public TreePriorityQueue()
   {
      tree = new TreeSet<E>();
   }

   /**
      Determines if queue is empty.
      @return true if the number of elements
      in the priority queue is 0; false otherwise
   */
   public boolean isEmpty()
   {
      return tree.size() == 0;
   }
```

```
/**
    Adds x to the priority queue; the number of
    elements in the priority queue is increased by 1.
*/
public void add(E x)
{
    tree.add(x);
}

/**
    Removes and returns the smallest item in the priority queue.
    The number of elements in the priority queue is decreased
    by 1. Throws unchecked exception if priority queue is empty.
    @return the smallest item in priority queue
*/
public E remove()
{
    Iterator<E> iter = tree.iterator();
    E r = iter.next();
    iter.remove();
    return r;
}

/**
    Returns the smallest item in the priority queue; the
    priority queue is unchanged. Throws unchecked
    exception if priority queue is empty.
    @return the smallest item in priority queue
*/
public E peek()
{
    Iterator<E> iter = tree.iterator();
    E r = iter.next();
    return r;
}

private TreeSet<E> tree;
}
```

Now, let's look at another data implementation called a *heap*.

17.9 Heaps

A *min-heap* is a binary tree with the following properties:

1. It is complete or almost complete, which means that every level of the tree is completely filled, except maybe the bottom level. If the bottom level is not filled, the nodes are in the leftmost positions (see Figure 16 in Section 16.9 of your text).

2. The object stored at each node is less than or equal to the values stored in its descendants. Figure 17 in Section 16.9 of your text illustrates this.

These properties are maintained with each addition to the heap. Figure 17.7 illustrates a min-heap.

Figure 17.7

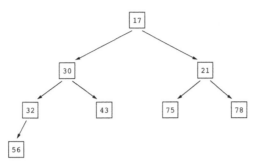

Figure 17.8 below inserts 25 into our heap. When an element is inserted in the heap, it is inserted in a vacant slot at the "end" of the tree representing the heap. After the insertion, the heap is readjusted (by swapping the new element "up" in the heap) so that the heap properties are fulfilled.

Figure 17.8

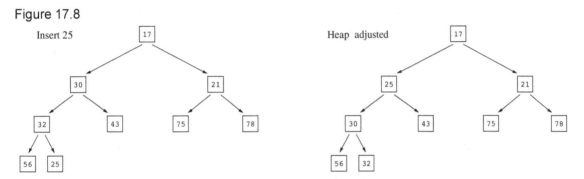

Figures 17 and 18 in Section 16.9 of your text illustrate creating a min-heap and inserting elements into the heap. It is easy to see that the element with the smallest value is the root of the binary tree.

The only element that we will remove from a heap is the root node. To remove the root, we replace the root with the "last" element in the heap and readjust the heap elements so that the min-heap properties are maintained (See Figure 19 in Section 16.9 of your text for a complete illustration of a node removal from the heap).

Figure 17.9

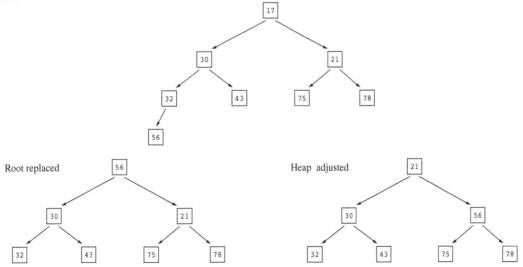

With the conclusion of each operation, the properties of a min-heap are satisfied. The algorithms used for insertions into and deletions from a heap are based on a complete binary tree, making each of the operations $O(\log(n))$.

Section 16.9 of your text implements a heap using an `ArrayList`. The elements from the heap are mapped to indices in an array list. The root of the heap is placed in index `1`. The left child of the node in position `x` is placed in index `2x` and the right child is placed in index `2x + 1`. Figure 20 in Section 16.9 of your text illustrates a heap mapping to an array and an `ArrayList` implementation of a heap follows it.

17.10 The Heapsort Algorithm

Heaps are also used to implement an efficient sorting algorithm, heapsort. This sorting algorithm is $O(n \log(n))$. There are *n* items in the heap. Each insertion and removal is $O(\log(n))$.

The heapsort inserts elements into a heap and removes them in sorted order. We use an array to store our heap elements. Of course, the original array of values does not represent a heap. To store the elements in the array, we number the heap elements from top to bottom, left to right, starting with 0 at the root. Those values are used as the subscripts into the array. The children of node *i* can be found at $2 * i + 1$ and $2 * i + 2$.

The idea behind the heapsort algorithm is to first reorder our array elements so that their order represents a heap as defined earlier. We do this by continuously adjusting our array elements until the heap properties are satisfied. We repeatedly remove the root element (replace the last non-sorted element in the array with the root element) and readjust our heap. This procedure results in our array having the smallest element in the last position. The heapsort algorithm is more easily implemented if we utilize a *max-heap* instead of a *min-heap* so that the largest value will be in the last position. A *max-heap* is a binary tree with the following properties:

1. It is complete or almost complete, which means that every level of the tree is completely filled, except maybe the bottom level. If the bottom level is not filled, the nodes are in the leftmost positions.

2. The object stored at each node is greater than or equal to the values stored in its children.

Let's look at a very simplified description of the heapsort algorithm. Figure 17.10 illustrates this pseudocode.

Start with a max-heap (an array) of size n.

```
// Invariant: h[n]. . .h[heapname.size() - 1] is sorted
for (int n = heapName.size() - 1; n > 0; n--)
{
    swap h[n] with root (h[0])
    readjust heap from 1 ... n−1
}
```

The diagrams in Figure 17.10 illustrate this algorithm. The shaded elements are the sorted portion of the heap (array). The algorithm consists of a `for` loop with two steps. The *swap* step exchanges the values in the root node and the last non-sorted element in the heap (array). After the swap, that last non-sorted array position now joins the sorted portion of the heap (array). The resulting tree representation needs to be readjusted to maintain the heap property that each node value is greater than or equal to the values stored in its children. The *readjust heap* is the second step in the `for` loop. While readjusting to maintain max-heap properties, if we need to demote a node, we swap it with its largest child.

Figure 17.10

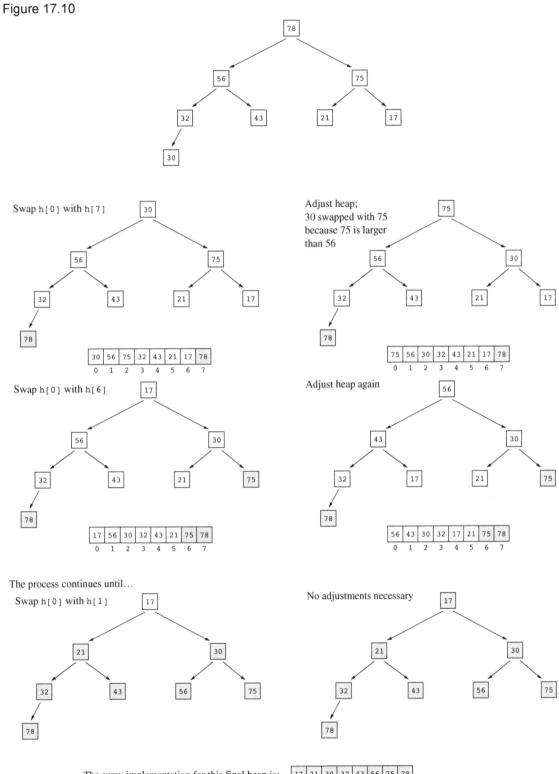

When we traverse the array beginning with the first array element, the elements visited are in increasing order. Section 16.10 of your text illustrates the heapsort and implements the heapsort using an array where the root of the heap is in position 0 in the array. The left child of the element in position x is in position $2x + 1$ and the right child of the element in position x is in position $2x + 2$.

17.11 Choosing a Container

How To 16.1 on page 737 of your text reviews how to pick the appropriate container (implementation) for your application. The questions you should ask yourself and the possible answers to each question are summarized below. As you read the questions and choose an answer, think about the container that you would use. The comments below the questions discuss possible choices.

Your container choices: array, array list, linked list, set, and map.

1. How will elements be accessed?
   a. The method of accessing doesn't matter in this application.
   b. Accessing elements needs to be by index for immediate retrieval (random access).
   c. The accessing will be done by key (like an ID number or a bank account number).
   d. Accessing is done by an index pair, such as a row and column.

2. Does order matter?
   a. Order doesn't matter.
   b. The order of the entries needs to be kept in the order they were entered.
   c. The entries need to be kept in sorted order.

3. Which operations need to be fast?
   a. It doesn't matter.
   b. Adding and/or removing elements needs to be fast.
   c. Finding an element needs to be fast.

- If the answers to all of the questions are "doesn't matter," then use an array list. It's an easy and straightforward implementation.
- If the answer to 1 is b, use an array or array list.
- If the answer to 1 is c, use a map.
- If the answer to 1 is d, use a two-dimensional array.
- If the answer to 2 is b, use an array, an array list, or a linked list.
- If the answer to 2 is c, use a tree set.
- If the answer to 3 is b, use a linked list.
- If the answer to 3 is c, use a set.
- If you need a set or a map, remember
  - To use a `HashSet` and a `HashMap`, the keys/values you are going to store must implement a `hashCode` method. Check to see that the class of your objects implements this method.
  - To use a `TreeSet` or `TreeMap`, the keys/values you are going to store must implement a `compareTo` method. Alternatively, you may provide a `Comparator`, although this method is not included in the AP subset.
- Sets do not contain duplicates. If your application is meant to include duplicates, a set is not your choice.

■ Expanded Coverage of Material That Is Not Found in the Text

- The method we used to implement our hash table involved *chaining*. We used an array of `ListNodes`. Each bucket in the array contained a linked list of nodes mapped (by their hash code) to that bucket. The linked list resembles a *chain*. When you are searching for a *key*, the hash code of the key (and therefore the appropriate bucket) is determined and the linked list in that bucket is searched. The chain is being traversed in searching for the key. Another method of storing elements in a hash table is called *linear probing*. With linear probing, each bucket contains at most one element. If an attempt is made to add an element to a bucket that already has an element in it, the new element would be added to the next available (empty) bucket.

■ Topics That Are Useful But Not Tested

- The `String` class, `Double` class, and `Integer` class provide a `hashCode` method that returns an integer hash code. When writing your own hash function, you may wish to call these methods. The `Coin` example in Section 16.4 of your text calls the `Double hashCode` method.
- Computing hash codes is covered in Section 16.4 of your text. Implementing `hashCode` will not be tested.

■ Things to Remember When Taking the AP Exam

- Sets do not contain duplicates. If you change an item in a set it may become the same as another item in the set. Moreover, this WILL upset the set data structure because it may change the hash code or the sort order!
- Sets are not ordered, unless they are `TreeSets`.
- Use an iterator or an enhanced `for` loop to list all elements in a set.
- An iterator for a `HashSet` does not return the elements in any specific order; an iterator for a `TreeSet` returns the elements using an inorder traversal.
- For a `HashSet`, an iterator can iterate through all elements in $O(n)$ time where n is the sum of the `HashSet` instance's size (the number of elements) and the number of buckets.
- You cannot add an element to a set at an iterator position.
- A hash function computes an integer value from an object.
- A good hash function will distribute entries uniformly in a hash table.
- A map associates keys with values.
- In a hash map, only the keys are hashed. In a tree map, only the keys are sorted.
- For `HashSet` and `HashMap`, the operations `add`, `remove`, and `contains` have an expected time of $O(1)$ and are $O(n)$ in the worst case.
- When a class redefines `equals`, it should redefine `hashCode` to be compatible. Implementing these functions is not tested on the AP Exam.
- If a binary search tree is balanced, locating, adding, and removing an element is $O(\log(n))$.
- To use a tree set or a tree map, the elements must belong to a class that implements `Comparable`.
- `TreeSets` and `TreeMaps` are implemented as balanced binary trees so the operations `add`, `remove`, and `contains` are $O(\log(n))$.

- For a `TreeSet` iterator, the first call to `next()` takes $O(\log(n))$ time.
- Know the difference between preorder, postorder, and inorder traversals of a binary tree.
- Removing an element from a priority queue will remove the element with the highest priority (minimal value).
- The heapsort algorithm is $O(n \log(n))$.

■ Key Words

You should understand the terms below. The AP CS Exam questions may include references to these terms. The citations in parentheses next to each term identify the page numbers where it is defined and/or discussed in *Java Concepts for AP Computer Science*, 5th ed.

balanced binary search
  tree (726)
binary tree (720)
binary search tree (720)
buckets (709)
children (720)
collision (708)
descendant (720)
hash code (707)
hash function (707)

hash map (705)
hash set (701)
hash table (707)
heap (740)
heapsort (751)
inorder (732)
key set (705)
map (705)
postorder (732)

preorder (732)
priority queue (739)
root (720)
set (701)
table size (710)
tree map (705)
tree set (701)
value set (705)

■ Connecting the Detailed Topic Outline to the Text

The citations in parentheses next to each term identify the page numbers where it is defined and/or discussed in *Java Concepts for AP Computer Science*, 5th ed.

- Sets (700–704)
- Maps (705–707)
- Hash Tables (707–715)
    - Using `HashSet` (714)
    - Implementing `HashSet` (710–714)
    - Using `HashMap` (707)
- Computing Hash Codes (715–719)
- Binary Search Trees (720–731)
    - Searching a Binary Search Tree (725)
    - Removing a Node from a Binary Search Tree (725–726)
- Tree Traversal (731–735)
- Using Tree Sets and Tree Maps (735–737)
- Priority Queues (739–740)
- Heaps (740–751)
- The Heapsort Algorithm (751–756)
- Choosing a Container (737–738)

■ Practice Questions

Multiple Choice

1. A hash function computes an integer value from an object. The goal of a good hash function is to:

    a. determine the size of the hash table.
    b. provide space for the object that is to be inserted.
    c. provide a method of dealing with collisions.
    d. provide a key for efficiently sorting the objects in the hash table.
    e. provide an integer value for the object so that the objects are uniformly distributed in the hash table.

Questions 2–4 refer to the incomplete binary search tree implementation given below. The class `Tree` is a binary search tree of `TreeNodes`. Refer to the *AB Quick Reference Guide* or Example 17.5 for the `TreeNode` implementation. The `Tree` method `printXxx` calls `xxxPrint` to print the values in the nodes of the binary search tree.

```
/**
    This class implements a binary search tree whose
    nodes are TreeNodes that hold objects that
    implement the Comparable interface.
*/
public class Tree
{
    // Constructs an empty tree.
    public Tree()
    {
        root = null;
    }

    // Other Binary Search Tree methods here

    public void printXxx()
    {
        if (root != null)
            xxxPrint(root);
    }

    public void xxxPrint(TreeNode current)
    {
        ListQueue q = new ListQueue();
        q.enqueue(current);
        while (!q.isEmpty())
        {
            Object temp = q.dequeue();
            current = (TreeNode) temp;
            System.out.print(current.getValue() + " ");
            if (current.getLeft() != null)
                q.enqueue(current.getLeft());
            if (current.getRight() != null)
                q.enqueue(current.getRight());
        }
```

```
        }

        private TreeNode root;
    }
```

The following declaration is made.

```
    Tree numbers = new Tree();
```

The following `Integer` values are inserted, in the order below, into an initially empty binary search tree, `numbers`.

```
    15 8 25 6 14 24 20 22 30 13 26
```

2. What is printed when the statement

```
    numbers.printXxx();
```

is executed in a client program of the `Tree` class?

   a. *6 8 13 14 15 20 22 24 25 26 30*
   b. *6 13 14 8 22 20 24 26 30 25 15*
   c. *15 8 6 14 13 25 24 29 22 30 26*
   d. *15 8 25 6 14 24 30 13 20 26 22*
   e. *15 25 8 30 24 14 6 26 20 13 22*

3. Suppose the statements

```
    if (current.getLeft() != null)
        q.enqueue(current.getLeft());
```

and

```
    if (current.getRight() != null)
        q.enqueue(current.getRight());
```

were exchanged. What would be printed when the statement

```
    numbers.printXxx();
```

is executed in a client program of the `Tree` class?

   a. *6 8 13 14 15 20 22 24 25 26 30*
   b. *6 13 14 8 22 20 24 26 30 25 15*
   c. *15 8 6 14 13 25 24 29 22 30 26*
   d. *15 8 25 6 14 24 30 13 20 26 22*
   e. *15 25 8 30 24 14 6 26 20 13 22*

4. Suppose the following methods were added to the `Tree` class above.

```
    public int mysterySum(TreeNode current)
    {
        if (current == null)
            return 0;
        else
            return (1 + mysterySum(current.getLeft())
                    + mysterySum(current.getRight()));
    }
```

```
public int mystery()
{
    return mysterySum(root);
}
```

The following `Integer` values are inserted, in the order below, into an empty binary search tree, `numbers`.

```
8 3 10 2 5
```

What would be printed when the statement

```
System.out.println(numbers.mystery());
```

is executed in a client program of the `Tree` class?

a. *0*
b. *1*
c. *5*
d. *28*
e. Nothing is printed, a run-time error occurs.

5. Which of the following statements about maps is **true**?

a. A `HashMap` can have two keys that map to the same value but two values cannot have the same key.
b. A `HashMap` can have two values with the same key but two keys cannot have the same value.
c. Each key in a `HashMap` must have a unique value and each value in a `HashMap` has a unique key.
d. A `HashMap` can have two values with the same key and two keys with the same value.
e. A `HashMap` can have values that do not map to any key.

Questions 6 and 7 refer to the problem statement below.

The following `Integer` values are pushed onto a stack, `s`. The values are pushed onto `s` in the order that they appear below (left to right).

```
1 7 4 6 10 9
```

6. Assume the following declaration has been made.

```
PriorityQueue<Integer> priQue = new PriorityQueue<Integer>();
```

Values are popped off the stack, `s`, and as each value is popped off the stack, it is inserted into the priority queue, `priQue`. The following code is then executed.

```
while (!priQue.isEmpty())
{
    System.out.println(priQue.remove())
}
```

The numbers printed to the screen would be:

a. *1 7 4 6 10 9*
b. *9 10 6 4 7 1*
c. *1 4 6 7 9 10*
d. *10 9 7 6 4 1*
e. *9 6 4 1 7 10*

7. The values are pushed onto `Stack` `s` in the order that they appear below (left to right).

    1 7 4 6 10 9

The values are then popped off the stack. As each value is popped off the stack, it is inserted into a binary search tree. The values in the tree are printed by visiting the nodes in the tree with a preorder traversal. The numbers printed to the screen would be:

a. *1 7 4 6 10 9*
b. *6 4 9 10 7 1*
c. *1 4 6 7 9 10*
d. *10 9 7 6 4 1*
e. *9 6 4 1 7 10*

8. Which of the following is **not** a fundamental operation for a `Set`?

a. Adding elements to the set.
b. Removing elements from the set.
c. Listing elements in the set.
d. Testing the set to see if an element is contained in the set.
e. Returning the number of times a given element appears in the set.

9. Which of the following statements is **true**?

a. A set iterator visits the elements in the order in which you inserted them.
b. When adding elements to a set, you should use the `add` method of the set iterator.
c. Elements can be removed from a set using the iterator method `remove` or the `Set` method `remove` that is defined by the class that implements `Set`.
d. You should not attempt to add duplicates to a set because an error will occur.
e. To insert an element in a particular place in the set, use the set iterator to find the set position.

10. Which of the following lines of code will add an association of a person and a university in the `Map friends`?

a. `friends.add("Mary");`
b. `friends.add("Mary", "University of Delaware");`
c. `friends.put("Mary", "University of Delaware");`
d. `friends.addValue("Mary", "University of Delaware");`
e. `friends.putValue("Mary", "University of Delaware");`

11. Which of the following describes how to print all of the keys, with their associated values, of a class that implements Map?

    a. Store a value and its associated key in a TreeNode and insert the TreeNode in a binary search tree. Then, traverse the tree using an inorder traversal.
    b. Store a value and its associated key in a TreeNode and insert the TreeNode in a binary search tree. Then, use a tree iterator to retrieve the values.
    c. Iterate through the set returned by the class's keySet method to retrieve the key and use the class's get method to retrieve the value associated with the key.
    d. Iterate through the set returned by the class's keySet method to retrieve the value and use the class's get method to retrieve the key associated with the value.
    e. Store the elements in an array list and the corresponding values in a set. Iterate through the array list and the set simultaneously to retrieve and print the keys and values.

12. If there are no collisions in the hash table, then locating a hash table element takes

    a. $O(1)$
    b. $O(\log(n))$
    c. $O(n)$
    d. $O(n \log(n))$
    e. $O(n^2)$

13. Consider the following sorting algorithms.

    I.   Merge sort
    II. Quicksort
    III. Heapsort

    In the worst case, which of the algorithms is $O(n \log(n))$?

    a. I only
    b. II only
    c. III only
    d. I and III only
    e. I, II, and III

14. The following Integers are added to an initially empty min-heap in the order they are listed. The heap properties are maintained with each insertion.

        9 25 32 90 15 4 23

    If the heap is represented by a binary tree and an inorder traversal is done on this binary tree, the resulting order of the visited Integers is:

    a. 9 32 15 90 4 25 23
    b. 4 9 15 23 25 32 90
    c. 90 32 25 23 15 9 4
    d. 90 15 25 4 32 9 23
    e. 9 15 32 4 23 25 90

15. Consider the following two methods for sorting a set of strings in descending order.

    Method 1
    - Construct an empty binary search tree.
    - Insert all strings into the binary search tree.
    - Repeatedly get the maximum element (by following the rightmost path) and remove it.

    Method 2
    - Construct an empty max-heap.
    - Insert all strings into the heap.
    - Repeatedly get the maximum element (stored in the root) and remove it.

    Which of the following statements is **true**?

    a. Method 2 is more efficient than Method 1 if the resulting trees are both balanced after inserting all elements.
    b. Method 1 is more efficient than Method 2 if the input set is already sorted.
    c. Method 1 has $O(n \log(n))$ efficiency in the best case.
    d. Method 2 has $O(n^2)$ efficiency in the worst case.
    e. Method 1 and Method 2 are both less efficient than selection sort.

16. Your job is to choose a data structure to implement polynomials whose coefficients are positive integers, such as $17x^4 + 4x^3 + 0x^2 + 6x^1 + 12x^0$.

    Here are three possible implementations.

    I. As a two-dimensional array of boolean values: coeff[c][i] is true if and only if $c * x^i$ is a term of the polynomial.
    II. As a tree map with `Integer` keys and values. If $c * x^i$ is a term of the polynomial, then we add the following correspondence to the map:

    ```
    coeff.put(new Integer(i), new Integer(c))
    ```

    III. As a hash set of objects of type

    ```
    public class Term
    {
        // Based on power
        public int hashcode(){. . .}

        // Based on power
        public boolean equals(Object obj){. . .}

        . . .
        private int coefficient;
        private int power;
    }
    ```

If *n* is the number of terms in the polynomial, which of the following statements is **false**?

a.   Implementation I requires more space than implementations II and III.
b.   Implementation II makes possible to print the polynomial by decreasing powers in $O(n \log(n))$ time.
c.   Implementation II requires $O(\log(n))$ time to find the coefficient of a term with a given power.
d.   Implementation III is impossible to carry out because one cannot define a hash code for terms.
e.   If the hash code is assumed to run in constant time, implementation III requires $O(1)$ time to find the coefficient of a term with a given power.

17. The principal advantage that heapsort has over the merge sort algorithm is

a.   Heapsort is related to priority queues.
b.   Heapsort doesn't require a second array for intermediate storage.
c.   Heapsort is a $O(n \log(n))$ algorithm.
d.   Heapsort uses binary search trees.
e.   Heapsort does not require recursion.

18. Consider the following max-heap:

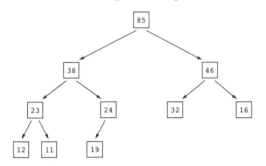

The array representation of this heap is

a.   11 12 16 19 23 24 38 46 85
b.   85 38 46 23 24 32 16 12 11 19
c.   12 11 19 24 24 32 16 38 46 85
d.   85 38 23 12 11 24 19 46 32 16
e.   None of the above—the tree doesn't fulfill the max-heap conditions.

19. Consider the following binary trees:

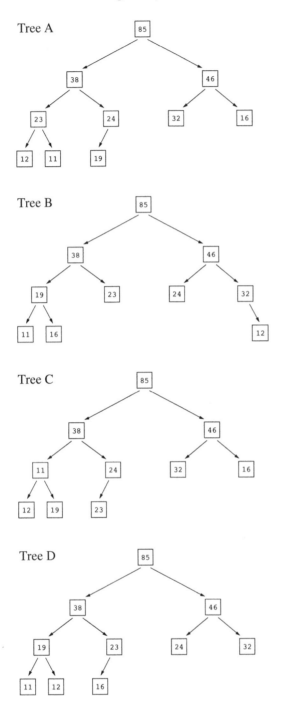

Which of the binary trees above are max-heaps?

a. All of the trees above are heaps.
b. A and B only
c. C and D only
d. B and D only
e. A and D only

20. Consider the following mystery function on a binary tree (not necessarily a binary search tree).

```java
public int mysteryHelper(TreeNode cur)
{
    if (cur == null)
        return 0;
    else
    {
        int r = mysteryHelper(cur.getLeft())
              + mysteryHelper(cur.getRight());
        if ((cur.getLeft() != null && ((Integer) cur.getLeft()
                .getValue()).compareTo(cur.getValue()) > 0) ||
            (cur.getRight() != null && ((Integer) cur.getRight()
                .getValue()).compareTo(cur.getValue()) < 0))
        {
            r++;
        }
        return r;
    }
}

public int mystery()
{
    return mysteryHelper(root);
}
```

What is the result of applying the function to the following tree?

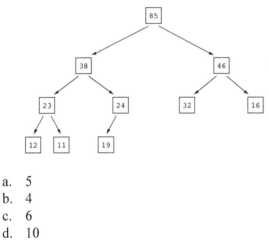

a. 5
b. 4
c. 6
d. 10
e. 306

Free Response Questions

1.   The class SetsWithOps contains set operations that include the methods setIntersection, setUnion, setDifference, isSubset, and isProperSubset. The one SetsWithOps constructor has two Set parameters. The method functionality is limited to sets of strings and is described in the comments of the incomplete SetsWithOps class below. You will be implementing the set methods as described.

```
import java.util.Iterator;
import java.util.Set;
import java.util.TreeSet;

public class SetsWithOps
{
   /**
      Constructor for set operations.
      @param s1 the first set to operate with
      @param s2 the second set to operate with
   */
   public SetsWithOps(Set<String> s1, Set<String> s2)
   {
      set1 = s1;
      set2 = s2;
   }

   /**
      Returns the elements that are in set1 and set2.
      @return the intersection of set1 and set2
   */
   public Set<String> setIntersection()
   {
      // Code goes here
   }

   /**
      Returns the elements that are in set1 or set2.
      @return the union of set1 and set2
   */
   public Set<String> setUnion()
   {
      // Code goes here
   }

   /**
      Returns the elements that are in set1 but not in set2.
      @return the difference of set1 and set2
   */
   public Set<String> setDifference()
   {
      // Code goes here
   }

   /**
      Returns true if all of the elements of set1 are also in
      set2, false otherwise.
      @return true if set1 is a subset of set2, false otherwise
   */
   public  boolean isSubset()
   {
      // Code goes here
   }

   /**
      Returns true if set1 is a subset of set 2 and not equal to
      set2.
```

```
        @return true if set1 is a proper subset of set2, false
        otherwise
    */
    public boolean isProperSubset()
    {
        // Code goes here
    }

    private  Set<String> set1;
    private  Set<String> set2;
}
```

a. You are to implement the `SetsWithOps` method `setIntersection`. The intersection of two sets is a set whose members are common to both sets. The method `setIntersection` will return the intersection of `set1` with `set2`, the two instance fields of this class. For example, if

> `s1` is the set `{"Ginger", "Harry", "Mary", "Thomas"}`

and

> `s2` is the set `{"Frank", "Harry", "Kevin", "Mary", "Nancy"}`

and the statements

```
SetsWithOps s = new SetsWithOps(s1, s2);
Set<String> set3 = s.setIntersection();
```

were executed, `set3` would contain `{"Harry", "Mary"}`.

If the two sets have no elements in common, an empty set is returned. Use the method header below to write the method `setIntersection`.

```
public Set<String> setIntersection()
```

b. You are to implement the `SetsWithOps` method `setUnion`. The union of two sets is a set whose members are in at least one of the sets. The method `setUnion` will return the union of `set1` with `set2`, the two instance fields of this class. For example, if

> `s1` is the set `{"Ginger", "Harry", "Mary", "Thomas"}`

and

> `s2` is the set `{"Frank", "Harry", "Kevin", "Mary", "Nancy"}`

and the statements

```
SetsWithOps s = new SetsWithOps(s1, s2);
Set<String> set3 = s.setUnion();
```

were executed, `set3` would contain `{"Frank", "Ginger", "Harry", "Kevin", "Mary", "Nancy", "Thomas"}`.

Use the method header below to write the method `setUnion`.

```
public Set<String> setUnion()
```

c. You are to implement the `SetsWithOps` method `setDifference`. The difference of `set1` minus `set2` is the set whose members are in `set1` but are not in `set2`. The method `setDifference` will return the difference of `set1` with `set2`, the two instance fields of this class.

For example, if

s1 is the set {"Ginger", "Harry", "Mary", "Thomas"}

and

s2 is the set {"Frank", "Harry", "Kevin", "Mary", "Nancy"}

and the statements

```
SetsWithOps s = new SetsWithOps(s1, s2);
Set<String> set3 = s.setDifference();
```

were executed, set3 would contain {"Ginger", "Thomas"}.

Use the method header below to write the method setDifference.

```
public Set<String> setDifference()
```

d. You are to implement the SetsWithOps method isSubset. The method isSubset will return true if every element of set2 is also an element of set1 where set1 and set2 are the two instance fields of this class. The set set1 may have exactly the same elements as set2. For example, if the statement

```
SetsWithOps s = new SetsWithOps(s1, s2);
```

was executed, then

s1	*s2*	*s.isSubset()*
{1,2,3,4,5}	{1,2,3}	true
{1,2,3,4}	{1,2,3,4}	true
{1,2,3,4,5}	{1,2,3,6}	false

Use the method header below to write the method isSubset.

```
public boolean isSubset()
```

e. You are to implement the SetsWithOps method isProperSubset. The method isProperSubset will return true if every element of set2 is also an element of set1 and set1 has some elements that are not in set2. For example, if the statement

```
SetsWithOps s = new SetsWithOps(s1, s2);
```

was executed, then

s1	*s2*	*s.isProperSubset()*
{1,2,3,4,5}	{1,2,3}	true
{1,2,3,4}	{1,2,3,4}	false
{1,2,3,4,5}	{1,2,3,6}	false

In writing isProperSubset, you may call the method isSubset described in part d of this problem. Assume isSubset works as intended regardless of what you wrote for part d. Use the method header below to write the method isProperSubset.

```
public boolean isProperSubset()
```

2. A concordance is an alphabetical word list for a passage of text. Each word in the concordance is mapped to an `Integer` indicating the frequency of the word's occurrence. The constructor of `Concordance` has one `String` parameter that identifies the text file to be read. An incomplete `Concordance` class is below.

```
public class Concordance
{
    /**
       Constructor.
       @param nameOfFile the text file being read
    */
    public Concordance(String nameOfFile)
    {
        concord = new TreeMap<String, Integer>();
        createConcordance(nameOfFile);
    }

    /**
       Create a TreeMap of words mapped to their
       Integer frequencies.
       @param fileName name of text file for concordance
    */
    public void createConcordance(String fileName)
    {
        // Code goes here
    }

    /**
       Prints the alphabetized list of words paired with their
       frequencies.
    */
    public void printConcordance()
    {
        // Code goes here
    }

    private Map<String, Integer> concord;
}
```

a. The method `createConcordance` will fill `concord`, a `TreeMap` of words mapped to their `Integer` frequencies. Complete the method `createConcordance` below. You may assume that all words in the passage are made up of lowercase letters.

```
public void createConcordance(String fileName)
{
    . . .
    while (inFile.hasNext())     // while more words to read
    {
        String word =           // read word from file
        // More code goes here
    }
}
```

b. Write the method `printConcordance` that will print the alphabetized list of words paired with their frequencies. If the text file contains the following text:

> *hickory dickory dock*
> *the mouse ran up the clock*
> *the clock struck one*
> *the mouse ran down*
> *hickory dickory dock*

`printConcordance` will print:

> *clock occurs 2 time(s).*
> *dickory occurs 2 time(s).*
> *dock occurs 2 time(s).*
> *down occurs 1 time(s).*
> *hickory occurs 2 time(s).*
> *mouse occurs 2 time(s).*
> *one occurs 1 time(s).*
> *ran occurs 2 time(s).*
> *struck occurs 1 time(s).*
> *the occurs 4 time(s).*
> *up occurs 1 time(s).*

Use the method header below in writing `printConcordance`.

```
public void printConcordance()
```

c. Suppose, in addition to the method `printConcordance`, you wish to include a method `printByFrequency` that would print the words ordered by frequency. The method `printByFrequency` will print:

> *down occurs 1 time(s).*
> *one occurs 1 time(s).*
> *struck occurs 1 time(s).*
> *up occurs 1 time(s).*
> *clock occurs 2 time(s).*
> *dickory occurs 2 time(s).*
> *dock occurs 2 time(s).*
> *hickory occurs 2 time(s).*
> *mouse occurs 2 time(s).*
> *ran occurs 2 time(s).*
> *the occurs 4 time(s).*

Words with the same frequency can be printed in any order. Describe the data structure(s) and algorithms that you would use to write `printByFrequency`. Comment on the time complexity of your algorithm.

CUMULATIVE REVIEW 3

Chapters 14–17

This review will focus on material in Chapters 14–17 but may include questions on material in previous chapters. You should consider this a mini-practice for the AP Exam. Look over the material in these chapters and read over the section *Things to Remember When Taking the AP Exam* below. Have available the Exam Reference Materials for the AP Exam that you will be taking. Because you will have reference materials available to you during the exam, you should become familiar with them now.

■ Things to Remember When Taking the AP Exam

General Guidelines
- It is a common error to use a while statement when an if statement should be used to check for the base case in a recursive function. Check your work!
- A recursive solution is not necessarily more efficient than an iterative solution to the same problem. For many problems, a recursive solution is shorter and/or clearer and thus a more efficient use of the programmer's time writing and testing the solution.
- Include an end condition for recursive solutions. Infinite recursions are usually undesirable.
- Write recursive solutions when the problem statement is defined recursively or when explicitly instructed to do so. Do not use recursion as a substitute for iteration.
- When given a particular algorithm, you should be able to count the number of times a specific statement is executed.
- The merge sort is more efficient than the insertion sort and selection sort algorithms but requires a temporary array.
- When given an algorithm similar to the binary search algorithm and an algorithm similar to the sequential search algorithm, you should be able to choose the algorithm that is more efficient for a specific set of data.
- Remember that an array has to be sorted in order to use binary search.
- Binary search generally is more efficient than sequential search if the array is sorted.
- When writing a sorting algorithm, there are many places where off-by-one errors can occur. Be careful when choosing between 0 and 1, < and <=, and a.length and a.length - 1 for loop initializations. Walk through your code carefully.
- The worst case for the quicksort algorithm occurs when the original array is in order or in reverse order and the pivot chosen is the first or last element.
- Be sure to check whether an array or an array list is empty before you try to remove an item from it.

AB Topics

- You should be able to throw the unchecked `IllegalStateException` and `NoSuchElement-Exception` in your own methods.
- Merge sort, quicksort, and heapsort are $O(n \log(n))$ algorithms. Insertion and selection sorts are $O(n^2)$.
- When the quicksort algorithm is performed on an array that is originally in order or in reverse order and the pivot chosen is the first or last element, running time is $O(n^2)$.
- Algorithms that are $O(n \log(n))$ are more efficient than algorithms that are $O(n^2)$.
- When given an algorithm, you should be able to classify it as $O(1)$, $O(n)$, $O(\log(n))$, $O(n^2)$, or $O(n \log(n))$.
- Algorithms are not classified as $O(2n)$, $O(3)$, or $O(n^2 + 2n + 1)$. These are $O(n)$, $O(1)$, and $O(n^2)$ respectively.
- Do not simply count loops when determining the big-Oh running time. Consecutive loop algorithms are most often $O(n)$. Nested loop algorithms tend to be $O(n^2)$.
- Inserting and deleting from a `LinkedList` is efficient because these operations do not require shifting the other elements in the list.
- Stacks are LIFO (last-in, first-out). Queues are FIFO (first-in, first-out).
- If an application requires many look-ups (searches), use an implementation that provides $O(1)$ access whenever possible. Specifically, use an array when you need random access to individual elements (e.g., sorting algorithms) and use a linked list when you frequently need to insert or remove in the middle of the list (e.g., simulation of cars on a freeway with entrance/exit ramps).
- Be sure to check whether the list data structure is empty before you try to remove an item from it.
- Become familiar with the `ListNode` class and the `TreeNode` class. The *AB Quick Reference Guide* that you will be given during the AP Exam includes the implementation of these classes but you should be familiar with their use before the exam.
- Be careful when implementing code that adds or removes nodes from a linked list. Ask yourself the following questions:
  - Does this code handle the empty list case?
  - Does this code handle the front of the list case?
  - Does this code handle the end of the list case?
  - Does this code handle the middle of the list case?
  - Does this code handle the list with only one node?
- Use a list iterator to access elements of a `LinkedList`. DO NOT use `get/set/insert`.
- Use an enhanced `for` loop to traverse arrays and lists. There is less of a chance (actually no chance) to make an off-by-one error!
- Check for `null` references! Whenever calling `p.next`, `p.data`, etc., ask yourself "Can p be empty? If so, am I checking for it? If not, why not?"
- Sets do not contain duplicates. If you change an item in a set it may become the same as another item in the set. Moreover, this WILL upset the set data structure because it may change the hash code or the sort order!
- Sets are not ordered except for `TreeSet`.
- Use an iterator to list all elements in a set.
- An iterator for a `HashSet` does not return the elements in any specific order.
- For a `HashSet`, an iterator can iterate through all elements in $O(n)$ time where *n* is the sum of the `HashSet` instance's size (the number of elements) and the number of buckets.
- You cannot add an element to a set at an iterator position.
- A hash function computes an integer value from an object.
- A good hash function will distribute entries uniformly in a hash table.
- A map associates keys with values.
- In a hash map, only the keys are hashed. In a tree map, only the keys are sorted.
- For `HashSet` and `HashMap`, the operations `add`, `remove`, and `contains` have an expected time of $O(1)$ and are $O(n)$ in the worst case.

- When a class redefines `equals`, it should redefine `hashCode` to be compatible. Implementing these functions is not tested on the AP Exam.
- If a binary search tree is balanced, locating, adding, and removing an element is $O(\log(n))$.
- To use a tree set or a tree map, the elements must be comparable.
- `TreeSets` and `TreeMaps` are implemented as balanced binary trees so the operations `add`, `remove`, and `contains` are $O(\log(n))$.
- For a `TreeSet` iterator, the first call to `next()` takes $O(\log(n))$ time.
- Know the difference between preorder, postorder, and inorder traversals of a binary tree.
- Removing an element from a priority queue will remove the element with the highest priority (minimal value).

■ Practice Questions

Multiple Choice

Questions 1 and 2 refer to the method `design`, given below. The method prints a design of *'s.

```
public static void design(int n)
{
    for (int i = n; i >= 1; i--)
    {
        for (int j = 1; j <= i; j++)
        {
            System.out.print("*");
        }
        System.out.println();
    }
}
```

1. In order for the method `design` to be guaranteed to print some *'s, which of the following is a correct precondition?

    a. $n \neq 0$
    b. $n < 0$
    c. $n \leq 0$
    d. $n > 0$
    e. $n \geq 0$

2. Which of the following methods will result in the same output as the method `design`?

    a. ```
        public static void design(int n)
        {
            System.out.println();
            if (n >= 1)
            {
                design(n - 1);
            }
            else
            {
                System.out.print("*");
            }
        }
        ```
        ```

b.
```java
public static void design(int n)
{
    if (n == 1)
    {
        System.out.println("*");
    }
    else
    {
        System.out.println();
        for (int j = 1; j <= n; j++)
        {
            System.out.print("*");
        }
        design(n - 1);
    }
}
```

c.
```java
public static void design(int n)
{
    if (n == 1)
    {
        System.out.println("*");
    }
    else
    {
        for (int j = 1; j <= n; j++)
        {
            System.out.print("*");
        }
        System.out.println();
        design(n - 1);
    }
}
```

d.
```java
public static void design(int n)
{
    if (n == 1)
    {
        System.out.println("*");
    }
    else
        for (int j = 1; j <= n; j++)
        {
            design(n - 1);
            System.out.print("*");
        }
}
```

e.
```java
public static void design(int n)
{
    if (n == 1)
    {
        System.out.println("*");
    }
    else
        for (int j = 1; j <= n; j++)
        {
            System.out.print("*");
            design(n - 1);
        }
}
```

3. The following code segments are intended to eliminate duplicates from an `ArrayList` of `Integers`.

    I.
    ```
    for (int i = 0; i < arr.size() - 1; i++)
    {
        if (arr.get(i).equals(arr.get(i + 1)))
        {
            arr.remove(i);
        }
    }
    ```

    II.
    ```
    int i = 0;
    while (i < arr.size() - 1)
    {
        if (arr.get(i).equals(arr.get(i + 1)))
        {
            arr.remove(i);
        }
        else
        {
            i++;
        }
    }
    ```

    a. Choices I and II work as intended for all `ArrayLists` of `Integers`.
    b. Choices I and II work as intended for `ArrayLists` of `Integers` that are sorted.
    c. Choices I and II work as intended for all non-empty `ArrayLists` of `Integers`.
    d. Choice I works as intended for `ArrayLists` of `Integers` that are sorted but Choice II does not.
    e. Choice II works as intended for `ArrayLists` of `Integers` that are sorted but Choice I does not.

4. **(AB)** The following code segment is intended to eliminate duplicates from an `ArrayList` of `Integers`.

    ```
    Iterator<Integer> iter = arr.iterator();
    Integer num = iter.next();
    while (iter.hasNext())
    {
        Integer num2 = iter.next();
        if (num.equals(num2))
        {
            iter.remove();
        }
        else
        {
            num = num2;
        }
    }
    ```

    Which statement about the code segment is **true**?

    a. This code segment works as intended for all `ArrayLists` of `Integers`.
    b. This code segment works as intended for all `ArrayLists` of `Integers` that are sorted.
    c. This code segment works as intended for all non-empty `ArrayLists` of `Integers`.
    d. This code segment works as intended for all non-empty `ArrayLists` of `Integers` that are sorted.
    e. This code segment eliminates only those values that are duplicates of the first value in the `ArrayList`.

5. **(AB)** Suppose it takes x milliseconds to sort a set of data using the selection sort algorithm. Approximately how long will it take to sort a data set that is four times as large?

    a. x milliseconds
    b. $4x$ milliseconds
    c. $16x$ milliseconds
    d. x^2 milliseconds
    e. There is no way to determine the answer.

Questions 6 and 7 refer to the following algorithm for sorting values in an array.

```java
public class Orderer
{
   public Orderer(int[] anArray)
   {
      a = anArray;
   }

   public void order()
   {
      for (int i = 0; i < a.length - 1; i++)
      {
         int position = findPosition(i);
         swap(position, i);
      }
   }

   private int findPosition(int from)
   {
      int pos = from;
      for (int i = from + 1; i < a.length; i++)
         if (a[i] < a[pos])
         {
            pos = i;
         }
      return pos;
   }

   private void swap(int i, int j)
   {
      int temp = a[i];
      a[i] = a[j];
      a[j] = temp;
   }

   private int[] a;
}
```

6. Which of the following statements is **true** about the `Orderer` method `order` above?

    a. This algorithm closely resembles the selection sort algorithm.
    b. This algorithm closely resembles the insertion sort algorithm.
    c. This algorithm closely resembles the merge sort algorithm.
    d. This algorithm reverses the order of the data in the array.
    e. This sort algorithm randomly reorders elements in the array.

7. If the array `a` contains the numbers 5, 2, 12, 6, and 72, how many times is the comparison

    `a[i] < a[pos]`

    made?

    a. 1
    b. 5
    c. 10
    d. 25
    e. 50

8. Which of the following statements about classes and interfaces are **true**?

    I.   Abstract classes can contain constructors.
    II. Interfaces can contain constructors.
    III. Classes that have no abstract methods can contain constructors.

   a. III only
   b. I and II only
   c. II and III only
   d. I and III only
   e. I, II, and III

9. Consider the `NumberGenerator` class defined below.

```
public class NumberGenerator
{
    public NumberGenerator(int numberOfPositions, int startNum)
    {
        digits = numberOfPositions;
        currentDigit = startNum;
        if (digits > 1)
        {
            tail = new NumberGenerator(digits - 1, currentDigit + 1);
        }
        else
        {
            tail = null;
        }
    }

    public String nextElement()
    {
        String r = "";
        if (digits == 1)
        {
            r = currentDigit + "";
            currentDigit++;
            return r;
        }
        r = currentDigit + tail.nextElement();
        if (!tail.hasMoreElements())
        {
            currentDigit++;
            tail = new NumberGenerator(digits - 1, currentDigit + 1);
        }
        return r;
    }

    public boolean hasMoreElements()
    {
        return (currentDigit <= MAXDIGITS)
            && (digits <= MAXDIGITS - currentDigit + 1);
    }

    private int digits;
    private NumberGenerator tail;
    private int currentDigit;
    private final int MAXDIGITS = 4;
}
```

What is the result of the following code segment?

```
NumberGenerator combs = new NumberGenerator(3, 0);
int count = 1;
while (combs.hasMoreElements() && count <= 5) // only printing 5
{
    System.out.print(combs.nextElement() + " ");
    count++;
}
```

    a. 012 013 014 023 024
    b. 000 001 002 003 004
    c. 010 012 013 014 020
    d. 000 111 222 333 444
    e. 012 013 014 022 023

For Questions 10 and 11, assume that the following declarations are made.

```
LinkedList<Integer> aList = new LinkedList<Integer>();
PriorityQueue<Integer> pq = new PriorityQueue<Integer>();
Stack<Integer> s = new Stack<Integer>();
Queue<Integer> q = new LinkedList<Integer>();
```

10. **(AB)** Suppose the following segment of code is executed.

```
aList.add(1);
aList.add(2);
aList.add(3);
aList.add(4);
aList.add(5);

ListIterator<Integer> iter = aList.listIterator();
while (iter.hasNext())
{
   Integer item = iter.next();
   s.push(item);
   q.enqueue(item);
}
System.out.print("Queue: ");
while (!q.isEmpty())
{
   System.out.print(q.dequeue());
}
System.out.println();
System.out.print("Stack: ");
while (!s.isEmpty())
{
   System.out.print(s.pop());
}
```

What would be printed?

  a. Queue: 12345
      Stack: 54321

  b. Queue: 12345
      Stack: 12345

  c. Queue: 54321
      Stack: 12345

  d. Queue: 54321
      Stack: 54321

  e. Queue:
      Stack:

11. **(AB)** Suppose the following segment of code is executed.

```
pq.add(new Integer(5));
pq.add(new Integer(9));
pq.add(new Integer(6));
pq.add(new Integer(4));
pq.add(new Integer(1));
pq.add(new Integer(7));

while (!(pq.isEmpty()))
{
    Integer num = pq.peek();
    if (num % 2 == 0)
    {
        s.push(pq.remove());
    }
    else
    {
        q.add(pq.remove());
    }
}
System.out.print("Queue: ");
while (!q.isEmpty())
{
    System.out.print(q.remove());
}
System.out.println();
System.out.print("Stack: ");
while (!s.isEmpty())
{
    System.out.print(s.pop());
}
```

What would be printed?

a. Queue: 5917
    Stack: 64

b. Queue: 1579
    Stack: 64

c. Queue: 5917
    Stack: 46

d. Queue: 1579
    Stack: 46

e. Queue: 596417
    Stack:

For Questions 12 and 13: Suppose that the implementation of add in the SomePriorityQueue class is

```
public void add(Object x)
{
    someDataImplementation.add(x);
}
```

and that the elements are added to this priority queue in random order.

12. **(AB)** Which choice for a data structure for `someDataImplementation` would yield the fastest retrieval time for the `SomePriorityQueue` method `peek`?

    a.　`java.util.LinkedList`
    b.　`java.util.ArrayList`
    c.　`java.util.HashSet`
    d.　`java.util.TreeSet`
    e.　`java.util.TreeMap`

13. **(AB)** Assuming that the choice of data type for `someDataImplementation` yields the fastest retrieval time for `peek`, the big-Oh efficiency for `peek` is

    a.　$O(1)$
    b.　$O(n)$
    c.　$O(\log(n))$
    d.　$O(n \log(n))$
    e.　$O(n^2)$

14. **(AB)** Suppose that the `Integers` 9, 5, 3, 7, 1 are added, in the order given, to an initially empty queue, `q`, and that the `Integers` 2, 4, 6, and 8 are added, in the order given, to an initially empty stack, `s`. Also suppose that `hp` is an initially empty min-heap and that the min-heap method `addToHeap` adds an element to the min-heap using the standard algorithm for inserting into a heap thus maintaining the min-heap properties after each insertion into the heap. After the following code is executed,

    ```
    while (!q.isempty())
    {
        hp.addToHeap(q.remove());
    }
    while (!s.isempty())
    {
        hp.addToHeap(s.pop());
    }
    ```

    which of the following min-heaps is a representation of `hp`?

    a.

    b.

c.

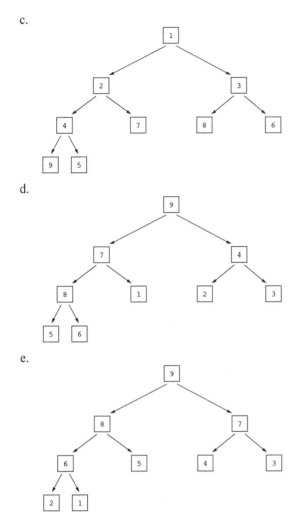

d.

e.

15. **(AB)** The linked list class, `java.util.LinkedList`, defines the method `addLast()`. The run-time efficiency of this `addLast` method is:

a.　$O(1)$
b.　$O(\log(n))$
c.　$O(n)$
d.　$O(n \log(n))$
e.　$O(n^2)$

Questions 16–18 refer to the following partial class declaration.

```java
public class LList
{
    public LList()
    {
        first = null;
    }

    public void addLast(Object obj)
    {
        ListNode newNode = new ListNode(obj, null);
        if (first == null)
        {
            first = newNode();
```

```
            }
            else
            {
                ListNode temp = first;
                while (temp.getNext() != null)
                {
                    temp = temp.getNext();
                }
                temp.setNext(newNode);
            }
        }

        public void addLastRecursive(Object obj)
        {
            first = addLastHelper(first, obj);
        }

        private ListNode addLastHelper(ListNode list, Object obj)
        {
            // Code goes here
        }

        // ... Other methods and data not shown
        private ListNode first;
    }
```

16. **(AB)** The linked list class, LList, defines the method addLast(). The run-time efficiency of this addLast method is:

   a. $O(1)$
   b. $O(\log(n))$
   c. $O(n)$
   d. $O(n\log(n))$
   e. $O(n^2)$

17. **(AB)** The LList method addLastRecursive, with its helper method addLastHelper, is intended to have the same result as the LList method addLast defined above. Which of the following is a correct implementation of addLastHelper?

   a.
```
        private ListNode addLastHelper(ListNode list, Object obj)
        {
            if (list == null)
            {
                return new ListNode(obj, null);
            }
            else
            {
                addLastHelper(list.getNext(), obj);
                return list;
            }
        }
```

   b.
```
        private ListNode addLastHelper(ListNode list, Object obj)
        {
            if (list == null)
            {
                list = new ListNode(obj, null);
            }
            else
            {
                list = (addLastHelper(list.getNext(), obj));
            }
            return list;
```

```
    }
c.  private ListNode addLastHelper(ListNode list, Object obj)
    {
        if (list == null)
        {
            return new ListNode(obj, null);
        }
        else
        {
            return addLastHelper(list.getNext(), obj);
        }
    }
d.  private ListNode addLastHelper(ListNode list, Object obj)
    {
        if (list == null)
        {
            return new ListNode(obj, null);
        }
        else
        {
            list.setNext(addLastHelper(list.getNext(), obj));
            return list;
        }
    }
e.  private ListNode addLastHelper(ListNode list, Object obj)
    {
        if (list == null)
        {
            return new ListNode(obj, null);
        }
        else
        {
            list.setNext(addLastHelper(new ListNode(obj, null), obj));
            return list;
        }
    }
```

18. **(AB)** Which of the following statements about the `LList` methods `addLast` and `addLastRecursive` is **true**?

    a. `addLastRecursive` is always more efficient than `addLast`.
    b. `addLast` is always more efficient than `addLastRecursive`.
    c. For small lists, there is no significant difference in efficiencies between `addLast` and `addLastRecursive`.
    d. `addLast` is only more efficient than `addLastRecursive` if the elements are added to the list in increasing order.
    e. `addLast` is only more efficient than `addLastRecursive` if the elements are added to the list in decreasing order.

19. You have been asked to write a program that will serve as a Spanish-English dictionary of commonly used words and phrases. If the input to your program is a word or phrase in English, your program should output the equivalent word or phrase in Spanish. Which of the following data structures would be the best choice if you will be adding information to your dictionary and doing many look-ups in the dictionary?

a. An array list of maps where each key is a string representing the English word or phrase and each value is the corresponding Spanish word or phrase.
b. A `HashMap` where each key is a string representing the English word or phrase and each value is the corresponding Spanish word or phrase.
c. A `TreeMap` where each key is a string representing the English word or phrase and each value is the corresponding Spanish word or phrase.
d. An unordered linked list of `Words` where a `Word` object has an accessor method that can return the Spanish form of the English word.
e. An ordered linked list of `Words` where a `Word` object that has an accessor method that can return the Spanish form of the English word.

20. Consider the incomplete `BinaryTree` class below.

```
/**
    This class implements a binary tree whose nodes hold objects that
    implement the Comparable interface.
*/
public class BinaryTree
{
    /**
        Constructs an empty tree.
    */
    public BinaryTree() {. . .}

    /**
        @return true if root == null, false otherwise
    */
    public boolean isEmpty() {. . .}

    /**
        Inserts a new node into the tree in order using the Binary
        Search Tree insert algorithm.
        @param obj the object to insert
    */
    public void insert(Comparable obj) {. . .}

    /**
        Prints the TreeNode values using an inorder traversal order.
    */
    public void inOrder() {. . .}

    public void swapBigAndSmall()
    {
        // Code goes here
    }

    private TreeNode root;
}
```

The `BinaryTree` method `swapBigAndSmall` is intended to exchange the largest and smallest values in the tree. For example, suppose the integers 15, 8, 25, 6, 14, 24, 20, 22, 30, 13, 26, were inserted into a tree in the order given. An inorder traversal of the tree would print:

6 8 13 14 15 20 22 24 25 26 30

After a call to `swapBigAndSmall`, an inorder traversal of the same tree would print

30 8 13 14 15 20 22 24 25 26 6

Which of the following code segments could be the body of `swapBigAndSmall` so that the intended task is completed?

I. ```
    TreeNode temp = root;
    TreeNode temp2 = root;
    ```
    ```

```
      while (temp.getLeft() != null)
      {
         temp2 = temp;
         temp = temp.getLeft();
      }
      TreeNode almostSmall = temp2;
      temp = root;
      temp2 = root;
      while (temp.getRight() != null)
      {
         temp2 = temp;
         temp = temp.getRight();
      }
      TreeNode almostBig = temp2;
      temp = almostSmall.getLeft();
      almostSmall.setLeft(almostBig.getRight());
      almostBig.setRight(temp);
```

II.
```
   TreeNode temp = root;
   TreeNode temp2 = root;
   while (temp.getLeft() != null)
   {
      temp2 = temp;
      temp = temp.getLeft();
   }
   TreeNode small = temp;
   temp = root;
   temp2 = root;
   while (temp.getRight() != null)
   {
      temp2 = temp;
      temp = temp.getRight();
   }
   TreeNode big = temp;
   Object tempValue = small.getValue();
   small.setValue(big.getValue());
   big.setValue(tempValue);
```

III.
```
   TreeNode temp = root;
   TreeNode temp2 = root;
   while (temp.getLeft() != null)
   {
      temp2 = temp;
      temp = temp.getLeft();
   }
   TreeNode almostSmall = temp2;
   temp = root;
   temp2 = root;
   while (temp.getRight() != null)
   {
      temp2 = temp;
      temp = temp.getRight();
   }
   TreeNode almostBig = temp2;
   almostSmall.setLeft(almostBig.getRight());
   almostBig.setRight(almostSmall.getLeft());
```

a. I only
b. II only
c. III only
d. I and II only
e. I, II, and III

Free Response

1. A combination can be thought of as an unordered list of elements. For example, consider individuals: Tom, Dick, Harry, and Romeo. To form a committee of three individuals from this group of four, we look at combinations. There are four such combinations: [Tom, Dick, Harry], [Tom, Dick, Romeo], [Tom, Harry, Romeo], and [Dick, Harry, Romeo]. The ordering of the members of the committee doesn't matter. The committee [Dick, Harry, Romeo] is the same committee as [Romeo, Dick, Harry] and so both orders would not be included in a list of all combinations.

    The `CombinationGenerator` class generates all combinations that can be formed with a given set of integers. The incomplete `CombinationGenerator` class is below.

    ```
    public class CombinationGenerator
    {
        /**
            Constructor creates a display of digits.
            @param numberOfPositions the number of positions diplayed
            @param startNum the lowest number appearing in the combination
            @param endNum the highest number appearing in the combination
        */
        public CombinationGenerator(int numberOfPositions,
               int startNum, int endNum) {. . .}

        /**
            @return the next combination display
        */
        public ArrayList<Integer> nextElement() {...}

        /**
            @return true if there are more combinations, false otherwise
        */
        public boolean hasMoreElements() {. . .}

        //  Private instance fields declared here
    }
    ```

    The program segment

    ```
    CombinationGenerator combs = new CombinationGenerator(3, 0, 4);
    while (combs.hasMoreElements())
    {
        System.out.println(combs.nextElement() + " ");
    }
    ```

    would print array lists of size 3, containing combinations of integer values from 0 to 4 inclusive:

    [0, 1, 2] [0, 1, 3] [0, 1, 4] [0, 2, 3] [0, 2, 4] [0, 3, 4] [1, 2, 3] [1, 2, 4] [1, 3, 4] [2, 3, 4]

    A high school wishes to use this program to generate combinations of players for the starting line-ups for its teams. For example, suppose there is a total of 8 members of the basketball team. A starting line-up consists of 5 players. The coach wants to generate all possible 5-player starting line-ups formed from the 8 members of the basketball team. For example, if the players are stored as a team in the array list as [James, John, Bob, Larry, Henry, Tom, Michael, Norman] then the combination generator

    ```
    CombinationGenerator combs = new CombinationGenerator(5, 0, 7);
    ```

    would generate all possible team combinations and the combination [0, 1, 2, 3, 7] would represent the team consisting of the players [James, John, Bob, Larry, Norman] (array list positions in the team). The incomplete definitions for the `Player` class and the abstract `Team` class are given below.

`Player` Class

```
public class Player
{
```

```java
    /**
        Constructor.
        @param firstName the player's first name
        @param lastName the player's last name
        @param jerseyNumber the player's jersey number
        @param position the player's starting position
    */
    public Player(String firstName, String lastName, int jerseyNumber,
        String position) {. . .}

    /**
        @return player name
    */
    public String getName() {. . .}

    /**
        @return player's jersey number
    */
    public int getJersey() {. . .}

    /**
        @return player's position
    */
    public String getPosition() {. . .}

    /**
        @return string representation of this player
    */
    public String toString() {. . .}

    // Other methods here
    // Private instance fields here
}
```

Team Class

```java
public abstract class Team
{
    /**
        Constructs Team.
        @param filename the file containing player information
        @param ratingFile the file containing rating information
        @param number the number of players on a team
    */
    public Team(String fileName, String ratingFile, int number)
    {
        myTeam = new ArrayList<Player>();
        getTeamInfo(fileName);
        ratings = setRatingInfo(ratingFile);
        numberInLineUp = number;
        startingLineUps = null;
    }

    /**
        Fills myTeam with player information from fileName.
        @param filename the file containing player information
    */
    private void getTeamInfo(String fileName) {. . .}

    /**
        @return string representation of all players on myTeam
    */
    public String toString() {. . .}
```

```
/**
   Prints player information of particular ArrayList of players.
   @param p the players to print information about
*/
public void printLineUpInfo(ArrayList<Player> p) {. . .}

/**
   @return the number of total members on team
*/
public int getTeamSize() {. . .}

/**
   @return rating of thisTeam
*/
public int getLineUpRating(ArrayList<Player> thisTeam)
{
   // Code goes here
}

/**
   Reads player rating information from file and stores in SomeDataType.
   @param filename the file containing rating information of players
   @return data structure holding correct pair rating information
*/
private SomeDataType setRatingInfo(String fileName)
{
   // Code goes here
   return playerRatings;
}

/**
   Creates array list of players in line-up.
   @param bb the ArrayList positions of the player numbers
   @return ArrayList of Players given player positions in
   ArrayList of Integers
*/
public ArrayList<Player> getPlayersInLineUp(ArrayList<Integer> bb)
{
   // Code goes here
}

/**
   Prints all valid starting line-ups.
*/
public void printValidStartingTeams()
{
   // Code goes here
}

/**
   @return the valid line-up that has the highest rating
*/
public ArrayList<Player> getBestTeam()
{
   // Code goes here
}

/**
   @return true if this line-up of players is valid, false otherwise
*/
public abstract boolean isLineUpValid(ArrayList<Player> p);
```

```
    private ArrayList<Player> myTeam;
    private SomeDataType ratings;
    private CombinationGenerator startingLineUps;
    private int numberInLineUp;
}
```

A basketball team is a team with 5 players in its starting line-up. An incomplete class definition for BbTeam is given below.

```
public class BbTeam extends Team
{
    public BbTeam(String fileName, String ratingFileName, int number)
    {
        super(fileName, ratingFileName, number);
    }

    /**
        @return true if this line-up has exactly 2 guards, 2 forwards,
        and 1 center, otherwise return false
    */
    public boolean isLineUpValid(ArrayList<Player> lineup)
    {
        // Code goes here
    }
}
```

a. Write the implementation of the Team method getPlayersInLineUp that will return the ArrayList<Player> chosen from myTeam that corresponds to its parameter, an ArrayList<Integer> that was generated by the CombinationGenerator. For example, if myTeam contains [James, John, Bob, Larry, Henry, Tom, Michael, Norman] and line-up contains [1, 2, 4, 5, 7] then getPlayersInLineUp would return [John, Bob, Henry, Tom, Norman]. Use the header below in writing getPlayersInLineUp.

    ```
    public ArrayList<Player> getPlayersInLineUp(ArrayList<Integer> bb)
    ```

b. Write the implementation of the BbTeam method isLineUpValid that returns true if the line-up is a valid starting line-up and false otherwise. A valid starting line-up for a Basketball team must have 2 forwards, 2 guards, and 1 center. Player positions returned by Player method getPosition will be one of the String values "center", "guard", or "forward". Use the header below in writing isLineUpValid.

    ```
    public boolean isLineUpValid(ArrayList<Player> lineup)
    ```

c. A coach wishes to list all possible valid line-ups for a basketball team. The following code segment is intended to do that task.

    ```
    BbTeam bb = new BbTeam("PlayerFileName", "RatingFileName", 5);
    bb.printValidStartingTeams();
    ```

    Write the implementation of the Team method printValidStartingTeams that will print the valid starting line-ups for the basketball team. Use the header below.

    ```
    public void printValidStartingTeams()
    ```

d. Explain why the class Team is an abstract class.

e. **(AB only)** Player ratings are recorded in a text file in the following format:

    0 55 7
    52 11 3

    where the first two integers on a line represent the jersey numbers of two players and the last integer on the line represents the rating (on a scale from 1 to 10 inclusive) of how well the two players play together. Jersey numbers are in the range 0 to 99 inclusive. If a pair of players is not listed in the file, they are assigned a default rating of 5. A player paired with him/herself is assigned a rating of 0. The Team method setRatingInfo reads the file information and fills some data structure with this rating information. An incomplete implementation of setRatingInfo is below.

```
private SomeDataType setRatingInfo(String fileName)
{
    final int defaultRating = 5;

    // Code goes here: Declare and initialize playerRatings here

    // fileName is open for reading
    while        //  (there is still information to read in the file)
    {
        readFromFile(jersey1);
        readFromFile(jersey2);
        readFromFile(pairRating);
        //  Code goes here
    }
    return playerRatings;
}
```

In determining the rating for a team, the sum of the ratings of all possible players on the team is calculated. Describe a data structure that you would use to store this rating information that would allow for quick retrieval of pair ratings.

f.   **(AB only)** Using the data structure chosen in part d, declare and initialize playerRatings.

g.   **(AB only)** Write the code that would replace the comment // *Code goes here* and fill playerRatings.

h.   **(AB only)** Based on the data structure chosen in part d, write the implementation of the Team method getLineUpRating that will return the integer rating of its parameter thisTeam. This rating is found by calculating the sum of the ratings of all possible players on thisTeam. You may assume that method setRatingInfo works as intended regardless of what you wrote for parts f and g.

```
public int getLineUpRating(ArrayList<Player> thisTeam)
```

i.   Write the implementation of the Team method getBestTeam that returns the valid line-up with the highest rating. You may assume that the methods written in previous parts of this problem work as intended. Use the header below in writing getBestTeam.

```
public ArrayList<Player> getBestTeam()
```

2.   **(AB only)** A polynomial is stored as a tree map with Integer keys and values. If $c * x^i$ is a term of the polynomial, then we add the following correspondence to the map:

```
poly.put(new Integer(i), new Integer(c))
```

The incomplete Polynomial class is below.

```
public class Polynomial
{
    /**
        Constructs an empty polynomial.
    */
    public Polynomial()
    {
        poly = new TreeMap<Integer, Integer>();
    }

    // Adds a term to this polynomial.
    public void addTerm(Integer exponent, Integer coefficient)
    {
        poly.put(exponent, coefficient);
    }
```

```
/**
    @return the String representation of this polynomial with the
    term having the largest exponent being first
*/
public String toString()
{
    // Code goes here
}


/**
    Evaluates a polynomial.
    @param x the value to substitute to the polynomial
    @return the value of the polynomial when x is substituted
*/
public double evaluatePolynomial(double x)
{
    // Code goes here
}


/**
    Adds two polynomials.
    @param other polynomial to add
    @return a polynomial that is the sum of this polynomial and other
*/
public Polynomial add(Polynomial other)
{
    // Code goes here
}


/**
    Multiplies two polynomials.
    @param other polynomial to multiply
    @return a polynomial that is the product of this polynomial and
    other
*/
public Polynomial multiply(Polynomial other)
{
    // Code goes here
}

    private TreeMap<Integer, Integer> poly;
}
```

a. Write the `Polynomial` method `toString` that returns the string representation of the polynomial. The representation is such that the term with the largest exponent is first and the other terms appear in decreasing exponent order. For example, `2x^5 + 4x^3 + 6x^2 + 7x^1 + 8` is one such string representation. Use the header below in writing `toString`.

    ```
    public String toString()
    ```

b. Write the `Polynomial` method `evaluatePolynomial` that will return the value of the polynomial found by substituting its `double` parameter into the polynomial. For example, if `p1` is the `Polynomial` representing $2x^5 + 4x^3 + 6x^2 + 7x + 8$, `p1.evaluatePolynomial(1)` would return 27. Use the header below in writing `evaluatePolynomial`.

    ```
    public double evaluatePolynomial(double x)
    ```

c. Write the `Polynomial` method `add` that returns the sum of this `Polynomial` and its `Polynomial` parameter. For example, if `p1` = $2x^5 + 4x^3 + 6x^2 + 7x + 8$ and `p2` = $3x^2 + 4x + 7$ then `p1.add(p2)` would return the `Polynomial` representing $2x^5 + 4x^3 + 9x^2 + 11x + 15$. Use the header below in writing `add`.

    ```
    public Polynomial add(Polynomial other)
    ```

d.   Write the `Polynomial` method `multiply` that returns the product of this `Polynomial` and its `Polynomial` parameter. For example, if p1 = $3x + 1$ and p2 = $2x + 3$ then `p1.multiply(p2)` would return the `Polynomial` representing $6x^2 + 11x + 3$. Use the header below in writing `multiply`.

```
public Polynomial multiply(Polynomial other)
```

CHAPTER **18**

The AP Exam Case Study

TOPIC OUTLINE

18.1 What Is a Case Study?
18.2 Why Are Case Studies Included in AP CS?
18.3 How Do I Use the Case Study During the School Year?
18.4 How Do I Prepare for the Case Study Questions on the AP Exam?
18.5 Where Do I Get the Case Study?

■ Topic Summary

18.1   What Is a Case Study?

A case study is a document that includes a problem statement, a program that solves the problem, and a narrative discussing the steps taken and the decisions made in developing the problem solution. Case studies have been used for years to teach law, medicine, business, and science. Case studies were added to the AP Computer Science curriculum in 1994. The AP CS Case Study contains a large program, written by experts, that is meant to serve as a good programming example. The narrative discusses the development of this program. Within the narrative there are exercises and analysis questions. Through these questions and the questions posed within the narrative, development options are explored as they would be before development decisions are made. This enables you, the student, to act as an apprentice in the programming situation. You will be learning from the experts as you work through the program. The case study narrative makes it clear that having a program that just "works" should never be the focus of a software system — the process of arriving at a solution is just as important as the final product itself. In Chapter 13 of this guide we discussed the software life cycle. This cycle consists of five distinct processes.

• Analysis
• Design
• Implementation
• Testing
• Deployment

The focus of the case study is to become familiar with each of these five processes as they relate to the particular case study problem. You will be able to study the different alternatives to a problem solution and you will understand why certain choices were made in each step of the software life cycle.

The sets of short answer questions posed throughout each section of the case study narrative guide you through the software life cycle for the case study problem. Do not skip these questions and do not "leave them for later." Completing the questions and the case study programming activities as you go through the case study document allows for an understanding of the complete development process.

18.2   Why Are Case Studies Included in AP CS?

The AP CS Exam consists of 40 multiple-choice questions and 4 free-response questions. Answering these types of questions would not necessarily indicate that you have ever worked with a program of any size. Since AP Computer Science parallels the first semester or two of university-level computer science courses, and since universities generally require the development and completion of larger programs, the case study offers a method for ensuring that AP CS students have some experience with a large program. This case study program requires you to read a very large program written by someone else. By working with the case study, you will gain experience modifying and extending a large program, and you will be exposed to a good programming example written by experts. The exercises throughout the case study deal with all stages of development and encourage you to think through design and implementation tradeoffs.

18.3   How Do I Use the Case Study During the School Year?

The case study will help develop critical thinking skills. You should begin reading the case study very early in the year. It is important that you become familiar with the current case study documents. If possible, you should visit the case study several times throughout the AP CS course. Do not wait until two weeks before the exam to look at the document for the first time. The case study will help you learn computer science concepts. Studying the case study will improve your performance throughout the course, not just on the case study exam questions. Complete all of the exercises, question sets, and programming activities as you go through the case study. These questions will help you understand the design decisions and programming alternatives. Research has indicated that the more time spent on the case study, the better the mastery of all AP CS material.

18.4   How Do I Prepare for the Case Study Questions on the AP Exam?

Familiarize yourself with the goal of the case study. Review the question sets before the exam. There are different requirements for the A and AB Exams. Be aware of the material that is covered on the AP Exam that you will be taking. You can find this information on the College Board Web site listed at the end of this chapter.

You will be given certain documents during the AP CS Exam. You may use these documents throughout the multiple-choice and free-response parts of the exam. These documents include the AP CS A or AB Quick Reference Guide and portions of the case study document. The case study materials will include the source code for the visible classes, a summary of class documentation for the classes whose code you are not responsible for knowing, and an index. All of these documents are available to you during the school year. Become familiar with these resources.

Be familiar with the classes that are included in the case study. Understand the constructors, accessor methods, and modifier methods for each class. Know the class dependencies and inheritance hierarchies. Be able to modify and extend the existing classes. You should have quite a bit of experience with this already if you have been faithfully completing the questions and exercises and implementing these changes in the case study.

Remember that there will be 5–10 multiple-choice questions and one free-response question directly related to the case study. These questions may include tasks such as:
- Extend the case study code by writing a new method, class, or subclass.
- Give a different design for a class.
- Design an entirely new class.
- Design a set of interacting classes. **(AB only)**
- Give an alternative choice of data structure.
- Implement a given method using an alternative data structure or approach.
- Develop test data for a particular implementation.
- Explain the interaction and dependencies among classes.
- Analyze given code, explaining how it might be made more efficient.
- Give the big-Oh analysis for a particular algorithm. **(AB only)**
- Modify classes based on an alternative problem description.

Do not wait until the exam to look at the case study resources! Time is very valuable during the exam period. Read the exam questions carefully. They may be simple modifications of problems that you have already done.

18.5   Where Do I Get the Case Study?

The case study consists of several parts. The required material is available for you to download from the College Board Web site. Important College Board links are listed below.

Information on the current case study:

> http://www.collegeboard.com/student/testing/ap/compsci_a/case.html?compscia

You can access general information about the Advanced Placement Program at:

> http://www.collegeboard.com/student/testing/ap/about.html

Current information about AP Computer Science:

> AP CS A: http://www.collegeboard.com/student/testing/ap/sub_compscia.html?compscia

> AP CS AB: http://www.collegeboard.com/student/testing/ap/sub_compsciab.html?compscia

APPENDIX

Exercise Solutions

■ Chapter 2

Answers to Multiple Choice Questions

1. a	4. b	7. e	9. d
2. b	5. c	8. e	10. d
3. e	6. e		

Notes on Answers

6. The entire body of the void method is a comment. There is no error but nothing is printed.

■ Chapter 3

Answers to Multiple Choice Questions

1. b	4. a	7. c	9. e
2. c	5. e	8. d	10. d
3. a	6. a		

Notes on Answers

9. Modifiers change the state of the object. I, II, and III all change the attributes (or state) of the Rectangle object. The correct anwer is e.
10. Accessors do not change the state of an object. The methods getY and getHeight return information about the object without changing the state. The correct answer is d.

■ Chapter 4

Answers to Multiple Choice Questions

1. c	4. a	7. e	9. a
2. d	5. e	8. d	10. b
3. d	6. e		

Notes on Answers

5. b1 and b2 are `BankAccount` objects.

```
b1.deposit(b2.getBalance());     // deposits 500 in b1
                                 // b1 balance now 1000
                                 // b2 balance now 500
b2.deposit(b1.getBalance());     // deposits 1000 in b2
                                 // b1 balance now 1000
                                 // b2 balance now 1500
```

6. b2 and b1 reference the same `BankAccount` object.

```
BankAccount b1 = new BankAccount(500);
BankAccount b2 = b1;    // balance of b1 and b2 is 500
b1.deposit(b2.getBalance());     // balance of b1 and b2 is 1000
b2.deposit(b1.getBalance());     // balance of b1 and b2 is 2000
```

Answers to Free Response

```
1a. public Employee(String firstName, String lastName, double moneyEarned)
    {
        myFirstName = firstName;
        myLastName = lastName;
        mySalary = moneyEarned;
    }

1b. public void raiseSalary(double byPercent)
    {
        double amountOfRaise = byPercent / 100 * mySalary;
        mySalary = mySalary + amountOfRaise;
    }

1c. public double calculateBonusAmount(double byPercent)
    {
        return (mySalary * byPercent / 100);
    }

2a. public Book(String name, String writer, double cost)
    {
        title = name;
        author = writer;
        price = cost;
    }

2b. public void giveDiscount(double byPercent)
    {
        double amountOfDiscount = byPercent / 100 * price;
        double newPrice = price - amountOfDiscount;
        price = newPrice;
    }
```

■ Chapter 5

Answers to Multiple Choice Questions

1. c	4. d	7. a	9. d
2. c	5. a	8. e	10. e
3. c	6. b		

Answers to Free Response

1a.
```
public double findGasUsed(double numMiles)
{
    return numMiles / mpg;
}
```

1b.
```
public void drive(double numMiles)
{
    mileage += numMiles;
    double gas = findGasUsed(numMiles);
    gasInTank -= gas;
}
```

2a.
```
public int totalInPennies()
{
    return (int) (PENNIES_PER_DOLLAR * getTotal())
}
```

2b.
```
public int getDollars()
{
    int amount = totalInPennies();
    return amount / PENNIES_PER_DOLLAR;
}
```

Alternate Solution

```
public int getDollars()
{
    return (int) getTotal();
}
```

2c.
```
public int getCents()
{
    int amount = totalInPennies();
    return amount % PENNIES_PER_DOLLAR;
}
```

■ Chapter 6

Answers to Multiple Choice Questions

1. d	5. d	9. e	13. a
2. b	6. d	10. c	14. e
3. e	7. e	11. d	
4. a	8. c	12. c	

Notes on Answers

1. This is an example of a *dangling-else*. The `else` goes with the closest `if` regardless of the indentation. Indentation does not control the flow of the program execution. The answer is d.

```
x = 6;
y = 19;
z = 2;    // x = 6, y = 19, z = 2
if (x > y)   // x is not greater than y so the following if-else
             // is not executed.
    if (z > x)
        z++;
    else
        z -= 5;
y += x;    // x = 6, y = 19 + 6 = 25, z = 2
```

4. The answer is a.

```
foo = word.substring(1, 3) = "om"
hoo = word.substring(4) = "ute"
if (foo.compareTo(hoo) < 0)   // true
{
    hoo += foo;   // hoo is now "uteom", foo is "om".
}
else
{
    foo += hoo;
}
```

7. The correct answer is e.

```
string2 = string1;   // string2 now references "Hello"
string1 += "There!";   // A new string is created. The variable string1
                       // references this new string ("HelloThere") and
                       // string2 still references "Hello".
```

8. Choice I is incorrect because a client program is trying to access private instance fields. Choice II is incorrect because `equals` is not specifically defined for the `Point` class, so the call to `equals` would return `true` if and only if p1 and p2 reference the same object. But p1 and p2 can have the same *x*- and *y*- coordinates and be referencing different objects. The correct answer is c.

9. Choices I and III are both correct because a class can access its private variables. Choice II is not correct because `equals` is not used with primitive types.

10. De Morgan's Law. The correct answer is c.

13. According to the precondition, the first parameter to the method `weeklyPay` must be between 0 and 168 inclusive. All three choices satisfy this precondition. The second parameter to this method must be greater than 0. Choice I is the only choice that violates this. The correct answer is a.

14. According to the precondition, the first parameter to the method `weeklyPay` must be between 0 and 168 inclusive. Both Choice I and Choice II check this boundary condition. The first parameter in Choice III is 40. This is a boundary condition on the branch of the conditional that will check for time-and-a-half pay. The correct answer is e.

Answers to Free Response

1a.
```
public double gasNeeded(double numMiles)
{
    return numMiles / mpg;
}
```

1b.
```
public boolean enoughGas(double numMiles)
{
    return gasNeeded(numMiles) <= gasInTank;
}
```

1c.
```
public void getGas()
{
    if (gasInTank < 0.5 * tankCapacity)
    gasInTank = tankCapacity;
}
```

1d.
```
public void drive(double numMiles)
{
    if (enoughGas(numMiles))
    {
        mileage += numMiles;
        gasInTank -= gasNeeded(numMiles);
    }
    else
    {
```

```
            double milesToGo = gasInTank * mpg;
            mileage += milesToGo;
            gasInTank = 0;
        }
    }
```

2a.
```
public double getDistanceFromOrigin()
{
    double d = Math.sqrt(x * x + y * y);
    return d;
}
```

2b.
```
public static Point findFarPoint(Point p1, Point p2, Point p3)
{
    double d1 = p1.getDistanceFromOrigin();
    double d2 = p2.getDistanceFromOrigin();
    double d3 = p3.getDistanceFromOrigin();

    double longest = d1;
    Point far = p1;
    if (d2 > longest)
    {
        longest = d2;
        far = p2;
    }
    if (d3 > longest)
    {
        longest = d3;
        far = p3;
    }
    return far;
}
```

■ Chapter 7

Answers to Multiple Choice Questions

1.	c	5.	c	9.	e	13.	c
2.	e	6.	a	10.	d	14.	b
3.	d	7.	c	11.	c	15.	c
4.	e	8.	c	12.	c	16.	d

Notes on Answers

4.   All loops result in the desired output. The values of the loop control variables appear in the first two columns of each table. The third column shows the printed result at the completion of each execution of the outer loop.

Choice I

i	j	Prints the value of i for each j
4	1	4
3	2, 1	33
2	3, 2, 1	222
1	4, 3, 2, 1	1111

Choice II

i	j	Prints 4 – i + 1 for each j
1	1	4
2	1, 2	33
3	1, 2, 3	222
4	1, 2, 3, 4	1111

Choice III

i	j	Prints 4 – i + 1 for each j
1	4	4
2	4, 3	33
3	4, 3, 2	222
4	4, 3, 2, 1	1111

5. The answer is c. For each execution of the `while` loop, a's value is increased by the last digit of the current value of n (n `%` 10 gives you the last digit of n). Then n is divided by 10 so that the new value of n is the old value of n without the last digit. This process continues until n `<= 0`.

9. Choice I checks each letter of the string `"aeiou"` for an occurrence in `word`. If that letter occurs (no matter how many times) `count` is incremented by 1. For example. if `word` = `level`, `count` would return 1. This choice is incorrect. The correct answer is e.

10. A loop invariant is a statement that is true before the loop is executed, at the beginning of each execution of the loop and after the loop terminates. In this problem, `p` and `i` are initialized to 1 and n is a positive integer.

```
while (i <= n)
{
   p = p * i;
   i++;
}
```

Clearly, the code calculates *n* factorial (*n!*). Eliminate choice e (the code is not calculating *n* to a power). Since *n* could begin with the value 1, choices a and b are incorrect. When the loop terminates, $i = n + 1$ so choice c is not correct. Choice d is the correct answer.

14. Assuming that the original number is a positive integer, the loop continuously divides by 2 (incrementing x each time this division is done) until the quotient is 0. When the loop terminates, number of divisions-by-2 made is x. Therefore, x is the smallest power of 2 such that $2^x \geq n$. The correct answer is b.

15. From the explanation of 14 above, 5 is the smallest power of 2 that is greater than or equal to 32. The body of the `while` loop is executed 6 times before `val` = `0`. The correct answer is c.

Answers to Free Response

```
1a. public void waitForYears(int y)
    {
       for (int i = 1; i <= y; i++)
       {
          double interest = balance * rate / 100;
          balance += interest;
       }
    }
```

```
1b. public void compoundTheInterest(int y, int n)
    {
        for (int year = 1; year <= y; year++)
        {
            for (int numTimes = 1; numTimes <= n; numTimes++)
            {
                double interest = balance * rate / 100 / n;
                balance += interest;
            }
        }
    }

2a. public Game()
    {
        myWheel = new Spinner(4);
    }

2b. public int spinTheWheel()
    {
        int number = myWheel.spin();
        if (number >= 2)
            return number;
        else return 0;
    }

2c. public double playRoulette(Purse myPurse)
    {
        double myMoney = myPurse.getTotal();
        double myEndMoney = 2 * myMoney;
        Coin aCoin;

        while (myPurse.coinCount() > 0 && myPurse.getTotal() < myEndMoney)
        // Comparing the int coinCount to 0 rather than
        // worrying about precision errors when comparing doubles
        {
            aCoin = myPurse.removeCoin();
            int r = spinTheWheel();    // Value of r is 0, 2, or 3
            for (int i = 1; i <= r; i++)
            {
                myPurse.add(new Coin(aCoin.getValue(), aCoin.getName()));
                // Actually add new coins to myPurse--not
                // references to the same coin!
            }
        }
        return myPurse.getTotal();
    }
```

■ Cumulative Review 1

Answers to Multiple Choice Questions

1. a	6. c	11. d	16. e	21. d
2. e	7. b	12. e	17. a	22. b
3. e	8. d	13. c	18. d	
4. d	9. d	14. d	19. d	
5. b	10. d	15. d	20. d	

16. The loop is executed 11 times. `vowels.substring(0)` evaluates to `"aeiou"`. Because the string `"aeiou"` is not found in `"mathematics"`, `-1` is added to `number` 11 times and the resulting value of `number` is `-11`. The correct answer is e.

19. One 6-sided die is rolled and its value is stored in `rand`. Four more dice are rolled. If the value on the rolled die is not equal to `rand`, `false` is returned. The method returns `true` only if all five dice result with the same value, `rand`.

Answers to Free Response Questions

1a.
```
public int numDigits()
{
    int num = myNum;
    int digits = 0;
    while (num > 0)
    {
        num = (num / 10);
        digits++;
    }
    return digits;
}
```

Alternate Solution
```
public int numDigits()
{
    String s = "" + myNum;
    return s.length();
}
```

Alternate Solution 2
```
public int numDigits()
{
    return toString.length();
}
```

1b.
```
public int sumDigits()
{
    int temp = myNum;
    int sum = 0;
    while (temp > 0)
    {
        sum += temp % 10;
        temp = temp / 10;
    }
    return sum;
}
```

1c.
```
public boolean isPerfect()
{
    int sum = 0;
    for (int i = 1; i < myNum / 2; i++)
    {
        if (myNum % i == 0)
        {
            sum += i;
        }
    }
    return (sum == myNum);
}
```

1d.
```java
public FunNumber reverseNum()
{
    int rev = 0;
    int digits = 0;
    int temp = myNum;
    while (temp > 0)
    {
        digits = temp % 10;
        rev = 10 * rev + digits;
        temp = temp / 10;
    }
    FunNumber reversedNumber = new FunNumber(rev);
    return reversedNumber;
}
```

Alternate Solution

```java
public FunNumber reverseNum()
{
    String s = toString();
    String newString = "";
    for (int i = s.length() - 1; i >= 0; i--)
        newString += s.substring(i, i + 1);
    FunNumber reversedNumber = new FunNumber(newString);
    return reversedNumber;
}
```

Alternate Solution 2

```java
public FunNumber reverseNum()
{
    String s = "";
    int temp = myNum;
    while (temp > 0)
    {
        s = (temp % 10) + s;
        temp = temp / 10;
    }
    return new FunNumber(s);
}
```

2a.
```java
public String getSuit()
{
    if (mySuit.equals("H"))
        return "Hearts";
    else if (mySuit.equals("C"))
        return "Clubs";
    else if (mySuit.equals("D"))
        return "Diamonds";
    else return "Spades";
}
```

2b.
```java
public String getDenomination()
{
    String temp = "";
    if (myValue < 11 && myValue > 1)
        temp = "" + myValue;
    else if (myDenom.equals("J"))
        temp = "Jack";
    else if (myDenom.equals("Q"))
        temp = "Queen";
    else if (myDenom.equals("K"))
        temp = "King";
    else if (myDenom.equals("A"))
```

```
            temp = "Ace";
        return temp;
    }
```

2c. `public int getValue()`
```
    {
        String values = "00234567890JQKA";

        if (myDenom.equals("10"))
            return 10;
        else
            return values.indexOf(myDenom);
    }
```

Alternate Solution

```
    public int getValue()
    {
        if (myDenom.equals("10"))
            return 10;
        else if (myDenom.equals("J"))
            return 11;
        else if (myDenom.equals("Q"))
            return 12;
        else if (myDenom.equals("K"))
            return 13;
        else if (myDenom.equals("A"))
            return 14;
        else
        {
            Integer num = new Integer(myDenom); // This form of the Integer
                                                // constructor is not part of the
                                                // AP subset.
            return num.intValue();
        }
    }
```

2d. `public String toString()`
```
    {
        return getDenomination() + " of " + getSuit();
    }
```

3a. `public boolean isPair()`
```
    {
        return (card1.getValue() == card2.getValue());
    }
```

3b. `public boolean sameSuit()`
```
    {
        return (card1.getSuit().equals(card2.getSuit()));
    }
```

3c. `public boolean sameColor()`
```
    {
        String temp1 = card1.getSuit();
        String temp2 = card2.getSuit();
        if ((temp1.equals("Spades") || temp1.equals("Clubs"))
            && ((temp2.equals("Spades") || temp2.equals("Clubs"))))
        {
            return true;
        }
        if ((temp1.equals("Hearts") || temp1.equals("Diamonds"))
            && (temp2.equals("Hearts") || temp2.equals("Diamonds")))
        {
            return true;
```

```
        }
        else
        {
            return false;
        }
    }
3d. public int getTotal()
    {
        int temp = card1.getValue();
        if (temp > 10)
        {
            if (temp == 14)
            {
                temp = 11;
            }
            else
            {
                temp = 10;
            }
        }
        int temp2 = card2.getValue();
        if (temp2 > 10)
        {
            if (temp2 == 14)
            {
                temp2 = 11;
            }
            else
            {
                temp2 = 10;
            }
        }
        return temp + temp2;
    }
```

■ Chapter 8

Answers to Multiple Choice Questions

1. d	5. b	9. d	13. d
2. d	6. a	10. d	14. d
3. e	7. b	11. d	15. c
4. b	8. e	12. b	

Notes on Answers

4. This method returns the number that has the longest sequence of consecutive repeated values in the array.

5. The statement B = A results in B referencing the same array that A references. When a change is made in B, the change also occurs in A.

9. Choice I checks references. To check if arrays have equal values, each element must be checked.

14. # indicates iterator position in people.

```
Iterator<Person> it = people.iterator();    // #ATLDK
it.next();    // A#TLDK
it.next();    // AT#LDK
Person temp = it.next();    // temp = Lara; ATL#DK
it.remove();    // AT#DK
temp = it.next();    // temp = David  ATD#K
System.out.println(temp.getName());    // David
```

Answers to Free Response

1a.
```
public FooList(int numLetters)
{
    fooLength = numLetters;
    possibleFoos = new ArrayList<String>();
}
```

1b.
```
public boolean found(String key)
{
    for (String foo : possibleFoos)
    {
        if (foo.equals(key))
            return true;
    }
    return false;
}
```

Alternate Iterator Solution (AB)

```
public boolean found(String key)
{
    Iterator<String> iter = possibleFoos.iterator();
    while (iter.hasNext())
    {
        String temp = iter.next();
        if (temp.equals(key))
            return true;
    }
    return false;
}
```

1c.
```
public void addFoo(String entry)
{
    if (entry.length() == fooLength && !found(entry))
    {
        possibleFoos.add(entry);
    }
}
```

1d.
```
public String removeRandomFoo()
{
    int choice = (int)(Math.random() * possibleFoos.size());
    String temp = possibleFoos.remove(choice);
    return temp;
}
```

2a.
```
private void fillBoard()
{
    for (int i = 0; i < size / 2; i++)
    {
        String word = possibleTileValues.removeRandomFoo();
        for (int j = 0; j < 2; j++)
        {
            int place = (int)(Math.random() * size);
            while (gameBoard[place] != null)
            {
                place = (int)(Math.random() * size);
            }
            gameBoard[place] = new Tile(word);
        }
    }
}
```

2b.
```
public void lookAtTile(int p)
{
    gameBoard[p].turnFaceUp();
}
```

2c.
```
public void checkMatch(int pos1, int pos2)
{
    if (gameBoard[pos1].equals(gameBoard[pos2]))
    {
        numberOfTilesFaceUp += 2;
    }
    else
    {
        gameBoard[pos1].turnFaceDown();
        gameBoard[pos2].turnFaceDown();
    }
}
```

2d.
```
public void printBoard()
{
    final int PADDING = 3;    // Spacing of tiles
    int spacing = possibleTileValues.getFooLength() + PADDING;
    for (int i = 0; i < size; i++)
    {
        if (gameBoard[i].isFaceUp())
        {
            String temp = gameBoard[i].showFace();
            System.out.print(format(temp, spacing));
        }
        else
        {
            System.out.print(format(i, spacing));
        }
        if (i % rowLength == rowLength - 1)
            System.out.println("\n");
    }
}
```

3a.
```
private void fillBoard()
{
    for (int i = 0; i < size / 2; i++)
    {
        String word = possibleTileValues.removeRandomFoo();

        for (int j = 0; j < 2; j++)
        {
            int row = (int)(Math.random() * rowLength);
            int col = (int)(Math.random() * rowLength);
            while (gameBoard[row][col] != null)
            {
                row = (int)(Math.random() * rowLength)
                col = (int)(Math.random() * rowLength)
            }
            gameBoard[row][col] = new Tile(word);
        }
    }
}
```

3b.
```
public void printBoard()
{
    final int PADDING = 8;    // for proper spacing of tiles
    int spaces = possibleTileValues.getFooLength() + PADDING;
    for (int row = 0; row < rowLength; row++)
    {
```

```
      for (int col = 0; col < rowLength; col++)
      {
         if (gameBoard[row][col].isFaceUp())
         {
            String temp = gameBoard[row][col].showFace();
            System.out.print(format(temp, spaces));
         }
         else
         {
            String temp = "[" + row + "][" + col + "]";
            System.out.print(format(temp, spaces));
         }
      }
      System.out.println();
   }
}
```

■ Chapter 9

Answers to Multiple Choice Questions

1. c	4. e	7. a	9. c
2. c	5. d	8. e	10. c
3. d	6. c		

Notes on Answers

4. Perimeter is not a behavior of a point.

7. change1 attempts to reassign the parameter reference inside the method body. Parameters to methods cannot change. The method change2 actually changes the state of the object, not the object reference. The order of parameters can also be confusing. student3 is passed to the first parameter stdt1 of change2 and student1 is passed to the second parameter stdt2 of change2.

Answers to Free Response

```
1a. public class Book
    {
       /**
          Constructor.
          Precondition: cost > 0
          Postcondition: Book object created
          @param name the book's title
          @param writer the book's author
          @param cost the book's price
       */
       public Book(String name, String writer, double cost) {. . .}

       /**
          @return the identification number of the book
       */
       public double getIdentificationNumber() {. . .}

       /**
          @return the author's name
       */
       public String getAuthor() {. . .}

       /**
          Precondition: newPrice > 0
          Postcondition: Book price is updated and now equals newPrice
```

```
        @param newPrice the new price for the book
    */
    public void setPrice(double newPrice) {. . .}

    /**
        @return the price of book
    */
    public double getPrice() {. . .}
}
```

1b.
```
private String title;
private String author;
private double price;
private int idNum;
private static int identification = 0;
```

1c.
```
/**
    Precondition: cost > 0
    Postcondition: Book object created
    @param name the book's title
    @param writer the book's author
    @param cost the book's price
*/
public Book(String name, String writer, double cost)
{
    if (cost <= 0) throw new IllegalArgumentException();    // AB only
    title = name;
    author = writer;
    price = cost;
    identification++;
    idNum = identification;
}
```

1d. Alternative 1: Throw an exception if the precondition is not met. The advantage is that control will be transferred to the exception handler and, if there isn't an exception handler, the program stops. There will be no data corruption. The disadvantage is that the program may stop prematurely.

Alternative 2: Assume the precondition is always satisfied. The advantage is that there is no extra work on the programmer's part. It is the responsibility of the calling method to check the precondition, not the method's responsibility. The disadvantage is that there may be data corruption or other failures that occur that will be the result of the caller's failure to satisfy the precondition.

2a.
```
public class Client
{
    /**
        Constructor.
        @param who the client
        @param inches the client's height
        @param lbs the client's weight
        @param sex the client's gender
    */
    public Client(String who, int inches, int lbs, String sex) {. . .}

    /**
        @return client name
    */
    public String getName() {. . .}

    /**
        @return client gender
    */
    public String getGender() {. . .}
```

```
        /**
           @return client height
        */
        public int getHeight() {. . .}

        /**
           @return client weight
        */
        public int getWeight() {. . .}

        // setRecommendedCalories omitted

        /**
           @return suggested calorie intake per day
        */
        public int getRecommendedCalories() {...}
    }
```

2b.
```
    private String name;
    private int weight;
    private int height;
    private String gender;
    private int caloriesPerDay;
```

2c.
```
    public void setRecommendedCalories(WeightCalculator plan)
    {
        final int CALORIES_TO_CUT = 500;

        int idealWeight = plan.getIdealWeight(gender, height);
        int calories = plan.getCalorieIntake(gender, height);
        if (idealWeight < weight)
        {
            calories -= CALORIES_TO_CUT;
        }
        caloriesPerDay = calories;
    }
```

■ Chapter 10

Answers to Multiple Choice Questions

1. d	4. e	7. a	9. b	
2. b	5. c	8. d	10. c	
3. c	6. c			

Notes on Answers

2. You cannot instantiate an interface. The correct answer is b.

3. skyRider2 is a `Flier` and a `Flier` is not an `Athlete` and does not implement the `Athlete` interface. The correct answer is c.

4. `Athlete` does not have a `fly` method. The compiler will complain. The correct answer is e.

5. When converting from an interface type to a class type, you must cast.

    `s = a;` will cause the compiler to complain.

    `s = (SkiJumper) a;` would be OK.

7. Recall the `Flier` interface and the `SkiJumper` class from Examples 10.1 and 10.2 in this guide.

```
    Flier f;
    Skijumper sj1 = new SkiJumper();
    f = sj1;    // This is OK.
    sj1 = f;    // This causes a compile-time error.
    sj1 = (SkiJumper) f;    // This is OK.
```

Answers to Free Response

1a. `public class SkiJumper implements Flier, Athlete, Comparable`

1b.
```
public int compareTo(Object obj)
{
    SkiJumper temp = (SkiJumper) obj;
    if (myNumberOfJumps < temp.myNumberOfJumps)
        return -1;
    if (myNumberOfJumps == temp.myNumberOfJumps)
        return 0;
    return 1;
}
```

Alternate Solution

```
public int compareTo(Object obj)
{
    SkiJumper temp = (SkiJumper) obj;
    return myNumberOfJumps - temp.myNumberOfJumps;
}
```

2.
```
public int compareTo(Object obj)
{
    Purse temp = (Purse) obj;
    if (getTotal() < temp.getTotal())
        return -1;
    if (getTotal() > temp.getTotal())
        return 1;
    return 0;
}
```

Alternate Solution

```
public int compareTo(Object obj)
{
    Purse temp = (Purse) obj;
    return getTotal() - temp.getTotal();
}
```

3a.
```
public interface Instrument
{
    void setSeatAssignment(String seat);
    String getSeatAssignment();
    void tune();
}
```

3b.
```
public class BrassInstrument implements Instrument
{
    public BrassInstrument(String theSeat)
    {
        mySeat = theSeat;
    }

    public String getSeatAssignment()
    {
        return mySeat;
    }

    public void setSeatAssignment(String seat)
    {
        mySeat = seat;
    }
}
```

```
    public void tune()
    {
        System.out.println("Tuning middle G");
    }

    private String mySeat;
}
```

■ Chapter 11

Answers to Multiple Choice Questions

1. c	4. d	7. e	9. b
2. d	5. e	8. e	10. e
3. d	6. a		

Notes on Answers

4. Think of the *is-a* relationship. "An `Employee` *is-a* `Manager`" is a *false* statement. The correct answer is d.

5. When using the *is-a* relationship statement, all choices are OK.

6. The actual type of the object referenced by `employ1` is `Manager` and the actual type of the object referenced by `employ3` is `Manager`. The `work` method called is that of the actual type of the objects, not the reference type.

8. The first statement in the subclass constructor should be a call to the superclass constructor. If it isn't, then the superclass default constructor (if it exists) will be executed before executing code in the subclass constructor.

Answers to Free Response

```
1a. public Person(String firstName, String lastName)
    {
        myFirstName = firstName;
        myLastName = lastName;
        myEmailAddress = myFirstName.substring(0, 1);
        if (myLastName.length() >= 5)
        {
            myEmailAddress += myLastName.substring(0, 5);
            // Substring expression would throw a StringIndexOutOfBoundsException
            // if the length of myLastName is less than 5.
        }
        else
        {
            myEmailAddress += myLastName;
        }
        myEmailAddress += "@jc.com";
    }
```

Alternate Solution

```
public Person(String firstName, String lastName)
{
    myFirstName = firstName;
    myLastName = lastName;
    myEmailAddress = myFirstName.substring(0, 1);
    int n = myLastName.length();
    if (n > 5) n = 5;
    myEmailAddress += myLastName.substring(0, n);
}
```

1b.
```
public String toString()
{
    return ("name = " + myFirstName+ " " + myLastName
        + "\nemail address = " + myEmailAddress);
}
```

1c.
```
public class Student extends Person implements Comparable
```

1d.
```
public Student(String firstName, String lastName)
{
    super(firstName, lastName);
    myGpa = 0;
    myNumberOfCredits = 0;
    lastIdAssigned++;
    myStudentId = lastIdAssigned;
}
```

1e.
```
public String toString()
{
    String s = super.toString();
    return s + "\nGPA = " + myGpa + "\nnumber of credits = "
        + myNumberOfCredits + "\nid = " + myStudentId;
}
```

1f.
```
public int compareTo (Object other)
{
    Student temp = (Student) other;
    if (myGpa < temp.myGpa) return -1;
    if (myGpa > temp.myGpa) return 1;
    return 0;
}
```

2.
```
public class Marathoner extends Runner
{
    public Marathoner(String firstName, String lastName)
    {
        super(firstName, lastName);
    }

    public void race(double raceLength)
    {
        final int MINIMUM_RACE_LENGTH = 10;
        final double MINUTES_PER_MILE = 8.5;
        final int MINUTES_PER_HOUR = 60;

        if (raceLength > MINIMUM_RACE_LENGTH)
        {
            super.race(raceLength);
        }
        else
        {
            double trainingTime = MINUTES_PER_MILE * raceLength
                / MINUTES_PER_HOUR;
            train(trainingTime);
        }
    }
}
```

3a. Course *has-a* ClassRoster
Course *has-a* Teacher
ClassRoster *has-a* Student
Person *has-a* HomeAddress

3b. Hierarchy Diagram

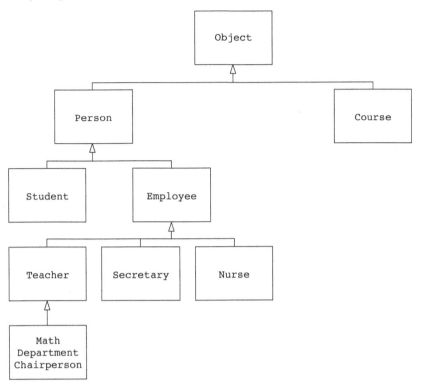

Note: MathDepartmentChairperson may be subclass of Employee. Nurse may be subclass of Teacher.

■ Chapter 12

Answers to Multiple Choice Questions

1. b	4. c	7. b	9. a
2. a	5. d	8. c	10. b
3. d	6. e		

Notes on Answers

2. There is a division by 0 error at runtime. The answer is a.
3. myLastName.substring(0,5) will cause a StringIndexOutOfBoundsException when called on a last name that has fewer than 5 characters. The answer is d.
4. "Tote" has fewer than 5 characters. The answer is c.
5. Since "John" is not found in positions 0, 1, 2, or 3, count is incremented in the loop and there is an attempt to check the next (non-existent) element in this array list.
7. workers.get(1) is not a Manager object. It was instantiated and added to the array list as an Employee object.
8. Choice II causes a ClassCastException and Choice IV causes an IndexOutOfBounds-Exception.
10. IOException is a checked exception.

Answers to Free Response Questions

```
1.  public class Teacher extends Person
    {
       public Teacher(String first, String last, double money)
       {
          super(first, last);
          if (money <= 0)
          {
             throw new IllegalStateException("Salary must be a
                   positive number.");
          }
          salary = money;
       }

       public void getRaise(double more)
       {
          if (more <= 0)
          {
             throw new IllegalArgumentException("Raise must be a
                   positive number.");
          }
          salary += more;
       }

       private double salary;
    }
```

```
2a. private int tossesRemaining;
```

```
2b. public CoinTosser()
    {
       tossesRemaining = (int)(Math.random() * 21);
    }
```

```
2c. public boolean hasMoreTosses()
    {
       return (tossesRemaining > 0);
    }
```

```
2d. public String nextToss()
    {
       if (hasMoreTosses())
       {
          tossesRemaining--;
          int toss = (int)(Math.random() * 2);
          if (toss == 1)
             return "HEADS";
          else
             return "TAILS";
       }
       else
          return ""; // A students
                     // AB students throw the following exception instead of
                     // returning the empty string
          // throw new NoSuchElementException("No tosses remaining.");
    }
```

■ Chapter 13

Multiple Choice Questions

1.	a	4.	d	7.	a	9.	b
2.	c	5.	e	8.	d	10.	a
3.	a	6.	e				

Notes on Answers

6. The best way to attack this problem is to dissect the various parts. The two parts described in the problem are Food Item and Drink Item. They both have a name and a price. Drink Item has a size. Based on this, we should be able to conclude that we need a `FoodItem` class and a `DrinkItem` class. We eliminate choice a. Because `FoodItem` and `DrinkItem` have common elements (name, price), they can inherit from `Item`. We now have to choose between c and e. Hamburgers and hot dogs differ only in name. They should not be separate classes so e is the best choice.

9. "Check trip" is the responsibility of `Trip`. The `Trip` class holds the responsibility of the trip as a whole. The `Ticket` class is responsible only for knowing about the ticket (whatever it is: airline, boat, etc). `HotelReservation` is responsible for knowing only about the hotel information.

10. Whole trips consist of transportation ticket, hotel reservations, car rentals, etc. These are represented by objects of different classes. There is an unknown number of these objects that constitute a trip. This indicates an array list (number of *objects* in trip list is *not fixed* so choice III is eliminated.). There may be various `CarRental` objects that are part of this trip so choice II is eliminated. Choice I is the only correct answer.

Answers to Free Response

```
1a. public class Car
    {
        public Car(String carMake, int yearMade, double miles)
        {
            make = carMake;
            year = yearMade;
            mileage = miles;
            price = 0;
        }

        public void setPrice(double howMuch)
        {
            price = howMuch;
        }

        public void addMiles(double milesDriven)
        {
            mileage += milesDriven;
        }

        public double getPrice()
        {
            return price;
        }

        public String getMake()
        {
            return make;
        }

        public int getYear()
        {
            return year;
```

```
       }

       public double getMiles()
       {
          return mileage;
       }

       public String toString()
       {
          String s = getYear() + " " + getMake()
                 + "\nMileage: " + getMiles() + " miles"
                 + "\ncosts $" + getPrice() + "\n";
          return s;
       }

       private String make;
       private int year;
       private double price;
       private double mileage;
   }
```

1b.
```
   public void addCar(Car aNewCar)
   {
       if (numberOfCars < MAX_CARS)
       {
          lot[numberOfCars] = aNewCar;
          numberOfCars++;
       }
       else    // AB students
       {
          throw new IllegalStateException("No room in lot.");
       }
   }
```

1c.
```
   public void printCarsInLot()
   {
       for (Car c : lot)
       {
          System.out.println(c);
       }
   }
```

1d.
```
   private ArrayList findMatchingCars(int year, String make)
   {
       ArrayList<Car> wantedCars = new ArrayList<Car>();
       for (Car c : lot)
       {
          if (c.getYear()== year && make.equals(c.getMake()))
             wantedCars.add(c);
       }
       return wantedCars;
   }
```

1e.
```
   public void printMatchingCars(int year, String make)
   {
       ArrayList<Car> carList = findMatchingCars(year, make);
       if (carList.size() == 0)
          System.out.println("No cars with your specifications are available.");
       else
       {
          System.out.println("Your requested list of available cars:");
          for (Car c : carList)
          {
             System.out.println(c);
```

```
        }
    }
}
```

Alternative loop using `Iterator`s (can replace the `for` loop):

```
Iterator iter = carList.iterator();
while (iter.hasNext())
{
    System.out.println(iter.next());
}
```

2a. (Note: Variable and method names may be different but should be descriptive.)

```
Class name: Employee
Methods:
    // Constructor
    public Employee(String firstName, String lastName)

    public String getName()    // Needed to return name of employee
                               // with highest total sales
    public double getCommission()
    public double getTotalSales()    // Needed to find employee with
                                     // highest total sales
    public int getId()    // Needed to remove employee from company
    public void addSale(double money)

Instance fields:
    private String myFirstName;
    private String myLastName;
    private int idNumber;
    private double totalSales;

Static variables:
    int nextAvailableId;
```

```
Class name: Company
Methods:
    public Company()    // Constructor
    public void addEmployee(Employee worker)
    public ArrayList getEmployeeList()
    public void removeEmployee(int idNum)
    public Employee getHighestSeller()

Instance fields:
    private ArrayList<Employee> employeeList;    // No static variables
                                                 // needed
```

2b. (Note: Variable names may be different but should be descriptive and consistent with part a.)

```
public class Employee
{
    private static int nextAvailableId = 0;

    Employee(String firstName, String lastName)
    {
        myFirstName = firstName;
        myLastName = lastName;
        nextAvailableId++;
        idNumber = nextAvailableId;
        totalSales = 0;
    }
}
```

2c. (Note: Variable names may be different but should be descriptive and consistent with part a.)

```
public class Company
{
    public Company()
    {
        employeeList = new ArrayList<Employee>();
    }

    private ArrayList<Employee> employeeList;
}
```

3a. `SmartPlayer` *is-a* `Player`
`HumanPlayer` *is-a* `Player`
`NimGame` *has-a* `HumanPlayer`
`NimGame` *has-a* `SmartPlayer`
`NimGame` *has-a* `NimPile`

3b. NimGame class

```
public class NimGame
{
    // Constructs game. Creates players and pile of marbles.
    public NimGame(int low, int high) {. . .}
    // Plays game.
    public void playNim() {. . .}

    private HumanPlayer human;
    private NimPile pile;
    private Player computer;
}
```

NimPile class

```
public class NimPile
{
    // Constructs marble pile for Nim with a random number of
    // marbles between a and b inclusive.
    public NimPile(int a, int b) {. . .}

    // Returns number of marbles in pile.
    public int getMarbles() {. . .}

    // n <= numMarblesInPile / 2
    public void takeMarbles(int n) {. . .}

    private int numMarblesInPile;
}
```

Player class

```
public class Player
{
    // Constructor
    public Player(String aName) {. . .}

    // Generic turn ... stupid player's strategy.
    public int takeTurn(NimPile pile) {. . .}

    // Returns name.
    public String getName() {. . .}

    private String name;
}
```

SmartPlayer class

```java
public class SmartPlayer extends Player
{
    public SmartPlayer(String n) {. . .}

    // Takes marbles using "smart" algorithm.
    public int takeTurn(NimPile pile) {. . .}
}
```

HumanPlayer class

```java
public class HumanPlayer extends Player
{
    public HumanPlayer(String n) {. . .}

    // Human decides the number of marbles to take.
    public int takeTurn(NimPile pile) {. . .}
}
```

3c. ## NimGame class

```java
public class NimGame
{
    // Constructs game. Creates players and pile of marbles.
    public NimGame(int low, int high)
    {
        System.out.print("What is the human player's name?");
        String nm = Utilities.readWord();
        human = new HumanPlayer(nm);
        boolean isStupid = (Utilities.getRandNumber(0, 1) == 1);
        String computerName = "ROBO COMPUTER";
        if (isStupid)
            computer = new Player(computerName);
        else
            computer = new SmartPlayer(computerName);
        pile = new NimPile(low, high);
    }

    // Plays game.
    public void playNim()
    {
        boolean computerHasTurn = (Utilities.getRandNumber(0, 1) == 1);
        if (computerHasTurn)
            System.out.println(computer.getName() + " goes first!");
        else
            System.out.println(human.getName() + " goes first!");
        while (pile.getMarbles() > 1)
        {
            System.out.println("\nMarbles in pile: " + pile.getMarbles());
            if (computerHasTurn)
            {
                int n = computer.takeTurn(pile);
                System.out.println(computer.getName() + " takes " + n
                    + " marbles");
            }
            else
            {
                human.takeTurn(pile);
            }
            computerHasTurn = !computerHasTurn;
        }
```

```
         if (computerHasTurn)
            System.out.println("Congratulations! You won!");
         else
            System.out.println("Sorry, you lost.");
      }

      private HumanPlayer human;
      private NimPile pile;
      private Player computer;
   }
```

NimPile class

```
   public class NimPile
   {
      // Constructs marble pile for Nim.
      public NimPile(int a, int b)
      {
         numMarblesInPile = Utilities.getRandNumber(a, b);
      }

      // Returns number of marbles in pile.
      public int getMarbles()
      {
         return numMarblesInPile;
      }

      // n <= numMarblesInPile / 2
      public void takeMarbles(int n)
      {
         numMarblesInPile -= n;
      }

      private int numMarblesInPile;
   }
```

Player class

```
   public class Player
   {
      // Constructor.
      public Player(String aName)
      {
         name = aName;
      }

      // Generic turn...stupid player's strategy.
      public int takeTurn(NimPile pile)
      {
         int n = Utilities.getRandNumber(1, pile.getMarbles() / 2);
         pile.takeMarbles(n);
         return n;
      }

      // Returns name.
      public String getName()
      {
         return name;
      }

      private String name;
   }
```

SmartPlayer class

```
public class SmartPlayer extends Player
{
   public SmartPlayer(String n)
   {
      super(n);
   }

   // Takes marbles using "smart" algorithm.
   public int takeTurn(NimPile pile)
   {
      int marbles = pile.getMarbles();
      int n = 0;
      if (Utilities.isPowerOfTwoMinusOne(marbles));
         n = Utilities.getRandNumber(1, marbles / 2);
      else
      {
         int p = Utilities.largestPowerOfTwoMinusOneBelow(marbles);
         n = marbles - p;
      }
      pile.takeMarbles(n);
      return n;
   }
}
```

HumanPlayer class

```
public class HumanPlayer extends Player
{
   public HumanPlayer(String n)
   {
      super(n);
   }

   public int takeTurn(NimPile pile)
   {
      int n;
      do
      {
         System.out.println("How many marbles do you take?");
         n = Utilities.readInt();
      }
      while (n <= 0 || n > pile.getMarbles() / 2);
      pile.takeMarbles(n);
      return n;
   }
}
```

■ Cumulative Review 2

Answers to Multiple Choice Questions

1. d	6. c	11. b	16. d
2. e	7. b	12. e	17. c
3. a	8. a	13. c	18. e
4. c	9. d	14. c	19. d
5. c	10. c	15. a	20. d

Notes on Answers

1. We start with `i = 1`. Mary is in position 1, so Joe is deleted. Now `i = 3`. Because Joe has been deleted, Harry is in position 3 and David is deleted. The size of the list is now 5. When `i` is increased to 5, the loop is not executed. The correct answer is d.

2. An array of size 31 would store the number of samples having 0, 1, 2, 3, ..., 30 left-handed people. `arr[0]` is the number of the 500 samples having 0 lefties; `arr[1]` is the number of the 500 samples that have 1 leftie, etc. The correct answer is e.

9. $n(n-1)/2$ is $O(n^2)$. Expanding the algebraic expression gives a quadratic expression. As n gets very large, the constants can be ignored. We classify this by the largest power of n. The correct answer is d.

14. When `getWorkDetail` is called, it is called from the `Person` method `work`. The implicit type of `this` in the `Person` class is `Person`. Therfore, the parameter type for `getWorkDetail` is `Person` and the correct answer is c.

15. The correct answer is a.

    `e2.printSalary(e2);` e2 is instantiated as a `Manager`. Even though e2's type is `Employee`, dynamic binding applies when determining whether the `Employee` `printSalary` or `Manager` `printSalary` method is called. Because e2 references a `Manager` object, the `Manager` `printSalary` method is called.

    `e1.printSalary(e1);` e1 is of type `Employee` and therefore the `printSalary` method (there is only one) of `Employee` is executed.

    `m1.printSalary(m1);` m1 is of type `Manager` and therefore the `Manager` `printSalary` method that has a parameter of type `Manager` is executed.

    `e1.printSalary(m1);` e1 is of type `Employee` and therefore the `printSalary` method (there is only one) of `Employee` is executed. Since m1 is of type `Manager`, which is a subclass of `Employee`, a `Manager` object can be passed to a parameter of type `Employee`.

Answers to Free Response Questions

1a.
```java
public Hand(int numCards)
{
   myHand = new Card[numCards];
   cardsInHand = 0;
}
```

1b.
```java
public void addCard(Card c)
{
   if (!isHandFull())
   {
      myHand[cardsInHand] = c;
      cardsInHand++;
   }
}
```

1c.
```java
public void printHand()
{
   for (Card i : myHand)
      System.out.println(i);
}
```

1d.
```java
public boolean isFlush()
{
   Card[] myCards = getHand();
   String suit = myCards[0].getSuit();
   for (int i = 1; i < MAX_CARDS; i++)
   {
      String cardSuit = myCards[i].getSuit();
      if (!(suit.equals(cardSuit)))
         return false;
   }
```

```
            return true;
      }
1e. public boolean isStraight()
      {
            sortCards();
            Card[] myCards = getHand();
            for (int i = 1; i < MAX_CARDS; i++)
            {
                if (myCards[i].getValue() - myCards[i - 1].getValue() != 1)
                    return false;
            }
            return true;
      }

1f. public boolean isStraightFlush()
      {
            return isFlush() && isStraight();
      }

1g. public boolean isRoyalFlush()
      {
            // Must call sortCards() if it was not called in isStraight.
            Card[] myCards = getHand();
            return isFlush() && isStraight()                         .
                  && ("Ace".equals(myCards[4].getDenomination())));
      }

1h. public boolean isFullHouse()
      {
            int countVal = 0; int countVal2 = 0;
            sortCards();
            Card[] myCards = getHand();
            int val = myCards[0].getValue();
            int val2 = myCards[MAX_CARDS - 1].getValue();

            for (int i = 0; i < MAX_CARDS; i++)
            {
                if (myCards[i].getValue() == val) countVal++;
                if (myCards[i].getValue() == val2) countVal2++;
            }
            return (countVal == 2
                  && countVal2 == 3
                  || countVal == 3
                  && countVal2 == 2)
      }

2a. public static double mean(int[] sampleData)
      {
            int sum = 0;
            for (int i : sampleData)
            {
                sum += i;
            }
            double avg = (double) sum / sampleData.length;
            return avg;
      }

2b. public static double variance(int[] sampleData)
      {
            double sum = 0.0;
            double avg = mean(sampleData);

            for (int i : sampleData)
            {
```

```
            double diff = (i - avg);
            sum += diff * diff;
        }
        return sum / (sampleData.length - 1);
    }
```

2c. ```
    public static double standardDeviation(int[] sampleData)
    {
        return Math.sqrt(variance(sampleData));
    }
```

2d. ```
    public static int mode(int[] sampleData)
    {
        // Find largest data value
        int largestValueInData = sampleData[0];
        for (int i : sampleData)
        {
            if (i > largestValueInData)
            {
                largestValueInData = i;
            }
        }
        // Create an array to tally sampleData values
        int[] b = new int[largestValueInData];
        // Tally sampleData values in array b
        // A value of 5 would increment b[5]
        for (int i = 0; i < sampleData.length; i++)
        {
            b[sampleData[i]]++;
        }
        // Find the largest tally amount
        // The index of the largest tally amount is a mode
        int large = b[0];
        int value = 0;
        for (int i = 1; i < b.length; i++)
        {
            if (b[i] > large)
            {
                large = b[i];
                value = i;
            }
        }
        return value;
    }
```

2e. ```
    public static double median(int[] sampleData)
    {
        int[] arr = sortValues(sampleData);
        int len = arr.length;
        if (len % 2 == 0)
            return (arr[len / 2] + arr[len / 2 - 1]) / 2.0;
        else
            return (arr[len / 2]);
    }
```

2f. ```
    public static void stemAndLeafPlot(int[] sampleData)
    {
        int[] arr = sortValues(sampleData);
        int j = 0;
        for (int i = 0; i <= 10; i++)
        {
            int stem = i;
            System.out.print(stem);
            if (stem < 10)
```

```
                  System.out.print("   | ");
            else
                  System.out.print("   | ");
            while (j < arr.length && stem == arr[j] / 10)
            {
                  int leaf = arr[j] % 10;
                  System.out.print(leaf + " ");
                  j++;
            }
            System.out.println();
      }
   }
```

3. Solutions will vary.

EMT class

```java
import java.util.ArrayList;

public class Emt
{
    public Emt(String emtLastName, String emtFirstName, String emtSs)
    {
        lastName = emtLastName;
        firstName = emtFirstName;
        ssNumber = emtSs;
        ceuCourses = new ArrayList<Course>();
    }

    public String getSsNumber()
    {
        return ssNumber;
    }

    public String getName()
    {
        return firstName + " " + lastName;
    }

    public int getRequiredCredits()
    {
        int totalRequired = 0;
        for (Course i : ceuCourses)
        {
            if (i.getIsRequired())
                totalRequired += i.getNumCeus();
        }
        return totalRequired;
    }

    public int getElectiveCredits()
    {
        int totalElectives = 0;
        for (Course i : ceuCourses)
        {
            if (!i.getIsRequired())
                totalElectives += i.getNumCeus();
        }
        return totalElectives;
    }

    public void addCourse(Course c)
    {
        ceuCourses.add(c);
```

```
   }

   public boolean completeRequirements()
   {
      return getRequiredCredits() >= CREDITS_NEEDED
            && getElectiveCredits() >= CREDITS_NEEDED;
   }

   public String toString()
   {
      String s = getName() + "\nSS#: " + getSsNumber() + "\n";
      for (Course c : ceuCourses)
         s += c.toString();
      return s;
   }

   private String ssNumber;
   private String firstName;
   private String lastName;
   private ArrayList<Course> ceuCourses;
   private static final int CREDITS_NEEDED = 48;
}
```

Course class

```
public class Course
{
   public Course(String name, int credits, String required)
   {
      courseName = name;
      numCeus = credits;
      isRequired = required.equals("required");
   }

   public boolean getIsRequired()
   {
      return isRequired;
   }

   public String getCourseName()
   {
      return courseName;
   }

   public int getNumCeus()
   {
      return numCeus;
   }

   public String toString()
   {
      String s = getCourseName() + " " + getNumCeus();
      if (isRequired)
         s += " required\n";
      else
         s += " elective\n";
      return s;
   }

   private String courseName;
   private int numCeus;
   private boolean isRequired;
}
```

■ Chapter 14

Answers to Multiple Choice Questions

1. e	4. b	7. c	9. a
2. b	5. c	8. d	10. d
3. c	6. d		

Notes on Answers

1. Each method results in a different output.

Method I	Method II	Method III
0	1	0
1	2	
2	3	
3	4	
4	5	
5		

4. The argument to the recursive method is the string minus its last character. The `return` statement returns the last character plus the result of the recursive call. This basically creates a string that is the reverse of the original string.

7-9. The `ArraySearcher` method `searchFor` is a *helper* method called by the client program. The recursive method is the method `search`. Helper methods are explained in Section 13.3 of your text. The method `search` is recursively called with half of the array, the lower half if `key` is less than `a[mid]` and the upper half if `key` is greater than `a[mid]`. The recursion ends when `key` is found (`a[mid] == key`) or there are no more values to check (`low >= high`). If `key` is not found, `-1` is returned. This method will work as intended only if the original array is in ascending order.

10. This is based on the triangle number problem explained in Section 13.1 of your text.

Answers to Free Response

```
1.  public static int gcd(int num1, int  num2)
    {
        if (num2 == 0)
            return num1;
        else
            return gcd(num2, num1 % num2);
    }
```

```
2a. public static double triangleArea(Point p1, Point p2, Point p3)
    {
        double x1 = p1.getX();
        double y1 = p1.getY();
        double x2 = p2.getX();
        double y2 = p2.getY();
        double x3 = p3.getX();
        double y3 = p3.getY();

        double area = Math.abs((x1 * y2)
                + (x2 * y3)
                + (x3 * y1)
                - (y1 * x2)
                - (y2 * x3)
                - (y3 * x1))
                / 2;
        return area;
    }
```

2b. ```
public double getArea()
{
    if (corners.size() < 3) return 0;

    Point p1 = corners.get(0);   // in diagram: p1 = c(0)
    Point p2 = corners.get(1);   // in diagram: p2 = c(1)
    Point p3 = corners.get(2);   // in diagram: p3 = c(2)
    double area = triangleArea(p1, p2, p3);   // Ax = area of xth triangle

    Polygon remainder = new Polygon();
    remainder.add(p3);   // r(0)
    for (int i = 3; i < corners.size(); i++)
        remainder.add(corners.get(i));
    remainder.add(p1);   // r(r.size() - 1)
    return area + remainder.getArea();
}
```

Illustrated calls to area of polygon:

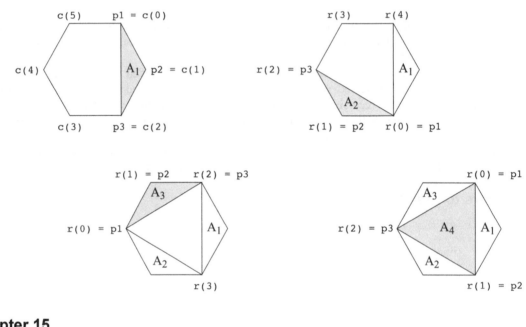

## Chapter 15

## Answers to Multiple Choice Questions

| | | | |
|---|---|---|---|
| 1. e | 4. d | 7. d | 9. b |
| 2. d | 5. a | 8. d | 10. c |
| 3. b | 6. e | | |

### Notes on Answers

1. The number of comparisons made by the selection sort is based on the number of elements in the array, not the order of the values. The correct answer is e.

2. Choice I is incorrect because it assumes that the elements in the array are all non-negative values.

3. The correct answer is b.
   Choice I. For each element in list ($x_i$), look at $x_i$. Now look at each element in list and count how many times $x_i$ occurs in list ($n$ comparisons for each of $n$ elements). So far this is $O(n^2)$. If the count is larger than 1, remove $x_i$. Removal may require shifting ($O(n$ for each element removed)).
   Total = $n^2 + n^2 = O(n^2)$
```

Choice II. Sort the array list with an efficient sort algorithm.($n \log(n)$). For each x_i in list, look at its next neighbor to decide whether it is present more than once. If it is, remove x_i. If we detect adjacent duplicates, we must shift the remainder of the array down, which is $O(n^2)$ in the worst case. So, this gives us a total of $O(n \log(n) + n^2) = O(n^2)$ algorithm.

Choice III. Sort the array list, list, with an efficient algorithm ($n\log(n)$). Traverse the array list looking at each x_i in list. Whenever the element after x_i is strictly larger than x_i, append x_i to a second (initially empty) array list, list2. Find the difference, diff, in the sizes of list and list2. Beginning with the last element of list, delete diff elements from list. Then, copy the elements of list2 back into list. Total = $n \log(n) + 3n = O(n \log(n))$.

8. This is a binary search but the array is not ordered so it does not work as is intended. The value 2 is never found. The correct answer is d.

9. The smallest power of 2 that is greater than or equal to 45 is 6 ($2^6 = 64$). The correct answer is b.

Answers to Free Response

1a.
```
private String sortWord()
{
    String s = "";
    for (int i = 0; i < originalWord.length(); i++)
    {
        int pos = i - 1;
        String wordLetter = originalWord.substring(i, i + 1);
        while (pos >= 0 && wordLetter.compareTo(s.substring(
            pos, pos + 1)) < 0)
        {
            pos--;
        }
        s = s.substring(0, pos + 1) + wordLetter + s.substring(pos + 1);
    }
    return s;
}
```

Alternate solution for 1a (outside AP subset)

```
private String sortWord()
{
    String s = "";
    int len = originalWord.length();
    char[] a = new char[len];
    for (int i = 0; i < len; i++)
    {
        a[i]= originalWord.charAt(i);
    }
    Arrays.sort(a);
    for (int i = 0; i < len; i++)
    {
        s += a[i];
    }
    return s;
}
```

1b.
```
public boolean checkAnagram(Word aWord, Word anotherWord)
{
    return (anotherWord.getSorted().equals(aWord.getSorted()));
}
```

1c.
```
public void printAnagrams(String key)
{
    Word newWord = new Word(key);
    for (int i = 0; i < wordList.size(); i++)
    {
```

```
            Word temp = wordList.get(i);
            if (checkAnagram(newWord, temp))
            {
                System.out.println(temp.getWord());
            }
        }
    }
```

2a.
```
public int compareTo(Object obj)
{
    String fullName = getName();
    Person other = (Person) obj;
    String otherFullName = other.getName();
    return fullName.compareTo(otherFullName);
}
```

2b.
```
private int minimumPosition(int from)
{
    int minPos = from;
    for (int i = from + 1; i < list.size(); i++)
    {
        Person ithPerson = list.get(i);
        Person minPerson = list.get(minPos);
        if (ithPerson.compareTo(minPerson) < 0)
            minPos = i;
    }
    return minPos;
}
```

2c.
```
private int minimumEmailPosition(int from)
{
    int minPos = from;
    Comparator comp = new PersonComparator();
    for (int i = from + 1; i < list.size(); i++)
    {
        Person ithPerson = list.get(i);
        Person minPerson = list.get(minPos);
        if (comp.compare(ithPerson, minPerson) < 0)
            minPos = i;
    }
    return minPos;
}
```

■ Chapter 16

Answers to Multiple Choice Questions

1. b	6. e	11. a	16. d
2. d	7. d	12. d	17. b
3. d	8. b	13. e	18. a
4. e	9. b	14. c	19. d
5. e	10. a	15. d	20. c

Notes on Answers

6. When `equals` is not defined for a class, the class inherits `Object`'s `equals` method and will return `true` if and only if node1 and node2 reference the same object.

11. Lookups need to have a quick retrieval time. The array provides this. In order to retrieve a value from a linked list, the list must be traversed. The stack and queue can not return a specific element, they can access only one element (the top or front element).

Answers to Free Response

1a. Add another instance field and modify the constructor.

1b. `public DLListNode getPrevious();`
     `public void setPrevious(DLListNode theNewPrevious);`

1c.
```
public DLListNode(Object initValue, DLListNode initNext,
        DLListNode initPrev)
{
    super(initValue, initNext);
    previous = initPrev;
}
```

1d.

Operation	Doubly Linked List
addFirst	$O(1)$
addLast	$O(1)$
removeLast	$O(1)$
removeFirst	$O(1)$
isEmpty	$O(1)$
Linear Traversal	$O(n)$
Random Access	$O(n)$

1e.
```
public DLListNode search(Object key)
{
    DLListNode temp = first;
    while (temp != null && !temp.getValue()).equals(key))
    {
        temp = (DLListNode) temp.getNext();
    }
    return temp;
}
```

1f.
```
public void removeOne(Object key)
{
    DLListNode temp = search(key);
    if (temp == null)    // Key isn't in list.
        return;
    if (temp == first)    // Is it the first node?
    {
        if (temp == last)    // Is it the only node?
            last = null;
        first = (DLListNode) first.getNext();   // first.getNext() returns a
                                                // ListNode so we need to cast
        if (first != null)
            first.setPrevious(null);
        return;
    }

    if (temp.getNext() == null)    // Deleting last node.
    {
        DLListNode hold = temp.getPrevious();
        hold.setNext(null);
        last = hold;
        return;
    }
```

```
        // Deleting a middle node.
        DLListNode hold = temp.getPrevious();
        hold.setNext(temp.getNext());
        hold = (DLListNode) temp.getNext();
        hold.setPrevious(temp.getPrevious());
        return;
    }
```

1g.
```
    public void removeAll(Object key)
    {
        while (search(key) != null)
        {
            removeOne(key);
        }
    }
```

2a.
```
    public static void displayBinary(int decimalNum)
    {
        final int BASE = 2;
        Stack<Integer> stck = new Stack<Integer>();

        while (decimalNum != 0)
        {
            int remainder = decimalNum % BASE;
            stck.push(new Integer(remainder));
            decimalNum /= BASE;
        }
        while (!stck.isEmpty())
        {
            Integer num = stck.pop();
            System.out.print(num);
        }
        System.out.println();
    }
```

2b.
```
    public static void displayOtherBase(int num, int base)
    {
        Stack<Integer> stck = new Stack<Integer>();

        while (num != 0)
        {
            int remainder = num % base;
            stck.push(new Integer(remainder));
            num /= base;
        }

        while (!stck.isEmpty())
        {
            Integer number = stck.pop();
            int numValue = number.intValue();
            String alpha = "ABCDEF";
            if (numValue >= 10)
            {
                int converted = numValue % 10;
                System.out.print(alpha.substring(converted, converted + 1));
            }
            else
            {
                System.out.print(numValue);
            }
        }
    }
```

3a. The appropriate data structure is a linked list. Arrays are not a good choice because the actual number of windows is not known. Array lists are inefficient because of the insertions and deletions to the top. Quite a bit of shifting would be necessary. Stacks add and delete from one end so `cycle` would not be an appropriate operation for a stack. Queues add to one end and delete from the other end. The `WindowManager` operation of `add` and `remove` both refer to the same end. Therefore a queue is not an appropriate choice.

Notes on 3b–3e: The instance field name could be something other than `windows` but should be descriptive. Knowledge of `java.util.awt.Rectangle` is not tested on the AP Exam.

3b.
```
public void add(Window w)
{
    windows.addFirst(w);
}
```

3c.
```
public void remove()
{
    windows.removeFirst();
}
```

3d.
```
public void cycle()
{
    if (windows.size() == 0) return;
    Window w = (Window) windows.removeFirst();
    windows.addLast(w);
}
```

3e.
```
public void print()
{
    Iterator iter = windows.iterator();
    while (iter.hasNext())
        System.out.println(iter.next());
    System.out.println();
}
```

■ Chapter 17

Answers to Multiple Choice Questions

1. e	6. c	11. c	16. d
2. d	7. e	12. a	17. b
3. e	8. e	13. d	18. b
4. c	9. c	14. d	19. e
5. a	10. c	15. c	20. b

Notes on Answers

2. After insertion of all values, the binary tree is:

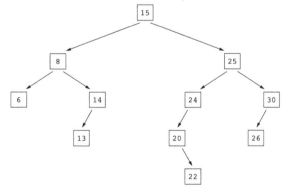

4. This method returns the number of nodes in a binary tree. The answer is c.
14. After insertion of all values, the binary tree is:

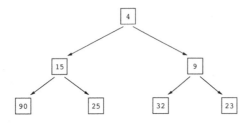

Answers to Free Response

1a.
```java
public Set<String> setIntersection()
{
    Set<String> set3 = new TreeSet<String>();
    Iterator<String> iter = set1.iterator();
    while (iter.hasNext())
    {
        String temp = iter.next();
        if (set2.contains(temp))
        {
            set3.add(temp);
        }
    }
    return set3;
}
```

1b.
```java
public Set<String> setUnion()
{
    Set<String> set3 = new TreeSet<String>();
    Iterator<String> iter = set1.iterator();
    while (iter.hasNext())
    {
        set3.add(iter.next());
    }
    iter = set2.iterator();
    while (iter.hasNext())
    {
        set3.add(iter.next());
    }
    return set3;
}
```

1c.
```java
public Set<String> setDifference()
{
    Set<String> set3 = new TreeSet<String>();
    Iterator<String> iter = set1.iterator();
    while (iter.hasNext())
    {
        String temp = iter.next();
        if (!(set2.contains(temp)))
        {
            set3.add(temp);
        }
    }
}
```

1d.
```java
public boolean isSubset()
{
```

```
        Iterator<String> iter = set1.iterator();
        while (iter.hasNext())
        {
           if (!(set2.contains(iter.next())))
           {
              return false;
           }
        }
        return true;
     }
```

1e.
```
    public boolean isProperSubset()
    {
        if (!(isSubset()))
        {
           return false;
        }
        else if (set1.size() != set2.size())
        {
           return true;
        }
        else
        {
           return false;
        }
    }
```

Alternate Solution

```
    public boolean isProperSubset()
    {
        return (isSubset() && set1.size() != set2.size());
    }
```

2a.
```
    public void createConcordance(String fileName)
    {
        . . .
        while (inFile.hasNext())  // while more words in file
        {
           String word = inFile.next();  // read word
           Integer temp = concord.get(word);
           if (temp == null)
           {
              concord.put(word, 1);  // autoboxing
           }
           else
           {
              concord.put(word, temp + 1);  // autoboxing
           }
        }
    }
```

2b.
```
    public void printConcordance()
    {
        Set<String> concordSet = concord.keySet();
        Iterator<string> iter = concordSet.iterator();
        while (iter.hasNext())
        {
           String word = iter.next();
           System.out.print(word + " ");
           System.out.println("occurs " +  concord.get(word) + " time(s).");
        }
    }
```

2c. A method similar to printConcordance would have the iterator traverse the set created by the TreeMap's keySet method to obtain the word and its frequency. A WordFreq class would be defined to have instance fields that hold word-frequency pairs. With each move of the iterator, a new WordFreq object would be instantiated and its two instance fields would be set. The WordFreq objects would then be inserted into one of the following data structures.

- A binary search tree implemented so that duplicates are possible according to the frequency. An inorder traversal would give the required results. Insertion of n WordFreq objects is $O(n \log(n))$. Traversal is $O(n)$.
- A priority queue implemented so that duplicates are possible and where the priority is the frequency. Executing remove repeatedly would give the desired results. Insertion is $O(n \log(n))$. Traversal is $O(n)$.
- An ordered linked list of nodes whose information field is the WordFreq object. Nodes would be inserted in order according to the frequency. A linear traversal of the linked list would give the required results. Insertion is $O(n^2)$ ($O(n)$ for each of n elements). Traversal is $O(n)$.
- An ordered ArrayList of WordFreq objects ordered by frequency. Insertion is $O(n^2)$. Traversal is $O(n)$.

The ones that won't work:
- A stack cannot maintain frequency order.
- A queue cannot maintain frequency order.
- A hash set does not maintain order.
- A hash map does not maintain order.
- A tree set cannot have duplicate values.
- A tree map cannot have duplicate keys.

■ Cumulative Review 3

Answers to Multiple Choice Questions

1. d	6. a	11. b	16. c
2. c	7. c	12. d	17. d
3. e	8. d	13. c	18. c
4. d	9. a	14. b	19. b
5. c	10. a	15. a	20. b

Notes on Answers

12. Because the elements are added in random order, a LinkedList and an ArrayList would require traversals to find the smallest element ($O(n)$ operations). A HashSet is not appropriate if we are concerned with order. A map is not appropriate because our objects do not have a mapping of key and value. A TreeSet is implemented using a binary search tree so the smallest element is returned with $O(\log n)$ efficiency. The answer is d.
17. Each recursive call needs to set the next field of the node. Answers a, b, and c will each end with one node in the list. Answer e will result in an endless loop. d is correct.
20. Choice I will swap references. If the leftmost node has a right child or the rightmost node has a left child, this option will not work. Choice III has the same problem and the additional problem of attempting to swap without using temp. Choice II is correct. Swapping values does not interfere with references.

Answers to Free Response Questions

1a.
```java
public ArrayList<Player> getPlayersInLineUp(ArrayList<Integer> bb)
{
    ArrayList<Player> someTeam = new ArrayList<Player>();
    for (Integer i : bb)
    {
        Player p = myTeam.get(i);
        someTeam.add(p);
    }
    return someTeam;
}
```

1b.
```java
public boolean isLineUpValid(ArrayList<Player> lineup)
{
    int numForwards = 0;
    int numGuards = 0;
    int numCenters = 0;
    for (Player i : lineup)
    {
        if (i.getPosition().equals("guard")) numGuards++;
        if (i.getPosition().equals("center")) numCenters++;
        if (i.getPosition().equals("forward")) numForwards++;
    }
    return numGuards == 2 && numForwards == 2 && numCenters == 1;
}
```

1c.
```java
public void printValidStartingTeams()
{
    bbLineUps = new CombinationGenerator(numberInLineUp, 0,
            getTeamSize() - 1);
    while (bbLineUps.hasMoreElements())
    {
        ArrayList<Integer> list = bbLineUps.nextElement();
        ArrayList<Player> p = getPlayersInLineUp(list);
        if (isLineUpValid(p))
        {
            System.out.println(p);
        }
    }
}
```

1d. The method `isLineUpValid` is defined differently for each type of team and each type of team has requirements for a starting line-up. All other methods are the same.

1e. `int[][] = new int[100][100]` would allow immediate access to a player pair rating.

1f.
```java
final int defaultRating = 5;
final int numRow = 100;
final int numCol = 100;
int[][] playerRatings = new int[numRow][numCol];
for (int row = 0; row < numRow; row++)
{
    for (int col = 0; col < numCol; col++)
    {
        if (row == col)
        {
            playerRatings[row][col] = 0;
        }
        else
        {
            playerRatings[row][col] = defaultRating;
        }
    }
```

```
      }
1g.  if (jersey1 != jersey2)
     {
         playerRatings[jersey1][jersey2] = pairRating;
         playerRatings[jersey2][jersey1] = pairRating;
     }

1h.  public int getLineUpRating(ArrayList<Player> thisTeam)
     {
         int total = 0;
         for (int i = 0; i < thisTeam.size(); i++)
         {
             for (int j = i + 1; j < thisTeam.size(); j++)
             {
                 total += ratings[thisTeam.get(i).getJersey()]
                         [(thisTeam.get(j)).getJersey()];
             }
         }
         return total;
     }

1i.  public ArrayList<Player> getBestTeam()
     {
         ArrayList<Player> bestTeam = new ArrayList<Player>();
         CombinationGenerator lineUps
             = new CombinationGenerator(numberInLineUp, 0, getTeamSize() - 1);
         int maxRating = 0;
         while (lineUps.hasMoreElements())
         {
             ArrayList<Integer> list = lineUps.nextElement();
             ArrayList<Player> p = getPlayersInLineUp(list);
             if (isLineUpValid(p))
             {
                 int rating = getLineUpRating(p);
                 if (rating > maxRating)
                 {
                     bestTeam = p;
                     maxRating = rating;
                 }
             }
         }
         return bestTeam;
     }

2a.  public String toString()
     {
         Set<Integer> st = poly.keySet();
         Iterator<Integer> iter = st.iterator();
         String s = "";
         while (iter.hasNext())
         {
             Integer exponent = iter.next();
             Integer coef = poly.get(exponent);
             if (exponent > 0)
             {
                 if (s != "")
                     s = coef + "x^" + exponent + " + " + s;
                 else
                     s = coef + "x^" + exponent;
             }
             else
             {
                 s = coef + "";
```

```
            }
        }
        return s;
    }

2b. public double evaluatePolynomial(double x)
    {
        double answer = 0;
        Set<Integer> s = poly.keySet();
        Iterator<Integer> iter = s.iterator();
        while (iter.hasNext())
        {
            Integer p = iter.next();
            Integer coef = poly.get(p);
            answer += Math.pow(x, p) * coef;
        }
        return answer;
    }

2c. public Polynomial add(Polynomial other)
    {
        Polynomial theSumPolynomial = new Polynomial();
        TreeMap<Integer, Integer> poly3 = theSumPolynomial.poly;

        Set<Integer> s1 = poly.keySet();
        Iterator<Integer> iter1 = s1.iterator();

        TreeMap<Integer, Integer> poly2 = other.poly;
        Set<Integer> s2 = poly2.keySet();
        Iterator<Integer> iter2 = s2.iterator();

        while (iter1.hasNext())    // Get terms with common exponents
        {
            Integer exponent = iter1.next();
            if (poly2.containsKey(exponent))
            {
                theSumPolynomial.addTerm(exponent, poly.get(exponent)
                        + poly2.get(exponent));
            }
            else
            {
                theSumPolynomial.addTerm(exponent, poly.get(exponent));
            }
        }

        while (iter2.hasNext())
        {
            Integer exponent = iter2.next();
            if (!poly3.containsKey(exponent))
            {
                theSumPolynomial.addTerm(exponent, poly2.get(exponent));
            }
        }
        return theSumPolynomial;
    }
```

```
2d. public Polynomial multiply(Polynomial other)
    {
        Polynomial theProductPolynomial = new Polynomial();
        TreeMap<Integer, Integer> poly3 = theProductPolynomial.poly;

        Set<Integer> s1 = poly.keySet();
        Iterator<Integer> iter1 = s1.iterator();

        TreeMap<Integer, Integer> poly2 = other.poly;
        Set<Integer> s2 = poly2.keySet();
        Iterator<Integer> iter2;

        while (iter1.hasNext())
        {
            Integer exponent1 = iter1.next();
            Integer coef1 = poly.get(exponent1);
            iter2 = s2.iterator();
            while (iter2.hasNext())
            {
                Integer exponent2 = iter2.next();
                Integer coef2 = poly2.get(exponent2);

                Integer prodExponent = exponent1 + exponent2;
                Integer prodCoef = coef1 * coef2;

                if (poly3.containsKey(prodExponent))
                {
                    prodCoef += poly3.get(prodExponent);
                }
                theProductPolynomial.addTerm(prodExponent, prodCoef);
            }
        }
        return theProductPolynomial;
    }
```

CPSIA information can be obtained at www.ICGtesting.com
Printed in the USA
BVOW10s0449010814

360759BV00009BD/25/P

9 780470 181614